Encountering The Holy Spirit

Paths of
Christian Growth and Service

FRENCH L. ARRINGTON

THOMAS J. DOOLITTLE, CONTRIBUTOR

study helps compiled by
Athena Arrington Hicks

Pathway
PRESS

Book Editor: Marcus V. Hand
Copy Editors: Cresta Shawver
Esther Metaxas

Library of Congress Catalog Card Number: 2003104018
ISBN: 0871482274
Copyright © 2003 by Pathway Press
Cleveland, Tennessee 37311
All Rights Reserved
Printed in the United States of America

To my son

Lee Arrington

a man who has made his father proud

and who is faithful in using

his gift of evangelism

Contents

List of Tables

Foreword

"Pentecostals don't write books," the professor harrumphed, "and if they did, I wouldn't read them!" I was astounded.

I have enjoyed five years of theological seminary classroom experience in three different institutions. The day this statement was made stands out with absolute clarity. It was during a course on the Acts of the Apostles, and it was in a non-Pentecostal school. Arriving at the Acts 2 account of the outpouring of the Holy Spirit, the professor sagely observed, "This is the John 3:16 of the Pentecostal churches."

He went on to share his opinion that the baptism in the Holy Spirit was always a corporate experience, since Scripture records the group experiences of the 120 in the Upper Room, the converts in Samaria, the household of Cornelius, and the disciples of John at Ephesus. Following the professor's obvious line of reasoning, one of the students asked that since 3,000 were converted on the Day of Pentecost, the whole city of Samaria responded to the gospel with joy, the Philippian jailer was saved along with his household, and so forth, could we also say that salvation was always a corporate experience?

The professor referred the student to some obscure textbook, and attempted to move along to his next point. Not to be put off, the student pursued the idea. "What would a Pentecostal writer say about it?" he asked. At this point, the professor made his erroneous and impugning broadside.

Well, Pentecostals do write books. And the one you hold in your hand is one of the best.

About a century ago the Holy Spirit was rediscovered. The birth of the Pentecostal Movement at the beginning of the 20th century focused attention on an aspect of theology long neglected or relegated to a few pages in textbooks. About 50 years later the appearance of the Charismatic Movement spurred a new resurgence of interest in the study of the person and work of the Spirit. Many books have appeared along the way.

I recall hearing Dr. David Allan Hubbard preach a sermon on the doctrine of the Holy Spirit in which he pointed out the absolute necessity of basing our understanding of the Spirit on what the Bible says. We can no more formulate a doctrine of the Spirit grounded only on our experience with Him, Hubbard said, than we could develop a doctrine of Creation based on our experience of a beautiful sunset or an autumn drive through the forest.

Dr. French Arrington approaches this book with the same conviction. Our grasp of the person and work of the Spirit may be informed and enlightened by our experience with Him, but undergirding that reality must be a thorough understanding of what God has revealed in His Word.

Encountering the Holy Spirit explores the development of the doctrine of the Holy Spirit in the Bible. As a faithful scholar and skillful exegete, Arrington leads us through the Old and New Testaments, unfolding the revelation of the Spirit's attributes and functions. After a thorough and exhaustive treatment of the Biblical teachings, he addresses matters of experience. The result is a *magnum opus* that is certain to take its place among the classics of Pentecostal scholarship.

Pathway Press invited French Arrington to write this book because of his sterling academic credentials, his years of experience sharing Biblical and theological truth with seeking students, and his warm heart. After undergraduate studies at the University of Chattanooga, he earned the M.Div. and Th.M. degrees at Columbia Theological Seminary and the Ph.D. from St. Louis University. He has written nine previous books, principally on New Testament subjects, and numerous articles. He is an editor of the *Life in the Spirit Study Bible* and *Life in the Spirit New Testament Commentary*, where he wrote the exposition of Luke/Acts.

Arrington has dedicated his life to the preparation of students for ministry and the enrichment of pastors. A pastor himself, his writings bear a stamp of practicality that adds to their critical value. Pathway Press is pleased to offer the rich fruit of his scholarly mind and his passionate heart.

—Bill George
Editor in Chief

With Gratitude

The gifts of the Spirit are crucial to whatever we undertake in ministry. The preparation and publication of *Encountering the Holy Spirit*, of course, is no exception. I am indebted to a number of people for the faithful exercise of their spiritual gifts in helping me to initiate and complete this book. Because of their wise counsel and assistance that have proved so crucially significant, I wish to express my appreciation.

First I want to thank Athena Arrington Hicks, my daughter, who has read the entire manuscript and made many splendid suggestions; and Dr. Thomas J. Doolittle, pastor of Solid Rock Church of God, Louisville, Kentucky, and a special friend over the years. He has shown special interest in this project from its inception to its completion, and has offered many valuable insights.

Special thanks go to Nyrone Hodge for his valuable research and skills in assisting with the preparation of the manuscript; to Drs. Rickie Moore and David Roebuck, two colleagues, for their wise advice and for recommending important resources; to Dr. Lois Beach for her support in this project; and to her late husband, Dr. Charles Beach, for his inspiring ministry through his spiritual gifts. He has touched the lives of so many.

I am also grateful to Pathway Press; Dr. Daniel F. Boling, general director of Publications; and Bill George, editor in chief, for their response to pastors who requested a book on the Holy Spirit. I thank them for inviting me to write it.

I express my heartfelt love and appreciation to those persons who have had a profound impact on my life and ministry:

My colleagues and students of colleges, universities, seminaries, and Pentecostal churches; their pastors here and abroad where I have preached and taught God's Word; and especially the congregation in Milledgeville, Georgia, where I was converted and filled with the Spirit. This congregation has continued to be an inspiration for many years.

My immediate and extended family, for the love that they have shown me through the use of their spiritual gifts. My immediate family: Frances, Athena and Lee for their inspiration, encouragement and sacrifices through the years; Athena and Gary Hicks, my daughter and son-in-law, for sharing computer expertise, and for Gary's assistance in formatting the manuscript; Lee and Traci Arrington, my son and daughter-in-law, for their love and encouragement during this project; and Travis and Trent, my grandsons, for all the joy that they bring me.

To my wonderful wife, Frances, I express my deep love and gratitude. She has gone through another writing project with me and has seen my research tools and books spread out for a year on the Ping-Pong table in our recreation room. Special thanks to her for helping with the book, putting up with the clutter and loving me through it all.

—French L. Arrington, Ph.D.

Introduction

The Holy Spirit is our life and power now, as He was for God's people in the age of the apostles and prophets. Through the ministry of the Spirit, God is particularly and personally involved in the life of a believer. The Holy Spirit's dynamic presence is evident in a rich variety of works—illumination, conversion, regeneration, sanctification, empowerment, spiritual gifts and glorification. They are all works of the one Spirit. His work is of such scope and has so many facets that the Biblical authors found that no single word was adequate to describe it. No rational explanation or single theology can fully describe the explosive and dynamic character of the Spirit's work. It is, first of all, a move of God in the world.

Since the Holy Spirit is so important to the Christian life and true spirituality, who is the Holy Spirit? The answer to this question is found in the New Testament, where the Holy Spirit clearly reveals Himself as a personal being. He performs many personal actions. The following are examples:

He creates (Genesis 1:2; Psalm 33:6).
He regenerates (John 3:5; Titus 3:5).
He teaches (John 14:26).
He directs (Acts 8:29; 13:2).
He testifies (John 15:26).
He guides (Romans 8:14).
He warns (1 Timothy 4:1).
He empowers (Acts 1:8; 4:1-8, 31).
He intercedes (Romans 8:26).
He inspires (2 Peter 1:21; 1 Corinthians 2:12, 13).

As a person He has emotions. He may be vexed or grieved (Isaiah 63:10; Ephesians 4:30). Also, through Him divine love is made manifest (Romans 5:5; 15:30). Furthermore, the Spirit has a mind and a will. Paul speaks of "the mind of the Spirit" in Romans 8:27, and he says that only the Spirit knows the deep things of God (1 Corinthians 2:10, 11). The Holy Spirit exercises

His will in distributing gifts "to each one individually just as He wills" (1 Corinthians 12:11), and by choosing the fields for evangelistic work (Acts 16:6, 7).

As well as affirming the personhood of the Holy Spirit, Scripture places the Holy Spirit on the same level with God the Father and God the Son (2 Corinthians 13:14; 1 Peter 1:2). The Spirit is, therefore, God and one of the three persons of the Holy Trinity. He is fully divine like the Father and the Son. The Father, Son and Holy Spirit together are one God, yet each person of the Holy Trinity has His own distinct identity and work. The three persons of the Trinity function and work together harmoniously to accomplish their work in the universe. The Father is the ultimate Creator of heaven and earth, and is the Lord of the universe, exercising continual care and control of it. Both the Holy Spirit and Christ are closely linked to the Father in Creation (Genesis 1:1, 2; Hebrews 1:1-3; 1 Corinthians 8:6).

They are also closely linked in our salvation. As the supreme act of His love, the Father sent His Son, Jesus Christ, into the world to reconcile sinful people to Himself (2 Corinthians 5:19). While on earth, Jesus, in order to accomplish the Father's mission, was both God and man so that He could meet our deepest spiritual needs. Jesus Christ meets these needs through God's gift of salvation. Since salvation is a gift, God has chosen to use His Holy Spirit to invite us to receive this gift. It is the Holy Spirit who communicates the good news of God's love and awakens the possibility of faith in our hearts. It is also the Holy Spirit who helps us to express the love of God to the world and empowers us for dynamic Christlike living.

The Holy Spirit empowered Jesus at the Jordan River, giving us a model for the Spirit's empowerment of the believer. In His baptism, Jesus stood in the river; the Holy Spirit in the form of a dove descended on Him, and the Father spoke audibly from heaven (Luke 3:21, 22). On that occasion the Holy Spirit empowered the Savior for His task of preaching the kingdom of God, healing the sick and delivering people from the bondage of sin (4:18ff). Similar to Christ's experience at the Jordan River, His disciples at Pentecost had an encounter with the Holy Spirit that empowered them eventually to take the gospel through Judea and Samaria to Antioch, Asia Minor, Greece and finally to Rome (see the Book of Acts).

Through the power of the Holy Spirit the disciples advanced the gospel to the different parts of the earth. Pentecostals and Charismatics appeal to the disciples' experience at Pentecost as the model for understanding their empowerment for worship and service by the Spirit. Among Charismatics and Pentecostals is a broad spectrum of doctrine and practice, but the term *Pentecostal*, as it is used in this work, refers to classical Pentecostalism. Classical Pentecostalism teaches that subsequent to conversion, believers should be baptized in (filled with) the Spirit and that the initial sign of the experience is speaking in unknown languages by the enablement of the Spirit (Acts 2:4).

The growth of Pentecostal churches during the past 100 years and the sheer magnitude and diversity of Pentecostalism today testify to the explosive dynamism of the Holy Spirit. Pentecostal and Charismatic spirituality has become a global phenomenon. God still gives the Spirit "without measure" (John 3:34), and the wind of the Spirit blows wherever He desires. Indeed, the fullness of the Spirit remains available to all—"for you and your children and for all who are far off" (Acts 2:39).

The critical element to the life, vitality and growth of the Christian church has been, and remains, the presence and power of the Spirit. To feel moved spiritually is no guarantee that you are moved by the Holy Spirit; Satan moves people, too. God's people need discernment so that they can distinguish between the Holy Spirit's presence and what comes from an evil spirit. A sure sign of the Holy Spirit's power in one's life is the ability to reach out to others with the gospel and to serve them in self-sacrificing love and compassion.

Pentecostals and Charismatics recognize that this world is a place where Satan is at work, seeking to destroy human lives. But they also see it as a place where God puts broken lives back together, delivering them from the bondage of sin, reorienting their priorities, restoring them to freedom, empowering them for service and giving them deep assurance as God's children. God does all of this through the powerful ministry of the Holy Spirit. The Spirit of God touches every facet of our lives. For those of us who have come to faith in Christ, we have already encountered the person of the Spirit through conversion and are now indwelt by Him, but there is another dimension of life in the Spirit. Pentecostals describe this dimension or encounter as "baptism in the Spirit." By Spirit baptism we are empowered to bear witness to the saving power of Christ and are made more open and sensitive to the operation of the gifts of the Spirit through us (1 Corinthians 12:4-11; Romans 12:6-8). If you have not encountered the Holy Spirit through conversion, my prayer is that you will come to know Christ as your Savior and experience the overwhelming presence and power of the Holy Spirit in your life.

This book examines Pentecostal teachings on the Holy Spirit and the gifts of the Spirit. The focus is on the experience of Spirit baptism and related matters: (1) the Spirit and the Old Testament; (2) the Spirit's role in conversion and spiritual fruit; (3) baptism in the Spirit following conversion; (4) baptism in the Spirit being accompanied by speaking in unknown languages; (5) reception of the Spirit and the results; (6) gifts of the Spirit; and (7) challenges facing Pentecostals and Charismatics, and their churches. The final chapter offers stories of individuals' encounters with the Holy Spirit.

This study is intended as a practical guide for Christians, and its basis is the Bible. Pentecostal understanding of the experience of baptism in the Spirit and the gifts of the Spirit is grounded in Scripture. A full understanding of the Holy Spirit's work in our lives and in the life of the church is learned through a combination of several means: the study of Scripture, the study of our historical roots in the Pentecostal/Charismatic Movements, listening and learning from the experiences of individuals in our Christian community, and experiencing a relationship with the Holy Spirit in our own lives.

A word of caution is in order for Pentecostals and Charismatics. It is not enough just to be able to trace our roots back to the Azusa Street Mission (1906) in Los Angeles, California, where historians often trace the origin of the Pentecostal/Charismatic Movements. Nor is it enough to rely on one's own personal experience of being filled with the Spirit in order to have a complete understanding of the work of the Holy Spirit. When we think of our personal relationship with the Spirit today, the crucial question should not be, "When was I filled with the Spirit?" but rather, "Am I now living a Spirit-filled life based on God's Word?" True Pentecostal and Charismatic spirituality demands commitment to the service of Christ, holy living and sincere worship of God. The study of God's Word and submission to the Holy Spirit's guidance are essential to living a Spirit-filled life.

Summary
- The Holy Spirit is a personal being who is one of the three persons of the Holy Trinity.
- The Holy Spirit is our life and power now, as He was for God's people in the age of the apostles and prophets.

Characteristics of the Holy Spirit

Member of the Holy Trinity	
2 CORINTHIANS 13:14; 1 PETER 1:2	He is fully divine.
GENESIS 1:1, 2; PSALM 33:6; cf. 1 CORINTHIANS 8:6; HEBREWS 1:1-3	He was active in Creation.
JOHN 3:3-8; 6:63; ROMANS 8:2-11; GALATIANS 3:2-5	He is active in our salvation.
ACTS 1:8; 2:1-4; 4:1-8, 31	He empowers believers.
Personal Being	
ACTS 16:6, 7; ROMANS 8:27; 1 CORINTHIANS 2:10, 11; 12:11	He has a mind and a will.
ROMANS 5:5; 15:30	He manifests divine love.
ISAIAH 63:10; EPHESIANS 4:30	He may be vexed or grieved.
GENESIS 1:2; PSALM 33:6	He creates.
JOHN 3:5; TITUS 3:5	He regenerates.
JOHN 14:26	He teaches.
ACTS 8:29; 13:2	He directs.
JOHN 15:26	He testifies.
ROMANS 8:14	He guides.
1 TIMOTHY 4:1	He warns.
ACTS 1:8; 4:1-8, 31	He empowers.
ROMANS 8:26	He intercedes.
1 CORINTHIANS 2:12, 13; 2 PETER 1:21	He inspires.

Introduction—Study and Discussion

1. What type of being is the Holy Spirit?

2. According to the Bible, as a personal being what are some of the actions of the Holy Spirit? (See Table—Intro.)

3. Discuss how the Holy Spirit functions with the other members of the Trinity. (See Table—Intro.)

4. Define *Pentecostalism*, as the term will be used in this book. (See Glossary.)

5. What should God's people pray for so that they can distinguish between the Holy Spirit's presence and an evil spirit's presence? (See 1 Corinthians 2:12-15; 1 John 4:1-6.)

6. What is the sure sign that the Holy Spirit's power is present in one's life? (See Galatians 5:22, 23; Acts 1:8; 1 Corinthians 12:8-10, 28-30.)

7. What primary source should we use when learning about the Spirit of God? (See 2 Timothy 3:16.)

8. Think about what you hope to gain from this study and any questions you hope to have answered.

Part One

The Spirit and
the Old Testament

*The earth was formless and void, darkness was over
the surface of the deep; and the Spirit of God was
moving over the surface of the waters* (Genesis 1:2).

1

The Witness of the Old Testament to the Holy Spirit

T he Holy Spirit is the same Spirit in the Old Testament as in the New Testament. The Hebrew word for "Spirit of God" is *ruach*, and the Greek word is *pneuma*. Both of them have three meanings—"wind," "breath" and "spirit." From the beginning, the Spirit is set apart from all created beings and first appears in the Biblical narrative of Creation. His powerful action is emphasized in the words "the Spirit of God was moving over the face of the waters" (Genesis 1:2, *RSV*).

In Psalm 33, the psalmist states that the Spirit's work is even broader, including not only earth but also the universe: "By the word of the Lord the heavens were made, and by the breath [or Spirit] of His mouth all their host" (v. 6). In the Psalms, all creation (earth, sea) and the inhabitants are ascribed to the Spirit: "Thou sendest forth thy Spirit, they are created" (104:30, KJV). The Spirit of God stands behind all creation and life (cf. Psalm 104:29, 30). Obviously, the work of the Spirit before the New Testament era was very important.

The references to the Holy Spirit in the Old Testament are limited in comparison to the number in the New Testament. Even so, He does appear in almost two-thirds of the Old Testament books.[1]

---

[1]Emil Brenner observes that the establishment of the monarchs in Israel seemed to interfere with divine guidance and that "Israel . . . was not originally a monarchy nor a hierocracy, but a pneumatocracy." The leader of Israel was expected to be called and empowered by the Spirit of God (cf. *Christian Doctrine of Creation and Redemption* [Philadelphia: Westminster, 1952], 274).

In the Old Testament three things stand out about the Spirit:

First, the emphasis is on His work and not on His nature. His mighty acts establish His deity. Therefore, we may speak of the Spirit as "God-in-action" or "God-on-the-move." The same holds true in the New Testament.

Second, in the Old Testament, as well as in the New Testament, the Spirit's work is marked by mystery and power. It was the mighty wind (*ruach*) that caused the waters of the Flood to subside (Genesis 8:1). Likewise, the wind (*ruach*) turned the waters into dry land before Israel at the Exodus (Exodus 14:21). The mysterious wind of God has incomparable power and can never be controlled by man. As Jesus reminded Nicodemus, "The wind [*pneuma*] blows where it wishes and you hear the sound of it, but do not know where it comes from and where it is going; so is everyone born of the Spirit [*pneuma*]" (John 3:8). So both the Old and New Testaments emphasize the power and mystery of God's Spirit.

Third, the work of the Holy Spirit in the Old Testament foreshadows and helps us to better understand much of what we read about Him in the New Testament. Consequently, the Old Testament's teaching about the Spirit of the Lord provides the background for the Christian doctrine of the personality, deity and the work of the Spirit. Several passages in the New Testament would be difficult to understand were it not for the light that is shed on them by the Old. We will now consider Old Testament teachings on the Holy Spirit that call attention to the Spirit's ministry, especially the powerful charismatic dimensions of His work that result in miracles and the operation of spiritual gifts and extraordinary power to do great feats.

THE POWER OF THE SPIRIT

Likely when we examine the Old Testament, one of the first things that catches our attention is the emphasis on the Spirit of the

Lord as a mighty force. Many of the Old Testament stories describe individuals who experienced the power of the Spirit. The Book of Judges reminds us of the extraordinary feats that were accomplished by those used by the Spirit. In response to the cry of the Israelites for deliverance, the Lord raised Othniel up as their deliverer. When the Spirit came upon him, he went out to war and prevailed against the oppressor (Judges 3:9, 10). In like manner, Gideon was merely an ordinary man until the Spirit of the Lord came on him (6:34). He became the instrument by which the Lord gave victory over the enemy.

Despite Samson's obvious character flaws, the Spirit inspired him and empowered him to do unusual feats. The Spirit began to stir in him when he was still a young man (13:25) and enabled him to tear lions asunder and to kill a thousand Philistines with the jawbone of an ass (14:6; 15:14-17). Due to Samson's actions with Delilah, he discovered that "the Lord had departed from him," and he no longer had enormous strength (16:20, 21). Because he had disobeyed God, he lost his charismatic power, but we are told repeatedly in the Book of Judges that the Spirit of the Lord came upon men and women in power. As a result the enemies of Israel were defeated, and God's kingdom was established and advanced.

The weakness of the judges (charismatic leaders in the Book of Judges) and the Israelites became the occasion for the Spirit of the Lord to give them boldness and enable them to overthrow their enemies, such as the Canaanites, Moabites, Midianites, Philistines and Ammonites (see Judges 1:4ff.; 3:9ff.; 6:11ff.; 10:1ff.; 15:1ff.).

Other accounts speak about prophets who experienced the power of the Spirit. As Elijah's successor, Elisha was empowered to perform extraordinary deeds. He divided the waters of the Jordan River (2 Kings 2:14) and demonstrated that he had the power to meet insult with a curse (vv. 23, 24).

Another way the Spirit worked in the physical realm was evident in miraculous transportations. When the Spirit of the Lord came upon Elijah, the Spirit swept him away against his will (1 Kings 18:12). Possibly the whirlwind that transported Elijah to heaven was the action of the Holy Spirit (see 2 Kings 2:11). The Spirit set Ezekiel on his feet (Ezekiel 2:2). He seemed to have had similar experiences to Elijah, but it is not always easy to decide whether the Spirit gave him a visionary trip or transported him physically to Jerusalem and then back to Babylon (3:12-14; 8:3; 11:1, 24; 43:5). Ezekiel's experience may be comparable to Paul's when the apostle was "caught up to the third heaven," not knowing whether he was "in the body or apart from the body" (2 Corinthians 12:2, 3). It appears that the Spirit also caught up Philip, the evangelist, and provided him with miraculous transportation similar to that of an Old Testament prophet (Acts 8:39, 40).

Indeed, the Spirit was active in the earliest of times. His deeds were amazing and inexplicable. Unexpectedly He broke in and empowered people to do extraordinary things.

THE GIFTS OF THE SPIRIT

The mighty acts of the Spirit should not cause us to overlook the wide range of His operations in the Old Testament. The Spirit strives with sinful people, trying to bring them to repentance (Genesis 6:3). The removal of the Spirit from the midst of wicked people in Noah's time resulted in their perishing in the Flood (Genesis 6:3, 5-7, 13). We also see other aspects of the Spirit's work, including regeneration (the new birth), sanctification (separation from what is sinful and consecration to what is righteous), His presence in the saints, and the bestowal of spiritual gifts. Old Testament believers were justified and regenerated (Genesis 15:6; Romans 4:1-25).

Because of Saul's disobedience, we are told that the Spirit of the

Lord departed from him (1 Samuel 16:14; cf. Judges 16:20). Acknowledging his sin, David prayed, "Do not cast me away from Your presence and do not take Your Holy Spirit from me" (Psalm 51:11). The term *Holy Spirit* occurs in the Old Testament only here in Psalms and in Isaiah 63:10, 11. The emphasis of the term *holy* is that the Spirit stands in contrast to David's sinful condition. So here we have another example that unconfessed sin results in the loss of the Holy Spirit.

These operations of the Spirit were inseparable elements of the great salvation provided by Christ's death and resurrection, but they were also made available to Old Testament believers before the coming of the Savior. Yet in the Old Testament, the Holy Spirit was not only active in bringing men and women to experience God's saving grace, but He also bestowed spiritual gifts. These are known in the New Testament as the *charismata* (gifts of grace). It may be easy for us to overlook this fact. The New Testament gives the prominence to the gifts of the Spirit, and as Pentecostals we link closely baptism in the Spirit and spiritual gifts. As a consequence, we may fail to see the presence of special endowments in the Old Testament community of faith.

The point has been made that the work of the Spirit in salvation in the Old Testament stands in close relationship to the same work in the New Testament. The bestowal of spiritual gifts is no exception (cf. 1 Corinthians 12). Not only was the Holy Spirit present in regenerating and sanctifying power, but also He was active through special gifts. An example of the Spirit's endowing individuals with gifts is the building of the Tabernacle and the making of the garments for the high priest. The Spirit came on certain men and equipped them for these specific tasks (Exodus 28:2, 3). Bezalel and those who worked with him received the gift of wisdom that gave them the divine knowledge and craftsmanship necessary for performing their duties (35:30, 31).[2] They did not rely on mere human skills and expertise but on their Spirit-given abilities to build the house of God. Supernatural endowments were essential for them to accomplish their tasks.

The Temple needed rebuilding after the 70 years of Babylonian captivity, but the circumstances were not favorable to undertake the work. Opposition came from without and dissension from within. Under those conditions, the reliance on political power and human strength could have been a temptation, but the Word of the Lord gave them assurance that all difficulties would be overcome by depending on divine power: "Not by might nor by power, but by My Spirit" (Zechariah 4:6). The work of the Lord can be done only if we are enabled by the Spirit.

More than human strength and ingenuity are needed to accomplish spiritual tasks. Because of the need for more than human resources, God gave the gift of government to such men as Moses, Joshua, David and Solomon (see Numbers 11:16, 17; Deuteronomy 34:9; 1 Samuel 16:13; 1 Kings 3:5-14). He gave the gift of working miracles and healings to Elijah and Elisha (2 Kings 2:9, 10). At times there occurred prophesying that was a kind of utterance similar to New Testament *glossolalia*, the speaking in tongues (1 Samuel 10:10-13; 18:10; 19:23, 24). As in the New Testament, the Spirit "came upon" individuals (Numbers 24:2; 1 Samuel 10:10) and He also "clothed" Himself with people (Judges 6:34; 2 Chronicles 24:20). In these verses, the Hebrew verb for *clothe* represents more than the Spirit's settling on a person. Rather, the Holy Spirit enters the person, who submits and gives the Spirit complete

---

[2] As to the manner that the *charismata* were received, we can only conclude that the Holy Spirit was not tied to any specific pattern in the matter. On one occasion the *charisma* might come through the laying on of hands, or at other times it was an answer to prayer (see 1 Kings 3:4-15). Frequently, the special gifts of the Spirit seem to have been given directly without any form of mediation. No definite pattern can be identified. The rule is that the Spirit gives as He wills.

control. The action of the Spirit may be described as His "clothing" the individual. A number of translations fail to reflect this meaning, but sometimes language such as "fills" and "full" are used to speak of the Spirit in regard to individuals (Exodus 31:3; Micah 3:8). These terms have a remarkable similarity to what appears in the New Testament and, in fact, anticipate the phrase "filled with the Spirit."

We must not, however, overlook two important differences between the Spirit's work in the Old and the New Testaments. First, in Old Testament times the Spirit came upon only a few (warriors, judges, kings and prophets), but in the new era every believer experiences the Holy Spirit. Second, the Spirit was only a temporary experience for the Old Testament leaders. Generally the Holy Spirit empowered people for a specific task and then withdrew. In contrast, all New Testament believers enjoy the permanent possession of the Spirit (Romans 8:9-16).

Truly the character of the Old Testament community was shaped by the presence of spiritual gifts. To remove them would alter the entire character of the Old Testament community of faith. A fundamental truth of the old era is that God is present with His saving power in human history. He exercises this power through men and women whom He has chosen and endowed with the Spirit. Gifts of the Spirit were given to them for the benefit of the entire covenant community. Leaders were an essential part of God's people and were equipped by the Spirit to serve the people. Their exploits and accomplishments were possible only because of the special endowments of God's Spirit. As a result, there is good reason to think that the Old Testament community of faith was a charismatic community and that the rich array of *charismata* that appear in the New Testament church was present in God's people in the Old Testament.

In New Testament times, the *charismata* were not a new development.[3] They were, however, no longer confined to a limited few, but were distributed to all of God's people (1 Corinthians 12:4-11). With regard to the gifts of the Holy Spirit, as with every work of God, we must see the New Testament as the fulfillment of the Old.

THE GIFT OF PROPHECY

Prophecy is such a common occurrence in the Old Testament that it demands special attention. The Spirit of the Lord is closely linked to this phenomenon, and the prophets were charismatic[4] personalities, endued with power by the Spirit. The prophetic *charisma*, therefore, pervades the Old Testament record and shows that prophecy was a significant aspect of the Spirit's work in the Old Testament community.

A fundamental characteristic of prophecy is that it can involve foretelling and forthtelling. The term *prophecy* primarily refers to foretelling or predictions, but a prophet may be both a foreteller of future events and a forthteller, proclaiming the Word of God to the people. A study of the prophetic books discloses that much of what the prophets wrote had nothing to do with future events. In large measure, they address their message to contemporary problems. Therefore, by definition a prophet (Greek: *prophētēs*) is one who

---

[3]There is a striking similarity between the *charismata* as they appear in the Old and New Testaments. But the connections between the *charismata* and personal holiness, to say the least, is ambiguous. An unregenerate person, such as Balaam, may possess *charismata*. There were limits on the use of spiritual gifts. They were never exercised in a base way or against the welfare of the community of faith. Balaam found that he could not use his prophetic gift to curse Israel. Saul's *charisma* of government was taken away because of his apostasy; and for the same reason, Samson's Charismatic strength was withdrawn, though later briefly restored (1 Samuel 16:14; Judges 16:20).

[4]The word *charismatic* is derived from the Greek *charisma* and has come to mean special work of the Spirit that is dynamic in nature. A Charismatic is a person endued by the Holy Spirit to perform a particular ministry.

speaks forth, a proclaimer and interpreter of divine revelation. True prophecy is always inspired by the Holy Spirit. Often we find the statement, "The Spirit came upon him and he prophesied." In the Old Testament, prophecy was a sign that the Holy Spirit had come upon a person.

When the Spirit came on the prophet, he brought a message from God. The message sometimes appeared to be strange and often came in mysterious forms. Sometimes ecstatic behavior was induced suddenly; sometimes the message was received through a dream or a vision (see Jeremiah 1:11ff.; Daniel 8:1ff.). At other times there was no apparent trance or hypnotic state, and the experience was not personally overwhelming. As a result, the prophet was able to behave in a more normal manner and communicate his message in intelligible speech or writing. What really mattered was the content of his message. Because of the direct inspiration of the Holy Spirit, he was always able to declare, "Thus says the Lord."

The first account that shows the Spirit's relationship to prophetic utterance is Numbers 11:16-30. The people complained about Moses. In response, the Lord took the Spirit that was on Moses and placed the same Spirit on the 70 elders, who then prophesied. Their prophesying was a sign that they shared in the leadership of the tribes and were equipped to deal with the people's complaints. The evidence of the Spirit's presence was prophecy. Only the Holy Spirit could supply what the elders needed to serve the people. The Spirit who had enabled Moses to bear the burdens of the people and to fulfill his task now was placed in these men. So the 70 elders were chosen by the Lord and equipped by the Spirit as leaders of God's people.

Prophecy indicated in a unique manner that the Holy Spirit was present. After Saul was chosen as king of Israel, God used Samuel to tell him that he would meet a group of prophets and that he too would prophesy (1 Samuel 10:5-10). The arrival of the Spirit confirmed to Saul all that Samuel said. Through the experience of the Spirit, Saul became a changed man—"a different person" (v. 6, *NIV*).

On a later occasion, Saul had another overpowering experience with the Spirit of the Lord (19:18-24). At that time, he had turned back to the old life of sin and had tried to kill David. The messengers he sent to apprehend David encountered a band of prophets; and the messengers themselves prophesied, frustrating their efforts to arrest David. Since they were planning evil, why did the Spirit of the Lord come upon them? The answer must lie in the sovereignty of God. The ways of God are not always according to our ways.

To emphasize it again, prophesying is a sign of the presence of the Spirit, but it is not necessarily an endorsement of the prophet's character. For example, the Spirit of the Lord came upon wicked Balaam, and he proclaimed oracles of blessings (Numbers 24:2-9). He was just a conduit used to convey the Spirit's message. Saul himself is another example of a person on whom the Spirit came, but at the time he was out of touch with the Lord. When those sent to arrest David failed, Saul went to see what was going on, and he himself was overwhelmed by the Spirit. "He also stripped off his clothes, and he too prophesied before Samuel and lay down naked all that day and all that night" (1 Samuel 19:24). He was in what we would describe as a trance, or hypnotic state. In that ecstatic condition, he was not aware of what he was doing and had become a channel through which the Spirit was working. In this ecstatic state for an entire day and night, Saul was unable to arrest David. So God gave David another chance to escape.

The great prophets of the eighth century, sometimes referred to as the "writing" or "classical" prophets, placed less emphasis on ecstasy. The Books of Isaiah through Malachi record their prophecies. They were all prophets, because the Spirit of the Lord came upon them. Among them, Ezekiel is an important example of a prophet whose life and message were controlled by the Spirit. He was conscious of the power of the Spirit in him and states that the Spirit entered him and set him on his feet (Ezekiel 2:2; 3:24); fell upon him (11:5); lifted him up (3:12, 14); took him away (v. 14); transported him (either physically or spiritually) to the Temple (11:1), to Jerusalem (8:3), to Chaldea (11:24), and to a valley where the Spirit would cause the dead bones to come to life (37:1-14). Over and over Ezekiel says, "The word of the Lord came to me saying" (6:1; 7:1; 11:14; 13:1; 16:1). The expression means that the Spirit came upon the prophet and personally empowered him, giving him a message for God's people.

What was really important was not that the prophet experienced a trance or ecstasy. Such manifestations from time to time did accompany prophecy; they were especially prominent among the early prophets. The important thing was that God had broken in, and the prophet had experienced the energizing presence of the Spirit, leaving no doubt that his message and deeds were directly from God. The Spirit had given the message to the prophet. As a result we see a close link between the Spirit and the Word of God (2 Samuel 23:2; Isaiah 59:21; Micah 3:8). So the Spirit was the source of divine revelation.

The Spirit's work is not only connected closely to prophecy but also to miracles. The Spirit is consistently recognized as the source of power, strength and miracles. The close link that exists between prophecy and the mighty works of the Spirit is evident in the miracles of the prophets like Elijah and Elisha (1 Kings 17–2 Kings 8). Miracles often served to credit the prophet and his message at a critical time in the history of God's people. During the ministry of Elijah, faith in the true God was threatened by the worship of Baal (1 Kings 18:20-39). Elijah's confrontation of the prophets of Baal proved the truth of the prophet's message that the God of Israel was the true God. We are told about similar exploits performed by Moses, Joshua, Saul, David and others. A general rule was that the Spirit broke in suddenly and anointed individuals to do extraordinary things.[5] Miracles served as signs of the presence of the Spirit. Yet, Jerome Boone, professor of Old Testament, states in his writings on

---

[5]Of course, miracles and divine healing were not always a matter of charismatic activity. At times God did work apart from the *charisma* of men.

the Holy Spirit that after the period of the kings there emerged a more comprehensive understanding of the Spirit's work. Boone writes: "The workings of God in Israel are no longer seen only as miraculous, mighty acts of God; the Spirit of God is understood to be actively involved in the daily lives of men and women in community."[6]

The conclusion that we can reach is that the Spirit was not tied to a particular pattern. The prophetic *charisma* and other gifts demonstrated the presence of the Spirit and usually were given immediately without any mediation. The Holy Spirit then operated through the gifts in many ways. Prophetic *charisma* and gifts were given to and exercised by the prophets and others. They were given to members who were a part of the community of faith, not to isolated individuals. They were for the benefit of the whole community.[7]

THE SPIRIT AND THE MESSIAH

In the Old Testament the dawn of a new day was expected. This day was expected to be accompanied by the charismatic activity of the Spirit of God, who would abundantly bless God's people. At the center of the coming age would be a child of peace with extraordinary names that belong only to God. This Son's government would be from the throne of David, eternal and unlimited in its dimensions (Isaiah 11:2-9). By the power of the Spirit, God's Son—"the Branch of Jesse," the Messiah—would be endowed with the charismatic gifts of wisdom, understanding, counseling ability, might, knowledge and spirituality. Further, the prophet Isaiah said that the

---

[6]R. Jerome Boone, "The Role of the Holy Spirit in the Construction of the Second Temple," *The Spirit and Mind* (Lanham, MD: University Press of America, 2000) 51.

[7]An exception to this is Balaam, who was not a member of the community of faith, but was allowed to use his prophetic *charisma* only for the benefit of Israel. The Holy Spirit maintained full control of the *charismata*, not permitting them to be used for the detriment of the community of faith.

Lord had put His Spirit upon this Leader: "Behold, My Servant, whom I uphold; My chosen one in whom My soul delights. I have put My Spirit upon Him; He will bring forth justice to the nations" (42:1). Again, the prophet predicted that the Father by the Spirit would grant the Messiah authority to do His work: "Come near to Me, listen to this: From the first I have not spoken in secret, from the time it took place, I was there. And now the Lord God has sent Me, and His Spirit" (48:16). Only through the power of the Spirit can we serve God. This truth also applied to the Messiah. The most comprehensive of Isaiah's prophecies expresses this theme:

> The Spirit of the Lord God is upon me, because the Lord has anointed me to bring good news to the afflicted; He has sent me to bind up the brokenhearted, to proclaim liberty to captives, and freedom to prisoners; to proclaim the favorable year of the Lord (61:1, 2).

Isaiah described his own experience, but one thing became clear later on in the New Testament: Isaiah's comments are also a prophetic description of the Lord's Anointed, the Messiah. At the beginning of His ministry, Jesus read this passage at a synagogue service in Nazareth and then declared, "Today this Scripture has been fulfilled in your hearing" (Luke 4:21; see also vv. 16-22). Jesus offered only this one comment, but this prophecy of Isaiah identified who Jesus was and summarized His Spirit-anointed ministry. As the fulfillment of the prophecy, Jesus understood Himself as having received the fullest endowment of God's Spirit, which had been recorded in Scripture: the spiritual gifts of wisdom, understanding, counseling ability, strength, knowledge and spirituality.[8]

Jesus, therefore, stands apart in comparison to Israel's great charismatic leaders: Moses, Joshua, David, Elijah, Elisha, Isaiah and Ezekiel. He is the Messiah, and throughout His ministry on

---

[8]Roger Stronstad, *The Charismatic Theology of Luke* (Peabody, MA: Hendrickson, 1984) 24-26.

earth He is uniquely a man of the Spirit. Without exaggerating, Jesus frequently says with authority, "Truly I say to you." He claims to speak the final truth of God. In Jesus, the anointing of the Spirit became a unique reality far exceeding the great charismatic prophets of the Old Testament. God did not give Jesus the Spirit by measure (John 3:34), but He was fully and uniquely endowed with the Holy Spirit. As the Old Testament prophets (especially Isaiah) foresaw, the Messiah would be extraordinarily equipped by the Holy Spirit for His ministry. The prophecy of Isaiah was fulfilled when the Holy Spirit descended upon Jesus and fully equipped Him for His ministry of preaching, healing the sick and setting free those in spiritual bondage (Isaiah 11:1ff.; 61:1ff.; Luke 3:21, 22; 4:18, 19).

THE PROMISE OF THE SPIRIT

In the Old Testament the Holy Spirit came upon kings, prophets and others in order for them to be used mightily by the Lord. The Spirit anointed only those who had a special task and mission in serving God's people. But God promised that He would initiate the age of the Spirit. In that age, the Spirit would uniquely equip the Messiah, but the power of the Spirit would not be limited exclusively to Him. In fact, the Messiah would make the gift of the Spirit available to all of God's people.

The special anointing of the Spirit was to become generally available to God's people as a whole and make possible the fulfillment of the intense longing of Moses: "Would that all the Lord's people were prophets, that the Lord would put His Spirit upon them!" (Numbers 11:29).

Men and women, through the coming of Christ and His pouring out of the Spirit, could experience in their lives what the prophets predicted for the last days. Through the prophets God promised the age of the Spirit, which was initiated in the new covenant and reached its climax in events of Pentecost (Acts 2). To place the new covenant and Pentecost in proper perspective, we must consider two important passages: Ezekiel 36:25-27 and Joel 2:28, 29.

The Ezekiel passage looks forward to a day when God will enter a new covenant or agreement with humankind. The new relationship that He is to forge with them will transform their hearts:

> Then I will sprinkle clean water on you, and you will be clean; I will cleanse you from all your filthiness and from all your idols. Moreover, I will give you a new heart and put a new spirit within you; and I will remove the heart of stone from your flesh and give you a heart of flesh. And I will put My Spirit within you and cause you to walk in My statutes, and you will be careful to observe My ordinances (36:25-27).

The prophet ascribes the change to the Spirit. God will sprinkle them with clean water and purify them from all the guilt and stain of their sins. He will give them a new heart, a disposition to be sensitive to His will, but He will do more than that. He will put His Spirit in them so that they may remain obedient to Him (cf. Jeremiah 31:31ff.). God's Spirit dwelling in the heart of the believer makes the spiritual renewal a reality: "I will put My Spirit within you" (Ezekiel 36:27).

This promise is clearly related to the New Testament doctrine of the new birth (regeneration), the inward spiritual renewal that results from the indwelling of the Holy Spirit. Jesus speaks about the need to be "born of water and the Spirit" (John 3:5), emphasizing a spiritual cleansing and renewal that occurs through the rebirth of the Spirit. Echoing this teaching of Jesus, Paul says that we have been saved "by the washing of regeneration and renewing by the Holy Spirit" (Titus 3:5).

The inward transformation that takes place with the new birth results in a change of lifestyle. The new life of obedience is made possible only through the indwelling of the Holy Spirit. Hence, the mark of all believers is that they are temples of the Holy Spirit (Romans 8:9-14; 1 Corinthians 6:19). The faith and life of the Christian are bound up with the Holy Spirit. No true believer is without God's Holy Spirit.

The prophecy of Ezekiel stresses that the Spirit purifies the people of their sins and indwells them. On the other hand, Joel's prophecy calls attention to another dimension of the Spirit's ministry. He does not talk about inner transformation, the change of lifestyle, or the indwelling of the Spirit, but about the Charismatic or Pentecostal anointing of the Spirit. Joel foretells what God will do in the last days:

> And afterward, I will pour out my Spirit on all people. Your sons and daughters will prophesy, your old men will dream dreams, your young men will see visions. Even on my servants, both men and women, I will pour out my Spirit in those days (Joel 2:28, 29, *NIV*).

Here the Spirit's activity is strikingly different from Ezekiel's prophecy. The pouring out of the Spirit upon all humankind would have dramatic results. Those who receive the experience will prophesy, dream and see visions. It is Charismatic or Pentecostal in nature, and produces extraordinary manifestations of God's Spirit, accompanied by audible and visible signs.

The Spirit comes upon people primarily to empower them to prophesy. Peter underscored this in His sermon at Pentecost (Acts 2:16-21). He said, "Your sons and your daughters shall prophesy" (v. 17); but then for emphasis he inserts and repeats "and they shall prophesy" (v. 18). On the Day of Pentecost, God initially fulfilled Joel's prophecy. The disciples "were all filled with the Holy Spirit" (Acts 2:4). They did not experience regeneration on that occasion, but the anointing of the Spirit for the purpose of offering a Spirit-filled, inspired witness to the whole world.

In the New Testament, both the prophecies of Ezekiel and Joel are fulfilled. The people of faith experienced the transformation of their hearts, a radical change in lifestyle, and the indwelling presence of the Holy Spirit in their lives. Yet at Pentecost, 120 believers experienced what Joel had predicted: the filling, the empowering of God's people by the Spirit. Obviously there is a basic difference between

TABLE 1-C
The Twofold Promise of God the Father

Indwelling of the Holy Spirit Through Regeneration (EZEKIEL 36:25-27)
• It is the work of the Holy Spirit within a believer. • The Holy Spirit cleanses, the evidence of which is a new heart and a new spirit.
Empowerment by the Holy Spirit (JOEL 2:28, 29)
• It is an outpouring of the Holy Spirit, an observable work of the Spirit. It is a gift, not a result of a believer's works. • The Holy Spirit gives power for Christian service, the evidence of which is prophecy, dreams and visions.

Ezekiel's and Joel's prophecies. Ezekiel emphasizes the indwelling of the Spirit and Joel the empowerment of the Spirit. In light of the distinction we, therefore, conclude that there are two aspects of the coming of the Spirit—His indwelling and His empowerment. In the Old Testament, the overall promise includes both the indwelling and the empowering of the Holy Spirit. Spiritual transformation and spiritual empowerment are two results of the work of the Holy Spirit in the age that dawned with the coming of Christ.

Beginning with the moment of Jesus Christ's conception by the Virgin Mary, the Holy Spirit was with Him. The Spirit descended upon Him after His baptism in the Jordan River (Matthew 3:16; Mark 1:9ff.; Luke 3:21ff.). From that time, the Holy Spirit anointed Him so that He could fulfill His mission.

Throughout Jesus' public ministry, He relied on the power of the Holy Spirit (Matthew 3:16; Luke 4:18, 19; Acts 10:38, 39). Nevertheless, the promise of the Holy Spirit for all Christians was not completely fulfilled until the Day of Pentecost. From that day, the Old Testament promise of pouring out the Spirit on all people ceased to be a promise and became a reality. Jesus' experience of the Spirit after baptism in the Jordan, together with the Spirit's anointing throughout His public ministry, initiates the new age of the Spirit and provides a model for all believers. Later at Pentecost we see the believers being indwelt and empowered by the Holy Spirit, both of which were promised them in the Old Testament.

To sum up this fulfillment of Old Testament prophecies, God promised that in the future He would create a new people through the inward renewal of their hearts. This renewal and spiritual transformation results from the indwelling of the Holy Spirit. This dimension of the Spirit is to be complemented by the outpouring of the Charismatic power of the Spirit on them. Among other things, the experience will equip them as witnesses to the gospel and intensify the work of the Spirit already indwelling them. The age of the Spirit will be characterized by two dimensions: the indwelling and empowering of the Spirit. People anointed by the Spirit will receive both moral and Charismatic power.

Summary

- The Holy Spirit has been present and active on earth from the beginning.

- The Holy Spirit's work of indwelling and empowering believers in the new age was prophesied in the Old Testament.

TABLE 1-A
Nature of the Spirit's Work in the Old Testament

Creation

GENESIS 1:2	During creation of the earth, the Spirit of God was moving over the face of the waters.
GENESIS 8:1	A mighty wind (*ruach*) caused the waters of the Flood to subside.
PSALM 104:29, 30	The Spirit of God stands behind all creation and life. The earth, the seas and all their inhabitants are ascribed to the Spirit.

Universal Work

PSALM 33:6	The Spirit's work is broad, including not only earth but also the universe.

Repentance and Regeneration

GENESIS 6:3	The Spirit strove with sinful people, trying to bring them to repentance.
GENESIS 15:6; ROMANS 4:1-25	Old Testament believers were justified and regenerated.
PSALM 51:11	Acknowledging his sin, David prayed, "Do not cast me away from Thy presence, and do not take Thy Holy Spirit from me."
EZEKIEL 36:25-27; cf. JEREMIAH 31:31-34	Ezekiel prophesied regarding the regeneration of Israel.

continued

TABLE 1-A (CONTINUED) **Nature of the Spirit's Work in the Old Testament**	
Removal From the Wicked	
GENESIS 6:5-7, 13	The removal of the Spirit from the midst of wicked people in Noah's time resulted in their perishing in the Flood.
Descent Upon Individuals	
NUMBERS 24:2; JUDGES 6:34; 1 SAMUEL 10:10; 2 CHRONICLES 24:20	The Spirit came upon individuals. He clothed Himself with people who submitted to Him and gave Him complete control.
EXODUS 31:3; MICAH 3:8	God filled individuals with His Spirit.
Empowerment	
JUDGES 1:4ff.; 3:9ff.; 6:11ff.; 10:1ff.; 15:1ff.	The Spirit of the Lord gave the judges boldness and enabled them to overthrow their enemies, including the Canaanites, Moabites, Midianites, Philistines and Ammonites.
Spiritual Gifts	
EXODUS 28:2, 3; 35:31	The Spirit equipped individuals with gifts for building the Tabernacle and making garments for the high priest.

continued

TABLE 1-A (CONTINUED) Nature of the Spirit's Work in the Old Testament	
ZECHARIAH 4:6	When the Temple needed rebuilding, there was opposition from outside and dissension from within. The word of the Lord gave the people assurance that all difficulties would be overcome by depending on the Spirit.
NUMBERS 11:16,17; DEUTERONOMY 34:9; 1 SAMUEL 16:13; 1 KINGS 3:5-14	God gave the gift of government to such men as Moses, Joshua, David and Solomon.
2 KINGS 2:9-14	God gave the gifts of working miracles and of healings to Elijah and Elisha.
Inspired Speech	
1 CHRONICLES 12:18; 2 CHRONICLES 20:14; 24:20	In 1 and 2 Chronicles, the Spirit of God is associated with inspired speech.
1 SAMUEL 10:10-13; 18:10; 19:23, 24	At times there occurred prophesying that was a kind of utterance similar to New Testament *glossolalia*, the speaking in unknown languages.
2 PETER 1:20, 21	The messages of the Old Testament prophets were given by the Holy Spirit.

TABLE 1-B
The Spirit's Work in Individuals' Lives in the Old Testament

Moses	
EXODUS 14:21	The wind (*ruach*) turned the waters into dry land before Israel during the Exodus.
NUMBERS 11:24, 25	The Lord transferred the Spirit from Moses to the 70 elders, and they prophesied.
NUMBERS 11:28, 29	Moses declared that he wished God would put His Spirit on all of His people, and that they would prophesy.
Othniel	
JUDGES 3:9, 10	In response to the cry of the Israelites for deliverance, the Lord raised Othniel up as their deliverer. When the Spirit came upon him, he went out to war and prevailed against the oppressor.
Gideon	
JUDGES 6:34	Gideon was merely an ordinary man until the Spirit of the Lord took control of him. He became the instrument by which the Lord gave victory over the enemy.

continued

TABLE 1-B (CONTINUED)
The Spirit's Work in Individuals' Lives in the Old Testament

Samson

JUDGES 13:25; 14:6; 15:14-17; 16:20, 21	The Spirit inspired Samson and empowered him to do unusual feats. When he was a young man, the Spirit enabled him to tear a lion apart and to kill a thousand Philistines with the jawbone of an ass. Due to his behavior with Delilah, Samson discovered that "the Lord had departed from him" and that he no longer had enormous strength.

King Saul

1 SAMUEL 10:1-10; 19:20, 23	Samuel anointed Saul. As the Spirit came upon Saul, he and his messengers prophesied.

King David

ACTS 1:16; 2:30	Peter reminded the people in Jerusalem that the Holy Spirit had spoken through the mouth of David.

Elisha

2 KINGS 2:14, 23, 24	Empowered by the Spirit to perform extraordinary deeds, Elisha divided the waters of the Jordan River and demonstrated the power to meet an insult with a curse.

continued

TABLE 1-B (CONTINUED)
The Spirit's Work in Individuals' Lives in the Old Testament

Elijah	
1 KINGS 18:12; 2 KINGS 2:11	When the Spirit of the Lord came upon Elijah, the Spirit swept him away against his will. The whirlwind that later transported Elijah to heaven was possibly the action of the Holy Spirit.

Ezekiel	
EZEKIEL 2:2; 3:12-14; 8:3; 11:1, 24; 43:5	The Spirit set Ezekiel on his feet; then the Spirit either gave him a visionary trip or transported him physically to Jerusalem—and then back to Babylon.

Notes

TABLE 1-C
The Twofold Promise of God the Father
For this table, see page 43.

CHAPTER 1—STUDY AND DISCUSSION

1. What is the Hebrew term used in the Old Testament to describe the Holy Spirit? What does it mean in English?
2. What is the Greek term used in the New Testament to describe the Holy Spirit? What does it mean in English?
3. Where does the Holy Spirit first appear in the Bible? (See Table 1-A.)
4. How much of the Old Testament contains references to the Holy Spirit?
5. What are three observations that can be made about the Holy Spirit's work in the Old Testament?

THE POWER OF THE SPIRIT

6. What are some examples from the Old Testament of extraordinary feats individuals accomplished because they were empowered by the Holy Spirit? (See Table 1-B.)

THE GIFTS OF THE SPIRIT

7. What are some examples of the Holy Spirit's works in the Old Testament? (See Table 1-A.)
8. What were some of the spiritual gifts (or *charismata*) that the Holy Spirit gave believers in the Old Testament? (See Table 1-A.)
9. What are some *similarities* in the relationship of the Holy Spirit with individuals in both the Old and New Testaments?
10. What are some *differences* in the relationship of the Holy Spirit with individuals in both the Old and New Testaments?

THE GIFT OF PROPHECY

11. What is a prophet? (See the Glossary.)

12. Give some examples of individuals prophesying in Old Testament times. (See Table 1-B.)
13. If an individual prophesies accurately, does it necessarily mean that God is endorsing the person's character? (See 1 Samuel 19:18-24; Numbers 24:2-9.)
14. Who were the "writing" or "classical" prophets? (See Isaiah through Malachi.)
15. There is a close connection between prophecy and miracles. Give some examples in which Old Testament prophets performed miracles. (See Table 1-B.)

THE SPIRIT AND THE MESSIAH

16. The Old Testament points to the dawn of a new age. What are some of the characteristics prophesied of this new age? (See Joel 2:28-32; Isaiah 40:26-36; 42:5-7; Jeremiah 31:31-34.)
17. Isaiah prophesied that the Messiah would come, and would be the center of the new age. According to Isaiah, how would the Messiah be equipped to do God's work on earth? (See Isaiah 42:1.)

THE PROMISE OF THE SPIRIT

18. According to the prophecies of Ezekiel 36:25-27 and Joel 2:28, 29, what would be two major aspects of the coming of the Holy Spirit? How were they to be fulfilled in New Testament times?

Part Two

Conversion and Spiritual Fruit

And now you also have heard the truth, the Good News that God saves you. And when you believed in Christ, he identified you as his own by giving you the Holy Spirit, whom he promised long ago (Ephesians 1:13, *NLT*).

2

Encountering the Holy Spirit in Conversion

The initial encounter with the Holy Spirit occurs at Christian conversion. Through this encounter, individuals experience a radical inward change, which is known as being "born again," "spiritual rebirth" or, to use the technical theological term, "regeneration." The Lord promised through the prophet Ezekiel this initial saving encounter with the Spirit: "I will give you a new heart and put a new spirit within you; and I will remove the heart of stone from your flesh and give you a heart of flesh. I will put My Spirit within you" (Ezekiel 36:26, 27). This message of spiritual transformation is of critical importance. Today, many people want something radically new in their lives. They find life empty and meaningless and want to avoid making the same old mistakes. What they desire is the personal experience of salvation—Christian conversion.

Conversion can be defined as "a turning to God away from sin, or wrongdoing, and relying solely upon Jesus Christ as Savior and Lord." It involves a human response to God's initiative and requires our acceptance and cooperation. The Biblical words *faith* and *repentance* indicate that conversion demands on our part an authentic response of turning to God and rejecting unrighteousness and evil. Paul taught that the necessary response to receive salvation is "repentance toward God and faith in our

Lord Jesus Christ" (Acts 20:21). Conversion, however, can only be accomplished by the help of the Holy Spirit.

A number of elements make up conversion, or entry into the Christian life: hearing the good news of salvation, having faith, being repentant for wrongdoing, receiving God's justification (forgiveness of sins), being adopted into God's family, and being sanctified (set apart for holy use). The focus of the discussion here will be the central role the Holy Spirit plays in the initial aspects of the spiritual process that initiates one into a new way of living.

THE HOLY SPIRIT AND CONVERSION
The Spirit's Call to Conversion

The Christian life begins with the hearing of the gospel, that is, the good news that we have forgiveness of sins through Jesus Christ. The hearing of this good news is then accompanied by faith and repentance. The Holy Spirit works through the preaching of the gospel. He invites people into a relationship with Christ and makes the story of Christ's sacrificial love effective, moving people to accept God's forgiveness and salvation (Romans 15:18, 19; 1 Corinthians 2:1-5). To truly hear the gospel, God's good news of salvation, is to hear the very Word of God. The Spirit takes this good news and makes it a personal reality in our hearts. Through His powerful inward ministry, the Holy Spirit gives power and life to the Word and illuminates the truth of God's saving plan, making it persuasive in our souls.

The Holy Spirit and Conviction of Sin

We can only fully understand the awfulness of sin when the Holy Spirit makes us aware of our wrongdoings in the light of God's redemptive work in Christ. Before conviction by the Holy Spirit, people usually have an awareness of right and wrong, but the Holy Spirit brings them to a deeper understanding of their sinfulness and spiritual condition. The Spirit deepens and intensifies people's awareness of the burden of not obeying God's laws and not following His will for their lives.

In Thessalonica, Paul's preaching was accompanied by the Holy Spirit. As a result, many of the people there came to a deeper understanding of sin and the truth of the gospel (1 Thessalonians 1:5, 6). Their conversion was not due to Paul's message alone, but to the message that was accompanied by the Holy Spirit, who brought deep conviction of the truth of God's plan for salvation. The same happened in Corinth. Paul's preaching was free of human wisdom and rhetoric, but it was accompanied by the demonstration of the Spirit's power that brought about the conversion of the Corinthians (1 Corinthians 2:1-5).

The Holy Spirit is active in the proclamation of the good news of salvation and opens the eyes of the unsaved to their spiritual condition, intensifying their awareness of their own moral corruption and need of Christ as Savior. To put it another way, He convinces the world of sin, of righteousness and of judgment (John 16:8). He does for unbelievers what they cannot do for themselves. The Spirit gives them spiritual sight, opening their hearts and eyes and unplugging their ears so that they can see their unsaved condition and truly hear the gospel and turn from their sin to God.

The Holy Spirit and Faith and Repentance

Turning from the old life of sin to the new life of God calls for faith and repentance. In fact, faith and repentance express the idea of conversion. As we have noted, the Holy Spirit exposes the condition of the human heart through the Word of God, preparing one to repent and believe. Therefore, the Holy Spirit prompts the unsaved to accept God's call to salvation by repenting of their sins and believing in Christ as Savior. The unsaved cannot save themselves, but conversion is a work of both God and of the individual. It requires human appropriation and cooperation, graciously made possible by the Holy Spirit. Paul taught that the necessary response to receive salvation is "repentance toward God and faith in our Lord Jesus Christ" (Acts 20:21). This verse sums up what it means to turn from sin to God.

Repentance is the willful rejection of sin and the life that displeases God. True repentance is demonstrated through a changed way of thinking and living. Faith goes hand in hand with repentance. They occur at the same time and are so inseparable that one includes the other; neither can be exercised without the other. Faith is permeated through and through with repentance, and repentance is permeated through and through with faith. Repentance and faith precede forgiveness of sins (Acts 5:31; 10:43; 13:39), but because faith and repentance result in salvation, they are inexplicably connected. Saving faith and repentance have the essential character of human response. The Holy Spirit inspires faith and leads us to repentance, but it is we ourselves who must believe, repent and receive. No one, not even God, will do that for us. To experience conversion demands an authentic response on our part—turning from sin to God and relying on the saving grace of Jesus Christ.

The Spirit's Work During Conversion

At the time of conversion a person experiences new birth (regeneration). Being "born again" and conversion should not be sharply distinguished. They are different terms used to describe the same experience, namely, salvation. One does not occur before the other. They are two ways of speaking of the new life in Jesus Christ. Both terms agree that the Holy Spirit plays a crucial role in the experience of conversion. Each term indicates that through the surrender of one's life to Christ, the living God transforms the human heart and bestows new life through the agency of the Holy Spirit.

The Central Role of the Spirit in Conversion

Like a journey, the Christian life has a beginning. It begins with conversion when one enters the Christian life. Conversion rests on the death and resurrection of Christ, who has secured salvation for those who believe. At conversion the Holy Spirit applies to us the saving benefits of Christ and transforms us. The Holy Spirit is absolutely essential to the experience of salvation, thus there can be no genuine conversion without the Spirit. This truth can be illustrated in a number of ways from the Scripture.

Biblical Illustrations of the Role of the Spirit in Conversion

As a broad term, *conversion* may include four Biblical concepts, each of which describes an aspect of the new life in Christ brought about by the Holy Spirit. These concepts show us how to understand the converting work of the Spirit.

New Birth. The change in the believer brought about by the Holy Spirit is of such magnitude that it can be compared to a new birth. Jesus' conversation with Nicodemus is the major passage on the new birth (John 3:1-21). The picture in this passage is that of beginning life all over again from infancy (1 Peter 2:2). The phrase *born again* is a physical image meant to help us understand that we have a new beginning and are spiritually born into a new sphere of life. This new sphere of life is known as the kingdom of God (John 3:3, 5; 1 Corinthians 15:50). To receive this new birth we must respond to God's Word, but the actual transformation comes from God the Father and the Holy Spirit. It can truly be said that the believer is "born again" (John 3:3)[1] and born "of the Spirit" (v. 6).

Paul reminds the Galatian Christians of their conversion by referring to Ishmael and Isaac. He first appeals to Ishmael, who was "born according to the flesh," but like Isaac, the Galatians

---

[1]The *NASB*, as well as several other versions, translate the Greek adverb *anōthen* in verse 3 as "again," but the context seems to support "from above," denoting the source of the new birth.

had been "born according to the Spirit" (Galatians 4:29). Their conversion, the radical spiritual change and transformation of their lives, had been accomplished by the Holy Spirit.

The gospel invites us into God's kingdom, but no one can enter without being "born of water and the Spirit" (John 3:5). Here "water" signifies cleansing and renewing as it does in Ezekiel 36:25-27. It is necessary to be cleansed, or renewed, by the Holy Spirit in order to enter into God's kingdom. Another way of putting it is "He [God] saved us . . . by the washing of regeneration and renewing by the Holy Spirit" (Titus 3:5). The Holy Spirit revolutionizes the believer's whole being. Such a spiritual change has a profound effect on the person. The believer's intentions, desires, affections and actions come under the influence of the Holy Spirit. Therefore, from the time of conversion, the Holy Spirit is crucial to the Christian life. What is experienced at the beginning of the Christian life can be properly described as a new birth.

Life From Death. Conversion is a spiritual restoration, or awakening, of a person from the dead. Scripture declares that the unsaved are dead in trespasses and sin (Ephesians 2:5; cf. John 3:36; Romans 5:15), but believers are "alive from the dead" (Romans 6:13). Outside of Jesus Christ, people are spiritually dead while their bodies are still alive. At their entry into the Christian life, they experience a spiritual resurrection, the result of the direct action of the Holy Spirit. As Paul says, the Spirit gives life to those who believe. Indeed "the Spirit of life" sets those who trust in Christ "free from the law of sin and of death" (Romans 8:2). So an essential aspect of the Spirit's work is the giving of life (2 Corinthians 3:6).

The believer has passed from death to life. Scripture urges Christians to consider themselves "dead to sin, but alive to God in Christ Jesus" (Romans 6:11). The dynamic change that has occurred involves not only a drastic break with sin, but also the imparting of spiritual life to believers by the Holy Spirit. Before conversion people walk in spiritual death, but in Christ they enjoy resurrection to a new life. This resurrection anticipates the resurrection of our bodies. As Christ was raised from the dead by the Holy Spirit, so will the Spirit give life to our mortal bodies (Romans 1:4; 8:11). In short, resurrection at conversion is the first step to ultimate resurrection.

Release From Darkness Into Light. The Holy Spirit is the Spirit of truth and enlightenment. Through the gospel, the Spirit brings light to hearts that were once darkened. In fact, darkness characterizes the way of unsaved people (Proverbs 2:13; Acts 26:18): their walk (1 John 1:6; 2:9-11), their works (Ephesians 5:11) and their understanding (Romans 1:21). In conversion the Spirit brings them out of darkness into the light of Jesus Christ. Paul thanked God for delivering Christians from "the domain of darkness" and qualifying them "to share in the inheritance of the saints in light" (Colossians 1:12, 13). Peter speaks of people whom God called "out of darkness into His marvelous light" (1 Peter 2:9).

The transition from total darkness into full daylight takes place when people believe the gospel. The Spirit of truth dispels darkness from their lives by revealing the light of Christ in their hearts and by helping them to understand the truth about Him (John 15:26; 1 John 2:20, 27). Again the Holy Spirit is central to conversion. Only He can remove darkness from the heart and open the eyes of the blind so that they can see "the glory of God in the face of Christ" (2 Corinthians 4:6).

Circumcision of Heart. According to Paul, believers have received circumcision of their hearts by the Holy Spirit. God gave to Abraham the physical mark of circumcision as a sign of the covenant (Genesis 17). The new covenant has been initiated by God in Jesus Christ, making outward physical circumcision irrelevant. The mark of the new covenant, the mark of being a child of God, is placed on the heart. No longer does outward circumcision identify one as a child of God. True circumcision is characterized by an inner change: "He is a Jew who is one inwardly; and circumcision is that which is of the heart, by the Spirit" (Romans 2:29).

God, who commanded outward circumcision in the Old Testament, was free to dispense with it; but now He calls for "circumcision made without hands" (Colossians 2:11) so that the old sinful nature may be cut off. The removal of sin is explained in Colossians further through a list of various examples of immorality, which God's people are told to put to death (3:5-11). Physical circumcision has been superseded by a superior reality. The Law was given on tablets of stone to Moses, but those "in Christ" have the law engraved by the Spirit upon the tables of their heart. The standard for God's people is internal rather than external. It is a matter of heart surgery, performed by the Holy Spirit and not by the written law (Romans 2:29). To those who have undergone inner transformation, an inner circumcision, Paul says, "We are the true circumcision, who worship in the Spirit of God and glory in Christ Jesus and put no confidence in the flesh" (Philippians 3:3). The condition of our hearts and a lifestyle of God's love in the world mark us unmistakably as God's people.

The Spirit's Indwelling at Conversion

From the beginning of life in Jesus Christ, the believer is indwelt by the Spirit. The believer receives the Holy Spirit at conversion, is born again of the Spirit, and becomes a child of God. No one can be a Christian without having the indwelling presence of God's Spirit (Romans 8:9; 1 Corinthians 6:19, 20). So, from conversion on, the Spirit takes up residence in the believer and His indwelling presence is a major aspect of the Christian's experience and life.

Receiving the Indwelling of the Holy Spirit

God has chosen to dwell in the believer on the earth. The Holy Spirit is God, who makes His home in those who believe in Jesus Christ. Writing to the believers in Corinth, Paul said, "You are the temple of the living God. As God has said: 'I will dwell in them and walk among them' " (2 Corinthians 6:16, *NKJV*). The Holy Spirit is God in us. When we believe in Jesus Christ, the Spirit becomes a reality in us. Therefore, by an act of faith in Christ, we receive the Spirit's indwelling presence (Galatians 3:2, 5, 14). Scripture identifies the unsaved as those "devoid of the Spirit" (Jude 19). Likewise, Paul says that the "natural man," the unsaved person, does not have the Spirit of God, and the things of God are foolish to him (1 Corinthians 2:6-16). In contrast, the opposite is true for believers. They have a continuing, intimate relationship with the Spirit, and the Spirit reveals to them deep truths about God.

The New Testament affirms that every Christian from the point of conversion is indwelt by the Holy Spirit. "Because you are sons, God has sent forth the Spirit of His Son into our hearts, crying, 'Abba! Father!' " (Galatians 4:6). "No one can say, 'Jesus is Lord' except by the Holy Spirit" (1 Corinthians 12:3). Having trusted in Christ, believers "were sealed . . . with the Holy Spirit of promise" (Ephesians 1:13). The presence of the Holy Spirit in their lives marks believers as belonging to God. If anyone does not have the Spirit, he does not belong to God (Romans 8:9). The indwelling Spirit leads and guides God's children (v. 14). The indwelling Spirit is vital to their prayer life because He intercedes in behalf of them (vv. 26, 27) and enables them to bear the fruit of the Spirit (Galatians 5:22, 23).

Biblical Terms for the Indwelling of the Spirit

The variety of terms used to describe the role of the Spirit indicates that no single term expresses adequately the work of the Spirit in the believer. Paul recognized that conversion cannot occur without the Holy Spirit's coming into the life of the believer. To explain the doctrine of the indwelling presence of the Holy Spirit, he uses three major terms: the *seal* of the Spirit, the *temple* of the Spirit, and the *pledge* of the Spirit. A brief examination of these terms will help us to understand the reality of the Spirit in every Christian.

Seal of the Spirit. At times Paul spoke of the indwelling of the Spirit as the *seal* of the Spirit. God, he said, has sealed (*sphragizō*) us and put His Spirit in our hearts "as a pledge" (2 Corinthians 1:22). Warning believers of the danger of grieving the Spirit and forfeiting future salvation, Paul told them that they had been sealed by the Holy Spirit for the day of redemption (Ephesians 4:30).

In Bible times, as in modern times, a seal (or signet) had a recognized meaning or significance. Widely used in maritime trade, the word *seal* would have been familiar to Christians living in the commercial centers of Corinth and Ephesus. In ancient times a seal served a variety of purposes, but Paul's use of the word expresses two basic ideas: ownership and certification. During Paul's lifetime, it was the custom that when a person purchased merchandise, the purchaser's seal was stamped on the goods for transit. To later claim the goods, the new owner needed only to show the signet that matched the stamp on the merchandise. His mark of ownership on the goods gave him the right to take possession of them.

In a similar fashion, God has set His seal of ownership on believers. He places His seal on them when they come to faith in Jesus Christ. The divine agent of the sealing is the Holy Spirit himself. The Spirit is the One by whom God has marked believers and claimed them as His own. By the indwelling Spirit, God places His stamp of ownership on the heart of Christians. This does not mean, however, that they are passive and have no active part in this change of ownership. Merchandise and other goods on which a seal was placed took no active part in the transaction. God, however, does not place His seal of ownership on us until we voluntarily surrender to Jesus Christ (John 1:12).

On the other hand, as God's seal of ownership, the Spirit certifies, or guarantees, that believers are the children of God. In ancient times, a seal certified the genuineness of a document (1 Kings 21:8-10). Abraham received the mark of circumcision as a seal of his faith. Circumcision did not create his faith, but it did attest that he stood in a right relationship with God. No one but the Holy Spirit gives validity to faith. "The Spirit Himself bears witness with our spirit that we are children of God" (Romans 8:16, *NKJV*). To believers, the Spirit brings the assurance of salvation and the guarantee of final honor and perfect happiness in heaven, provided they embrace their new life in the Spirit and follow the way of Jesus Christ.

Temple of the Holy Spirit. The Temple (*naos*) in Jerusalem had been understood to be the earthly "dwelling" of the God of Israel. For Paul, God's temple was no longer a building located on a piece of land. In his writings, Paul applies the term *temple* to the individual believer and to the community of believers, both of which are indwelt by the Holy Spirit. Because the Spirit dwells in the heart of each believer, Paul asked the Corinthians, "Do you not know that your body is a temple of the Holy Spirit?" (1 Corinthians 6:19). Those believers were guilty of loose living. They were not taking seriously the reality that the Spirit had taken up residence in each of them and that their lack of love and purity was grieving Him. Living in them, the Spirit saw whatever was in their hearts—whether envy, bitterness, hatred and lust or whether love, joy, hope and holiness. He also saw what they did—whether boasting, backbiting and slander or whether loving, serving one another and walking in humility before the Lord. The indwelling of the Spirit as the Spirit of holiness illuminates the human heart and seeks to bring human nature—body, soul and spirit—into conformity with Jesus Christ.

What is true of the individual Christian holds true for the community of believers. The community is also the temple of the Spirit, a special dwelling place for the third person of the Holy Trinity. The church is not merely another kind of fellowship; it is a fellowship created by the Holy Spirit (2 Corinthians 13:14) and indwelt by the Spirit. Paul refers to the community, the local church, as the corporate dwelling place of the Spirit when he inquires in 1 Corinthians 3:16, "Do you not know that you are a temple of God and that the Spirit of

God dwells in you?" (*NKJV*). Strife, schism and false teaching were threatening the very existence of the Christian community in Corinth. He warns them that false doctrine and divisions could destroy God's temple, the local church. As His corporate sanctuary, the Spirit permeates with His presence the community of believers. He not only dwells in us but also among us, seeing and hearing what goes on in the gathered community, the temple of the living God.

Pledge of the Spirit. Here we have a different perspective on the indwelling of the Spirit in the Christian. At conversion the believer receives the Spirit as a pledge (*arrabōn*). The use of this word *pledge* in Biblical times indicated that part of the purchase price was paid in advance. So the Spirit is a pledge, a down payment, the first installment of what God has prepared for those who love Him. For this reason, the word *pledge* takes on a prophetic significance and assures us of the final installment of our salvation in the future. What the Holy Spirit begins in conversion, He will bring to completion when believers receive their spiritual bodies (Romans 8:23; 1 Corinthians 15:35ff.). The apostle Paul was keenly aware that the Holy Spirit is the pledge of our eternal inheritance. God, he said, "put his Spirit in our heart as a deposit (*arrabōn*), guaranteeing what is to come" (2 Corinthians 1:22, *NIV*). Again he wrote, "Having believed, you were marked in him with a seal, the promised Holy Spirit, who is a deposit (*arrabōn*) guaranteeing our inheritance" (Ephesians 1:13, 14, *NIV*). Life for the believer in this present age of suffering and adversity is blessed with the joy and peace of the Holy Spirit, but these blessings are only the first installment of the perfect joy and peace of heaven.

The indwelling of the Holy Spirit is God's way of assuring us of better things to come. Salvation is a gift from God, and we will receive it in full when Christ comes the second time. The new life we have through the Spirit is a pledge of eternal life, but full payment will be received when we are liberated from all present frailties. Our mortal bodies will be transformed so that they will be like Christ's glorious body (Philippians 3:21).

The Spirit's Witness to Our Conversion

To receive the Spirit at conversion is to be adopted as children into God's family (cf. Galatians 4:4-6). As children in God's family, we share a level of intimacy with our heavenly Father that is similar to the relationship that His eternal Son has with Him. The testimony of the Holy Spirit affirms our standing as children of God. Characteristic of the ministry of the Spirit is the way He illuminates the truth and meaning of the Scriptures and leads individuals to Christ. Equally characteristic is the fact that He touches us in the deep places of our hearts and grants us assurance and a better understanding of our position as members of God's family. This is what Paul had in mind when he wrote: "The Spirit Himself testifies with our spirit that we are children of God" (Romans 8:16).

Divine Assurance of the Pardon of Sin

By the Spirit we are convicted of sin and led to faith in Christ. The result is that we are acquitted of all of our wrongdoings and mistakes and are declared to be sons and daughters of God. Our past sins and guilt are completely wiped out. Debts against us for withholding obedience to God have been cancelled. Our past is past and done with.

The Spirit bears witness to the truth: "Therefore there is now no condemnation for those who are in Christ Jesus" (Romans 8:1). Only the Holy Spirit makes known to us that we have been cleared of all condemnation in the high court of heaven. The Spirit testifies that our sins and failures of the past have no claims on us. This means that no one, not even Satan, can bring any charge against us for the sins that God has forgiven. Satan will try to make us feel paralyzing shame over sins that God has blotted out and will attempt to make us doubt that they have been put away. He delights in tempting us to look back on our former lives and grieve over past sins and failures, which God has already forgiven and forgotten.

But the Holy Spirit bears good news. His testimony is that our sins have been put so far away from us that on the Day of Judgment, God himself will not be able to find them. Our sins have been blotted out. That indeed is the message of Romans 8:33, 34: "Who shall bring a charge against God's elect? It is God who justifies. Who is he who condemns? It is Christ who died, and furthermore is also risen, who is even at the right hand of God, who also makes intercession for us" (*NKJV*).

Divine Assurance of Adoption

The Holy Spirit is spoken of as the Spirit of adoption. He testifies to "our spirit that we are children of God" (v. 16) and assures us that we enjoy all of the rights and privileges of heirs of God and coheirs with Christ. "The love of God has been poured out within our hearts through the Holy Spirit" (5:5). The witness of the Spirit takes away the doubts and fears that have resulted from adversity and teaches us to rejoice in tribulation. Our assurance is prompted by the witness of the Holy Spirit. "For you did not receive the spirit of bondage again to fear, but you received the Spirit of adoption by whom we cry out, 'Abba, Father' " (Romans 8:15, *NKJV*). And again, "Because you are sons, God has sent forth the Spirit of His Son into our hearts, crying, 'Abba! Father!' " (Galatians 4:6).

The Spirit inspires our hearts with trust and confidence in the heavenly Father. He assures us that we are born of God and that we have the privilege of calling God "Father." So when we are adopted into the family of God, the Spirit begins to touch our spirit and to testify that we are sons and daughters in God's family. None other but the Holy Spirit makes us aware of our right to call God by His close, intimate family name, which is "Abba, Father."

Therefore, the Holy Spirit is the key to conversion. From the beginning of the Christian life, He is responsible for bringing us into the family of God to which we were once aliens and strangers (Ephesians 2:12). The very reception of the Spirit makes us children of God. Upon entering our hearts, He begins to teach us to address

God by His close, intimate family name, "Abba, Father," bearing witness to the great love the Father has for us and imparting to us blessed assurance that we have been forgiven, restored and redeemed. Indeed, the Holy Spirit is crucial to every dimension of our salvation.

THE SPIRIT'S FRUIT IN OUR LIVES

For the Christian, not only does life begin with the Spirit, but one's entire walk as a Christian is a matter of walking with the Spirit. The Spirit initiates a specific way of living and from then on cultivates Christian graces in believers and empowers them to live the Christian life. Their salvation is complete in Christ (Colossians 2:10), but they need to "grow in the grace and knowledge of our Lord and Savior Jesus Christ" (2 Peter 3:18). Paul prayed that the Gentile believers would mature in the grace and knowledge of Christ. He wanted them to respect the presence of the Holy Spirit in their daily lives; therefore, he prayed for them to grow in the love of Christ (Ephesians 1:15; 3:2; 4:2, 3). This growth, when it occurs, conforms one to the likeness of Jesus Christ, for Christ dwells in the heart of believers by the Holy Spirit.

As a result of this spiritual growth and maturity, all believers are to bear "the fruit of the Spirit" (Galatians 5:22, 23) or "the fruit of righteousness" (Philippians 1:9-11). These Christlike graces in their lives reveal the indwelling presence of the Holy Spirit. Like natural fruit, the fruit of the Spirit does not reach maturity overnight. No believer in his own strength can produce the spiritual fruit, but the Holy Spirit cultivates His fruit in us as we daily submit ourselves to the Lord. First, believers bear the good fruit because the Spirit and His nature have been planted in their hearts. Second, they bear this fruit because they put real effort into cultivating spiritual graces in their lives (2 Peter 1:5-8).

Paul prays for his readers to live the Christian life, "bearing fruit in every good work" (Colossians 1:10). His prayer is for a full range of Christian obedience. This obedient lifestyle is not purely a matter of believers striving to live the Christian life, but is also the result of the Spirit's work in the believer. Christians rely upon the Spirit to put to death selfish desires and actions (Galatians 5:16-21) and to bear fruit that expresses their new life in Christ and promotes the fellowship of believers. As believers submit themselves to God's will through the help of the Spirit, their lives are conformed to Christ.

Paul indicates that daily living that conforms to Christ is the fruit of the Spirit. Such a life consists of nine interpersonal attitudes and actions that enhance a Christian's personal life and fellowship with other believers (vv. 22, 23). These nine graces of the Spirit, not to be understood as exhaustive, focus on the personal relations of Christians with one another.

Love (*agapē*) stands at the head of the list since it is the most important. Christ is the best example about whom Paul says, "the Son of God, who loved me, and gave himself for me" (Galatians 2:20, KJV). Prompted by the Holy Spirit, love is self-giving action for the benefit of others and involves much more than affectionate feelings (1 Corinthians 13).

Joy (*chara*) is an important aspect of the Christian life. As a spiritual grace in the believer's life, joy does not depend on outward circumstances. The Thessalonian Christians had "received the word in much tribulation with the joy of the Holy Spirit" (1 Thessalonians 1:6). Paul tended to connect joy with fellowship of believers. Paul had joy because of the progress that his converts were making in learning to have confidence and trust in God (Philippians 1:25, 26; 2 Corinthians 2:3). Joy that the Holy Spirit cultivates in the hearts of believers arises out of their knowing Christ and enhances their fellowship with one another.

Peace (*eirēnē*) suggests the idea of total well-being and is a mark of God's children. Through His cross, Christ removed barriers that divide people into hostile groups, bringing them together into one body, the church (Ephesians 2:14-16). The Holy Spirit fosters personal peace that is to be evident in believers' interpersonal relationships. Good relationships are never automatic. Because of this, believers are urged to "seek peace and pursue it" (1 Peter 3:11).

Patience (*makrothumia*) expresses the idea of long-suffering. The Lord is long-suffering and slow to anger (Exodus 34:6; Psalm 103:8). Thus the grace of the Holy Spirit is revealed when one refuses to be provoked, or to retaliate when hurt or taken advantage of (Matthew 5:44). Long-suffering is a characteristic of Christian love. Such love suffers long and is patient and kind (1 Corinthians 13:4). Therefore, patience is the staying power of love in our dealings and relationships with others.

Kindness (*chrēstotēs*) can be described as an attitude of goodness that puts love into action. God's kindness is evident throughout the Bible, but is especially evident in His gracious attitude and actions toward sinners (Romans 2:4; Ephesians 2:7). Christian kindness is essential to the forgiveness of each other. As God has treated us, so we are to treat others: "Be kind to one another, tender-hearted, forgiving each other, just as God in Christ also has forgiven you" (Ephesians 4:32).

Goodness (*agathōsunē*) expresses the idea of generosity. This spiritual grace is generous kindness to others and stands in contrast to envy, which is an attitude that begrudges others' success and prosperity. The Holy Spirit cultivates the practice of magnanimous generosity—that is, doing good to others in useful ways, especially to the household of faith (2 Thessalonians 1:11).

Faithfulness (*pistis*), at times, in the Bible indiates faith by which we accept Christ (Romans 3:22; Galatians 2:16). At other times it indicates faithfulness, which is a spiritual grace in the daily life of the Christian (Galatians 5:22). Being faithful is being steadfast, dependable and trustworthy. Paul emphasizes God's faithfulness again and again (Romans 3:3; 1 Corinthians 1:9). Likewise, God's people are to be faithful. The Holy Spirit cultivates in their hearts faithfulness to God and to each other.

Gentleness (*prautēs*) is closely related to meekness (*epieikeia*) and means "strength under control." Paul addressed the Christians in Corinth "by the meekness and gentleness of Christ" (2 Corinthians 10:1). However, in his interactions with them, he did not hesitate to rebuke those who were causing trouble. Correction expressed through gentleness does not allow for the loss of self-control. Since human passions are stronger than human will, only the Holy Spirit can tame the passions of the heart and produce self-control, so that we can show gentleness to all people (Titus 3:2).

Self-Control (*egkrateia*) is having mastery over one's own desires (2 Peter 1:5, 6; 1 Corinthians 9:25; Galatians 5:24; Titus 2:12; 1 Peter 1:13). The Holy Spirit gives Christians strength to control sexual and other sensual desires and to resist temptation, so that they may live pure lives that are not corrupted by the evil in the world.

The nine fruit of the Spirit, or spiritual graces, grow together like a beautiful cluster of fruit. The Spirit plants in believers the motivations and abilities for Christian living, but like a vine planted in the earth, the bearing of fruit is not automatic. The vine must be watered and nourished by the sun and soil in order to produce good fruit. Believers must see to it that they receive proper spiritual nourishment by living a balanced Christian life. Such a life will include a balance of prayer, worship, study, service, fellowship with other believers, physical care and rest. Paul gives us two captivating descriptions of the Spirit's role in nurturing beautiful graces in the lives of believers:

We are led by the Spirit (Romans 8:14). The Spirit manifests the Christlike life in us as we are led by Him. He inspires our hearts and minds to do what is good and right. As we allow ourselves to be led by Him, He adorns our lives with graces that identify us as God's children.

We walk in the Spirit (Galatians 5:16). It is similar to being led by the Spirit, but in the New Testament, walking emphasizes a way of life. As we walk in the power of the Spirit, we march in line with Him and walk the steps that the Spirit walks. As we follow the Spirit, the fruit of the Spirit flourishes in our lives.

CONCLUSION

The Christian life is rooted and grounded in the Holy Spirit. To be converted to the gospel is to receive the Holy Spirit. No one can receive "life in Christ" apart from the work of the Holy Spirit (Galatians 3:2, 3). God has placed the Spirit into our hearts. His presence assures us that we are children of God with all the rights and privileges of being members of His great family (Romans 8:16). By the power of the Spirit, we put to death selfish desires and evil deeds (v. 13). The fruit of the Spirit in our lives offers concrete evidence of the Christian life (see Romans 14:17; Galatians 5:22, 23; 2 Peter 1:5-7). Finally, "the one who sows to the Spirit will from the Spirit reap eternal life" (Galatians 6:8). Eternal life flows from the Holy Spirit.

Summary

- The Holy Spirit invites people to come to Christ and initiates them into the body of Christ.

- The Holy Spirit is active in the events leading to conversion, during the experience of conversion, and in the new life that follows conversion.

- The Holy Spirit gives believers spiritual graces through which they express Christ's love in the world.

TABLE 2-A **The Spirit's Work in Conversion**	
The Spirit is active in events that lead to conversion, during conversion and in the new life that follows conversion.	
The Spirit's Call to Conversion	
The Holy Spirit invites us to meet Christ. JOHN 16:5-15	
JOHN 16:8; 1 CORINTHIANS 2:1-5; 1 THESSALONIANS 1:5, 6	The Holy Spirit convicts us of our sin, making us aware of our wrongdoings and our need for Christ.
ACTS 5:31; 10:19-43; 13:39; 20:21; ROMANS 2:4	The Holy Spirit inspires people to accept God's invitation to repent, to have faith in Christ, and to live in eternity with Him.
The Spirit's Work During Conversion	
The Holy Spirit applies to us the saving benefits of Christ and transforms our lives. GALATIANS 4:6, 28, 29	
ROMANS 5:15; 8:1, 2; 2 CORINTHIANS 3:6; EPHESIANS 2:5; cf. JOHN 3:36	We receive a new birth.
JOHN 6:63; ACTS 10:43; 13:39; 20:21	We receive spiritual awakening from a life of death.
PROVERBS 2:13; ACTS 26:18; ROMANS 1:21; 13:12; EPHESIANS 5:11; COLOSSIANS 1:12, 13; 1 PETER 2:9; 1 JOHN 1:6; 2:9-11	We are released from darkness into the light.

continued

TABLE 2-A (CONTINUED)	
The Spirit's Work in Conversion	
GENESIS 17; ROMANS 2:29; COLOSSIANS 2:11; 3:5-11	We receive a "circumcision of the heart," that is, a changed heart as sign of our new life in Christ.

The Spirit's Indwelling at Conversion

The Holy Spirit makes His home in those who believe in Jesus Christ.
ROMANS 8:9, 14, 26, 27; 1 CORINTHIANS 12:3, 6-13;
2 CORINTHIANS 6:16; GALATIANS 3:2, 5, 14; 4:6; 5:22, 23; JUDE 19

1 KINGS 21:8-10; ROMANS 8:16; 2 CORINTHIANS 1:22; EPHESIANS 4:30	Those who follow Christ are sealed with the Spirit.
1 CORINTHIANS 6:19; cf. 2 CORINTHIANS 13:14	Those who follow Christ are the temple of the Holy Spirit.
2 CORINTHIANS 1:22; 5:5; EPHESIANS 1:13, 14; cf. HEBREWS 6:4, 5	Those who follow Christ receive the Holy Spirit as a pledge, or promise, of the blessings that are to come.

The Spirit's Witness to Our Conversion

The Holy Spirit affirms our standing as children of God.
ROMANS 8:16; GALATIANS 4:4-6

ROMANS 8:1, 33, 34	The Spirit gives us divine assurance that we have been pardoned of all of our sins.
ROMANS 5:5; 8:15; GALATIANS 4:6	The Spirit gives us assurance that we have been adopted into God's family.

TABLE 2-B
The Spirit's Fruit in Our Lives

The life of the Christian is a matter of walking with the Spirit, growing in the grace and knowledge of Christ as we walk.

GALATIANS 5:22, 23; EPHESIANS 1:15; 4:2, 3;
PHILIPPIANS 1:9-11; COLOSSIANS 1:10; 2 PETER 1:5-8

Love

1 CORINTHIANS 13; GALATIANS 2:20	Love is self-giving action for the benefit of others.

Joy

PHILIPPIANS 1:25, 26; 1 THESSALONIANS 1:6	Joy that the Holy Spirit cultivates in the hearts of believers arises out of their knowing Christ, and it enhances their fellowship with one another.

Peace

EPHESIANS 2:14-16; 1 PETER 3:11	Peace suggests the idea of total well-being in personal and community life.

Patience

EXODUS 34:6; PSALM 103:8; 1 CORINTHIANS 13:4	Patience is the expression of long-suffering love for others.

Kindness

ROMANS 2:4; EPHESIANS 2:7; 4:32	Kindness is an attitude of goodness that puts love into action.

continued

TABLE 2-B (CONTINUED)
The Spirit's Fruit in Our Lives

Goodness	
2 THESSALONIANS 1:11	Goodness is generous kindness to others and prompts one to be pleased when others are blessed and are successful in life.
Faithfulness	
ROMANS 3:3; 1 CORINTHIANS 1:9	Faithfulness is a state of being steady, dependable and trustworthy.
Gentleness	
2 CORINTHIANS 10:1; TITUS 3:2	Gentleness, a spiritual grace closely related to meekness, indicates having one's strength under control.
Self-Control	
ACTS 24:25; cf. 2 PETER 1:5, 6	Self-control is having mastery over one's own desires.

The Holy Spirit nurtures beautiful graces in the lives of believers, as we follow His lead and walk with Him on our journey through life.

ROMANS 8:14; GALATIANS 5:16

Notes

77

Chapter 2—Study and Discussion

The Holy Spirit and Conversion

The Spirit's Call to Conversion

1. When does our initial encounter with the Holy Spirit occur? (See Table 2-A.)
2. What are two actions that the Holy Spirit performs in our call to conversion? Please give examples of these actions in the Bible. (See Table 2-A.)
3. What is a definition for the word *repentance*? (See Glossary.)
4. What is a definition for the word *faith*? (See Glossary.)

The Spirit's Work During Conversion

5. What is the central role of the Holy Spirit in conversion? (See Table 2-A.)
6. What saving benefits of Christ does the Holy Spirit give us when we accept Jesus Christ as our Savior and follow Him? Look up some passages in the Bible that describe these spiritual blessings. (See Table 2-A.)

The Spirit's Indwelling at Conversion

7. When does the Holy Spirit come to live in a person? (See Table 2-A.)
8. Please give some examples from the New Testament that discuss the Spirit's making His home in those who believe in Jesus Christ. (See Table 2-A.)
9. In the Bible, there are a variety of phrases that describe the Spirit's indwelling of believers. What are a few of these? Please give examples from the Bible. (See Table 2-A.)

The Spirit's Witness to Our Conversion

10. According to Romans 8:16, what does the Holy Spirit do for us? (See Table 2-A.)

11. What are two ways that the Holy Spirit affirms our standing as children of God? Give examples from Scripture that describe the Spirit's affirmations. (See Table 2-A.)

THE SPIRIT'S FRUIT IN OUR LIVES

12. What role does the Holy Spirit play in the Christian's daily walk? (See Galatians 5:22, 23; Ephesians 4:2, 3; Philippians 1:9-11; 2 Peter 1:5-8.)

13. What are "fruit of the Spirit" or "spiritual graces"? (See Glossary.)

14. For each of the spiritual fruit (graces) listed in the box below, please do the following:

> Love, Joy, Peace,
> Patience, Kindness, Goodness,
> Faithfulness, Gentleness, Self-control

(See Table 2-B.)

a. Read passages from the Bible about each fruit.

b. Describe some characteristics of each fruit.

c. Think of how you have expressed the fruit in your own life.

d. How would you like to express these spiritual graces in the future?

15. How should we cultivate spiritual fruit, or graces, in our lives? (See Romans 8:14; Galatians 5:16.)

16. Think of a change you might make in your life that would cause your Christian walk to be more spiritually balanced and would create nourishment for the Spirit's fruit to flourish.

CONCLUSION

17. What promise does God give us in Galatians 6:8?

Part Three

Spirit Baptism

All Scripture is inspired by God and is profitable for teaching, for reproof, for correction, for training in righteousness (2 Timothy 3:16).

3

Understanding the Bible

The rise of the Pentecostal and Charismatic Movements has prompted much dialogue and debate about the role of the Holy Spirit in Christian experience. The interpretation of baptism in the Spirit, which stands at the heart of classical Pentecostalism, has been the major focal point in the debate. Pentecostals understand that Spirit baptism[1] is distinct from and subsequent to (follows) conversion and that its purpose is empowerment for ministry and service. In addition to the Holy Spirit's coming to dwell in us at conversion, baptism in the Spirit is another blessing that God promises to all believers. The Gospel of Luke and the Book of Acts support the Pentecostal doctrine of Spirit baptism. To get a clearer picture, we must first consider some of the basics that will guide us in understanding this distinctive doctrine of being baptized in (filled with) the Spirit.

BIBLICAL INTERPRETATION

Pentecostal Principles for Interpreting the Bible

From the beginning of the modern Pentecostal Movement,

---

[1]The term *Spirit baptism* is used as a shorthand way of speaking of "baptism in the Spirit" or "filled with the Spirit."

Spirit-filled believers have seen the Bible as the Word of God and have taken it at face value. It has been the standard by which they have lived and the basis for their expecting to encounter the supernatural manifestations of Scripture. Their experience with the Holy Spirit definitely has shaped their understanding of the Bible, that it "not only represents witness to God, but it is the very Word of God." [2] Still committed to this view of Scripture, Pentecostal scholars have become more adept at translating matters of the Spirit than some of the earlier interpreters. Following sound principles of interpretation is vital to the examination of Spirit baptism as a second and subsequent normative experience for Christians. These principles will provide the framework for this study and will guide us through our exploration of the Scriptures.

Interpretation and Authority of Scripture

In order to speak with confidence about our beliefs, we need an authoritative source, and that source is the Bible. The Holy Spirit is its divine author, and as God's Word it is fully reliable. The key passage in the Bible regarding its authorship is 2 Timothy 3:16: "All Scripture is inspired by God and is profitable for teaching, for reproof, for correction, for training in righteousness." Furthermore, Paul believed that "whatever was written in earlier times was written for our instruction" (Romans 15:4; cf. 1 Corinthians 10:11). Pentecostals believe that the Holy Spirit does not contradict Himself in Scripture. They also believe that the experiences of the apostles are recorded as lessons for us. Luke recorded them in the Book of Acts for our instruction.

The Biblical Text as a Whole

Sound Biblical exposition must take seriously the Scriptures

---

[2]Kenneth J. Archer, "Pentecostal Hermeneutics: Retrospect and Prospect," *Journal of Pentecostal Theology* 8 (1996) 67.

as a whole. Study of the whole Scripture guards against reading into a passage what is not there. Such a practice helps ensure that our understanding of Scripture is controlled by the teaching of the Scripture itself and not by our immediate desires. With a holistic, disciplined approach to study, we can fully embrace God's Word as the rule and practice in our lives.

Particular Emphases of Biblical Authors

Each book of the Bible is unique, with each of its human authors emphasizing different aspects of the faith. For example, Matthew emphasizes the doctrine of the church. John emphasizes the deity and humanity of Christ. Paul's emphasis falls on justification by faith, and Luke emphasizes the charismatic, dynamic aspects of the Spirit's ministry. None of them contradicts another; however, the authors should be understood in the light of their particular emphases. A Biblical writer is therefore best understood according to his own terms and uniqueness and in context with the whole of God's Word. This is to say, when people read or hear an author's teachings, they should then relate that author's teachings to the teachings of other Biblical writers and to the whole of Scripture.

Literary Form

A full range of literary forms can be found in the Bible—historical narrative, legal code, poetry, parables (storytelling), apocalyptic writings, wisdom literature, gospels, epistles, and so forth. Pentecostals recognize Luke/Acts as an example of historical narrative. In sound interpretation, 1 Corinthians is interpreted as an epistle and Luke/Acts as a historical narrative. Luke, in his Gospel and in Acts, intends to present more than a historical account of the life and ministry of Jesus Christ and the early church. He uses history as a means of teaching Christian doctrine. As the Old Testament narratives served as instructional lessons, the historical accounts about the outpouring of the Holy Spirit in Acts are intended by Luke to instruct the church on the normative for Christian experience. The apostle Paul indicates his understanding of historical narratives as instruments of instruction when he writes about the wilderness experience of Israel that is recorded in the Old Testament: "Now these things happened to them as an example, and they were written for our instruction, upon whom the ends of the ages have come" (1 Corinthians 10:11). He makes no distinction between Scripture that teaches doctrine and Scripture that simply records history (cf. Romans 15:4). Pentecostals and Charismatics who approach the Scripture with an understanding that historical narratives serve to teach doctrine are more likely to come to a better understanding of the teachings regarding the Pentecostal experience in the Book of Acts.

The Grammatical-Historical Method of Interpretation

The presence of the Holy Spirit in one's life does not mean that a person receives knowledge of the Scriptures apart from study and research. The Holy Spirit and the Charismatic experience should not lead Pentecostals to disregard the historical context of a Scripture passage nor the grammatical significance of it. Literary form is important because we do not interpret an epistle as we do poetry. This literary aspect of interpretation, however, should not place form over content.

Likewise, emphasis on illumination by the Holy Spirit should not deny the importance of historical setting and grammar when interpreting Scripture. All these elements have an essential and proper place in Biblical interpretation. God made us in His image. Because of our being in His image, we have a human intellect that distinguishes us from His other creatures. God expects us to use our minds in understanding the Bible. Pentecostals must guard against rejecting the rational in favor of the experiential. Serious interpretation of the Bible includes both. Since analytical thinking is as important as feelings and experiences, Pentecostals must be committed to developing and exercising all of their mental skills.

Experience and the Illumination of the Holy Spirit

The Holy Spirit illuminates the Scripture, informing and enlightening those who engage in serious and sober study of God's Word. This process of spiritual understanding points to the importance of the experiential and spiritual elements in interpreting the Word of God. The experience of Spirit baptism and illumination by the Spirit have a place in the interpretation process.[3] The Scriptures are spiritual, so they must be understood spiritually—that is, by the present help of the Holy Spirit. Paul himself teaches that the Spirit's illumination is necessary in order to grasp the fullest significance of the Biblical text. The full meaning of the gospel remains unclear until the Holy Spirit, who has full knowledge of the deep things of God, illuminates its truths to us (1 Corinthians 2:6-16). The Holy Spirit bridges the time gap between inspiration in the past and interpretation in the present. Therefore, just as Scripture has the stamp of the Spirit upon it, sound interpretation also has the imprint of the Spirit upon it.[4] In short, what the Spirit has given should be interpreted by the Spirit.

Other Viewpoints on Interpreting the Bible

Early Pentecostals insisted that what they had experienced was the "Bible pattern." For them, this pattern included Spirit baptism that is distinct and separate from conversion. They believed that the purpose of this baptism was to equip God's people with power for mission and ministry. Their argument, however, failed to persuade many evangelical Christians. For these Christians,

---

[3]See French L. Arrington, "Hermeneutics, Historical Perspectives on Pentecostal and Charismatic," *Dictionary of Pentecostal and Charismatic Movements*, eds. Stanley M. Burgess, Gary B. McGee and Patrick H. Alexander (Grand Rapids: Zondervan, 1988) 382-384.

[4]Roger Stronstad, *Spirit, Scripture and Theology* (Baquio City, Philippines: Asia Pacific Theological Seminary Press, 1995) 74.

baptism in the Spirit was not subsequent to conversion, but the same as regeneration and transformation, symbolized in water baptism. Though admired by many for their spiritual fervor, Pentecostals and Charismatics have not been without their critics, especially for the way they understand Scripture. Let us consider three objections that have been proposed:

Understanding Historical Narrative

Since the Book of Acts is written in historical narrative form, the argument is that Acts must be seen merely as history and not as a basis for doctrine. According to this view, it is improper to establish doctrine from the Acts accounts of the outpouring of the Spirit (2:1-42; 8:14-24; 10:1-48; 19:1-7). It is clear that Luke does record a narrative description of the Day of Pentecost. On that day those present spoke in tongues, an experience subsequent to the Spirit's work of salvation in their lives. Embracing the view that current Christian doctrine cannot rest on these accounts erodes away the pillars upon which Pentecostals' doctrine of the Holy Spirit is built. This view that the Book of Acts only records history, although difficult to understand in light of the Holy Spirit's work in Acts, objects to Spirit baptism as distinct from conversion and sees the two terms as describing the same experience. Such an assumption denies that Biblical narratives establish a precedent for what should be fundamental to Christian experience and doctrine.

Let us consider two arguments that have been proposed to support the view that conversion and Spirit baptism are not distinct experiences:

Non-Pentecostals often say there is no Scriptural statement that the disciples' experience is for all believers and that tongues will accompany Spirit baptism. Equally true is the fact that there is no statement that God exists in three persons, nor that Christ is fully man and fully God in Scripture; but we conclude from the teaching of Scripture that both are true. How else could we justify the doctrine of the Trinity and that Christ is both human and divine, yet one person? The New Testament makes no statement about either of these Biblical doctrines.

A second argument of non-Pentecostals is that Pentecostals are inconsistent in their interpretation of Acts. They point out that Pentecostals insist on "historical precedent" as a basis for their doctrine of a post-conversion experience of empowerment by the Spirit. If they were consistent, they would also follow the examples of selling properties in order to combine their financial resources (4:32-37) or of casting lots to make decisions (1:21-26). The reason Pentecostals do not follow these practices is that nowhere in the New Testament are we told that God directed the church as a whole to do these things. The disciples themselves took the initiative in these matters, possibly being led by the Spirit to perform particular actions in particular situations. These activities, however, were not reoccurring patterns among the early believers; they were local practices limited to the church in Jerusalem. Being filled with the Spirit, however, is an experience for all believers, not limited to any ethnic group or geographical location: "For the promise is for you and your children and for all who are far off, as many as the Lord our God will call to Himself" (Acts 2:39). The experience is divinely initiated activity and commanded by God (Luke 24:49; Acts 1:8; 2:14ff.).

Luke's Intent in Writing the Book of Acts

What was Luke's purpose in writing Acts? The answer often given is that his intent was to provide an account of the spread of the gospel over the Roman world, but it was not meant to teach baptism in the Holy Spirit as an experience for believers today. In the Book of Acts, Luke does give an account of the spread of the gospel, but in this account, he also introduces other key doctrinal themes. These themes include the power of the Holy Spirit for ministry, forgiveness of sin, salvation, prayer, resurrection and ascension of Jesus, divine providence, revelation in creation, and the Day of Judgment. In Acts, Luke illustrates and emphasizes these themes through specific historical examples. The impact of the gospel on the Roman world cannot be understood apart from the power of the Spirit's being poured out at Pentecost and on other occasions.

Most interpreters regard Acts 1:8 as the key verse that summarizes the Book of Acts. The two main clauses of this verse are closely related and must not be separated from one another: "You will receive power when the Holy Spirit comes on you; and you will be my witnesses" (*NIV*). The command to go into the world with the gospel still holds true. Therefore, it is reasonable to conclude that just as the spiritual power that Jesus had promised to His disciples was needed for spreading the gospel in New Testament times, it is also needed to carry out the church's mission in the world today.

Luke intends in Acts to record history *and* to teach doctrine. These are also his purposes in writing the Gospel of Luke. Further, the Gospel of Luke and the Book of Acts are a single work of the same author. Acts must not be separated from the study of Luke's Gospel. This one work (Luke/Acts) gives an account of the origin and spread of the gospel. Luke's Gospel tells about the life and ministry of Christ, and the Book of Acts about the life and ministry of the early church. The unity of the third Gospel and Acts demands that both books be interpreted together so that we can recognize the unity of the historical and doctrinal themes of both books. It is inconsistent to insist, as do some interpreters, that the Gospel of Luke teaches doctrine but to deny the same for the Book of Acts. Luke/Acts underscores the doctrinal and experiential importance of being led and empowered by the Spirit to render effective ministry today.

Distinction Between Conversion and Spirit Baptism

Some Christians' viewpoint that baptism "in" the Spirit is not distinct from conversion is often related to the previous views that we have discussed. From a little different perspective, their argument attempts to identify Spirit baptism as a part of conversion. According to this view, those who experienced the outpouring of the Spirit in Acts were representative groups who experienced God's saving grace on those occasions. Proponents of this view often propose that Luke's purpose is not to describe a separate and distinct experience apart from conversion, but simply to show the spread of the gospel and to demonstrate that God's grace is for all people: the Jews in Jerusalem (ch. 2), the Samaritans (ch. 8), the Gentiles (ch. 10) and the disciples of John the Baptist (ch. 19).

This position overlooks several things:

1. *It overlooks the fact that the disciples at Pentecost had already been converted.* Scripture does not indicate the precise time of their conversion; but as believers indwelt by the Holy Spirit, they went to Jerusalem as Christ had instructed them (Luke 24:49). Then, as He had promised, they were empowered by the Spirit on the Day of Pentecost for a charismatic ministry (Acts 2:6ff).

2. *It overlooks the fact that Paul was saved on the road to Damascus and that later he was filled with the Spirit (9:17).* Though converted and indwelt by the Spirit, he needed to be empowered by the Spirit to fulfill his new vocation in life: "bear My name before the Gentiles" (v. 15).

3. *It overlooks the fact that the 12 men in Acts 19:1-7 were already Christians before Paul met them.* However, through Paul's ministry they received the charismatic power of the Holy Spirit as the believers had on the Day of Pentecost.

BIBLICAL TERMINOLOGY
The Term *Baptism* in the Bible

There are three types of baptism discussed in the Bible: conversion baptism, water baptism and Spirit baptism. Each of these baptisms requires that there be an agent who does the baptizing, an element in which the baptism takes place, and a candidate who is baptized.

Conversion baptism occurs when one comes to faith in Jesus Christ. Repenting and turning away from sin, he or she is "baptized" or incorporated into the body of Christ, the church, by the Holy Spirit, consequently being placed "in Christ." Paul speaks of baptism at the time of conversion in 1 Corinthians 12:13 and Galatians 3:26, 27. In conversion baptism, the Holy Spirit is the agent inviting us to Christ and baptizing us into the body of Christ. Jesus Christ is the element, and the new believer is the candidate.

Water baptism signifies what happened at the moment of conversion. It is, therefore, a visible sign of the participant's dying and rising with Christ, illustrating the end of the old life and the beginning of the new life in Christ (Acts 8:13, 16, 34-38; Romans 6:1-14). In water baptism, the minister is the agent, the water is the element, and the people are the candidates. For example, in Biblical times John the Baptist served as the agent of water baptism, immersing people in water; the water of the Jordan River was the element; and the candidates were those who asked to be baptized.

Spirit baptism is a shorthand way of speaking of "baptism in the spirit." This is a distinct and empowering experience for mission and worship subsequent to conversion (Acts 1:8; 2:1-4; 8:15-17; 10:44-46; 19:1-7). In Spirit baptism, Jesus Christ is the agent, the Spirit is the element, and the candidates are followers of Jesus Christ. Since in Spirit baptism the Holy Spirit is the element into which believers are immersed, we call Spirit baptism being "baptized *in* the Spirit."

A Variety of Terms for Spirit Baptism

Luke/Acts emphasizes the dynamic presence of the Holy Spirit. Many of the references to the Spirit tell about His coming in power and provide examples of His encounters with people.

Luke uses a variety of words and phrases to describe these encounters. A number of the terms are used interchangeably and are more or less synonyms, but they do suggest the profound, powerful and spiritual richness of the Pentecostal anointing (empowerment) by the Spirit. Consequently, the various terms are ways of defining what it means to be baptized in the Spirit:

Baptism in the Spirit (Acts 1:5; 11:16)

The image of Spirit baptism comes from the practice of water baptism by immersion. The verb *baptize* generally means "to dip." Like a garment dipped in water, the believer who receives the Pentecostal experience is immersed in the Spirit. That person's life is permeated and saturated with the power of the Spirit for service and for living a holy life (a life in which one endeavors to follow God's will in all aspects of living). Therefore, Spirit baptism is immersion. However, it is not immersion in liquid, but it is immersion in the Spirit.

Promise of the Father (Acts 1:4; Luke 24:49)

This phrase focuses on the activity of the Father. Baptism in the Spirit is seen as a promise that God himself made (Greek subjective genitive). Peter, at Pentecost, interpreted the outpouring of the Spirit as the fulfillment of the promise that God gave through the prophet Joel. The same promise had been given through Isaiah (44:3) and Ezekiel (36:27; 37:14). The Father was the source of the promise, and that promise included both the indwelling of the Spirit in every believer and the experience of immersion in the Spirit. The Father began to fulfill His promise to pour out the Spirit "on all people" at Pentecost (Acts 2:17, *NIV*). The modern Pentecostal/Charismatic Movement bears witness to the continuation of this fulfillment.

Promise of the Spirit (Acts 2:33, 39)

The word *promise* refers to, and is the same as, the Holy Spirit (Greek genitive of apposition). The Holy Spirit is the Spirit that

God the Father promised to send. To experience the fulfillment of this promise is to receive the fullness of the Spirit. The exalted Christ himself received the promised Holy Spirit. Then Christ, in turn, poured out the Spirit at Pentecost. For the 120 disciples, the promised Holy Spirit ceased to be a promise and became a reality.

The Spirit's Coming (Luke 1:35; 3:22; Acts 1:8; 19:6) or Falling Upon (Acts 8:16; 10:44; 11:15)

In a vivid way, both expressions signify the arrival of the Spirit. We are told that "the Holy Spirit came on them" (Acts 19:6) and "the Holy Spirit fell upon" (10:44). The phrase "came on" means about the same thing as "clothed with" (Luke 24:49) and suggests the continuing powerful presence of the Spirit. However, the "falling" of the Spirit emphasizes the suddenness, the forcefulness of Spirit baptism. At Pentecost, the Spirit came or "fell" suddenly and with great force—"like a violent rushing wind" (Acts 2:2).

The Spirit's Being Poured Out by God (Acts 2:17, 18, 33; 10:45)

"Being poured out" is the way that Joel 2:28, 29 and Zechariah 12:10 described the coming of the Spirit. The picture is not that of sprinkling, but of a deluge. God does not give the Spirit sparingly, but as the word *outpouring* suggests, without measure. There is a streaming down, a deluge, and an abundance of the Spirit from above.

Gift of the Spirit (Acts 2:38; 10:45; 11:17)

The gift is the Spirit (Greek genitive of apposition). The word *gift* emphasizes that Spirit baptism is free and the consequence solely of God's grace. As salvation is a gift of God, so is "baptism" or "immersion" in the Spirit. It is not a result of our own efforts, so no one can boast (Ephesians 2:8, 9). Peter explained clearly that God is the giver of Spirit baptism. Speaking in reference to the Gentiles' receiving the fullness of the Spirit, he declares, "God gave to them the same gift as He gave to us also after believing in the Lord Jesus Christ" (Acts 11:17).[5]

Receiving the Spirit (Acts 2:38; 8:15, 17, 19; 10:47; 19:2)

God takes the initiative in pouring out His Spirit. For this reason Spirit baptism is explained primarily from the standpoint of the Giver rather than from the standpoint of the receiver. Nevertheless, to receive this spiritual blessing demands human response and cooperation with God. The verb *receive* (active voice) indicates the importance of human response to this divine initiative. Many of the early believers "received" the power of the Holy Spirit, clearly indicating an accompanying human response to God's initiative. Receiving the Holy Spirit is a necessary component of being "filled with the Spirit." What God gives is to be received by faith.

Filled With the Spirit (Acts 2:4; 4:8, 31; 9:17; 13:9, 52)

The verb *fill* points to penetration and diffusion throughout every part, whereas the verb *baptize* suggests submergence in the Spirit. "Filling" indicates a full penetration and diffusion of the Spirit. Both terms can be used interchangeably. They both emphasize totality, pointing to the Spirit who claims the Spirit-filled believer in totality (Acts 1:8; 2:4). Nevertheless, the term *baptize* seems to refer more to the initial aspect of the experience, whereas *filling* has a broader application. The term *filling* may describe the experience of believers who receive the initial fullness of the Spirit or believers who receive spiritual renewal. A person may experience spiritual "filling" or renewal many times throughout life (Acts 4:31; 13:50-52; cf. Ephesians 5:18). Those who continue living a Spirit-filled life can properly be

---

[5]The term *gift* of the Spirit discussed here indicates the Father's gift of the Holy Spirit to believers. The "gifts of the Spirit" or "spiritual gifts" discussed later in this book refer to special gifts given by the Holy Spirit to those who have received the Father's "gift of the Spirit."

described as "full of the Spirit" (Luke 4:1; Acts 6:3, 5; 7:55; 11:24).

The different terms for Spirit baptism are used to describe various perspectives on the outpouring of the Spirit, but each term refers to the same experience. Many of the terms are used interchangeably in the following four major accounts in Acts:

- **Pentecostal Account (Acts 1:1–2:42)**
  baptize (1:5); come (v. 8); fill (2:4); pour (vv. 17, 18, 33); receive (v. 38)

- **Samaria Account (8:14-24)**
  receive (vv. 15, 17, 19); fall upon (v. 16)

- **Cornelius Account (10:1–11:18; 15:7-11)**
  pour (10:45); receive (v. 47); fall upon (v. 44; 11:15); baptize (v. 16); give (v. 17; 15:8)

- **Ephesus Account (19:1-7)**
  receive (v. 2); come (v. 6)

Luke uses terms that are rich and diverse to describe the experience of abundant spiritual empowerment. The variety of terms indicates that Spirit baptism is a dynamic, complex experience. No single term adequately explains its significance. At the heart of the Pentecostal experience lie a momentous event and a dynamic reality of the presence and power of God. This gift of God's power, Spirit baptism, provides spiritual empowerment even beyond what has been experienced in conversion.

Differences in the Terms
"Baptism BY, IN and WITH the Holy Spirit"

As discussed earlier, a variety of terms is often used in the Bible to refer to Spirit baptism. Within Pentecostal/Charismatic churches and communities, phrases commonly used to describe encounters with the Spirit may include "baptized by the Spirit," "baptized in the

Spirit," "baptized with the Spirit," "filled with the Spirit," "the Spirit falls on," and "the Spirit is poured out." The following discussion seeks to clarify the meaning of each of these phrases and to determine the best language to most accurately describe encounters with the Holy Spirit. The best place to start our examination of terminology is to explore the usage of Greek terminology in the Bible.

How Context Affects the Meaning of Terms

One issue in determining the correct terminology is to look at the usage of the Greek terms within their context. If we examine the context in which terms are used, we often find that meanings of words and phrases vary according to how the author has used them in the text.

The Question of the Meaning of the Greek Word *En*

The Greek word *en* is a preposition used in the Bible in connection with the word *baptize*. When we examine the usage of this term, a pivotal question arises: Does the New Testament make a distinction between being baptized *by* the Holy Spirit and being baptized *in* the Holy Spirit? The Greek word *en* can be translated either as "by" or "in" the Holy Spirit.[6] The term one chooses to use can indicate that the Holy Spirit is either the agent by whom we are baptized or is the element into whom we are immersed.

In the Gospels and Acts, seven passages contain the verb *baptize* with the preposition *en* and the noun *Holy Spirit* or *Spirit* (Matthew 3:11; Mark 1:8; Luke 3:16; John 1:33; Acts 1:5, 8; 11:16). When examining these passages for answers about terminology, these are the questions to be addressed: (1) Should the preposition in all

---

[6]The Greek preposition *en*, when it is used with the dative case, should be taken either as instrumental (*by, with*) or locative (*in*). No New Testament writer speaks about a "baptism *of* the Holy Spirit"; but "baptism *en* the Holy Spirit" can mean either baptized *by* the Holy Spirit into the body of Christ (the church) at conversion or baptized *in* the Spirit (filled with, immersed into) following conversion.

these passages be translated "in"? (2) Do these verses teach a baptism in the Spirit that empowers the believer for service? The intent here is not to split theological hairs on the basis of Greek grammar, but to help us understand the nature of baptism in the Spirit, emphasizing that it is an experience in which the believer is totally immersed in the Spirit.

Baptism BY One Spirit (Conversion Baptism)

Paul's terminology when discussing the Holy Spirit in 1 Corinthians is similar to that used by John the Baptist, Jesus and Peter in their discussions of the Holy Spirit in the Gospels and in the Book of Acts. Paul uses the term *one Spirit*, which is similar to the more common designation of *Holy Spirit* in the Gospels. Paul, when referring to the Spirit along with the concept of baptism, precedes the verb *baptize* with the phrase "by [*en*] one Spirit."

Although Paul's terminology in 1 Corinthians 12:13 is similar to the language used in the Gospels and Acts, upon examination one can see that the context is different and that this context affects the meaning of what is being communicated. For example, in 1 Corinthians 12:3 we read, "No one speaking by [*en*] the Spirit of God says, 'Jesus is accursed.' " Another way to say this might be that "no one being led or empowered *by* the Spirit of God denies the deity of Jesus." The context here implies that the Holy Spirit is the agent or doer. Likewise in verse 9 where Paul is identifying a number of spiritual gifts, he says, "To another faith by [*en*] the same Spirit, and to another gifts of healing by [*en*] the one Spirit." These verses indicate that the gifts are received *by* or *from* the Spirit. The Holy Spirit is actually the giver of the gifts; He is the doer of the action.

In order to glean this meaning, it is necessary to understand both verses 3 and 9 of 1 Corinthians 12 and to consider their immediate context. Look also at verse 13 where Paul emphasizes "*by* one Spirit": "For by one Spirit we were all baptized into one body,

TABLE 3-E **Distinctions Among Frequently Used Terms**	
Conversion Baptism	**Spirit Baptism**
Baptism BY the (Holy) Spirit	Baptism IN the (Holy) Spirit
Regeneration by the (Holy) Spirit	Being filled with the (Holy) Spirit

Baptism WITH the (Holy) Spirit

A less descriptive term, the role of the Holy Spirit being unclear. The terms above are preferred.

Baptism OF the (Holy) Spirit

A phrase that makes the Holy Spirit the agent of Spirit baptism rather than the element of it. The phrase is not used in the Greek New Testament to refer to being filled with the Spirit.

whether Jews or Greeks, whether slaves or free." From these three verses (3, 9, 13), we see that the Holy Spirit is the agent or the active person in conversion as well as in the giving of spiritual gifts. Thus the Greek word *en* in these verses is best translated to English as *by* rather than *in*. This usage of the word *by* clearly indicates that the Spirit is the doer of the spiritual work being accomplished.

Baptism IN Water (Water Baptism) and Baptism IN the Holy Spirit (Spirit Baptism)

On the other hand, if we look at the Biblical accounts of conversion and water baptism, we see in context that John the Baptist baptized only in (*en*) water, immersing the candidates in the Jordan River. In contrast, Jesus, John's superior, was the One who would immerse believers in (*en*) the Holy Spirit, empowering them for mission and service (Matthew 3:11). *(For additional explanation of the Greek word* en, *please see Table 3-C at the end of this chapter.)*

Distinctions Among Frequently Used Terms

Following are two sets of terms that, while being similar in wording, have distinct meanings. Careful usage of these terms is necessary when trying to understand and communicate the richness of the Holy Spirit's work in the life of the Christian church. *(For descriptions of additional terms used to describe encounters with the Holy Spirit, please see the previous section covering "A Variety of Terms for Spirit Baptism" or the Glossary in the back of the book.)*

Baptism BY the Spirit, Regeneration by the Spirit and Conversion Baptism. These terms, along with other terms such as "being saved," "being born again," "being converted," "coming to Christ," "giving one's heart to God" and "becoming a Christian" are all commonly used to describe the encounter of being "baptized *by* the Spirit" into Jesus Christ.

The main question regarding the meaning of "baptized *by* the Spirit" is this: Does the New Testament make a distinction between "baptized *in* the Holy Spirit" for empowerment and being "baptized *by* the Holy Spirit" into the body of Christ at the moment of conversion? In the light of the previous discussion on the importance of context, look at 1 Corinthians 12:13: "By [*en*] one Spirit we were all baptized into one body, whether Jews or Greeks, whether slaves or free, and we were all made to drink of one Spirit." *En* or *by* in this case designates the Holy Spirit as the agent or the doer of this baptism. The experience of being baptized into Christ of which Paul is speaking is different from the baptism in the Spirit about which John the Baptist, Jesus and Peter spoke in the Gospels and Acts (Matthew 3:11; Mark 1:8; Luke 3:16; John 1:33, Acts 1:5, 8; 11:16). The baptism to which they referred is being baptized in the Holy Spirit, a distinct experience from conversion. This baptism following conversion will be defined further in the next section on "baptism *in* the Spirit."

As a number of versions indicate, "by one Spirit" is the preferred reading of 1 Corinthians 12:13, because it is the Holy Spirit who initiates the salvation experience. The Spirit, and only the Spirit, enables people to confess that Jesus is Lord (v. 3). Through the agency of the Spirit, we are brought into the community of believers; or as Paul says, "baptized into one body," the body of Christ, the church (v. 13). By the agency of the Spirit, we are plunged into Christ at the moment of conversion (cf. Romans 6:3; Galatians 3:27). When we receive the Pentecostal experience of Spirit baptism, we are baptized *by* Christ *in* the Spirit, but when we receive Christ we are incorporated into or united with the community of believers *by* the Holy Spirit.

This baptism of which Paul speaks in 1 Corinthians 12:13 is the spiritual experience by which the Spirit unites believers to Christ and to one another. It is also this baptism at conversion that Paul has in mind in Ephesians 4:5 where he speaks of "one baptism." The New Testament refers to a number of baptisms, but there is only one by which penitent sinners may be united with Christ and the community of faith. Upon hearing the Word of God and being drawn by the Holy Spirit, we accept God's Word by faith and turn from self and sin to Jesus as our Savior. In the Book of Titus, Paul describes the spiritual reality of being baptized into Christ by the Holy Spirit, or what is often referred to as "being born again," "being saved" or "being converted." At that moment, we are joined to Christ by the Holy Spirit, and God saves us "by the washing of regeneration and renewing by the Holy Spirit" (Titus 3:5).

Baptism IN the Spirit, Filled with the Spirit and *Spirit Baptism.* These three phrases describe the Holy Spirit's special blessing of empowerment for living, which is promised to all believers. Each phrase indicates the same type of spiritual encounter; but each offers a slightly different insight into this profound and moving experience with God's Spirit.

Baptized IN the Spirit is the most descriptive terminology to describe Spirit baptism, which occurs following conversion. As Acts 2:33 indicates, Spirit baptism is accomplished by Jesus *in* the Holy Spirit. Jesus is the baptizer; He immerses the Christian in the Holy Spirit. The term *baptize* means "to immerse" or "to dip."

This picture of being submerged makes *in* preferable to *with*. The phrase "baptized in the Holy Spirit" is much more descriptive of the Holy Spirit's role than the phrase "baptized with the Holy Spirit." In the King James Version of the Bible, the word *with* used with the word *baptized* suggests someone being in the presence of the Spirit. Several other versions of the Bible also use the word *with* when referring to Jesus Christ's baptizing someone *with* the Spirit (Matthew 3:11; John 1:33).[7] When the Holy Spirit is mentioned in conjunction with the word *with*, the Spirit himself is the element. Jesus is the doer of the action, and the Holy Spirit is *with* the believer. Modern usage of the word *with* often brings to mind being in the company of someone. If we take into consideration the limitations of these meanings for the word *with*, it becomes clear that the word *in* describes much more effectively the role of the Holy Spirit. We are not just baptized with the Holy Spirit present, we are actually immersed in the Holy Spirit. Although *with* is not incorrect, "baptized *in* the Spirit" is more descriptive and, therefore, the preferred phrase to describe Spirit baptism.

Filled WITH the Spirit is another way of speaking of being baptized in the Spirit or receiving the gift of the Spirit. The verb *filling* (*pimplēmi*) is closely linked with the Holy Spirit (Luke 1:41, 67; Acts 2:4; 4:8, 31; 9:17; 13:9). The emphasis is on the

---

[7]Cf. the King James Version, the *New King James Version,* the *Revised Standard Version, Phillips,* and the *New International Version.*

infusion of the Spirit into the inner life of believers, similar to God's filling the Temple with His presence. Indeed, the experience is a total penetration of the Spirit into all areas of one's life with an overwhelming sense that God has come in His fullness.

Spirit baptism is a contemporary, shorthand way of speaking of "baptism in the Spirit" or being "filled with the Spirit."

CONCLUSION

Spirit baptism is an intense spiritual experience and is properly described as being baptized *in* the Holy Spirit or being filled *with* the Spirit. It is necessary to use different language to indicate the distinction between this experience and being baptized into Christ *by* the Holy Spirit at conversion, since we encounter the Holy Spirit in both experiences. We saw that John the Baptist, Jesus and Peter used certain terminology when speaking about baptism *in* the Holy Spirit or being filled with the Spirit. Paul used similar terms when speaking of the Holy Spirit in 1 Corinthians 12:13, but his comments refer to baptism *by* the Holy Spirit into Christ at conversion. Translating Paul's use of the preposition *en* to the English *by* in verse 13 fits the context and makes the translation more readily understandable than other possibilities.[8] It is Christ who baptizes in the Holy Spirit and the Holy Spirit who baptizes into Christ. "If this distinction is not maintained, we have the strange idea that Christ baptizes into Christ."[9] By clearly defining terms and making these distinctions among meanings, we are better able to understand and

---

[8]Donald A. Johns understands that 1 Corinthians 12:13 refers to a post-conversion experience and that the reference is not to initiation into the body of Christ but "initiation into the charismatic ministry." See "Some New Directions in the Hermeneutics of Classical Pentecostalism's Doctrine of Initial Evidence," *Initial Evidence*, ed. Gary B. McGee (Peabody, MA: Hendrickson, 1991) 160-61.

[9]Anthony D. Palma, *Baptism in the Spirit* (Springfield, MO: Gospel Publishing House, 1999) 14.

communicate the rich and varied encounters with the Holy Spirit that we experience in our own lives and in the life of our Christian communities.

Summary

- The Bible is our standard for living and the basis for our expecting supernatural manifestations of God's love and power in our lives.

- The Bible teaches us through Old Testament prophecies, the words of Jesus, and stories in the Book of Acts that the Holy Spirit offers each of us a special blessing of empowerment for living.

	TABLE 3-A **Good Biblical Interpretation Practices**
1	The Bible is the authoritative source and "is profitable for teaching, for reproof, for correction, for training in righteousness" (ROMANS 15:4; 2 TIMOTHY 3:16).
2	The Bible is to be studied as a whole.
3	Each Biblical author is to be understood in light of that person's particular emphasis.
4	Taking into account literary style is important for interpreting the Bible.
5	Taking into account the historical setting and grammar is also important for interpreting the Bible.
6	The Holy Spirit is to be allowed to inform and enlighten us as we read and study God's Word.
Notes	

TABLE 3-B **Viewpoints on Biblical Interpretation of Spirit Baptism**	
The Day of Pentecost	
Classical Pentecostal	The disciples' experience on the Day of Pentecost and other encounters with the Spirit recorded in the Book of Acts are to be models for Christian doctrine and practice.
Other	There is no Scriptural statement that the disciples' experience on the Day of Pentecost is for all believers or that tongues will accompany Spirit baptism.
Spiritual Practices in Acts	
Classical Pentecostal	*General spiritual practices* recorded in the Book of Acts are meant to be models for Christians today. *Unique practices* applied to a particular occasion for a particular people, not generally practiced by the general church, are to be examples of the Spirit's unique work within each Christian community.
Other	Pentecostals are inconsistent in their interpretation of Acts, adopting some New Testament practices and not others.
Historical Narrative in Acts	
Classical Pentecostal	The Book of Acts is written in historical-narrative form in order to record history and to be a basis for doctrine.
Other	The Book of Acts is written in historical-narrative form in order to record history, but is not to be a basis for doctrine.

continued

TABLE 3-B (CONTINUED) Viewpoints on Biblical Interpretation of Spirit Baptism	
Luke's Main Intent in Acts	
Classical Pentecostal	In the Book of Acts, Luke's main intents were: • *To provide a historical account* of the spread of the gospel over the Roman world • *To introduce key doctrinal themes*, such as the power of the Holy Spirit for ministry, salvation, prayer, resurrection and ascension of Jesus, divine providence, revelation in creation, and the Day of Judgment
Other	In the Book of Acts, Luke's main intent was to provide a historical account of the spread of the gospel across the Roman world.
Baptism in the Spirit	
Classical Pentecostal	Conversion and baptism in the Spirit are distinct spiritual experiences.
Other	Baptism in the Spirit is part of the conversion experience.
Notes	

TABLE 3-C
The Greek Word *EN* in Context

Conversion Baptism—Baptized by (*en*) One Spirit
The Holy Spirit is the doer and the agent in conversion, as well as the giver of spiritual gifts.

Apostle Paul	"For by [*en*] one Spirit we were all baptized into one body" (1 CORINTHIANS 12:13). "No one speaking by [*en*] the Spirit of God says, 'Jesus is accursed'" (1 CORINTHIANS 12:3). "To another faith by [*en*] the same Spirit, and to another gifts of healing by [*en*] the one Spirit" (1 CORINTHIANS 12:9).

Water Baptism—Baptized in (*en*) Water
John the Baptist baptized in (en) water.

John the Baptist	"I baptized you with [*en*] water" (MARK 1:8). "John answered them saying, 'I baptize in [*en*] water'" (JOHN 1:26).
Jesus	"'John baptized with water, but you shall be baptized with [*en*] the Holy Spirit'" (ACTS 11:16).

Spirit Baptism—Baptized in (*en*) the Holy Spirit
Jesus immersed believers in (en) the Holy Spirit.

John the Baptist	"He will baptize you with [*en*] the Holy Spirit and fire" (MATTHEW 3:11). "And I did not recognize Him, but He who sent me to baptize in water said to me, 'He upon whom you see the Spirit descending and remaining upon Him, this is the One who baptizes in [*en*] the Holy Spirit'" (JOHN 1:33).
Jesus	"You shall be baptized with [*en*] the Holy Spirit not many days from now" (ACTS 1:5).

TABLE 3-D
A Variety of Terms for Spirit Baptism

Baptism in the Spirit

ACTS 1:5; 11:16 See *Wycliffe Bible.*	*Baptism in (en) the Spirit* indicates that a person is permeated and saturated with the power of the Spirit. He or she is immersed in the Spirit.

Promise of the Father

LUKE 24:49; ACTS 1:4	Baptism in the Spirit is a promise that God made to believers.

Promise of the Spirit

ACTS 2:33, 39	The Spirit is the promised blessing that God the Father promised He would send.

The Spirit's Coming and the Spirit's Falling Upon

LUKE 1:35; 3:22; 24:49; ACTS 1:8; 19:6	The Spirit's *coming* indicates that individuals are clothed with the Spirit and that the Spirit is continually present in a powerful way.
ACTS 8:16; 10:44; 11:15	The *falling* of the Spirit emphasizes the suddenness and forcefulness of Spirit baptism.

Gift of the Spirit

ACTS 2:38; 10:45; 11:17	The word *gift* emphasizes that Spirit baptism is free and the consequence solely of God's grace.

continued

TABLE 3-D (CONTINUED) **A Variety of Terms for Spirit Baptism**	
Receiving the Spirit	
ACTS 2:38; 8:15, 17, 19; 10:47; 19:2	God takes the initiative in pouring out His Spirit. For this reason our part in the experience is described as *receiving*.
Filled With the Spirit	
ACTS 2:4; 4:8, 31; 9:17; 13:9, 52	The word *filling* indicates a full penetration and diffusion of the Spirit throughout a person's being.
Notes	

TABLE 3-E **Distinctions Among Frequently Used Terms**
For this table, see page 99.

CHAPTER 3—STUDY AND DISCUSSION

1. What relationship do classical Pentecostals believe baptism in the Spirit has with the conversion experience?

BIBLICAL INTERPRETATION

Pentecostal Principles for Interpreting the Bible

2. What are the six basic principles that Pentecostal scholars use to interpret the Bible? (See Table 3-A.)

3. According to 1 Corinthians 10:11, what did Paul state was the reason for historical narrative (or the telling of history) in the Bible?

Other Viewpoints on Interpreting the Bible

4. What are some differences in opinion between how many Pentecostals and others interpret Spirit baptism in the Bible? (See Table 3-B.)

BIBLICAL TERMINOLOGY

The Term *Baptism* in the Bible

5. What types of baptism are taught in the Bible? Give an example of each. (See Table 3-C.)

A Variety of Terms for Spirit Baptism

6. What are some terms used to indicate Spirit baptism in the Bible? (See Table 3-D.)

Differences in the Terms "Baptism BY, IN, and WITH the Holy Spirit"

7. Why is it important to read a Bible verse in context?

8. How does the meaning of the Greek word *en* change according to context? (See Table 3-C.)

9. What is the difference between the terms "baptized BY the Spirit" and "baptized IN the Spirit"? (See Tables 3-C, 3-E.)

For I will pour out water on the thirsty land and streams on the dry ground; I will pour out My Spirit on your offspring and My blessing on your descendants; and they will spring up among the grass like poplars by streams of water (Isaiah 44:3, 4).

4

Spiritual Empowerment
After Conversion

C lassical Pentecostals have affirmed a second work of the
Spirit subsequent to—that is, following—the experience
of conversion. The question arises, Is there a distinction
between the work of the Spirit in salvation and the experience of
being filled with the Spirit? Many people make no distinction
between the two and believe that being filled with the Spirit, or
being baptized in the Spirit is the same as conversion to Christ.
The following remarks reflect this view that to be "born again" is
the same as baptism in the Spirit:

> The NT refers to many and various experiences of the Spirit and
> actions of the Spirit in the Christian life, but none which is a dis-
> tinctively further or second experience which all new Christians
> should be encouraged to seek. In contrast, the gift of the Spirit
> is the most fundamental aspect of the event or process of
> becoming a Christian, the climax of conversion-initiation.[1]

> I appeal to you not to urge upon people a baptism with the
> Spirit as a second and subsequent experience entirely distinct
> from conversion, for this cannot be proved from Scripture.[2]

These statements serve as a reminder that the Pentecostal/

---

[1]James D.G. Dunn, "Baptism in the Spirit: A Response to Pentecostal
Scholarship on Luke-Acts," *Journal of Pentecostal Theology* 3 (1993) 5.
[2]John R.W. Stott, *The Baptism & Fullness of the Holy Spirit* (Downers
Grove, IL: InterVarsity Press, 1964) 59.

Charismatic doctrine of Spirit baptism still is questioned widely in the Christian community. There are a few people, however, who do not necessarily refer to themselves as "Pentecostals" or "Charismatics," but who see special empowerment by the Spirit as a postconversion experience. An example is Edward Schweizer, who writes: "According to Acts 2:38 the Spirit is imparted to those who are already converted and baptized." In his comment about the disciples' experiences in Acts 19:1-7, he says, "Luke is telling about Christians who have not experienced the outpouring of the Spirit."[3] In reference to the same disciples, G.W. Lampe observes, "They may have been Christians of a pre-Pentecostal kind, comparable in their religious state with the twelve before Pentecost."[4]

The central issue here is, Can Spirit baptism be equated with conversion (regeneration)? Our focus is twofold: (1) The New Testament teaches the reality and the desirability of Spirit baptism for all believers. (2) The experience of Spirit baptism is distinct and separate from conversion. It may take place immediately upon conversion or at a later time. The emphasis is on the fact of the experience as subsequent to, or following, the conversion.

Students of Scripture have recognized that the books of the Bible are characterized by unity and diversity, and that Biblical authors have different emphases. As a result, one Biblical author will treat more extensively a particular doctrine than another author will. For example, if we want an explanation for justification by faith, we would turn to Paul's letters, especially to Romans and Galatians where this doctrine is treated in depth. Should we want to study the doctrine of the deity and humanity of Christ, then John's Gospel would be a good source. Not that the other New Testament writers fail to tell us

---

[3]Eduard Schweizer, "pneuma, pneumatikos," *Theological Dictionary of the New Testament,* vol. 6, ed. Gerhard Friedrich (Grand Rapids: Eerdmans, 1968) 412, 413.

[4]G.W. Lampe, "Acts," *Peake's Commentary on the Bible,* eds. Matthew Black and H.H. Rowley (London: Nelson, 1962) 916.

about the person of Christ, but the uniqueness of His person is a major emphasis in the fourth Gospel. On the other hand, if we decide to study the charismatic work of the Holy Spirit as the One who equips and empowers for service, the writings of Luke should be a major consideration.

Paul and John in their writings also indicate that the Holy Spirit empowers believers for service and ministry, but they tell us more about the role of the Holy Spirit in terms of salvation than does Luke (John 3:3ff.; 16:8, 9; Romans 8:9; 1 Corinthians 6:11; Titus 3:5). Luke contributes more to our understanding of Spirit baptism and the charismatic anointing that makes service more effective. Biblical writers complement rather than contradict one another. Paul, John and Luke each has his own complementary perspective and emphasis on the Holy Spirit. Luke's Gospel and the Book of Acts tell us more than the other New Testament books about the anointing of the Spirit. The proper way to interpret Scripture is to understand a particular author or writing and then relate it to other parts of Scripture.

ESTABLISHING LUKE'S INTENT

The question of Luke's intent is a fundamental issue, especially in regard to his account of the ministry of the Spirit. Did Luke so design Luke/Acts as to teach that Spirit baptism is a distinct experience from conversion and is for every believer? No doubt the narrative of Luke/Acts does encourage each believer to receive the Pentecostal gift. In Acts, Luke states that the outpouring of the Spirit at Pentecost as the fulfillment of Joel's prophecy is for "all people" (Acts 2:17-21, *NIV*; see also Joel 2:28-32, *NIV*). It is self-evident that Luke expected the community of faith in his day to experience what the believers at Pentecost had experienced—"your sons and daughters will prophesy" (Acts 2:17, *NIV*). At Pentecost the disciples received a prophetic experience, and the believers present became a potential community of prophets. Luke expected that this potential would be realized in the church of his day just as Moses had desired, and that God's people would become prophets during his time (Numbers 11:29). Though a number of passages can be chosen to support the conclusion that following conversion believers today can receive spiritual empowerment to communicate God's truths, we will limit our consideration to three texts.

The Spirit-Anointed Ministry of Jesus
Luke 3:21, 22

The Spirit-anointed ministry of Jesus began at the Jordan River. After He was baptized in the waters of Jordan and was praying, the Holy Spirit descended upon Him and equipped Him for ministry. A little later Jesus gives an explanation of this experience in the Nazareth synagogue (Luke 4:16-30). Jesus' encounter with the Holy Spirit provided the pattern for the rest of His ministry and a pattern or model for the ministry of believers. This model is that Jesus was empowered by the Spirit at the river Jordan, and He continued to be empowered for His ministry on earth. Likewise, believers today may receive spiritual empowerment for the work they are to do.

Before relating the story of Jesus' anointing with the Spirit, Luke had already told of the Spirit's empowering John the Baptist, Elizabeth, Zacharias and Simeon for prophetic ministry (1:15, 41, 67; 2:25-28). These individuals prophesied because they were "filled" with the Spirit. Jesus' anointing by the Holy Spirit at the time of His baptism must also be understood as an empowering for prophetic ministry, but Jesus' task was a unique prophetic task, as Isaiah had predicted (11:1, 2; 42:1). Upon empowerment, the Holy Spirit remained on Jesus, giving Him ongoing power for prophetic ministry. The Old Testament prophets and others were temporarily endowed with the Spirit; but in contrast to them, the Spirit remained on Jesus. Wherever He went during His earthly ministry, the

Spirit's anointing rested on Him "without measure" (John 3:34). Taking a bodily form as a dove, the Spirit made His descent on Jesus unmistakably visible. As a result of this anointing by the Spirit, Jesus was equipped to overcome the power of Satan and to resist the wilderness temptations (Luke 4:1-13). Jesus' spiritual anointing was the beginning of a new era, the age of the Spirit. This event initiated Jesus' ministry and continues to serve as a model for a Spirit-anointed ministry today. An empowered ministry, which includes bold witnessing to Christ and mighty works, flows out of the Spirit's anointing (4:18, 19; Acts 10:38).

Before Jesus' anointing at the Jordan River, the Holy Spirit had been active in His life. At the very beginning of Jesus' life as a human on earth, the creative work of the Spirit made possible His birth to a virgin (Luke 1:35; Matthew 1:18, 20). The direct agency of the Holy Spirit in His birth strongly suggests that Jesus was indwelt by the Spirit from birth, a spiritual blessing similar to that received by John the Baptist at birth (Luke 1:15). Yet, Jesus later had an additional, distinct encounter with the Spirit at the Jordan River. His baptism in water there identified Him with humanity, but the descending of the Spirit upon Him was a distinct and separate experience that anointed Him for His ministry of preaching the gospel, healing the sick and casting out demons.

Jesus Christ's anointing with the Spirit identified Him as the baptizer in the Spirit—about whom John the Baptist had spoken (Luke 3:16). Echoing John's words, Jesus promised His disciples that they would be immersed in the Spirit (Acts 1:4, 5). He assured them of an experience and ministry patterned after His own experience and ministry recorded in Luke 3:21, 22 and 4:16-19 (cf. Acts 1:8). At His ascension into heaven, Jesus received the promised Holy Spirit from the Father for distribution to His disciples and all believers (Acts 2:33, 39). Later the Day of Pentecost was the beginning of this fulfillment of the universal outpouring of the Spirit that had been foretold in Joel 2:28-32. The outpouring of the Spirit on the Day of Pentecost is universal in that it introduced the age of special anointing for all who come to faith in Christ, an anointing that continues to affect the physical and spiritual world in which we live.

According to Luke, when an individual experiences anointing with the Spirit, or receives Spirit baptism, that person is experiencing a specific, special encounter with God. This spiritual encounter is in addition to one's entering into the body of Christ at conversion. The kind of language Luke uses to describe the experience indicates that during this special encounter, one enters into more personal intimacy with the Spirit. Again, the Pentecostal experience is more than having the presence of the Spirit in the Christian life; it is an experience patterned after Jesus' own experience of Spirit anointing and empowerment for ministry. For believers, spiritual anointing (or Spirit baptism) follows their conversion just as Jesus' anointing at the Jordan followed the creative activity of the Spirit in His birth.

Praying for God's Gift of the Holy Spirit
Matthew 7:11; Luke 11:13

These verses in the Gospels of Matthew and Luke speak of God's gifts to His children. Luke assures his readers that when they engage in persistent prayer, they will receive not only "good gifts," but the greatest gift—the Holy Spirit. Matthew writes, "If you then, being evil, know how to give good gifts to your children, how much more will your Father who is in heaven give what is good to those who ask Him!" (7:11). Luke writes, "If you then, being evil, know how to give good gifts to your children, how much more will your heavenly Father give the Holy Spirit to those who ask Him?" (11:13). The promise that the Father will give the Holy Spirit to those who persist in prayer began to be fulfilled at Pentecost. Luke's first readers were Christians such as Theophilus and others.[5]

In the Book of Acts, Luke encouraged these Christians to ask for the Spirit—the Pentecostal anointing of the Spirit that will enable them to be powerful witnesses (Luke 12:12; Acts 1:8). A prominent theme in the Old Testament is to seek the Lord (Deuteronomy 4:29; Isaiah 55:6; 2 Chronicles 7:14; 11:16; Psalm 4:6; 27:8; 83:16); but Luke, in the Book of Acts, shifts the focus to seeking God's Spirit, the Holy Spirit. He urges his readers to "keep on asking, keep on seeking, and keep on knocking" (my translation of Luke 11:9). He promises that God will respond by filling them with the Spirit and granting them anointing power for service.

Praying for a special blessing from the Holy Spirit is appropriate for all Christians, who in love and obedience to Jesus would naturally respond by desiring a deeper relationship with God. Indeed, bold and obedient prayer characterized the response of the disciples at Pentecost (Acts 1:14). The disciples were being obedient by responding to Jesus' command in Luke 11:13 and 24:49.

Luke describes Jesus' teaching as "the word of God" (5:1). People crowded around Him to hear it. Jesus let His disciples know that those who hear the Word of God and do it are His spiritual family (6:46-49; 8:11-15). Obedience to His instructions to persist in prayer for the gift of the Spirit indicates the spiritual condition of the disciples. They were repentant believers and keepers of the Word of God. Their prayers resulted in their and other believers' being filled with the Spirit (Acts 2:4; 4:23-31; 8:14-17).

Although Spirit baptism is a profound encounter between God and an individual, it may also occur in response to one's joining with others in prayer (Acts 8:14-17; 9:17; 19:1-7). In the Bible, we are encouraged to pray for one another, build each other up, and draw

---

[5]French L. Arrington, *The Acts of the Apostles* (Peabody, MA: Hendrickson, 1988) xxxvi-xxxvii.

121

strength and encouragement from our Christian family (Ephesians 6:18; James 5:16). Engaging in prayer with spiritual brothers and sisters can assist us in our efforts to focus on spiritual matters and to accept the move of the Spirit in our lives.

In Acts, those who prayed for the gift of the Spirit were already Christians. At Pentecost the Holy Spirit was poured out on 120 servants of the Lord: "my servants, both men and women" (Acts 2:18, *NIV*). Luke's gift of the Spirit, therefore, does not refer to the work of the Spirit in the new birth, but to an anointing with the Spirit. The receipt of this anointing may require much prayer and results in inspired speech, prophecy, dreams, visions, signs, wonders (v. 17), and a more intense dedication to holy living (v. 42). Consequently, Spirit baptism is an answer to prayer and is experienced by those who are already converted.

God's Gift of the Spirit for All Believers
Acts 2:38, 39

We are reminded again that the Holy Spirit is a gift (Luke 11:13). Luke's intent in Acts 2:38, 39 is to teach that the Pentecostal gift is for all believers. It is stated explicitly that "the promise is for you and your children and for all who are far off, as many as the Lord our God shall call to Himself" (v. 39; cf. Luke 24:49; Acts 1:4). This promise has its origin in Joel 2:28: "I will pour out my Spirit on all people. Your sons and daughters will prophesy" (*NIV*). Non-Pentecostals often understand this promise recorded in Joel in light of Jeremiah 31:33ff. and Ezekiel 36:25ff., which refer to the salvation experience rather than to the empowering of believers for service after conversion. The focus of Joel 2 is not on conversion, but on God's promise to restore the Spirit of prophecy. This promise was initially fulfilled later at Pentecost (Acts 2:4).

In the Old Testament the promise of the Spirit had two aspects: the indwelling of the Spirit through regeneration (Ezekiel 36:25-27) and the empowering of the Spirit (Joel 2:28, 29). Luke does not deny or ignore the work of the Spirit in the salvation experience. He recognizes that the promise does include the promise of salvation as Joel had predicted (Joel 2:32; Acts 2:21). Luke states, "Everyone who calls on the name of the Lord will be saved" (Acts 2:21). Therefore, as Peter indicates, "the promise" includes salvation for those of his audience who were not saved (v. 39). But the promise embraced more than the experience of salvation. Luke focuses primarily on the second aspect of the promise: the anointing of the Spirit for powerful witnessing.

How Luke describes individuals before Pentecost reminds us of his focus. He gives no details about the salvation experience of the people described in the early chapters of his Gospel. We read about John the Baptist's being filled with the Holy Spirit from his mother's womb and about Elizabeth's, Zacharias', Simeon's and Mary's experiences with the Holy Spirit. Their personal devotion is praised, but nothing is said about their personal salvation before their experiences with the Holy Spirit. Rather, Luke stresses prophetic utterances and Spirit-inspired witnessing. Whereas Paul and John in their writings deal more extensively with the link between the Spirit and salvation, Luke focuses on the Spirit and witnessing.[6] No doubt, Luke is aware of other aspects of the work of the Spirit. After all, he had been a traveling companion of Paul's

---

[6]Paul's, John's and Luke's views of the Spirit are complementary. Paul offers a fuller exposition of the work of the Spirit. He helps us understand that the Spirit is the source of cleansing (1 Corinthians 5:5ff.; Romans 15:16), righteousness (Galatians 5:5ff.; Romans 2:29; 8:1-17), intimate fellowship with God (Romans 8:14-17), as well as power for mission (Romans 15:8ff.; Philippians 1:18ff.). Therefore, Paul emphasizes both *soteriological* (an adjective for *soteriology*, a term used for the Biblical doctrine of salvation) and Charismatic aspects of the Spirit. John speaks about Spirit baptism (John 1:33). In John 14–16 Jesus promises the Holy Spirit. John 20 should not be seen as the fulfillment of the promise; the fulfillment begins in Acts. Luke's perspective is more limited than Paul's or John's, with his emphasis primarily on the charismatic dimensions of the Spirit.

and would have been exposed to the apostle's understanding of the Holy Spirit. He chose to concentrate on the dynamic and charismatic aspects of the Holy Spirit, linking Spirit baptizing with power for witnessing as a subsequent experience to conversion. The receiving of spiritual power is an indissoluble link to equipping the church to proclaim that Jesus came to save.

NARRATIVE EXAMPLES IN ACTS

Jesus said that the heavenly Father will give the Holy Spirit to those who ask Him (Luke 11:13). The Holy Spirit descended on Jesus as He had prayed (Luke 3:21). The Spirit also came upon the disciples while they devoted themselves in "one accord" to prayer (Acts 1:14, KJV; 2:1). In light of these accounts, we may conclude that empowerment by the Spirit will not be given indiscriminately to seekers and nonseekers, but only to those who desire a deeper relationship with God and persist in prayer. In Acts, Luke provides narrative examples of believers' receiving the anointing of the Spirit as an answer to prayer. In Scripture the dominant way of teaching is the use of narrative, or story. Luke, aware of the dynamism and Pentecostal manifestations of the Spirit, penned an account of the life and ministry of the early church that was filled with excitement and suspense. Many of the events he records in Acts have a theological purpose, showing the spread of the gospel throughout the Roman world by the presence and power of the Holy Spirit. The themes of evangelism and empowerment are so interlocked that they cannot be understood apart from each other. The words of Jesus in Acts 1:8 proclaim God's missionary strategy and relate the spread of the gospel with the power of the Spirit: "You will receive power when the Holy Spirit comes on you; and you will be my witnesses" (*NIV*).

Later in the Book of Acts, Luke's examples of the outpouring of the Spirit demonstrate the fulfillment of Acts 1:8 and serve to inspire others to receive the gift of the Spirit in order to become empowered witnesses. Other aspects of the Spirit's ministry are also included; but in the Book of Acts, Luke's major focus is the charismatic, dynamic aspects of the Spirit's work. The first example of the disciples' having this charismatic encounter with the Holy Spirit is on the Day of Pentecost (2:1-13). Later Luke gives four other examples in which believers have similar experiences to that of the disciples at Pentecost (8:4-24; 9:17; 10:44-48; 19:1-7). These accounts are particularly instructive and worth our effort in examining them.

1ST NARRATIVE ACCOUNT

The Disciples' Encounter With the Spirit on the Day of Pentecost

Acts 2:1-13

Acts 2 opens with an account of the Day of Pentecost. The coming of the Spirit upon the disciples occurred at an assigned time, just as the coming of Christ occurred at a particular time (Galatians 4:4). When the time in God's plan arrived, He sent the Holy Spirit as the fulfillment of the Pentecostal promise. It was a unique, historical event. As the Exodus from Egypt, the giving of the Law at Sinai and the coming of Christ in the flesh were events in salvation history, so was this first outpouring of the Spirit for empowerment of believers as witnesses. Through each of these historical events, God was actively carrying out His redemptive purposes for the salvation and spiritual growth of humankind. Thus the coming of the Spirit at Pentecost was the fulfillment of the divine purpose, and represents the breaking-in of God into the world and the church.

Pentecost was pivotal in salvation history. It marked the climax of Jesus' ministry (Acts 2:33) and was the fulfillment of Joel's prophecy that spoke about the outpouring of the Spirit as the decisive sign of the coming age. Just as miraculous signs introduced the Israelites' Exodus, Moses' encounter with God on Mount Sinai, Jesus' birth at

Bethlehem, and Jesus' death at Calvary, so the Day of Pentecost was also accompanied by the miraculous. The sound of a mighty, rushing wind and the tongues like fire were supernatural manifestations emphasizing the greatness of the occasion. Following are a couple of major observations regarding Spirit baptism as it relates to the Day of Pentecost and the Book of Acts:

A Model for Later Outpourings of the Spirit

Pentecost was a model for later outpourings of the Spirit. The disciples' encounter with the Spirit in Acts 2 is a fulfillment of prophecy, but it is also a paradigm, a pattern, a model for personal experience. The Acts 2 account provides the pattern (what scholars describe as the "paradigmatic" or "programmatic") for later outpourings of the Spirit. In fact, Bible scholar Max Turner, in his article on Spirit endowment, contends that Acts 2 is programmatic for many events recorded in Acts and for Luke's doctrine of the Spirit in particular.[7] At every pivotal point in missionary outreach, Luke reports a reoccurrence of the outpouring of the Spirit similar to the experience of the disciples in Jerusalem. The writer, Stronstad, puts it well:

> Just as the anointing of Jesus (Luke 3:22; 4:18) is a paradigm for the subsequent Spirit baptism of the disciples (Acts 1:5; 2:4), so the gift of the Spirit to the disciples is a paradigm for God's people throughout the "last days" as a charismatic community of the Spirit a prophethood of all believers (Acts 2:16-21).[8]

The key to understanding the subsequent outpourings of the Spirit seems to lie in Acts 2. The pattern is not simply dependent on a few passages in Acts, but it includes Luke's perspective prior to Pentecost. The source of this pattern is Jesus' own experience at the Jordan River and the full scope of theology of the

---

[7] Max B. Turner, "Spirit Endowment in Luke-Acts: Some Linguistic Considerations," *Biblical and Historical Essays From London Bible College* (London: London Bible College, 1981) 45-63.

[8] Roger Stronstad, *The Charismatic Theology of St. Luke*, 8-9.

Spirit in Luke/Acts. It is through this framework that we can understand the Charismatic experience of the disciples at Pentecost and the later outpourings of the Spirit (Acts 8:14-20; 9:17; 10:44-49; 19:1-7). This spiritual outpouring, beginning on the Day of Pentecost, is not a matter of regeneration (new birth) or conversion, but is an additional spiritual blessing of power for worship, prophetic witnessing, service and Christlike living. Such is the character of the Pentecostal gift. The Acts 2 account provides the pattern for the personal experience of being baptized in the Spirit; the nature of the experience is charismatic. Therefore, Spirit baptism is an additional spiritual blessing to be received following one's conversion experience.

Order of Conversion and Spirit Baptism

Pentecost provides the order of conversion and Spirit baptism. Since the events on the Day of Pentecost are models for us today, the second concern here is this: Was the experience of the disciples on the Day of Pentecost "subsequent to" (following) their conversion? If those disciples had died before their baptism in the Spirit, would they have gone to heaven? The answer is obvious—yes, they would have. To argue otherwise would raise questions about the accuracy of Scripture. On one occasion, Jesus told 72 of His disciples to "rejoice that your names are recorded in heaven" (Luke 10:20). These followers, prior to the Day of Pentecost, had experienced personal salvation. Spirit baptism did not automatically happen at conversion, but later the 120 disciples were filled with the Spirit on the Day of Pentecost. Subsequent to conversion, they received a special endowment of power, inspiring witnessing and godly living. The character of the Pentecostal gift offers a strong argument for the doctrine of subsequence. For Luke, Spirit baptism is logically distinct from conversion and is an experience available to be received by every believer. As in the Old Testament, the anointing of the Spirit at Pentecost is primarily vocational in purpose and result. It is not a salvation anointing that makes one a member of God's family, but a special subsequent anointing that fills, equips and initiates the believer into Spirit-empowered service.

2ᴺᴰ NARRATIVE ACCOUNT
The Samaritans' Encounter With the Spirit
Acts 8:4-24

The narrative of the Samaritans' encounter with the Holy Spirit in Acts 8 is the most striking example of the doctrine of subsequence in the Book of Acts. This story about the Spirit baptism of the Samaritan converts is particularly instructive for Pentecostals, but can be troublesome for non-Pentecostals who believe that baptism in the Spirit is a part of conversion. On one occasion, Philip, one of the seven Spirit-filled deacons (Acts 6:5) and a spiritually gifted evangelist (21:8), had gone to Samaria. The Samaritans believed the preaching of Philip. Although they were baptized in water by him, they did not receive Spirit baptism until some time later, after Peter and John arrived. Acts 8:15, 16 tells us that Peter and John "prayed for them that they might receive the Holy Spirit. For He had not yet fallen upon any of them; they had simply been baptized in the name of the Lord Jesus." Many interpreters are puzzled by Luke's language "might receive the Holy Spirit." They fail to recognize that the reference is to a charismatic experience separate and subsequent to receiving salvation. This spiritual blessing is for those already "in Christ" and is a full immersion in the power of the Holy Spirit.

Encountering the Spirit as a Distinct Blessing

The question arises, Does not faith and repentance automatically result in the reception of the Holy Spirit? Again, we must note that Luke does not deny the work of the Holy Spirit in salvation; he simply does not emphasize it. Luke does recognize that Christ introduced the days of universal salvation, in which "everyone who calls on the name of the Lord will be saved" (Acts 2:21; cf. 10:43). Rather than stressing the role of the Spirit in salvation, Luke presents the gift of the Spirit as an anointing for worship and service. Pentecostals and Charismatics have recognized the difference between the promise of the Spirit in Ezekiel 36:25-27 and the promise in Joel 2:28, 29. As a result they have taught that all believers are indwelt by the Spirit from the moment of conversion (Romans 8:9; 1 Corinthians 6:19), and that baptism in the Spirit is a separate blessing offered to believers.

Other Viewpoints on the Samaritans' Encounter With the Spirit

The teaching of Acts 8:4-25 clearly indicates that the Samaritans were Christians before they received the baptism in the Holy Spirit. Those who identify the gift of the Spirit here with conversion have proposed a number of arguments:

Some assume this incident represents a unique exception to believers' receiving the fullness of the Spirit at conversion. According to this view, God suspended the normal rule of bestowing the Spirit upon one's coming to faith in Christ during conversion. They propose that because the church had reached a decisive turning point in its mission outreach, making a strategic missionary move beyond Jerusalem, God withheld the Spirit until Peter and John arrived in Samaria. Some believe that this "exceptional" incident was simply meant to show that the church was laying aside prejudices against the Samaritans (prejudices common among the Jews) and that these despised Samaritans had been accepted and received as members of the church.

This conclusion that the Samaritans' baptism in the Spirit was an exception has a number of serious problems. The first problem is the assumed exception. No exception is hinted at in the Biblical account of the outpouring of the Spirit on the Samaritans. Many commentators who take this view believe that the Spirit is tied to water baptism, but Luke regularly separates the ordinance of water baptism from Spirit baptism (Acts 2:4; 8:15-17; 9:17, 18; 10:44-48).

The second problem is that the Samaritans did not likely need more assurance of their membership in the church than what they had already received. They had experienced supernatural miracles and great joy upon seeing Philip cast out demons and heal the sick (8:7, 8). They already had been baptized in water, symbolizing their experience of salvation. Their assurance of inclusion in the body of Christ was not dependent on contact with the apostles from Jerusalem. The Samaritan believers were already indwelt by the Spirit and had their sins forgiven before Peter and John laid hands on them for an anointing of the Spirit. In this narrative, as well as in the rest of the New Testament, the believers' forgiveness of sins is not discussed as being dependent on being baptized in the Spirit.

Some scholars propose that the Samaritans were not Christians until the apostles arrived from Jerusalem. In other words, they think that the Samaritans' initial response to Philip's preaching of the gospel was defective, and that they were not genuinely saved until Peter and John arrived. The main argument that proponents of this position use to support their claim focuses on Acts 8:12: "But when they believed Philip preaching the good news about the kingdom of God. . . ." They only gave intellectual assent because "they believed Philip" rather than "they believed in the Lord." So the claim is that they experienced no genuine conversion under the ministry of Philip. They gave mental approval to his message, but did not come to real saving faith until Peter and John laid hands on them.

This position fails to take into account Luke's statement that the news reached Jerusalem that Samaria "had received the word of God [*dechomai ton logon*]" (Acts 8:14). A study of this expression confirms that the Samaritans had been saved. The same expression appears in Acts 11:1, which refers to the conversion of Cornelius and his friends. It also occurs in 17:11, which tells about people in Berea who "received the word with great eagerness." Likewise a similar expression is used to describe those who received Peter's message at Pentecost (2:41). Philip's message was not deficient, nor is there a hint that the Samaritans misunderstood it. He proclaimed Christ to them (8:5) and "the good news about the kingdom of God and the name of Jesus Christ" (v. 12). His message consisted of the central elements of the gospel (*kērugma*). He preached a saving message, and the Samaritans who believed it were saved. For Luke, believing the message of an evangelist who was guided by the Spirit to speak the truth was to believe the message of God (cf. Acts 16:14).

Bringing Into Focus the "Doctrine of Subsequence"

As Pentecostals and Charismatics understand, Acts 8:4-24 provides solid ground for making a distinction between believing Christ and receiving the baptism in the Spirit. At this point a summary of the Samaritans' encounter with the Spirit and a few observations should bring into focus the doctrine of subsequence.

The Samaritans listened intently to Philip's preaching, and his message was clear to them. If the Samaritans had not understood the message, then Peter and John would have clarified it in their teaching. There is no suggestion that they had to make up for a deficiency in Philip's preaching. He had proclaimed Christ to the Samaritans and had explained the good news about God's kingdom (8:5, 12), no doubt including Christ's death and resurrection. The fact that the Samaritans believed Philip as he preached indicates that they had a genuine saving faith. Their great joy was the direct consequence of their experience of salvation (v. 8; cf. v. 39; 13:52; Romans 14:17; 15:13).

Philip's message was confirmed by powerful miracles, which included the lame being healed and demons being cast out. He was mighty in deed as well as in word. His prophetic actions gave the Samaritans the assurance of the saving power of his message.

The Samaritans who believed the gospel had been baptized in the name of Christ (Acts 8:12). Baptism in the name of Christ indicates that their baptism was a Christian baptism. It is unthinkable that

Philip would have baptized them if they had not been genuinely converted. Water baptism is the sign that sins have been forgiven and new life has been received.

The apostles in Jerusalem received news that the Samaritans "had received the word of God" (v. 14). A similar report announced the conversion of the Gentiles in Caesarea (Acts 11). The reception of the Word is another way of referring to conversion (2:41; 17:11, 12).

When Peter and John heard of the Samaritans' conversion, they came to Samaria where they discovered that the Holy Spirit "had not yet fallen upon any of them" (8:16). No doubt the endorsement of the Jerusalem leaders of the acceptance of the Samaritans into the church was desirable, especially in light of the longstanding rift between the Jews and Samaritans. So whatever other purpose the visit of Peter and John to Samaria served, it clearly showed that neither water baptism nor conversion is Spirit baptism. They had been converted and baptized, but not yet filled with the Spirit.

Peter and John laid their hands on the Samaritans and "they were receiving the Holy Spirit" (8:17). In Acts, there are two other occasions in which the laying on of hands is linked to the reception of the Holy Spirit. Ananias laid hands on Paul (9:17) and Paul laid hands on the Ephesian believers (19:6).[9] Hands were also laid on the seven men appointed to serve the widows (6:6) and on Paul and Barnabas when the church at Antioch commissioned them as missionaries (13:3; cf. 1 Timothy 4:14; 2 Timothy 1:6). None of these passages teach or suggest that salvation is received by the laying on of hands.

---

[9]Some Biblical scholars interpret the laying of hands on the Samaritans, on Paul, and on the Ephesian disciples as an ordination or commissioning ceremony. Nothing appears in the three accounts that clearly supports this interpretation. I prefer to understand these accounts in light of Numbers 11:16ff., where the Lord transferred the Spirit on Moses to Israel's elders. They received a blessing, being empowered to serve as leaders of the people. This view is in accord with the text of Acts that God does use human instruments to mediate His blessings. In some cases the laying on of hands is linked with ordination or commissioning.

Acts, however, shows that on some occasions, individuals received the fullness of the Spirit with the imposition of hands.

The experience of the Samaritans when Peter and John prayed for them was not the spiritual transformation that comes with faith in Christ as Savior, but it was a powerful anointing by the Spirit. Their experience of the Spirit after conversion and baptism in water strongly supports the doctrine of subsequence.

3ʀᴅ NARRATIVE ACCOUNT
Saul's Encounter With the Spirit in Damascus
Acts 9:1-19

In Acts 9, Luke gives the first of his three accounts of Saul's (the apostle Paul's) conversion and call (cf. 22:3-16; 26:9-18). On the road to the city of Damascus, the risen Lord appeared to Saul of Tarsus and transformed him. Obeying the command the Lord gave him, Saul went into Damascus. After three days of fasting and prayer (cf. Luke 11:13), devout Ananias visited him. Laying hands on Saul, Ananias said, "Brother Saul, the Lord Jesus, who appeared to you on the road by which you were coming, has sent me so that you may regain your sight and be filled with the Holy Spirit" (Acts 9:17). Some scholars interpret this event as marking Saul's conversion. This view assumes that Saul's conversion takes place in Damascus and that his being filled with the Spirit is just part of his conversion experience.

Contrary to the position that Paul's conversion occurred in the city of Damascus, other scholars believe that Saul was converted on his way to the city. Here are some observations that support the position that Saul's conversion occurred before he reached Damascus:

Ananias addressed Saul as "brother," meaning that he was more than a fellow Jew; he was also a fellow believer. Culturally, it was natural to use this address in a Christian context. As a Christian, Saul had accepted Jesus as his Savior and had been renewed and indwelt by the Holy Spirit. He was now a brother in Christ. Paul calls Jesus "Lord" (*kurie*, v. 5). This title can express respect, meaning "Sir," but there is strong support of the translation "Lord." Of the passages in which the word *kurie* is used, 10 of them refer to the "Lord" Jesus and therefore indicate a more profound meaning than the polite "Sir" (1:6, 24; 4:29; 7:59, 60; 9:10, 13; 10:14; 11:8; 22:19). Paul's confession of Jesus as "Lord" indicates he was converted by his encounter with Jesus on the road to Damascus.

Godly Ananias makes no appeal to Saul to repent and to accept the Lord as Savior. He did instruct Saul to be baptized in water, a symbol of the washing away of his sins (Acts 22:16) and encouraged him to be filled with the Spirit. It is recognized that he needed to be filled with the Spirit to fulfill the prophetic task of preaching the gospel to the Gentiles. Luke is silent regarding the time when Saul was filled with the Holy Spirit. Most likely he received the fullness of the Spirit when Ananias placed his hands on him.

Ananias laid hands on Saul in prayer for him to be filled with the Spirit, not for him to be saved. No place in the Scripture is the laying on of hands associated with the imparting of salvation. Paul's change of heart had already occurred on the road to Damascus. The archenemy of the Christian church of that day had "died" and was made a new man (cf. Galatians 2:20; 2 Corinthians 5:17, 18). It is logical to conclude that Ananias laid hands on this new man in order to pray for God's spiritual blessing in his life.

Paul's experience on the road to Damascus included his call as an apostle to the Gentiles (Acts 9:15; cf. 26:16-18; Galatians 1:5-16). It is unbelievable that Christ would have chosen him as a servant had he not yet been converted. His conversion and call were interlocking realities.

The phrase "filled with the Spirit" (plēsthēs pneumatos hagiou) used in the story of Saul and Ananias is also used to describe the experience of the disciples on the Day of Pentecost (Acts 2:4). Before then it was also used to describe the empowerment of John the Baptist for ministry (Luke 1:15). Nowhere does Scripture use this term as a synonym for salvation.

At least three days passed following Saul's initial conversion encounter with God to the time when he was filled with the Spirit. This time lag indicates the occurrence of two separate spiritual experiences. It is evident that Luke's main concern is God's calling and equipping of Saul for missionary work. Saul's Spirit-anointed preaching that followed his experience in Damascus is a clear sign that he had been filled with the Spirit. He "grew more and more powerful and baffled the Jews living in Damascus by proving that Jesus is the Christ" (Acts 9:22, *NIV*). The work of the Spirit in Saul's life while traveling to, and during his stay in, Damascus has two dimensions—conversion and filling with the Spirit for service.

4ᵀᴴ Narrative Account

The Gentiles' Encounter With the Spirit in Caesarea

Acts 10:1–11:18

The importance of this story is evident from the space that Luke devotes to this account. The narrative relates the breaking down of the walls of religious and racial prejudice and reaches its climax in the outpouring of the Spirit (10:44-48). Cornelius was a Gentile who had separated himself from paganism. He was a godly man who devoted himself to constant prayer and generosity (v. 2). Cornelius had a vision in which he was instructed to send for Simon Peter, who was staying in the city of Joppa.

In the meantime, Peter had a vision in which God told him to eat food that he considered unclean. When he refused, God taught Peter that nothing God creates is impure. Through the vision, Peter came to realize that God loves everyone and that He does not show favoritism. When Cornelius' servants arrived in Joppa, Peter went with them to Caesarea and shared the love of Christ with Cornelius and his Gentile household. Luke reports that while Peter was preaching, "the Holy

Spirit fell upon all those who were listening to the message" (v. 44). Peter concludes that Cornelius and his household had received the Holy Spirit because they spoke in tongues and exalted God (v. 46).

Cornelius' Relationship With God

The experience of Cornelius and his household raises the question of their relationship with God before Peter preached to them. Among Pentecostals there are two views.

Some believe that as Peter gave his sermon, both Cornelius and his household were saved and filled with the Spirit. On that occasion, they simultaneously believed the gospel and experienced a special outpouring of the Spirit similar to what had been received by the disciples at Pentecost (11:17; 15:8, 9). According to this view, full immersion in the Spirit followed their conversion immediately. Some appeal to Acts 11:14 to support the interpretation that Cornelius was a devout Jew who feared God, but was not yet a follower of Christ until he received Peter's message.[10] This view holds that Cornelius, his family and close friends had a double experience that included conversion, immediately followed by Spirit baptism.

An alternative interpretation embraced by a few Pentecostals supports the view that these Gentiles converted prior to Peter's visit. The support for this view is threefold: (1) Peter assumes that these God-fearing Gentiles were acquainted with the life and ministry of Christ (Acts 10:37, 38). (2) Philip the evangelist lived in Caesarea (8:40; 21:8). He or some other Christian could have shared the gospel with them. (3) Nothing is said about Peter's calling Cornelius and his people to repentance; they were already saved. God had granted them repentance that leads to life (11:18) before Peter arrived.[11] Nevertheless, if one does not take this view but

---

[10]See Anthony Palma, *Baptism in the Holy Spirit,* p. 26, and Donald Gee, *Pentecost* (Springfield, MO: Gospel Publishing House, 1969) 20ff.

[11]Cf. French L. Arrington, *The Acts of the Apostles,* 112, 113.

believes instead that Cornelius and his friends were not saved prior to Peter's visit, then their conversion and receiving of the fullness of the Spirit occurred on the same occasion, one immediately following the other. It was the same occasion, but two separate events.

Observations Regarding Cornelius' Encounter With the Spirit

Many non-Pentecostals believe that these Gentiles experienced conversion and nothing more. They see the gift of the Spirit as being the same as the work of the Spirit in the new birth during conversion. Their assumption is that there is no reception of the Spirit beyond the experience of salvation. The following comments and observations come from a Pentecostal perspective regarding the gift of the Spirit to the Cornelius household.

The gift of the Spirit was given to Cornelius and his friends for empowerment, not for salvation. The terms Luke employed to refer to their spiritual encounter are not used anywhere else in the Book of Acts to describe conversion. The description of what happened uses such expressions as "the Holy Spirit fell upon" (Acts 10:44), "the gift of the Holy Spirit" (v. 45; cf. 11:17), "poured out on" (10:45), and "baptized with the Holy Spirit" (11:16). These expressions are synonymous with "filled with the Holy Spirit"—the phrase used to describe the anointing of the disciples at Pentecost and Saul's experience (2:4; 9:17). The same holds true for "receiving of the Spirit," which appears in the Samaria narrative (8:15, 17, 19). Further, the incident at Samaria speaks about the Holy Spirit's "fall[ing] upon" Christians (v. 16), as well as the experience being "the gift of God" (v. 20). None of these terms are used in Acts to speak of the salvation experience. Empowerment by the Spirit presupposes salvation.

Luke emphasizes the Gentiles' reception of the Spirit's anointing. He does not focus on the time that Cornelius was forgiven of his sins. He describes Cornelius' encounter with the Spirit, just as he does that of Elizabeth, Zacharias and Simeon—not in terms of personal salvation but in terms of spiritual empowerment (Luke 1–2). The story of Cornelius and his friends is not about the gift of salvation but about the gift of the Spirit for service. The Spirit is necessary to both, of course.

At times Spirit baptism follows water baptism (Acts 2:38; 8:14-17), *but here the anointing of the Spirit precedes it.* Clearly baptism in water does not effect salvation or spiritual empowerment.

Peter learned this lesson: "God is not one to show partiality" (Acts 10:34). God had accepted Cornelius and his friends; therefore, He loves and accepts both Jews and Gentiles. Their receiving the power of the Spirit taught the lesson that God's impartiality applies not only to salvation, but also to all His gifts. They received the same prophetic gift bestowed on the believers at Pentecost (2:4ff.), on the Samaritans (8:14-17) and on the apostle Paul (9:17).

The promise of the Pentecostal gift for bold Christian living and evangelism had been fulfilled to these Gentiles. Their experience stands parallel to the experience of the believers in Jerusalem, Samaria and Damascus. This story of Cornelius and his friends is a dramatic example that the prophetic gift of the Spirit is for all believers.

5ᵀᴴ NARRATIVE ACCOUNT
The Disciples' Encounter With the Spirit in Ephesus
Acts 19:1-7

When Paul arrived in Ephesus, he found some who were already disciples. The presence of these people raised two concerns for the apostle: (1) Had they received the Holy Spirit? (2) Were they disciples of John the Baptist or disciples of Jesus? Paul knew that all followers of Jesus have the Holy Spirit (Romans 8:9); so the two questions are interrelated. These disciples had believed, but had not yet been filled with the Spirit. Among modern Biblical scholars, debate has been intense regarding who these men were and their spiritual status.

The Disciples' Relationship With God

On his third missionary journey, Paul met "some disciples" in Ephesus (Acts 19:1). Luke consistently uses *disciples* to refer to Christians (6:1, 7; 9:1, 19, 26; 11:26; 14:21, 22). The only exception is 9:25, where the reference is to the disciples of Paul. Further, some scholars who believe that the term *disciples* does not refer to Christians, appeal to the word *some* (Greek *tines*). The word *tines* in singular form is often translated "certain" and has been used to explain the spiritual standing of these men. The pronoun *some* appears in the following passages to refer to known Christians: Ananias (9:10), Tabitha (9:36) and Timothy (16:1). So the indefinite pronoun *some* fails to support the argument that these disciples were simply followers of John the Baptist. There is solid basis for taking "some disciples" to refer to Christians. Luke is not absolutely certain about their number. He says "about twelve men" (19:7), or a small number of disciples in Ephesus. Various interpretations have been proposed to explain the spiritual status of these Ephesian disciples:

Some scholars think that the Ephesian disciples were merely followers of John the Baptist, but not followers of Christ. This view simply passes the 12 off as members of a "John the Baptist" sect with no real commitment to Jesus Christ. Since they had not received the Holy Spirit, it is claimed that these disciples were not saved, not regenerated. They could not be Christians because of their complete ignorance of the Holy Spirit. Paul's question, however, about their reception of the Spirit had nothing essentially to do with their salvation. Those who deny that the Ephesian disciples were believers identify the gift of the Holy Spirit with the Spirit's work in salvation.

Other scholars think that they were half-believers. They had come under the influence of the gospel, and because of that they were called disciples. In particular, the content of their faith and their understanding of Christian doctrine were limited. Contrary to this position, Paul does not ask them about their faith or their doctrine, but about their baptism. They had been baptized by John the Baptist.

John's preaching was a saving ministry. He had urged people to repent and to believe in Jesus as the Coming One. His baptism symbolized the washing away of sins by the regenerating work of the Spirit. The Ephesian disciples were believers in Christ and were indwelt by the Holy Spirit. They must not be seen as partially saved or as half-believers but as Christians, though perhaps they were in need of additional instruction.

Pentecostal scholars indicate that the Ephesian disciples were genuine Christians. Paul addressed them as believers when he asked, "Did you receive the Holy Spirit when you believed?" (Acts 19:2). This question has to do with their reception of the Holy Spirit after belief on the occasion of their conversion experience. If Paul had thought that they were disciples of John the Baptist and nothing more, no doubt his question would have been different. These disciples had not received the Pentecostal gift of the Spirit as Paul and others had. Their spirituality was similar to that of Jesus' followers prior to the Day of Pentecost. Indeed, they had been converted and indwelt by the Holy Spirit, but they had not yet received the Spirit's anointing of power subsequent to their experience of salvation.

The spiritual standing of the Ephesian disciples could be similar to that of Apollos (Acts 18:24-28). Though a believer, his knowledge seems to have been incomplete. He had received instruction about the way of the Lord, spoke with great power by the Spirit, and taught accurately about Jesus. Apollos, however, was "acquainted only with the baptism of John" (v. 25). Priscilla and Aquila "took him aside and explained to him the way of God more accurately" (v. 26). Indeed Apollos was a believer, but who is there among us who does not need a better understanding of our faith? [12]

---

[12]Unlike the disciples at Ephesus, Apollos may have already been filled with the Spirit. Some authorities take *spirit* (*pneuma*, v. 25) to refer to Apollos' own spirit, but it can be taken to refer to his spiritual empowerment. In other words, powerfully equipped by the Holy Spirit with the same prophetic authority linked to Peter's ministry at Pentecost.

The Holy Spirit's Encounter With the Disciples

Like all believers the Ephesian 12 were indwelt by the Holy Spirit (Romans 8:9). Much attention has been devoted to Paul's question: "Did you receive the Holy Spirit when you believed?" (Acts 19:2). The words "when you believed" (*pisteusantes*) can also be translated "after you believed." [13] No matter how we translate it, the "receiving" of the Spirit is to be understood in terms of what happened at the Jordan River, Pentecost, Samaria and Damascus (Luke 3:21, 22; Acts 2:4ff.; 8:15, 17, 19; 9:17; 10:47). The question is not about salvation, but what is basic to Luke/Acts, namely, the Spirit's anointing with power. They had believed. If Paul had doubts about their faith, he would have asked about the reality of it. What prompted his question we are not told, but it was not out of concern for the genuineness of their faith. He perceived that their need was for the charismatic anointing of the Spirit.

The reply of the Ephesian believers to Paul's question was negative. They had not heard about the Holy Spirit. But if we assume that they were merely disciples of John the Baptist, they would have heard about the Holy Spirit. John himself had preached that Jesus would baptize in the Holy Spirit (Luke 3:16). Also, they would have most likely known something about the Spirit from the Old Testament. Their response, therefore, indicated not that they were ignorant of the existence of the Holy Spirit, but that they had not

---

[13]Much has been written about the Greek participle *pisteusantes*. The action of a participle relates to the leading verb. The present participle normally indicates simultaneous action with that of the leading verb, but the aorist participle, of which *pisteusantes* is, indicates prior action to that of the leading verb. In Acts 19:1-7 two other aorist participles appear, and the normal translation of both of them also indicates prior action to that of the leading verb: "After they heard [*akousantes*], they were baptized" (v. 5) and "After Paul placed [*epithentos*] hands on them, the Holy Spirit came on them" (v. 6). Apart from Greek grammar, the context determines the time relationship of a participle to the leading verb. The context strongly supports that *pisteusantes* indicates prior action to the leading verb *elabete* ("did you receive").

heard about the outpouring of the Holy Spirit on the Day of Pentecost. What they had not known or experienced was the special anointing of the Spirit following their conversion. They had come under the influence of the tradition of John the Baptist and had believed in Christ, but they had not been filled with the Spirit.

After Paul had questioned them about their Pentecostal experience, they received the fullness of the Spirit. This spiritual fullness they received followed their baptism in the name of the Lord Jesus and Paul's laying hands on them. As Ananias laid his hands on Paul, the apostle was filled with the Spirit (Acts 9:17). Similarly Paul placed his hands on the Ephesian disciples, and they were filled with the Spirit. Their experience is not only significant for showing that Spirit baptism is distinct and subsequent to conversion, but also for demonstrating that Paul, like Luke, expects believers to receive this additional spiritual blessing of being filled with the Holy Spirit. In light of Paul's emphasis in his letters on the Charismatic ministry of the Spirit, it is understandable that when he saw no evidence of the Spirit in the Ephesian disciples, he asked them if they had received the Holy Spirit.

Some Observations

The outpouring of the Spirit on the 12 Ephesians makes it clear that Paul's teaching and practice agree with the charismatic theology of Luke. This is as we might expect, since Paul and Luke worked together in the ministry. There are the famous "we" passages in Acts that indicate that the person who wrote these passages accompanied Paul to Rome (16:10-18; 20:5–21:18; 27:1–28:16). The one behind the first-person pronouns *we* and *us* most likely was Luke (Colossians 4:14; 2 Timothy 4:11; Philemon 24). Probably, Paul told Luke about the outpouring of the Spirit on the Ephesian believers during their travels together a few years after the incident (Acts 20:5–21:18).

The account of the Ephesian believers teaches us, among other things, how the apostles and others ministered to those who had been saved, but had never been filled with the Spirit. The Spirit baptism that was promised by the prophet Joel, John the Baptist and Jesus became a reality for the 12 disciples at Ephesus.

CONCLUSION

Jesus ministered in the power of the Holy Spirit (Luke 4:14). Likewise His followers from the Day of Pentecost on would minister in the power of the Spirit. The outpouring of the Spirit on the Day of Pentecost was an outpouring of the Spirit's power from Jesus to the believers. On that occasion, their experience was distinct from the experience of regeneration. Therefore, Spirit baptism should be identified as an additional gift, separate from the gift of salvation that we receive at conversion.

We have examined five accounts in Acts of people being filled with the Spirit. Four of the accounts (Jerusalem, Samaria, Damascus and Ephesus) involved individuals who were already clearly identified as being believers. At Caesarea the experience could have occurred immediately upon Cornelius' and his household's believing the gospel; but at Samaria, Damascus and Ephesus, there was a clear lapse of time between conversion and the filling with the Spirit. In Jerusalem, the Spirit also came upon those who were already believers in Jesus Christ. The New Testament does not tell us precisely when they became believers. However, it does tell us that they went to Jerusalem obeying Christ and believing two promises: "You are to stay in the city until you are clothed with power from on high" (Luke 24:49), and "You will receive power when the Holy Spirit comes on you" (Acts 1:8, *NIV*).

The postconversion experience of the Spirit is spoken of as a "gift" (Acts 2:38; 8:20; 10:45; 11:17). That description is a reminder that Spirit baptism is neither earned nor is it a reward. It comes from the Lord as a result of His grace. Every divine blessing we receive is a matter of divine grace. Even so, persistent prayer has its place in the reception of the fullness of the Spirit. As Jesus promised, "How much more will your heavenly Father give the Holy Spirit to those who ask Him?" (Luke 11:13).

The Pentecostal gift of the Holy Spirit was first received in Jerusalem. On that occasion, Peter spoke to at least 5,000 people who had gathered because of extraordinary events. Those who repented and were baptized in the name of the Lord Jesus were promised the gift of the Holy Spirit. "For the promise is for you and your children . . . as many as the Lord our God will call to Himself" (Acts 2:39). It has become clear from the outpouring of the Spirit at Samaria, Damascus, Caesarea and Ephesus that the Pentecostal experience is still available to all believers, regardless of the age or place in which they live. All who have been born of the Spirit may be anointed by Him. Being filled with the Spirit subsequent to salvation is the Pentecostal view, and I believe that it is the Biblical view. "The ideal paradigm for New Testament faith was for the new convert also to be baptized in the Holy Spirit at the very commencement of his or her Christian life."[14]

Summary

- The New Testament teaches the reality and the desirability of Spirit baptism for all believers.

- The experience of Spirit baptism is distinct and separate from conversion. It may take place immediately upon conversion or at a later time.

[14]Douglas A. Oss, "A Pentecostal/Charismatic View," *Are Miraculous Gifts for Today?* ed. Wayne A. Gruden (Grand Rapids: Zondervan, 1996) 225.

TABLE 4-A **Jesus Christ and the Holy Spirit**	
LUKE 1:26ff.	The direct agency of the Holy Spirit in Jesus' birth strongly suggests that Jesus was indwelt by the Spirit from birth.
LUKE 1:35	The creative work of the Holy Spirit made possible Jesus' birth to a virgin.
LUKE 3:21, 22	The Holy Spirit descended upon Jesus and equipped Him for ministry. Jesus' encounter with the Holy Spirit provided the pattern for the rest of His ministry and a pattern, or model, for the ministry of believers.
LUKE 3:16	Jesus Christ's anointing with the Spirit identified Him as the baptizer in the Spirit, about whom John the Baptist had spoken.
ACTS 1:4, 5	Jesus promised His disciples that they would be immersed in the Spirit.
LUKE 3:21, 22; 4:16-19; cf. ACTS 1:8	Jesus assured His disciples of an experience and ministry patterned after His own experience and ministry.
ACTS 2:33, 39	At Jesus' ascension into heaven, He received the promised Holy Spirit from the Father for distribution to His disciples and all believers.
JOEL 2:28-32; ACTS 2	On the Day of Pentecost, Jesus poured out the Spirit of God as the prophet Joel had foretold.

TABLE 4-B **Praying for God's Gift of the Holy Spirit**	
LUKE 11:13	When believers engage in persistent prayer, they will receive not just good gifts, but the greatest gift—the Holy Spirit.
MATTHEW 7:11	"If you then, being evil, know how to give good gifts to your children, how much more shall your Father who is in heaven give what is good to those who ask Him!"
LUKE 11:13	"If you then, being evil, know how to give good gifts to your children, how much more shall your heavenly Father give the Holy Spirit to those who ask Him?"
LUKE 12:11, 12; ACTS 1:8	Luke encourages Christians to ask for the anointing of the Spirit that will enable them to be powerful witnesses.
LUKE 11:5-10	Luke encourages Christians to keep on asking, seeking and knocking. He promises that God will respond by filling them with the Spirit.
ACTS 1:14	On the Day of Pentecost, the disciples engaged in bold and obedient prayer.
ACTS 2:4; cf. 4:23-31; 8:14-17	The disciples' obedient prayer on the Day of Pentecost resulted in their being filled with the Spirit.
ACTS 9:17; 19:1-7	We are to encourage one another and to pray for God's blessings in each other's lives.
JOEL 2:28; LUKE 24:49; ACTS 1:4; 2:38, 39	The gift of the Holy Spirit is for all believers.

	TABLE 4-C **Narrative Examples of Spirit Baptism**

1	**The Disciples' Encounter With the Spirit** **on the Day of Pentecost** (ACTS 2:1-13)

Jesus Christ sent His Holy Spirit to fulfill His promise to empower believers for bold witnessing and living. The Holy Spirit came into the room where they were praying, accompanied by a rushing, mighty wind; and tongues of fire appeared above the disciples' heads. The believers spoke in other languages as the Spirit empowered them.

2	**The Samaritans' Encounter With the Spirit** **(ACTS 8:4-24)**

The Samaritans converted to Christianity in response to Philip's sharing of the love of Jesus with them. When the disciples in Jerusalem heard of the Samaritans' conversion, they sent Peter and John to visit them. When Peter and John laid their hands on the Samaritans and prayed for them, the Samaritans were filled with the Holy Spirit.

3	**Saul's Encounter With the Spirit in Damascus** **(ACTS 9:1-19)**

On the road to Damascus the Lord spoke to Saul, blinding him. Responding to the Lord's voice, Saul accepted Christ, converting to Christianity. The Lord instructed Saul to travel on to the city of Damascus, where Ananias laid hands on him in prayer. Saul regained his sight and received the baptism in the Holy Spirit.

continued

TABLE 4-C (CONTINUED)
Narrative Examples of Spirit Baptism

4	The Gentiles' Encounter With the Spirit in Caesarea (ACTS 10:1–11:18)

Cornelius was instructed in a vision to send for Simon Peter, who was staying in the city of Joppa. Meanwhile, Peter had a vision in which God told him to eat food he considered unclean. When Peter refused, God taught him that nothing He creates is impure. Through the vision, Peter came to realize that God loves everyone and that He does not show favoritism.

When Cornelius' servants arrived in Joppa, Peter went with them to Caesarea and shared the love of Christ with Cornelius and his Gentile household. While Peter was talking, the power of the Holy Spirit came on the Gentiles. They spoke in tongues and praised God.

5	The Disciples' Encounter With the Spirit in Ephesus (ACTS 19:1-7)

While Paul was in Ephesus, he found some disciples. He asked them if they had received the Holy Spirit. They indicated that they had not heard of the Holy Spirit, but that they had been baptized with John's baptism. Paul placed his hands on them, and the Holy Spirit came upon them. They spoke in other languages and prophesied.

Notes

CHAPTER 4—STUDY AND DISCUSSION

1. Who is eligible to receive the blessing of spiritual empowerment (Spirit baptism) according to Acts 2:38, 39?

2. When does God give this special blessing of spiritual empowerment in relation to our conversion experience? (See Acts 2:38; 19:1-7.)

ESTABLISHING LUKE'S INTENT

3. Did Luke design the Gospel of Luke and the Book of Acts to teach that Spirit baptism is a distinct experience from conversion and is for every believer? (See Acts 2:17-21; Joel 2:28-32.)

The Spirit-Anointed Ministry of Jesus

4. Since the life of Jesus Christ is to be a model for our lives, we can conclude that we may receive the Holy Spirit, as Jesus did for empowerment in ministry. Describe in your own words this event that initiated Jesus' ministry. (See Luke 3:21, 22.)

5. Before this event, how was the Holy Spirit already active in Jesus' life? (See Luke 1:15, 35.)

6. After this event, what were and continue to be some ways in which the Holy Spirit and Jesus work together? (See Table 4-A.)

Praying for God's Gift of the Holy Spirit

7. What should we do in order to receive the gift of the Spirit? Give some examples from Scripture. (See Table 4-B.)

God's Gift of the Spirit to All Believers

8. How do we know that God's gift of the Holy Spirit is for every Christian? (See Joel 2:28; Acts 2:38, 39.)

NARRATIVE EXAMPLES IN ACTS

1st Narrative Account:
The Disciples' Encounter with the Spirit
on the Day of Pentecost

Read Acts 2:1-13 and Table 4-C.

9. What did the coming of the Spirit on the Day of Pentecost mark? (See Acts 2:33.)

10. The Day of Pentecost became a model, or pattern, for what?

11. How do we know from the events on the Day of Pentecost that Spirit baptism follows conversion? (See Luke 10:20.)

2nd Narrative Account:
The Samaritans' Encounter with the Spirit

Read Acts 8:4-24 and Table 4-C.

12. Pentecostal scholars believe that the Samaritans were baptized in the Spirit following their conversion.

    How do some individuals, who do *not* believe that Spirit baptism is a separate blessing from conversion, explain the Samaritans' spiritual encounter?

    How does Acts 8:4-24 provide solid ground for making a distinction between conversion and Spirit baptism?

3rd Narrative Account:
Saul's Encounter with the Spirit in Damascus

Read Acts 9:1-19a and Table 4-C.

13. How do we know that Saul's conversion occurred on the road to Damascus and that he was later filled with the Spirit?

4th Narrative Account:
The Gentiles' Encounter with the Spirit in Caesarea

Read Acts 10:1–11:18 and Table 4-C.

14. What are two major spiritual focuses of this story?

15. Among Pentecostals, what are two viewpoints regarding Cornelius' household's relationship with God?

16. How do we know that Cornelius' house received a special, distinct spiritual blessing? (See Acts 10:44, 45; 11:16.)

17. In the story of Cornelius' household, in what order did the three baptisms occur?

    Please number:

    _____ Baptism by the Spirit (Conversion Baptism)

    _____ Water Baptism

    _____ Baptism in the Spirit (Spirit baptism)

18. What lesson about race and cultural differences can we learn from this story? (See Acts 10:34.)

5th Narrative Account:
The Disciples' Encounter with the Spirit in Ephesus

Read Acts 19:1-7 and Table 4-C.

19. How do we know that the disciples were already Christians?

20. What happened when Paul laid hands on them and prayed for them?

CONCLUSION

21. Read Acts 2:38; 8:20; 10:45 and 11:17. From these verses, what do we learn about Spirit baptism?

*The Jewish believers who came with Peter were amazed
that the gift of the Holy Spirit had been poured out upon
the Gentiles, too. And there could be no doubt about it,
for they heard them speaking in tongues and praising God*
(Acts 10:45, 46, *NLT*).

5

Initial Physical Sign
of Spirit Baptism

"Speaking in other tongues," or speaking in languages that are unknown to the speaker, as "the initial physical sign (evidence)" of Spirit baptism remains the most mysterious and controversial of classical Pentecostal beliefs. This belief has disturbed and baffled many, and as a result has given rise to much debate regarding the work of the Spirit. Such debate can be understood in light of the sharp division of opinion on the Day of Pentecost. Some of the observers said, "We hear them in our own tongues speaking of the mighty deeds of God" (Acts 2:11). But others mocking said, "They are full of sweet wine" (v. 13).

From the outset, speaking in languages unlearned by the speaker provoked differences of opinion. A variety of opinions regarding the Day of Pentecost and "tongues" continue to this day. Therefore, it comes as no surprise to hear questions such as these: "What about tongues as the initial evidence?" "What is the connection between baptism in the Spirit and tongues?" "Must I speak in tongues to be filled with the Spirit?"

These kinds of questions are raised so often that they reflect the fact that we have failed to provide adequate Biblical and theological support for our view of *glossolalia* (Greek word meaning "speaking in tongues"). The ultimate source for faith and practice is the Scripture. Although the Scriptures may not directly address all questions, we need to listen carefully to them and the doctrinal implications they present.

SPIRIT-INSPIRED SPEECH BEFORE PENTECOST

In the Old Testament, the Holy Spirit manifested Himself in a variety of ways. Most of what is said about the Spirit's ministry in the New Testament appears in one form or another in the Old Testament. The most characteristic manifestation of the Spirit was to give inspired utterances. When the Lord transferred the Spirit from Moses to the 70 elders, they prophesied (Numbers 11:24, 25). Likewise, the Spirit inspired Balaam to prophesy (23:5; 24:2). After Saul was anointed by Samuel, the Spirit came upon him. He prophesied (1 Samuel 10:1-10; 19:23) and so did his messengers (19:20). In 1 and 2 Chronicles, the Spirit of God is associated with inspired speech (1 Chronicles 12:18; 2 Chronicles 20:14; 24:20).

The prophetic writings are ascribed to the inspiration of the Holy Spirit. The messages of the prophets were not a result of the prophets' own interpretation, nor did the prophecies originate with human will. They were given by the Holy Spirit (2 Peter 1:20, 21). Peter reminded the people in Jerusalem that the Holy Spirit had spoken through the mouth of David (Acts 1:16; 2:30). Prophecy during Old Testament times was evidence that the Spirit had come upon particular individuals. Particularly, Spirit-inspired utterances are linked to Joel's prediction that all God's people would prophesy (2:28, 29) and to the famous reply of Moses that all God's people might prophesy (Numbers 11:28, 29).

At the beginning of the New Testament era, the Holy Spirit continued to give oral inspiration to individuals. When Elizabeth was filled with the Spirit, she spoke out with a loud voice, pronouncing a Spirit-inspired blessing on Mary (Luke 1:41, 42). Hearing the blessing, Mary exclaimed, "My soul exalts the Lord, and my spirit has rejoiced in God my Savior" (vv. 46, 47). As a result of prophetic inspiration, Zacharias gave a Spirit-inspired song of God's great plan of salvation (vv. 67-79). At the time of the Savior's birth, a number of people broke out in spontaneous praise. The shepherds returned from the stable, "glorifying and praising God" (2:20). Moved by the Spirit, Simeon went to the Temple. When he saw the child, Jesus, Simeon spoke a prophetic prayer of praise that was inspired by the Holy Spirit (vv. 25-32).

In each of these examples, the Holy Spirit came upon individuals prompting them to speak out. In view of this, the Spirit-inspired utterances in the Old Testament and similar experiences of people prior to Pentecost recorded in Luke 1–4 have a close connection. In the Old Testament, such experiences were limited to a few; but in Acts, Luke's account of the outpouring of the Spirit shows how that changed. The experience became wider and far more inclusive (Acts 2:38, 39).

Spirit-Inspired Utterances in Acts

In Acts, the various accounts of the initial infilling of believers with the Spirit raises the question of whether speaking in other tongues (or languages) is an essential aspect of baptism in the Spirit. Pentecostals have supported the doctrine of tongues by appealing to a pattern of events recorded in Acts. From the earliest days of the Pentecostal Movement, Pentecostals began with the Scripture. Through inductive study of the accounts in Acts, they concluded that speaking in tongues accompanied the experience of Spirit baptism. Using the inductive approach is proper for establishing the importance of tongues as the initial evidence or sign of Spirit baptism. This sign continues to this day and will continue to the end of time. The need, therefore, is not only to consider tongues as the Biblical pattern for the evidence of Spirit baptism, but also their purpose and meaning for our personal lives and for our worship and service.[1]

1ST NARRATIVE ACCOUNT

The Disciples' Encounter With the Spirit
on the Day of Pentecost

Acts 2:1-21

Jesus' disciples obeyed His command to wait in Jerusalem until they were clothed with power from above (Luke 24:49). Three miraculous signs accompanied the outpouring of the Holy Spirit: "a noise like a violent, rushing wind," "tongues as of fire," and speaking "with other tongues." The wind and the fire can be described as *theophanies*, manifestations of the Spirit, and were like the supernatural signs that introduced Moses' encounter with God on Mt. Sinai (Exodus 19:18, 19); Jesus' birth at Bethlehem (Matthew 1:18–2:12; Luke 2:8-20); and Jesus' death at Calvary (Matthew 27:51-53; Luke 23:44). The signs of wind and fire

---

[1]We know from Scripture that God loves us and meets us where we are, regardless of our nationality, ethnicity, culture, physical limitations, disabilities or mode of communication. The Bible relates only the experience of speaking in audible languages as the sign of the initial outpouring of the Spirit. However, we can conclude from the Bible's description of the nature of God and from Biblical narratives regarding Jesus' ministry and His followers' experiences that when God gives the gift of Spirit baptism, He will work in and speak through each individual in a unique way. This is according to His plan. For example:

- God might choose to heal a particular disability permanently, allowing His Spirit to work in new ways in a person's life (Mark 3:2-5; Luke 13:10-13; John 4:46-54).

- God might choose to temporarily suspend one's limitations, allowing His Spirit to work differently through that person for a particular period of time (Judges 15:14-20; Matthew 14:26-33.).

- God might work within one's disabilities, limitations or mode of communication, demonstrating the presence of His Spirit in unique ways (Exodus 4:14-17; 2 Corinthians 12:7-10).

marked the Day of Pentecost as having great historic significance in God's plan. These two signs are never mentioned again in Acts; no hint is given that they occurred in later outpourings of the Spirit. The supernatural signs of wind and fire served to introduce a new era, the age of the Spirit.

A Definition of "Speaking in Other Tongues"

As a reoccurring sign in Acts, speaking in other tongues was a vital sign of the disciples' being filled with the Spirit (10:46; 19:6). "And they were all filled with the Holy Spirit and began to speak with other tongues, as the Spirit was giving them utterance" (2:4). The word *utterance* is the rendering of the Greek that means "to speak authoritatively" (*apophthengomai*). It is used in the Greek Old Testament to refer to inspired speech of soothsayers (persons who predict future events) and prophets. Their words can be a result of either divine or demonic inspiration (Ezekiel 13:9, 19; Micah 5:12; Zechariah 10:2). The word appears only three times in the New Testament. In Acts 2:14 it is used to introduce Peter's address to the crowd (he "declared to them"), indicating that he spoke to them with great prophetic authority. Indeed, his speech was an inspired prophetic word.

In this light, tongues at Pentecost can be properly described as prophetic and as conforming to the pattern of vv. 17, 18: "Your sons

---

1 (cont'd) An example of God's choosing to work through one's mode of communication is His speaking through someone, using non-audible language, such as sign language. This type of communication is often referred to as "manual speaking in tongues." Pastors and missionaries ministering to those who have hearing disabilities have reported that some people who have been unable to hear spoken language or to speak audibly have spoken in audible tongues, while others have spoken using their hands. The difference between communication from God expressed through audible, vocal language and communication expressed using other means is simply the mode of communication. The essence of the communication is the same as if it were being expressed in audible language. The individual being blessed is actually expressing the thoughts of the Holy Spirit.

and daughters will prophesy" (*NIV*). The space devoted to speaking in tongues is contrasted with that given to the signs of the tongues of fire and the mighty rushing wind. The latter are mentioned only in verses 2 and 3. Speaking in other tongues (*lalein heterais glōssais*)[2] is introduced in the fourth verse and dominates the account to the end—even carrying over into Peter's sermon. Clearly, Luke understands that an essential aspect of the disciples' being filled with the Spirit was their speaking in other tongues.

The languages spoken at Pentecost were real human languages, but languages that the disciples had never learned. This kind of miraculous manifestation has been referred to as *xenolalia*, speaking in a foreign language. In the other accounts of this manifestation in Acts, we find no reference to foreign languages (10:46; 19:6). Nevertheless, to speak in tongues (*lalein glōssais*) is to speak a language. That is the way Paul understood speaking in tongues. He emphasized it as a spiritual gift and insisted that this gift must be accompanied by the gift of interpretation for the local congregation to be edified (1 Corinthians 12:7-10; 14:1ff.). Inspired speech may come not only in human language unknown by the speakers, but also may be given in heavenly languages. Paul seems to suggest the gift of tongues may be "with the tongues . . . of angels,"

---

[2]The adjective *other* (*heterais*) is used here to describe the phenomenon of tongues, but in Acts 10:46 and 19:6 it does not appear. No real significance should be ascribed to its absence in these passages. In the New Testament the manifestation of speaking in tongues is spoken of in a number of ways: to speak in other tongues (Acts 2:4), to speak in tongues (Acts 10:46; 19:6; 1 Corinthians 12:30; 14:5, 6, 18, 23), to speak in a tongue (1 Corinthians 14:2, 4, 13), to speak in the tongues of men and of angels (1 Corinthians 13:1), to speak in new tongues (Mark 16:17), kinds of tongues (1 Corinthians 12:10, 28), tongues (1 Corinthians 13:8; 14:22), and a tongue (14:14, 19, 26). Therefore, in his discussion of spiritual gifts (1 Corinthians 12–14) Paul uses a number of variations. Compare also 1 Corinthians 14:21 where he quotes Isaiah 28:11, "By men of strange tongues [*en heteroglōssois*] and by the lips of strangers [*en cheilesin heterōn*] I will speak to this people."

likely heavenly languages by which men speak to God in prayer (1 Corinthians 13:1; 14:2, 14-16).

A Definition of "Interpretation of Tongues"

The gift of interpretation of tongues indicates that tongues, whether human or heavenly, are translated for the edification, or spiritual enlightenment, of the congregation. The gift of interpretation indicates that speaking in tongues is done in a language and points to the translation from one language to another. No such conversion was needed on the Day of Pentecost, since the disciples spoke in the languages of the various national groups present.

Significance of Speaking in Other Tongues

The central significance of Pentecost is that "they were all filled with the Holy Spirit and [all] began to speak with other tongues, as the Spirit was giving them utterance" (Acts 2:4). A way of restating this is, *All who were filled with the Holy Spirit spoke in tongues, as the Spirit enabled them.* No one was excluded; the speaking in tongues was the sign that they had received the fullness of the Spirit. Speaking in tongues was the manifestation of a Person, the person of the Holy Spirit. It is His nature and character to speak, and true to Himself, He spoke through the disciples at Pentecost. Spirit-inspired utterances were expected "in the last days," which were initiated by the coming of Christ and the outpouring of the Holy Spirit. According to Peter the experience of the disciples pointed to the fulfillment of Joel's prophecy (Acts 2:16-21).

Spirit Baptism, a Gift in the Last Days

In applying the ancient prophecy of Joel, Peter characterizes the gift of the Spirit in two ways. First, it is a gift of the last days. Peter interprets "afterward" of Joel 2:28 (*NIV*) as "in the last days" (Acts 2:17). The Jews divided time into two ages: this age and the coming age. The latter age was the age of fulfillment, which the prophet Joel predicted. The messianic age, the age of the Spirit, the age of fulfillment, the "last days" had dawned. Peter says that the manifestation at Pentecost begins the fulfillment of God's promise of the Spirit, but it was only one of the many manifestations of the Spirit in the last days.[3]

Speaking in Other Tongues as Prophecy

Second, Peter identifies speaking in other tongues as a manifestation of inspired prophecy. In citing the words of Joel, he says, "Your sons and daughters will prophesy," and he goes on to add for emphasis "and they will prophesy" (vv. 17, 18, *NIV*). There are a number of elements in Joel's prophecy, such as the age of fulfillment, the universality of the outpouring of the Spirit, great signs and wonders in heaven and on earth, and the promise of salvation to all who call on the Lord. None of these elements receive the emphasis that Peter gives to prophetic utterance—clearly the key feature to the fulfillment of Joel's prediction. At Pentecost, tongues are a form of prophecy that serve as a sign of the Spirit's advent, or coming.

What is the basis for identifying tongues as a form of prophecy? Of course, speaking in tongues is not exactly the same as prophesying. However, both are manifestations of the Spirit and involve the Spirit's coming upon a person and inspiring the person to speak out. The essential difference is that prophecy is given in the speaker's language, whereas tongues are uttered in a language unknown to the speaker. Both of these manifestations operate through inspired speech, so speaking in tongues can be called a special form of prophecy in terms of the way it functions. Indeed, on the Day of Pentecost the disciples' speaking in tongues was a fulfillment of Joel's prophecy that the Lord's servants would prophesy. But on the same occasion, Peter preached his famous sermon in inspired speech

---

[3]Stronstad, *Charismatic Theology of Luke*, p. 56. Pentecost was not the first or the last of manifestations of prophetic inspiration in the New Testament. Luke also records other incidents of prophetic inspiration. See Luke 1–2 and Acts 10:44-46; 19:6.

("declared" v. 14, *apophthengomai*), taking the form of a word of prophecy, but in language Peter himself understood (Acts 2:14-36).

The Experience of Speaking in Other Tongues

The utterances of the disciples at Pentecost can be properly described as prophetic and as prompted by the Holy Spirit. Acts 2:4 says that they "began to speak with other tongues, as the Spirit was giving them utterance." Some sincere Pentecostals have appealed to the word *began* (*archomai*) for their understanding that the disciples initiated the speaking. The idea is that you start speaking in tongues, and then the Holy Spirit takes over. But the word *began* here is an example of redundancy, in which more words than necessary are used. This grammatical construction is not unusual in Greek and other languages. We could eliminate the word *began* and still express the sense of the sentence. If we do, then "they began to speak with other tongues" becomes "they spoke with other tongues." Another Biblical example of this construction is Luke 3:8, where John the Baptist tells the multitude that comes out to be baptized by him, "Do not begin to say to yourselves." The removal of "begin to" does not really change the meaning, and the command would read, "Do not say to yourselves."

At Pentecost the disciples spoke in tongues "as the Spirit was giving them utterance"—not under their own impetus but under the impetus of the Holy Spirit. The conjunction *as* (*kathōs*) can be rendered "just as," "to the degree that" or "in so far as."[4] It was the Holy Spirit who enabled them to speak in the languages of the pilgrims who were present in Jerusalem. The Holy Spirit spoke through the disciples, giving them the utterance. The utterances of the disciples were in a variety of foreign languages as indicated by the catalog of nations (Acts 2:9-11) and by Joel's prophecy: "Your

---

[4]Bauer-Arndt-Gingrich-Danker, *A Greek-English Lexicon of the New Testament and other Christian Literature*, 3rd ed. (Chicago: Univ. of Chicago Press, 1979) 493-94.

sons and daughters will prophesy" (Joel 2:28; Acts 2:17, 18, *NIV*). Indeed, the disciples' speaking in tongues was a fulfillment of Joel's prophecy and reminds us of the prophetic character of the Pentecostal gift.

2ᴺᴰ NARRATIVE ACCOUNT
The Samaritans' Encounter With the Spirit
Acts 8:14-20

The Samaritans listened intently to Philips' preaching of Christ. They also observed that in conjunction with his Spirit-anointed proclamation, he performed great miracles. Being mighty in works as well as in word, he was able through the power of the Holy Spirit to make demons powerless, forcing them to leave their victims. Through his ministry, many who were lame and paralyzed received healing for their bodies. As a result, the Samaritans believed Philip's message and were saved. They experienced great joy and were baptized in water as a sign that their sins had been washed away (Acts 8:8, 12).

The Samaritans were converted, but they had not received the Holy Spirit (v. 15). "He had not yet fallen on any of them" (v. 16). In the New Testament, "receiving the Spirit" is a term that is used with more than one meaning and must be determined in light of the particular writer's intent. Luke's emphasis is different than Paul's. Luke refers to this experience in the same way he refers to "being filled with the Spirit" or "baptized in the Spirit," the Spirit's "coming" or "falling upon" people, and "the gift" or "the promise of the Spirit." On the other hand, Paul's perspective in Romans 8:9 and 1 Corinthians 6:16 differs from Luke's. Paul has in view the indwelling of the Spirit in each believer, but Luke focuses on a subsequent experience in which the believer is equipped by the Spirit for service. Interpreting Scripture in terms of the author's intent is a sound rule of Biblical interpretation.

In Acts 2:4 and 10:46, the immediate result of the disciples' being filled with the Spirit was that they spoke in tongues. Likewise, when Peter and John laid hands on the Samaritan believers, those believers had a postconversion experience of the Spirit. Nothing, however, is said about *glossolalia* as the result of their experience. Yet, it is clear from the account that something extraordinary took place on this occasion. If not, why would Simon offer money for the power to confer the Spirit? He had already witnessed miraculous signs that accompanied the ministry of Philip (v. 6). What was it that convinced him that the Samaritans had received the power of the Spirit?

Luke does not provide the details. There must have been a spiritual manifestation that was different from the miracles performed by Philip. We are told that "Simon saw [*idōn/horaō*] that the Spirit was bestowed through the laying on of the apostles' hands" (v. 18). The Greek verb *horaō* has the basic meaning of "to see," but it can also mean "to perceive," indicating more than visual perception. Simon did not only observe, but he understood what was happening before his eyes and ears.[5] Something immediate and easily perceptible was manifested—an audible, visual manifestation. What could have arrested Simon's attention? What spiritual manifestation would have been different from the miracles that he had seen occur in the ministry of Philip? *Glossolalia* fits the occasion, for that sign would have occurred immediately and would have signified the Spirit's control and power. Yet the account is silent on this point.

Can we maintain that tongues are the initial physical evidence of Spirit baptism? Is it Luke's intent to teach that speaking in another language is an essential sign of the experience? It is true that there

---

[5]William G. MacDonald, *Glossolalia in the New Testament* (Springfield, MO: Gospel Publishing House, 1964) 6-7. In the same context Peter says to Simon, "I see [*horaō*—the same verb in Acts 8:18] you are in the gall of bitterness and in the bondage of iniquity" (v. 23). His seeing was perceptual rather than merely visual.

is no statement in the New Testament that says tongues are the normative sign of Spirit baptism. Neither does Scripture state that the Bible is completely reliable for faith and practice, but it is strongly implied. The Book of Acts strongly indicates that Luke intends to teach that tongues are the initial sign of baptism in the Spirit. Otherwise, it would be difficult for a person to know that he or she has been filled with the Spirit.

As we have noted, Luke identifies this sort of manifestation with the gift of the Spirit in two of his major accounts (Acts 2:1-21; 10:44-48). These two accounts bracket the Acts 8 outpouring of the Spirit. It is not likely that Luke would have thought it necessary to mention tongues specifically in connection with the experience of the Samaritans. Those who reject that the Samaritan believers spoke in other tongues fail to explain what captured Simon's interest. The silence of Luke on some of the details, especially on tongues in Samaria, is not surprising since that sign was common to the other stories of believers being filled with the Spirit (Acts 2:1-4; 10:44-46; 19:1-7). Commenting on the Samaritans' experience of the Spirit, the New Testament scholar Ernst Haenchen, who does not subscribe to the Pentecostal view of Spirit baptism, says that the gift of the Spirit is here "recognizable by the sign of *glossolalia*."[6]

Simon "saw" something. The account of the outpouring of the Spirit on the Samaritans occurs between the outpouring on the Day of Pentecost and the outpouring in the city of Caesarea, both of which were linked to *glossolalia*. That miraculous, visible, audible sign, according to classical Pentecostals, is what gripped the attention of Simon. This view is not an argument due to silence in the Bible. It fits well the context (Acts 2:4; 10:45, 46) and is harmonious with Luke's perspective that tongues provide demonstrative proof of Spirit baptism.

---

[6]Ernst Haenchen, *The Acts of the Apostles*, trans. Bernard Noble and Gerald Shinn (Philadelphia: Westminster, 1971) 304.

This manifestation as the initial sign of the experience fits the prophetic character of the Pentecostal gift. Similar to first-century Jews, Luke identifies the gift of the Spirit as a source of prophetic inspiration. For example, the rabbis interpreted Isaiah 44:3 ("I will pour out My Spirit on your offspring") and Joel 2:28ff. as referring to the outpouring of the Spirit of prophecy on Israel.[7] The Spirit provides the impetus for inspired speech. From the outset of his Gospel, Luke draws attention to the Spirit-inspired speech of Elizabeth (1:41-43), Zacharias (1:67) and Simeon (2:25-28). It is underscored in Jesus' sermon at Nazareth (4:18, 19) and Peter's sermon at Pentecost (Acts 2:17, 18). Therefore, the Pentecostal gift is the source of prophetic inspiration that includes intelligible speech and *glossolalia*. But because of its unusual and undeniable demonstrative character, speaking in tongues is well suited to serve as physical evidence of Spirit baptism.

3ᴿᴰ NARRATIVE ACCOUNT
Saul's Encounter With the Spirit in Damascus
Acts 9:17

After Saul's (Paul's) conversion and call, he entered the city of Damascus. God sent Ananias to him so that he might regain his sight and "be filled with the Spirit." Luke is silent about the time that Paul was baptized in the Spirit and any manifestations that may have accompanied the experience. Most likely, Paul received the gift of the Spirit when Ananias laid his hands on him. Luke, however, does not mention his speaking in tongues.

Nevertheless, what we know about Spirit baptism from the Book of Acts and about Paul's later practices strongly suggest that he

---

[7]Cf. Robert P. Menzies, "Coming to Terms With an Evangelical Heritage"—Part 2: "Pentecostals and Evidential Tongues," *Paraclete:* 28/4 (Fall 1994) 5; and also Aboth de Rabb:Nathan A. 34.

spoke in other tongues when he was filled with the Spirit. Like the narrative about the Samaritans, Saul's experience in Damascus occurs between the outpourings of the Spirit in Jerusalem and in Caesarea. Evidently, Luke did not think it was necessary to give all the details of Paul's experience, since it was consistent with the earlier outpouring of the Spirit. Paul himself, in his first letter to the Corinthians, affirms that he spoke in tongues, a manifestation he ascribes to the Spirit (12:10, 11; 14:18). According to Acts, Paul's charismatic experience parallels that of Peter's (2:4; 4:8, 31; 9:17; 13:9, 52). It is logical and completely proper, therefore, to conclude that Paul spoke in tongues as Ananias laid hands on him. Paul's experience was not an exception to the model for Spirit baptism, which had taken place on the Day of Pentecost. His spiritual encounter included the sign of speaking in other tongues, verifying by an audible, visible sign his reception of the Pentecostal gift.

4ᵀᴴ NARRATIVE ACCOUNT
The Gentiles' Encounter With the Spirit in Caesarea
Acts 10:44-48

At the house of Cornelius in Caesarea, Gentiles were filled with the Spirit. The believing Jews who had come with Peter were surprised "because the gift of the Holy Spirit had been poured out on the Gentiles also" (Acts 10:45). This account fits well with Luke's perspective on the outpouring of the Spirit at Pentecost. Similarities between the experience of the household of Cornelius and that of the disciples in Jerusalem are striking. The following observations make these similarities apparent:

No doubt, exalting and praising God are closely related to speaking in tongues. Luke uses similar terms in both accounts: "speaking with tongues" (2:4; 10:44) and "exalting [*megalunō*] God" (2:11; 10:46). In verse 46, the word *and* (*kai*) may be used in the phrase "speaking in tongues and exalting God" as an explanation. If so, then the exalting (*megalunō*) of God indicates that the content of speaking in tongues included the praising of Him. The noun form of the verb *megalunō* appears in 2:11, where the onlookers say, "We hear them in our own tongues speaking of the mighty deeds [*megaleia*] of God." The verb form appears also in Mary's hymn of praise: "My soul exalts [*megalunō]* the Lord" (Luke 1:46). In Acts 19:17, the people magnify (*megalunō*) the name of the Lord Jesus. Thus, speaking in tongues may often involve thanksgiving and praise to God for His mighty acts and blessings in Jesus Christ (1 Corinthians 14:2, 14, 15).

Peter identifies the gift of the Spirit to Cornelius and his household with the events at Pentecost. In showing the church at Jerusalem that the promise of the Spirit had been fulfilled to these Gentiles, Peter declared, "The Holy Spirit fell upon them just as He did upon us at the beginning" (Acts 11:15). Then he added that "God gave to them the same gift as He gave to us also after believing in the Lord Jesus Christ" (v. 17). Peter, at the Jerusalem Council, says that God gave the Holy Spirit to Cornelius "just as He also did to us" (15:8). Furthermore, common terms occur in both accounts, such as "baptized in the Holy Spirit," "poured out," "gift" and "speaking with tongues." The Gentiles at Caesarea received the same Spirit baptism as did the believers at Pentecost (10:47).

The disciples at Pentecost and Cornelius and his friends responded in a similar way: speaking in tongues. The outward, visible and audible manifestation of *glossolalia* convinced Peter and the six Jewish Christians from Joppa that these Gentiles had been received into God's family and had been immersed in the Spirit (v. 23; 11:12). Such inspired speaking was the evidence or the sign of their Spirit baptism: "For they were hearing them speaking with tongues and exalting God" (10:46). The manifestation of glossolalia had important apologetic value. How would they have known that the household of Cornelius had been filled with the Spirit without that observable manifestation? Since the Holy Spirit had manifested Himself in the same manner at Pentecost, the miraculous, audible speech provided significant proof that the Spirit had fallen upon Cornelius and his friends. They had received the same prophetic gift of the Spirit as the believers at Pentecost. The Pentecostal manifestation of tongues was undeniable evidence of the Gentiles' immersion in the Spirit.[8]

5ᵀᴴ Narrative Account
The Disciples' Encounter With the Spirit in Ephesus
Acts 19:1-7

The Spirit baptism of the 12 believers in Ephesus shows that Paul's and Luke's understanding of the work of the Spirit is complementary rather than contradictory. In his letters, Paul emphasizes that the receiving of the Spirit is essential to the salvation experience (Romans 8:9, 15; Galatians 3:2, 14; Ephesians 1:13). But Paul's question to the Ephesian believers, "Did you receive the Holy Spirit when you believed?" (Acts 19:2) indicates that receiving the Spirit at conversion could also have for him another meaning, namely the Pentecostal gift of the Spirit. I am fully convinced that Luke reported accurately what happened. He did not put the words on Paul's lips nor revise the question so that it would conform to his own Charismatic doctrine of the Spirit. Luke is a historian and a reliable one at that (see 2 Timothy 3:16).

In the account of the 12 disciples in Ephesus, we are told that

---

[8]According to Acts 11, Peter does not mention tongues directly in his defense of what had happened at Caesarea, but the sign of tongues is strongly implied by his reference to the events of Pentecost (vv. 15, 17). The mention of the phenomenon in 10:46 makes reference to tongues unnecessary in chapter 11. What happened at Caesarea reminded Peter of the words of the Lord in Acts 1:5, "John baptized with water, but you shall be baptized with the Holy Spirit" (11:16).

Paul laid his hands on them. Peter and John had laid their hands on the Samaritans when they received the Holy Spirit (Acts 8:17). Likewise, Ananias had laid his hand on Paul, who was then filled with the Spirit (9:17). So now Paul lays his hands on the 12 men, and they also are filled with the Spirit: "The Holy Spirit came on them, and they began speaking with tongues and prophesying" (19:6). The terms used here are similar to the earlier accounts of believers being filled with the Spirit: "receive the Holy Spirit," "the Holy Spirit came on," and "speaking with tongues." In fact, the words *came* (from *erchomai*) and *on* (*epi*) parallel that of Acts 1:8.

One noteworthy observation about 19:6 is that they spoke in tongues and prophesied. Paul's question to the 12 Ephesian believers assumes that they were expected to know whether or not they had received the Holy Spirit when they "believed." Indeed, the immediate consequence of their being filled with the Spirit was the Charismatic manifestations of tongues and prophecy. Some have interpreted this to mean that not all spoke in tongues. A few spoke in tongues, and the others prophesied. They conclude, therefore, that either tongues or prophecy can serve as the sign of Spirit baptism. I offer two observations:

1. *If prophecy is another option as the sign of the Pentecostal gift, Luke does not suggest it elsewhere in Acts.* Sound Biblical interpretation avoids basing a doctrine on one passage of Scripture. As we have noted, Acts 2 provides the paradigm for Spirit baptism. Peter clearly indicates that *glossolalia* at Pentecost fulfilled Joel's prediction. It is true that *glossolalia* is a special kind of prophetic, Spirit-inspired speech, but is not in itself prophecy. Tongues are given in a language not known to the speaker and usually require interpretation for the manifestation to influence people directly, whereas prophecy is spoken in a language understood by both the speaker and the hearer. Both tongues and prophecy are prophetic.

2. *The phrase "and prophesied" does not mean an additional or optional sign of Spirit baptism.* The events of the Day of

Pentecost show a close relationship between speaking in tongues and prophesying. In verse 6, the Greek (*te . . . kai*) specifies a closer connection and relationship than does the simple *and* (*kai*).[9]

No doubt, it can be debated whether Luke is referring to two separate manifestations or to the same spiritual reality. But prophetic activity had been promised for the last days (Joel 2:28). In light of the spiritual encounters of the disciples at Pentecost and of Cornelius' household in Caesarea, we can conclude that these people at Ephesus similarly spoke in tongues and gave praise to God after they received the Pentecostal power of the Spirit (Acts 2:4, 11; 10:46). Like the earlier outpouring on the Day of Pentecost, speaking in tongues was the initial evidence of the Pentecostal experience of the Ephesian believers and can properly be described as a special form of prophecy.

Paul expected that believers would be filled with the Spirit. The outpouring of the Spirit upon the Ephesian believers makes it clear that Paul's teaching and practice both affirm the charismatic theology of Luke. This outpouring of the Spirit illustrates the charismatic nature of the church. Wherever the gospel was preached—from Jerusalem to Ephesus, in large cities or in more remote areas like Ephesus—believers received the Pentecostal gift of the Spirit accompanied by the observable phenomenon of tongues.

CONCLUSION

Throughout Biblical history, inspired utterances have occurred when the Spirit came upon people. Spirit-inspired speech appears in

---

[9]Blass-Debrunner-Funk, *A Greek Grammar of the New Testament and Other Early Christian Literature*, 230. Palma, *Baptism in the Spirit*, p. 49, apparently understands that the *te . . . kai* sharpens the distinction between "speaking in tongues and prophesying." He offers this translation: "The Holy Spirit came upon them. Not only did they speak in tongues, but they also prophesied." His position is that the Ephesian believers spoke in tongues and they also prophesied, but only tongues were the initial sign that they had been endowed with power for ministry, thereby corresponding to the previous accounts (2:4; 10:46).

the Old Testament, at the beginning of the New Testament (Luke 1–4), and in the accounts recorded in the Book of Acts. Speaking in tongues is a special form of inspired, prophetic speech. Its appearance on the Day of Pentecost and on subsequent occasions fulfilled Joel's prophecy that all of God's people in the last days would prophesy. Joel's prediction and the outpouring of the Spirit in Acts have provided the Biblical basis for the association of speaking in tongues with Spirit baptism. From the earliest days of the Pentecostal Movement, Pentecostals have believed that accompanying Spirit baptism is this normative manifestation. Since the Book of Acts places a strong emphasis on tongues and is a distinctive source for understanding Pentecostal/Charismatic spirituality, there are a number of matters that deserve our consideration.

Viewpoints on Tongues as "The Initial Physical Evidence." Tongues as "the initial physical evidence" manifest the larger and deeper experience of Spirit baptism. This view has been controversial from the beginning of the Pentecostal/Charismatic Movements in the early part of the 20th century. Those in disagreement with Pentecostals and Charismatics have focused their debate on the validity of tongues for the church today. Some individuals view tongues as a response to the overwhelming presence of the Spirit, but insist that tongues are now outdated, no longer having any meaning for modern people. Others believe that tongues are a spiritual gift for the edification of the church, but are not the initial sign of Spirit baptism. They believe that tongues are just a teaching of Pentecostal and Charismatic churches, not relevant for their own lives. Still others see the initial-evidence doctrine as limiting the freedom of the Spirit, arguing that the Spirit moves as He wills and manifests Himself accordingly.

In recent years, Pentecostal scholars have begun to respond to such viewpoints. They have appealed to the outpouring of the Holy Spirit at Pentecost as the model for later outpourings. On the basis of inductive Bible study, they discern a pattern of *glossolalia,* beginning with Acts 2:4 and reoccurring in 10:46 and 19:6. Today, this approach is known as narrative theology, in which storytelling is used to teach doctrine. Indeed, storytelling is a widely used technique in Scripture, including Luke/Acts. Deriving normative doctrine and practices from narratives is a valid exercise. Some of the most important documents of the Christian faith, the four Gospels, consist of narratives of the life and teachings of our Lord. A widespread practice in many cultures of the world is the telling of something three times in order to establish the matter. Luke's three accounts of tongues accompanying Spirit baptism provide adequate basis for us to expect the same in our experience of the Spirit.[10] When we are baptized in the Spirit, speaking in tongues may be compared to the visible tip of an iceberg. This manifestation of the Spirit is a reliable sign of a much larger and deeper spiritual reality.

The Phrase "Initial Physical Evidence." Questions have been raised regarding the use of the phrase "initial physical evidence," because it does not appear in Scripture. The word *initial* should not be taken to refer to the first work of the Spirit in a person. From the moment of salvation, the believer is indwelt by the Holy Spirit. Many Pentecostals and Charismatics regard tongues not as the physical sign of the first, but of the second stage of the Spirit's ministry in the believer. The "initial" physical evidence is to be understood as the immediate proof (sign) of having received Spirit baptism. The phrase "initial physical evidence" is a human attempt to state the significance of the audible, visual manifestations that occurred in Acts at the outpouring of the Spirit. Like all theological formulations, it has limitations—especially if the focus is on "evidence," which can easily result in the confusion of the actual gift of the Spirit with the sign. Tongues are the evidence of the Pentecostal dimension of the

---

[10]Donald A. Johns, "Some New Directions in the Hermeneutics of Classical Pentecostalism's Doctrine of Initial Evidence," *Initial Evidence*, ed. Gary B. McGee (Peabody, MA: Hendrickson, 1991) 163.

work of the Spirit, not the gift itself. The gift is the Spirit's power that strengthens the believer's commitment to evangelism and intensifies devotional and worship life.

Caution should be taken against developing an overly extreme passion for "evidence." Our passion should be for the fullness of the Spirit and a deeper relationship with God, not merely for tongues. If the focus is only on tongues, then the emphasis is in the wrong place. On the other hand, it is unfair to try to write off the experience simply as a desire for "certainty." God in His wisdom has given tongues as a valid sign of the gift of the Spirit. We should be careful not to criticize the ways in which God chooses to move in our lives. After all, tongues are the outward sign of a genuine encounter with the Holy Spirit.

Omission of "Tongues" in Some Biblical Narratives. In the Book of Acts on a number of occasions, the only sign associated with Spirit baptism is tongues. Even so, some question whether tongues will invariably occur. They observe that Luke records instances in which believers are said to be "filled with the Spirit" or of being "full of the Spirit," but no mention is made of tongues. Some individuals, therefore, ask why speaking in unknown languages should be viewed as the only possible initial evidence of being filled with the Spirit. The response of Pentecostal scholars is threefold:

1. *Luke felt no need to provide all the details for all five instances of Spirit baptism recorded in Acts.* He observes the manifestation of tongues in Acts 2, 10 and 19, and must have determined that the three references were sufficient to indicate that the manifestation normally would accompany Spirit baptism as the initial sign of the experience. Another example of where Luke does not provide all the details has to do with conversion. He does not explicitly discuss faith and repentance in the account of Paul's conversion on the road to Damascus (Acts 9:1ff). Neither does Luke indicate specifics about the faith and repentance of Cornelius and his household

(10:1ff.). When telling individuals' conversion stories, Luke does not always state the requirements of faith and repentance for receiving salvation, nor does he indicate that all who were saved repented and believed. One can conclude from certain passages in Acts that all did repent and did receive salvation (2:37ff.; 3:11ff.; 10; 16:31ff.), just as one can conclude that all spoke in other languages—the sign that they were filled with the Spirit (8:14ff; 9:17-19).

2. *The "initial evidence" doctrine applies only to the initial experience of being filled with the Spirit* (Acts 2:4; 10:46; 19:6). Paul, however, focuses on "tongues" as also having value in private prayer and as being a spiritual gift for the edification of the local church (1 Corinthians 12–14). But when a person uses the phrase "initial evidence" to describe tongues, there is an implied essential connection between tongues and Spirit baptism. Speaking in a tongue unknown to an individual indicates the occurrence of the larger experience of being filled with the Spirit. One way many Pentecostals have described the manifestation is that it is a sign of yielding oneself completely to God. Scripture sees the tongue as a very unruly member of our bodies (James 3:8), and speech as an index of the heart: "For the mouth speaks out of that which fills the heart" (Matthew 12:34). Because of this, tongues manifest the sovereignty of the Spirit in the life of the believer and the yielding and obedience that is involved in the experience of Spirit baptism.

As true as that may be, tongues also indicate and manifest a deeper and more profound reality—the Holy Spirit's union with and empowerment of the believer. It is the Holy Spirit who speaks through the believer in tongues (Acts 2:4). His speaking demonstrates the presence and power of God and that Spirit baptism is a real spiritual experience. This spiritual manifestation, therefore, is actually part of being filled with the Spirit and is the initial physical sign of this profound empowering experience for service, living and worship. Functioning as the initial evidence, speaking in another tongue is the outward sign of this profound hidden experience of the Holy Spirit.

3. *Because tongues have a striking and demonstrative character, they are suited well as evidence of Spirit baptism.* The gift of the Spirit, as Joel predicted, is a prophetic experience; and *glossolalia* is a form of prophetic speech. There is strong, Biblical support for linking the coming of the Spirit with prophetic speech (Numbers 11:29; 1 Samuel 10:6, 10-12; 19:23, 24; Ezekiel 11:5; Joel 2:24ff.; Acts 2:17, 18). But why did God choose *glossolalia* as the sign of the coming of the Spirit? Could He not have chosen inspired speech or charismatic revelation that was understandable? None of these manifestations would have provided the audible, visible evidence that speaking in a language *unknown* to the speaker does.

Many of us can think of occasions where inspired utterances were given; but when the utterances are spoken in the speaker's native language, it requires more discernment on our part to decide what is inspired and what is not. Our judgment regarding the spirituality of this kind of speech is approximate and tenuous, whereas *glossolalia* is more demonstrative and extraordinary in its manifestation than prophecy is, indicating by a unique audible and visible sign the reception of the Pentecostal gift. Tongues may be spoken in either an earthly or a heavenly language. If the utterance is an earthly language, the language may be described as a prayer language not understood by the speaker. However, other persons present may understand the language (Acts 2:5-12). Because of its unusual character, this manifestation has been questioned by some and overvalued by others. To be immersed in the Spirit is an overwhelming and definite encounter with the person and power of the Holy Spirit. Tongues appropriately and uniquely serve as the initial sign of this charismatic experience because of its demonstrative and extraordinary character.[11]

Tongues, a Normal Sign of Spirit Baptism. From what we have said, it can be concluded that speaking in tongues, according to Pentecostal belief, accompanies Spirit baptism as the normative

---

[11]Menzies, 6.

sign. But the question can be raised: Can a person be Pentecostal without having spoken in tongues? The answer is yes. You can be a member of a Pentecostal church but never have been baptized in the Spirit with the initial evidence of speaking in tongues. The issue goes much deeper than this, however. Does the New Testament teach that a believer may be baptized in the Spirit, without having spoken in tongues? As we have observed, the Book of Acts places a strong emphasis on tongues and suggests that it is the definitive sign of being filled with the Spirit.

Yet there are those who argue that not in every instance does this sign accompany Spirit baptism. They claim that the Pentecostal position on tongues goes beyond New Testament evidence. For support they point to 1 Corinthians 12:30, where Paul asks, "All do not speak with tongues, do they?" The negative (Greek, *mē*) that Paul employs makes it clear that he anticipates the answer: "No, all do not speak in tongues." This appears to contradict the Pentecostal belief that all speak in tongues at the time they are baptized in the Spirit. Paul's question deals with ministries and spiritual gifts in the context of worship. In that context the manifestation of tongues must be accompanied by interpretation so that the congregation may be spiritually edified. All believers do not have the gift of tongues for the purpose of edifying (spiritually enlightening) the congregation. The Holy Spirit distributes the spiritual gifts so that there is a balance of ministries (1 Corinthians 12:7-11).

This does not deny the place of *glossolalia* at a personal, noncongregational level, such as one's private devotions or as the sign of Spirit baptism. Paul speaks about tongues as a way a speaker may edify himself (1 Corinthians 14:4). The *all* (Greek, *pantes*) of Acts 2:4 carries much weight in support of tongues as the normative sign of being filled with the Spirit. Because *all* serves as the subject of both clauses, an appropriate translation is, "They were all filled with the Spirit and [all] began to speak with other tongues." Believers normally experience tongues as the sign of being filled with the Spirit.

Tongues, an Indication of the "Last Days." The manifestation of tongues in our own lives reminds us not only of the experiences of those at the first Christian Pentecost, but also that we are living in the "last days." The new era of the Spirit began on the Day of Pentecost (John 3:39; Acts 2:33). That was an event of the last days predicted by the prophet Joel (2:28-32). The "powers of the age to come" (Hebrews 6:5) had dawned with the coming of Christ and the outpouring of the Spirit. The era of the Spirit is the period between the first and the second coming of Christ. Tongues demonstrated the breaking-in of the age to come, the kingdom of God. They, along with the tongues of fire and the sound of violent wind, were extraordinary manifestations of God's presence (Acts 2:1ff.).

As a form of prophetic speech, tongues signifies that the community of believers has been empowered for the missionary task in the last days. Until Jesus returns, Spirit-baptized believers receive power to live in an unbelieving and suffering world and are called to a prophetic ministry that reaches all people—young and old, men and women, rich and poor (Acts 2:17, 18). Speaking in tongues is a specific prophetic manifestation that the prophet Joel predicted would occur in the last days. For the last days, it seems that God has given a new form of prophetic speech, speaking in tongues, that reveals the presence of God's kingdom, the fullness of which remains a matter of hope.

To conclude, the purpose of the initial-evidence doctrine is not to establish a set of rules indicating how the Spirit fills people. Rather, it is to be faithful to Scripture and to encourage people to expect the sign when they experience the glory and the power of Spirit baptism. Where the belief in the initial evidence has been abandoned, the magnificence, richness and power of the Pentecostal experience will gradually disappear. At the same time, the focus should not be on the evidence. To place the emphasis primarily on the sign of speaking in other tongues can lead to the confusion of the sign with the actual gift of Spirit baptism.

An imbalance of focus may lead to the seeking of tongues, rather than the empowerment of the Spirit for Christian living and service. After we are filled with the Spirit, we must not focus so strongly on outward signs that we neglect to recognize and appreciate many other aspects of the Holy Spirit's work, such as His quiet moves and empowerment in our everyday lives. Tongues as the "initial evidence should not be so much that 'we have the Spirit,' but that the Spirit 'has us' as participants in the work of the kingdom." [12] The foremost emphasis, therefore must be placed on receiving God's blessing of the gift of the Holy Spirit. The sign will follow.

Summary

Through prophecies of the Old Testament and narrative accounts in the Book of Acts, we can conclude that speaking in languages not known by the speaker, is the initial physical sign of Spirit baptism.

[12]Frank D. Macchia, "The Question of Tongues as Initial Evidence," *Journal of Pentecostal Theology* 2 (1993) 121.

TABLE 5-A	
Characteristics of "Tongues"	
ACTS 2:11; 1 CORINTHIANS 13:1; 14:2, 14-16	The phrase "speaking in other tongues" indicates speaking in *languages that are unknown to the speaker*. Tongues may be either earthly or heavenly languages.
ACTS 2:4; 10:46; 19:6	Tongues are the *initial physical sign* that someone is being filled with the Holy Spirit. As the initial sign, they indicate spiritual empowerment. Prayer and praise accompany tongues, the sign of Spirit baptism.
JOEL 2:28, 29; ACTS 2:18	Tongues are a form of *prophetic language* inspired and enabled by the Holy Spirit.
ACTS 2:4, 11; 10:44, 46; 1 CORINTHIANS 14:2, 14, 15	Tongues are a form of *prayer and praise* to God.
JOEL 2:28; ACTS 2:16-21	On the Day of Pentecost, tongues and other spiritual signs *ushered in the age of the Spirit* (the last days) in which we live today.
ACTS 2:16-36	The manifestation of tongues in our own lives *reminds us* not only of the experiences of those at the first Christian Pentecost, but also that we are living in "the last days."
Wind: ACTS 2:2 Flames: ACTS 2:3 Tongues: See Table 5-C	In the Book of Acts, *more space is devoted to the discussion of tongues than to the other two signs* that occurred on the Day of Pentecost. The wind and flames of fire as signs of the Spirit's arrival are only mentioned once.

continued

TABLE 5-A (CONTINUED) Characteristics of "Tongues"	
1 CORINTHIANS 14:2, 14, 15, 27, 28	Tongues may be *prayer language*. Tongues as prayer language are a spiritual manifestation that occurs in private devotions. Prayer-language tongues are similar to tongues as the initial sign of Spirit baptism in that both are accompanied by prayer and praise. On both occasions, the person is personally edified (enlightened or encouraged) when he or she speaks in tongues.
1 CORINTHIANS 12:10, 30	Tongues may be a *gift of the Spirit* for the church. When accompanied by interpretation, tongues can be a gift from the Holy Spirit for the edification of the church in worship.
1 CORINTHIANS 14:5, 26-28	The gift of *interpretation of tongues* is for the *edification, or spiritual enlightenment*, of the congregation. It is a spiritual gift that enables one to give the significance of a message in tongues, whether human or heavenly.
LUKE 24:49; ACTS 1:8; GALATIANS 5:16-23; 2 PETER 1:5-8	A major focus of our prayers should be to seek a deeper relationship with God, requesting the empowerment of the Holy Spirit. The focus should be on *spiritual development and empowerment for service*.
Notes	

TABLE 5-B
Spirit-Inspired Language
Before the Day of Pentecost

Spoken Prophecy in the Old Testament

NUMBERS 11:24, 25	When the Lord transferred the Spirit from Moses to the 70 elders, they prophesied.
NUMBERS 23:5; 24:2	The Spirit inspired Balaam to prophesy.
1 SAMUEL 10:1-10; 19:19-23	After Saul was anointed by Samuel, the Spirit came upon him and he prophesied. Also, his messengers prophesied.
1 CHRONICLES 12:18; 2 CHRONICLES 20:14; 24:20	God is associated with inspired speech.

Written Prophecy in the Old Testament

2 PETER 1:20, 21	Prophetic writings are ascribed to the inspiration of the Holy Spirit.
ACTS 1:16; 2:30	Peter reminded the people in Jerusalem that the Holy Spirit had spoken through the mouth of David.

Old Testament Prophecy About Future Inspired Language

JOEL 2:28, 29; ACTS 2:17, 18	Joel predicted that people from all walks of life would prophesy.
NUMBERS 11:28, 29	Moses expressed his desire for all of God's people to prophesy.

continued

TABLE 5-B (CONTINUED)	
Spirit-Inspired Language Before the Day of Pentecost	
Inspired Speech in the New Testament	
LUKE 1:41, 42	When Elizabeth was filled with the Spirit, she spoke out with a loud voice pronouncing a Spirit-inspired blessing on Mary.
LUKE 1:46-55	Mary sang a song of praise in response to Elizabeth's pronouncement.
LUKE 1:67-79	Zacharias was filled with the Spirit and prophesied about God's plan of salvation.
LUKE 2:20	At the time of the Savior's birth, the shepherds returned from the stable "glorifying and praising God."
LUKE 2:25-32	Moved by the Spirit, Simeon went to the Temple. When he saw the child, Jesus, Simeon spoke a prophetic prayer of praise.

In the Old Testament, the filling with the Spirit seems to have been limited to Israel's leaders (prophets, priests and kings). From Acts 2 on, the experience is available to all of God's people.

Notes

Table 5-C
Narrative Examples of
Spirit-Inspired Utterances in Acts

1	The Disciples' Encounter With the Spirit on the Day of Pentecost

Jesus commanded His disciples to wait in Jerusalem until they were clothed with power from above (LUKE 24:49).

On the Day of Pentecost the disciples "were all filled with the Holy Spirit and began to speak with other tongues, as the Spirit was giving them utterance" (ACTS 2:4).

The tongues on the Day of Pentecost were the beginning of the fulfillment of Joel's Spirit-inspired prophecy from the Old Testament (JOEL 2:28, 29; ACTS 2:17, 18).

2	The Samaritans' Encounter With the Spirit

The Samaritans had become Christians but had not been filled with the Spirit. Peter and John laid hands on them, and they received the blessing of spiritual empowerment. Something extraordinary occurred, prompting Simon, the magician, to offer to pay money for the power that he had witnessed (ACTS 8:14-20).

3	Saul's Encounter With the Spirit in Damascus

After Paul (Saul) was converted, he entered the city of Damascus. Ananias laid hands on him in prayer, and most likely this was the occasion when he received the gift of Spirit baptism and spoke in tongues as well. We can conclude this because his spiritually empowered ministry began immediately following this event. Also, Paul himself indicated in his first letter to the Corinthians that he normally spoke in tongues (ACTS 9:17; 1 CORINTHIANS 14:18).

continued

TABLE 5-C (CONTINUED) **Narrative Examples of Spirit-Inspired Utterances in Acts**

4	The Gentiles' Encounter With the Spirit in Caesarea

When Cornelius and his household were filled with the Spirit, they praised God and spoke in tongues. Peter identified their spiritual encounter with the events of the Day of Pentecost (ACTS 10:44-48; 11:15-18).

5	The Disciples' Encounter With the Spirit in Ephesus

While Paul was in Ephesus, he found some disciples and asked them if they had received the Holy Spirit. They indicated they had not heard of the Holy Spirit, but that they had been baptized with John's baptism. Paul laid hands on them, and the Holy Spirit came upon them. They spoke in other languages and prophesied (ACTS 19:1-7).

Notes

CHAPTER 5—STUDY AND DISCUSSION

1. What is the initial physical sign that someone is receiving the blessing of Spirit baptism? (See Acts 2:4; 10:46; 19:6.)

2. Give a definition for "speaking in other tongues." (See the section in this chapter: "1ˢᵗ Narrative Account: The Disciples' Encounter with the Spirit on the Day of Pentecost–Acts 2:1-21"; Table 5-A.)

3. What types of language might one use when prompted by the Spirit to speak? (See Tables 5-A, 5-B and 5-C.)

4. Which of these types does the apostle Paul describe as "speaking in other tongues"? (See Acts 2:11; 1 Corinthians 13:1; 14:2, 14-16.)

5. Might an individual speak in tongues on occasions following his or her encounter with the Spirit in Spirit baptism? (See Table 5-A.)

6. What is the difference between speaking in other tongues as the initial sign of Spirit baptism and speaking in tongues as a gift of the Spirit for the Christian community? (See Table 5-A.)

7. What is the difference between speaking in other tongues, and the interpretation of tongues? (See Table 5-A.)

SPIRIT-INSPIRED SPEECH BEFORE PENTECOST

8. What are some examples of Spirit-inspired language in the Old Testament? (See Table 5-B.)

9. What are some of the incidences recorded in the New Testament in which Spirit-inspired speech occurred before the Day of Pentecost? (See Table 5-B.)

SPIRIT-INSPIRED UTTERANCES IN ACTS

10. Name some incidences from the Book of Acts in which the Holy Spirit inspired individuals to speak. (See Table 5-C.)

1ˢᵗ Narrative Account:
The Disciples' Encounter With the Spirit
on the Day of Pentecost
(Acts 2:1-21)

11. Joel prophesied that Spirit baptism would be a gift "in the last days." What did he mean by "last days"? (See Table 5-A and the Glossary.)

12. Discuss why speaking in other tongues is considered a form of prophetic speech. (See Joel 2:28, 29; Acts 2:18.)

2ⁿᵈ Narrative Account:
The Samaritans' Encounter With the Spirit
(Acts 8:14-20)

13. How do we know that the Samaritans had not received the gift of Spirit baptism before Peter and John prayed for them? (See Acts 8:14-17; Table 5-C.)

14. Peter and John prayed for the Samaritans, and they received the gift of Spirit baptism. How do we know that something extraordinary happened at this time? (See Acts 8:17, 19; Table 5-C.)

3ʳᵈ Narrative Account:
Saul's Encounter with the Spirit in Damascus
(Acts 9:17)

15. This account of Ananias' praying for Saul does not specifically state that Saul received the blessing of Spirit baptism or spoke in other tongues on this particular occasion. How do we

know that he probably did receive Spirit baptism on this day? (Paul: see Acts 9:17-19; 1 Corinthians 12:10, 11, 14-18; Peter: see Acts 2:4; 4:8, 31; 9:17; 13:9, 52; Table 5-C.)

4th Narrative Account:
The Gentiles' Encounter With the Spirit in Caesarea
(Acts 10:44-48)

16. What aspect of speaking in other tongues does Acts 10:46 indicate? (See Table 5-C.)

17. How do we know that the Gentiles in Caesarea spoke in other tongues? (See Acts 10:47; 11:15, 17; Table 5-C.)

5th Narrative Account:
The Disciples' Encounter With the Spirit in Ephesus
(Acts 19:1-7)

18. How do we know that the disciples in Ephesus had not already received the blessing of Spirit baptism? (See Acts 19:1-4; Table 5-C.)

19. When Paul laid his hands on the disciples, what happened? (See Acts 19:6; Table 5-C.)

20. Why do classical Pentecostal scholars conclude that prophecy in one's native language is not the first sign of Spirit baptism?

CONCLUSION

21. How do Pentecostal scholars explain the omission of the phrase "tongues" in some Biblical narratives?

22. Where should our focus be when we pray for the blessing of Spirit baptism? (See Table 5-A.)

23. Can those who have not yet received the gift of Spirit baptism and spoken in other tongues be Pentecostals?

And they sent Barnabas to Antioch. When he arrived and saw the evidence of the grace of God, he was glad and encouraged them all to remain true to the Lord with all their hearts. He was a good man, full of the Holy Spirit and faith, and a great number of people were brought to the Lord (Acts 11:22-24, *NIV*).

6

The Reception and Results of Spirit Baptism

B aptism in the Holy Spirit is an intensely personal experience. Scripture teaches that the Spirit indwells all believers from the time of their conversion, and that through the experience of Spirit baptism, they have a second personal encounter with the Holy Spirit. During this experience, He fills them and empowers them for service, worship and living. The prophet Joel prophesied about this edifying and empowering experience. When people receive what Joel promised, the Holy Spirit comes to them in a way that they can recognize. They experience a new contact with God and a fresh sense of spiritual vitality and power.

This contact is an encounter with the very present God, giving the believer a keen sense of the daily presence of God in the midst of the pressures and adversities of life. The work of the Holy Spirit in conversion is absolutely necessary for salvation, but Spirit baptism is distinct from the Spirit's work in which He brings men and women to faith in Christ. There are two kinds of experience—conversion and Spirit baptism. Both are the result of the Spirit's work (cf. Acts 8:9-24).

This two-step pattern is supported by the earthly life of Jesus. Throughout the life of Jesus on the earth, the Holy Spirit was present with Him. Before Jesus' birth, an angel informed Mary that she would have a child and that the Holy Spirit would come upon her (Luke 1:35). Prior to the time of her and

Joseph's coming together in marital union, "she was found to be with child by the Holy Spirit" (Matthew 1:18). Later, the Holy Spirit came upon Jesus and anointed Him at the very beginning of His public ministry (Luke 3:21, 22). As a result He was "full of the Holy Spirit" when He entered the wilderness (4:1), and after 40 days there He returned to Galilee "in the power of the Spirit" (v. 14). The empowerment of Jesus by the Spirit provides a pattern for believers' experience of the Spirit. The twofold encounter of the Spirit is also justified by particular passages in the Book of Acts that give accounts of people who were converted and subsequently filled with the Holy Spirit (see Acts 2:1ff.; 8:9-24; 9:17; 10:44-46; 19:1-7).

The Pentecostal gift of the Spirit penetrates every area of our lives—body, soul and spirit. Observe what is involved in this profound encounter with the Holy Spirit.

RECEPTION OF SPIRIT BAPTISM
Being Filled With the Spirit

Pentecostals teach that Spirit baptism is distinct from the work of the Spirit in regeneration (the new birth). At this point I raise the question: What is necessary to be filled with the Spirit? Scripture does not give us specific instructions for receiving the fullness of the Holy Spirit. Perhaps the following suggestions will prove helpful.

For All Believers

Baptism in the Spirit is for all believers. This intense experience is for every person who has faith in Jesus. The promise of the Spirit's fullness was fulfilled at Pentecost to 120 disciples, but the powerful experience was not limited to those first believers. The promise was not only to those who were the closest—"you and your children"—but also to "all who are far off, as many as the Lord our God will call to Himself" (Acts 2:39). A part of God's plan is for all believers to be filled with the Spirit. As Joel predicted, there would be a great outpouring of the Spirit in the last days. As a result, barriers such as age, gender and social status would be set aside and all God's servants could receive this prophetic, empowering experience (Joel 2:28, 29). These spiritual encounters in the last days stand in distinct contrast to those recorded in the Old Testament. No longer would the Spirit come to only a select few, such as rulers, priests and prophets.

The Lord now desires that all believers be filled with the Spirit. The story that Luke records in the Book of Acts shows that the encounter with the Holy Spirit at Pentecost was a continuing, repeatable event. It occurred on both the individual (Acts 9:17) and group levels (2:1-4; 4:31; 8:17ff.; 10:44-46; 19:1-7). Unlike the Incarnation, the death of Christ and His resurrection, which were onetime events, the outpouring of the Spirit would occur an unlimited number of times.[1] What happened at Pentecost was promised to all generations of Christians to come. Because of Jesus' words in both Luke 24:49 and Acts 1:4, and the promise of Peter in his sermon at Pentecost, the same promise has continued through the ages of time and is for believers today. It is an encounter with the Holy Spirit meant to empower and renew God's people. The individual seeker, therefore, must be a child of God and must believe that this extraordinary experience is indeed for him or her.

A Gift of God

Baptism in the Spirit is a gift of God. This spiritual encounter is described as the gift of the Holy Spirit (Acts 2:38; 10:45) and the gift of God (8:20). By definition, a gift is not bestowed on the basis of merit. It is a mistake to think that though salvation is by grace,

---

[1]The repeatability of receiving spiritual empowerment should not be taken to detract from the uniqueness of the coming of the Holy Spirit at Pentecost. That event was a new and powerful act of God, but it was only the first of many that came later.

immersion in the Spirit is by works. Whatever we receive from God is a matter of grace, not works. The gift of the Holy Spirit cannot be earned, no matter how great and noble the effort. If God were to bestow Spirit baptism on the basis of personal worth and merit, then the perplexing question would be: What degree of spiritual worthiness or perfection is required to qualify a person for the experience? This experience is appropriately referred to as the "gift of God." It is an act of God's grace. He gives this gift freely out of the abundance of His generosity, but it is not a gift that He normally bestows on both seekers and nonseekers. God gives Spirit baptism to believers who earnestly seek it—to those who "ask . . . seek . . . knock" (Luke 11:9-13). He will not withhold the Spirit's anointing from His children who ask the heavenly Father for this gift.

If we must speak of a condition for receiving Spirit baptism, like other blessings that God gives, the requirement is faith.[2] Genuine faith expresses itself in prayer, yielding, sensitivity and obedience. The receiving of the wondrous experience, therefore, does not require the personal attainment of a high standard of spirituality, but it assumes an ongoing response to the Lord in terms of devotion and obedience. God acts and fills the believer with the Holy Spirit. On the other hand, the believer must respond in order to receive the fullness of the Spirit. God does not impose the gift of the Spirit upon believers. He takes the initiative in giving, and His children can only

---

[2]The gift of the Holy Spirit is not conferred by the means of water baptism. At Samaria and Ephesus, the gift of the Spirit follows water baptism (Acts 8:12-17; 19:4-6), but at Caesarea the gift of the Spirit precedes it (10:44-48). In a number of the Acts accounts of the bestowal of the Spirit, nothing is said about water baptism. It apparently took place entirely apart from that ordinance (2:1ff.; 4:8, 31; 13:9, 52). Likewise the laying on of hands was not required. It is mentioned in connection with Spirit baptism of the Samaritans (8:17), Saul (9:17) and the Ephesians (19:6). Nowhere is it stated as a requirement. In fact, the Book of Acts gives no indication that the combination of water baptism and the laying on of hands can confer the Holy Spirit. In the Acts narratives, the freedom of the Spirit is emphasized.

receive what He has first given. To receive the Pentecostal gift of the Spirit requires the response of faith. From faith springs obedience. The Spirit is given "to those who obey Him" (Acts 5:32).

Dedication, Preparation and Petition

Prayer and praise lead to Spirit baptism. We have emphasized that Spirit baptism is given to those who are already believers. As believers engage in worship, it provides the proper environment for receiving the Holy Spirit. Worship and prayer are often the context and preparation for the outpouring of the Spirit.[3] Scripture disclos-es that frequently the Pentecostal experience has been received dur-ing prayer. Jesus himself began praying after His baptism in the Jordan River; and as He prayed, the Holy Spirit descended upon Him (Luke 3:21, 22). Therefore, He was praying when the Spirit anointed Him for His ministry. The Spirit's descent upon Him occurred with Jesus' prayer, not with His baptism. Soon after His experience at the Jordan River, He is described as "full of the Holy Spirit" (4:1). Jesus instructed His disciples to pray for the Holy Spirit: "If you then, being evil, know how to give good gifts to your children, how much more will your heavenly Father give the Holy Spirit to those who ask [keep on asking] Him?" (11:13). Believers are responsible to ask their heavenly Father to empower them by the Holy Spirit. God will respond to deep, earnest, persistent prayer. The assurance that God hears the prayers of His children should encourage those who are uncertain and perplexed because of the fear that what they will receive will not be the genuine empower-ment of the Holy Spirit.

In the Book of Acts, we also see an intimate link of prayer and worship with the coming of the Holy Spirit. The Spirit was given at Pentecost as an answer to prayer. The disciples "were continually

---

[3]R. Hollis Gause, *Living in the Spirit: The Way of Salvation* (Cleveland, TN: Pathway Press, 1980) 79ff., 82, 93ff.

devoting themselves to prayer" (Acts 1:14; cf. Luke 24:52, 53). They obeyed the command of Jesus to stay in the city of Jerusalem until they were endued with power from on high (Luke 24:49). Engaging in prayer and praise prepared them to be baptized in the Spirit.

On other occasions, prayer and praise were important to the out-pouring of the Holy Spirit. The disciples experienced opposition from the Jews soon after Pentecost. They prayed for boldness to preach the gospel and to minister in Jesus' name (Acts 4:29, 30). God answered their prayer by granting them a fresh filling of the Spirit (v. 31). In answer to Peter's and John's prayers, the Samaritan believers received the Holy Spirit (8:14-17). While Paul was praying and fasting, God directed Ananias to him (9:9-11). At the laying of Ananias' hands on him, Paul's sight was restored and he was filled with the Holy Spirit (vv. 17, 18). The angel of God spoke to Cornelius and said, "Your prayers . . . have ascended as a memorial before God" (10:4). As a result of Cornelius' petitions, the Holy Spirit fell upon him and his household (v. 44).

These examples show that prayer and praise provide the spiritual atmosphere and environment in which God grants the fullness of the Spirit to those who trust in Christ. Our heavenly Father delights in answering the petitions of those who ask Him for Spirit baptism. Pentecostals have rightly insisted that speaking in tongues accompanies this experience, but we need to guard against the error of making tongues, rather than God, our pursuit. This error prompts believers to pray to speak in tongues rather than to be filled with the Spirit. Of course, the believer can expect to speak in tongues as the initial sign of this new encounter with the Holy Spirit. A genuine hunger for God will prompt us to engage in praise and prayer for a personal encounter with God and will prepare us not to settle for anything less than the fullness of the Holy Spirit. The immediate effect of the outpouring of the Spirit on the disciples at Pentecost and on the believers at Caesarea was their praising and worshiping God in languages that they did not know

(Acts 2:11; 10:46; cf. 1 Corinthians 14:16, 17). Our prayers and praise of God in our own language can provide the atmosphere for us to be filled with the Spirit and facilitate our praising God in *glossolalia* as a response to experiencing the intense presence of God.

According to God's Will

God gives Spirit baptism according to His sovereign purpose. So far we have emphasized the importance of faith, prayer and praise in receiving the Pentecostal gift of the Spirit. The human context and atmosphere are important, but more basic to the Pentecostal experience is the will of God. All things, including God's giving of the Holy Spirit, work out according to His divine purpose. The outpouring of the Holy Spirit in Jerusalem reminds us of this truth. Long ago, God planned to manifest the Spirit on the Day of Pentecost. When that day arrived, He gave the Holy Spirit. The promise to pour out the Spirit was fulfilled according to God's timetable. The first words of Acts 2:1 suggest this: "When the day of Pentecost had come. . . ." On that occasion, the divinely ordained time for the manifestation of the Spirit was fulfilled.

God, therefore, has an overall plan for history and He carries it out according to His will. Baptism in the Spirit is a gift of God, but the time for bestowing the gift is always in the hands of the Giver. God gives when He wills, but He does respond to praise and prayer in accordance with His own will. There is a continuing mystery about God's plan and the working out of it. For that reason, His timing for giving the Pentecostal encounter with the Spirit may be different from our timing or expectation. Weeks or, in exceptional cases, years may pass before a believer receives the Pentecostal experience. The spiritual condition of the believer may be a factor, but the Lord does not disclose why His timing may be different from ours. It is clear from both the Book of Acts and church history that outpourings of the Spirit can occur at unexpected times. Although the timing of receiving Spirit baptism is unpredictable, the sincere seeker should not be filled with self-condemnation if the experience does not take place when expected. On the human side, as we have noted, it is through faith that the Pentecostal experience is received and that prayer and praise provide the atmosphere for the coming of the Spirit. Sometimes there may be those occasions of special visitations by the Lord when many people are filled with the Spirit.[4] At those times, the most favorable conditions exist for believers to be filled with the Spirit.[5]

A Continual Blessing

Baptism in the Spirit is not necessarily a onetime event. The Book of Acts clearly teaches that the experience of being filled with the Spirit may occur multiple times. God may refill His people because of different times and different circumstances and new challenges facing them. Nowhere does the New Testament teach that "once filled, always filled." Most Pentocostals understand that there is one baptism in the Spirit but many fillings. As we have already observed, Luke employs a variety of terms to describe the dynamic presence of the Holy Spirit, but two expressions—"filled with the Holy Spirit" and "full of the Holy Spirit"—help us to understand that being filled with the Spirit is not a onetime experience. It is a repeatable experience, intended "to empower and renew the people of God continuously."[6]

---

[4]Palma, *Baptism in the Spirit,* 63.

[5]Some have questioned the old-fashioned Pentecostal-style of "tarrying meetings." For them, such meetings seem unnecessary. Since the Holy Spirit was poured out on the Day of Pentecost, their question is: Why wait now for the Holy Spirit to come? Early Pentecostals knew how to seek for Spirit baptism, and they were unwilling to settle for anything less than an endowment of the Spirit. They "tarried" or engaged in prayer for a long length of time in order to focus on God and become more receptive to His work in their lives. They realized that it often takes a lot of effort and time to move from being focused on oneself to being truly focused on God, on hearing His voice, and on submitting one's life to Him.

[6]Frank D. Macchia, "The Baptism in the Holy Spirit: A Pentecostal Viewpoint," *Transforming Power*, ed. Young Chul Han (Cleveland, TN: Pathway Press, 2001) 154.

Definition of "Filled [*pimplēmi*] With the Holy Spirit"

To be baptized in the Spirit and to be filled with the Spirit are two ways of referring to the same experience (Acts 1:4; 2:4). The phrase "filled with the Holy Spirit" is also used in two additional ways.

1. *The phrase may refer to a fresh empowerment of the Spirit to meet a specific need.* For example, Peter had received an initial filling of the Spirit at Pentecost, but later he and John were brought before the Jewish authorities after the healing of a man who could not walk. They were asked by the authorities by what power had they healed the lame man. To meet the challenge of this situation, God gave Peter a renewed filling of the Spirit. Luke describes it in these words: "Then Peter, filled with the Holy Spirit, said to them . . ." (Acts 4:8). On that occasion, Peter was given by the Holy Spirit prophetic boldness and the words to speak in trying circumstances. This fresh filling of the Spirit was a fulfillment of Jesus' promise to believers that under persecution "the Holy Spirit will teach you in that very hour what you ought to say" (Luke 12:12; cf. Matthew 10:17-20; Mark 13:9-11).

Similar to Peter's and John's experience, the community of believers was facing persecution. Those believers had already been filled with the Spirit on the Day of Pentecost. But now they found themselves in a demanding situation, and they prayed, "Enable your servants to speak your word with great boldness" (Acts 4:29, *NIV*). God answered their prayer: "They were all filled with the Holy Spirit and began to speak the word of God with boldness" (v. 31). This encounter with the Spirit was a renewal and an enhancement of their initial filling with the Spirit, so that they could meet the challenges confronting them. Spirit-filled believers may receive additional fillings to cope with particular needs and difficult circumstances.

The repetitive characteristic of being filled with the Spirit is also demonstrated in the experience of Paul. Soon after his conversion and call to ministry, Paul had been filled with the Spirit (Acts 9:17). At the beginning of his missionary work, Paul confronted a practitioner of magic, a false prophet by the name of Elymas (13:4-12). Paul took strong prophetic action by pronouncing upon him divine judgment. At that time, his action was prompted by the inspiration of the Spirit. Luke describes him as having been "filled with the Holy Spirit" (v. 9). The Spirit came upon Paul to enable him to defeat this enemy of the gospel.

Indeed after being baptized in the Spirit, there may be special fillings. In terms of our Western understanding, if something has been filled, it cannot be filled more. But according to the Bible, a Spirit-filled believer may receive additional fillings with the Spirit. "One filling is not incompatible with another."[7] The new fillings impart to believers spiritual power to face threats and dangers and to continue to bear witness to Jesus Christ. Many Pentecostals have testified to having experienced a number of fillings of the Spirit in times of special need.

2. *The phrase "filled with the Spirit" is also used to indicate another meaning—a continuing, ongoing, charismatic empowerment and inspiration of the Holy Spirit.* This ongoing reality of the Spirit-filled life is mentioned in Acts 13:52: "The disciples were continually filled with joy and with the Holy Spirit." The occasion was Paul's and Barnabas' departure from Pisidian Antioch. The disciples whom they left behind underwent extreme persecution. At the same time, the Holy Spirit was ministering to their spiritual needs. As a result, they were being filled with joy and the Holy Spirit. The verb *were filled* (*eplērounto*, an imperfect tense) refers to ongoing action in past time ("were being filled"). The Spirit was continually filling and empowering them day by day. Earlier, these believers at Antioch had been immersed or baptized in the Spirit,

---

[7]I. Howard Marshall, *The Acts of the Apostles* (Grand Rapids: Eerdmans, 1980) 355.

but throughout the period of persecution they were being empowered and inspired by the Holy Spirit. For them, filling with the Spirit was not only an initial experience, but also it was an ongoing reality and a daily encounter with the Holy Spirit.

The Holy Spirit is free to move again and again. Paul was convinced of this and that believers who have been baptized in the Spirit may continue to be filled with the Spirit. He exhorted the Ephesian believers to "be filled with the Spirit" (Ephesians 5:18). The verb *be filled* (*plērousthe*, a present progressive tense) emphasizes ongoing action. Paul called for them to keep on being filled with the Spirit. Whether it was an individual or the whole Christian community, being filled with the Spirit's presence and power is the state of being thoroughly permeated by the Spirit of the living God. In verses 19-21, we have some examples of the results of a total, dynamic, ongoing filling with the Spirit. They are (1) "speaking to one another in psalms and hymns and spiritual songs"; (2) being joyful, singing and making music in our hearts to the Lord; (3) "always giving thanks for all things in the name of our Lord Jesus Christ to God, even the Father"; (4) "[being] subject to one another in the fear of Christ."

"Being filled to the full by the Spirit's presence"[8] shapes the lives of believers and permeates their whole existence, including their worship, their interpersonal relationships, their homes and their work. The constant renewal of the Spirit makes it possible for God's people to engage in genuine worship that is filled with singing and praising the Lord. Through such worship, believers express an overflowing joy. This joy is a personal joy in the Holy Spirit. Constant renewal in the Spirit also helps us to set aside a complaining and grumbling attitude and prompts us to endeavor to give thanks to God in the name of Christ in every situation. With the

---

[8]J. Wesley Adams, "Ephesians," *Full Life Bible Commentary* (Grand Rapids: Zondervan, 1999) 1073.

Spirit's help, we are able to look honestly at the hardships of life, grieve our losses, allow others to encourage us, and press on. We are able to do what needs to be done, as the Spirit gives us the assurance that God makes all things work together for our good (Romans 8:28). This comfort and hope that the Spirit gives helps us to be thankful at all times. Furthermore, Spirit-filled believers do not seek to manipulate and control others, but in humility they submit themselves to one another out of reverence for Christ. In like manner, Spirit-filled believers promote unity of the church and encourage fellow believers (Colossians 3:15-17).

Paul's command to keep on being filled with the Spirit strongly suggests that the Spirit can run dangerously low in a Christian's life, especially when we move away from the Spirit, getting caught up in the cares of life. Out of a sense of emptiness, many have had a desire for a fresh encounter with the Holy Spirit and to be filled with the Spirit day by day. Such a personal ongoing relationship enables us to experience the fullness of the Spirit in all areas of our lives—body, soul and spirit. Out of a profound sense of the daily presence of God, we are empowered by the Holy Spirit to live the Christian life and to share the good news of Jesus Christ. Likewise, a community of believers filled with the Spirit will find that not only their relationship with God but also their relationships with one another are saturated with the presence of God. They have profound assurance that God is at work in them and among them, and they are being flooded by His presence.

Definition of "Full [plērēs] of the Holy Spirit"

The phrase "full of the Holy Spirit" emphasizes a state of being. In the New Testament, it is used only by Luke. He speaks of Jesus as being "full of the Holy Spirit" (Luke 4:1) and indicates that it was a qualification for the seven deacons (Acts 6:3). One of the deacons, Stephen, is specifically described as "a man full of faith and of the Holy Spirit" (6:5; 7:55) and so is Barnabas (11:24). It may be impossible to make a hard-and-fast distinction between the phrase "full of the Holy Spirit" and being constantly "filled with the Spirit" (Acts 13:52; Ephesians 5:18). Both indicate a continual state in which the believer is inspired and empowered by the Holy Spirit. Yet, the phrase "full of the Holy Spirit" seems to suggest that the Holy Spirit is in full control of our lives. This phrase especially points to a deepened relationship to God. Such a relationship with God produces a remarkable quality of life.

The inner control of the Holy Spirit is not only demonstrated by powerful witnessing and miraculous deeds, but also by a manifestation of Christian graces in personal devotion and spirituality in daily life. Luke, therefore, understands that a person full of the Spirit will manifest the graces and virtues such as wisdom (Acts 6:3), faith (v. 5; 11:24), grace and power (6:8). Similarly, a person may be filled with wisdom (Luke 2:40), joy (Acts 2:28; 13:52), wonder and amazement (2:12; 10:45). All these graces are associated with those who are described as "full of" or "filled with" the Holy Spirit. In contrast, Luke also speaks of those who are "full of" deceit and fraud (13:10), and those who are "filled with" rage (19:28), jealousy (5:17) and confusion (19:29). We read of a man who was "full of leprosy" (Luke 5:12, KJV). His entire life was controlled by this disease. Furthermore, we are told that Satan filled Ananias' heart to lie to the Holy Spirit (Acts 5:3). He was dominated and controlled by the Evil One.

It is not hard for us to understand the meaning of "full of the Holy Spirit." Luke connects graces and virtues with those who are full of, or filled with, the Holy Spirit. Just like Jesus, the Spirit-filled are habitually controlled and empowered by the Spirit of the living God. This is a continual state of the believer that stands in contrast to someone governed by another spirit such as the spirit of pride, divisiveness, criticism and selfishness. The mark of being full of the Spirit speaks of a particular quality of life that distinguishes the believer as one pervaded in a total way by the Holy Spirit. The powerful sense of the Spirit's immediate presence impacts the inward and outward life of the believer. There is a total penetration of the Holy Spirit into all areas of a person's life and of a community of believers when they are full of the Spirit.

RESULTS OF SPIRIT BAPTISM

The Pentecostal experience has had a tremendous spiritual impact on the lives of individuals and churches. The benefits or the results of the experience speak for themselves. Yet Pentecostals and Charismatics need to take care not to overstate the value or the results of baptism in the Holy Spirit. To make claims for this experience that cannot be supported Biblically or experientially diminishes the strength of the Pentecostal position. A true Pentecostal position regarding what happens when one is filled with the Spirit should attempt to describe accurately the results and to avoid overstatement. Also, Pentecostals should endeavor to appreciate and not overlook or deny spiritual activity and ministry that have occurred in believers' lives before they have received Spirit baptism. God has saved them; they are indwelt by the Holy Spirit. A number of them are called to the ministry and among them are those who have had effective ministries, but who have not yet received the Pentecostal experience. Because of their personal devotion to Christ and their rich prayer lives, they have had fruitful ministries. Their ministries are reminders that all the power and all the spiritual gifts for ministry do not necessarily follow baptism in the Spirit. The charge that those who have not been filled with the Spirit have no power and gifts for ministry lack support in the Scriptures.

As we have noted, the Old Testament indicates that people like Samuel, Saul, David, Deborah and Gideon were given extraordinary abilities by the Spirit. Others, like Elijah and Elisha, were empowered to perform miraculous deeds (see pp. 29ff.). Before the outpouring of the Spirit on the Day of Pentecost, Jesus' disciples were empowered for their ministry and were granted gifts for the workings of miracles. On one occasion, 70 of His disciples healed the sick and cast out demons (Luke 10:17-20). The view that none of the anointing and gifts for service precedes baptism in the Spirit is indefensible.

In no way does this fact deny the importance of the Pentecostal experience. Baptism in the Spirit adds spiritual power. Never having received that experience, some have served the Lord well. Only through Spirit baptism can these greater works be done. The Pentecostal experience is something more—something is added to what God has already done. When this experience is received, there comes a profound sense of God's presence, a greater spiritual vitality in life and ministry, a deeper consecration, and a more active compassion and love. Indeed, Pentecostals have a spiritual dimension that the entire Christian world needs. The results of Spirit baptism clearly indicate that the experience is a wonderful provision of God that adds greatly to Christian life and ministry.

A Profound Sense of God's Immediate Presence

Baptism in the Spirit results in a profound awareness of God's nearness. God's revealing Himself to the believer makes the believer keenly aware that God is really present. This striking sense of God's closeness impacts our lives, particularly in terms of prayer and praise to God and ministry to others. The powerful sense of God's daily presence stimulates joy, praise and witnessing (Acts 2:11, 44; 4:31; 5:19, 20, 32; 10:44-46). Out of Spirit baptism flows life that is lived to its fullest in dynamic communion with God.

The Pentecostal experience, therefore, brings us into an intense fellowship with the triune God—Father, Son and Holy Spirit—

making us more aware that the living God has broken into this world and that He is at hand. There is a profound sense that God is present in love and power. As Paul says, "The love of God has been poured out within our hearts through the Holy Spirit" (Romans 5:5). In this verse, Paul appears to be describing Spirit baptism. God's love being poured out is what was happening when the Holy Spirit came on the Day of Pentecost (Acts 2) and when He came on the house of Cornelius (10:45, 46). One's encounter with the Spirit is an affirmation of God's being present in His love and power. The day-by-day effect of this experience is a powerful sense of God's immediate presence. As a result, there is deeper reverence for the Father, Son and Holy Spirit, and more fervent worship of the triune God.

Power for Witnessing

The primary result of Spirit baptism is power to evangelize the world. Acts 1:8 provides the Biblical basis for this emphasis: "You will receive power when the Holy Spirit comes on you; and you will be my witnesses . . . to the ends of the earth" (*NIV*). The direct result of "receiving power" is being "witnesses . . . to the ends of the earth." The best commentary on these two related themes is the Book of Acts. Jesus promised marvelous power (*dunamis*) that works miracles (Acts 3:12; 4:7; 6:8), that brings conviction through testimony and preaching the gospel (2:14ff.; 4:33), and that gives authority over Satan (10:38). Jesus' promise is tied to baptism in the Spirit: "You will receive power when the Holy Spirit comes on you" (*NIV*). Both power (*dunamis*) and witness (*martus*) point to empowerment by the Spirit to share the gospel with the lost. The focus is on being witnesses. The power that Jesus' disciples received transformed them into such witnesses.

The promise of Acts 1:8 draws our attention to "you will be." The full intent of this verse includes not only being witnesses, but also being doers, bringing into view the worldwide mission of the church. This worldwide mission involves not only going to other countries or giving money to foreign missions, but also caring for our neighbors and sharing the good news of salvation with them. The basic reason for the coming of the Spirit was to enable the church to carry out the Great Commission. Having "the ends of the earth" as its evangelistic goal protects the church from becoming introverted and turned in on its own life.

The global mission of the church was initiated on the Day of Pentecost. Sharing the love of God and explaining His love to the lost are correct responses to the additional power and ability that we receive through baptism in the Holy Spirit. Most likely, for Jesus' disciples, the phrase "to the ends of the earth" meant Rome, but it is prophetic of the growth of the church and the global spread of the gospel in the last days until Christ returns (Acts 1:8, *NIV*).

For the last hundred years, the church has experienced dramatic growth. At the heart of the worldwide growth of the church in the 20th century has been the outpouring of the Holy Spirit. All church growth in this century cannot be ascribed to Pentecostals and Charismatics, but the great contributions of the Pentecostal/ Charismatic Movements to the evangelization of the world testify to the reality of the power of Spirit baptism. On the other hand, we dare not deny the great sacrifices and contributions made by missionaries and others who were not baptized in the Spirit. God is to be praised for all churches and mission agencies that have been committed to taking the gospel to the ends of the earth. To say that these missionaries know nothing about the power of the Holy Spirit would be untrue. The difference between them and Pentecostals or Charismatics is a matter of degree. By the power of the Spirit, we have been specially equipped for the task of witnessing and mission. Yet, the power given by the Holy Spirit to the disciples at Pentecost must not be limited to just reaching the lost.

Power for Doing Mighty Works

Being filled with the Spirit not only results in bold and powerful witnessing but also in the workings of miracles. The ministry of signs and wonders pushes evangelism forward and confirms that Jesus Christ has the power of God to save individuals. Jesus promised His disciples: "You will receive power when the Holy Spirit comes on you" (Acts 1:8, *NIV*). As the Book of Acts makes clear, this power included marvelous ability to work miracles (*dunameis*). During His early ministry, Jesus gave His disciples the power to heal the sick and to cast out demons (Mark 16:17, 18; Luke 9:1, 2; 10:17). Before Jesus returned to heaven, He promised the same power to those who were baptized in the Holy Spirit. After His ascension, He began to fulfill the promise and gave His disciples power to perform great signs and wonders.

Being filled with the Spirit, the early believers performed miracles and drove out demons (Acts 2:43; 5:12). Peter's anointing was so extraordinary that the falling of his shadow on the sick brought them healing (5:15, 16). "Stephen, a man full of faith and the Holy Spirit . . . was performing great wonders and signs among the people" (6:5, 8). Handkerchiefs and aprons that had touched the body of Paul brought healing and deliverance from evil spirits (19:11, 12). Likewise, empowered by the Holy Spirit, Philip also healed many who were paralyzed and lame and cast out evil spirits (8:6, 7).

Baptism in the Spirit enabled them to give a powerful witness to Jesus Christ and to perform mighty works. The Holy Spirit confirmed their testimony through external signs and wonders. These powerful demonstrations attested to the truth of the gospel. Therefore, the early Christians' ministry following the Day of Pentecost was characterized by persuasive proclamation and mighty deeds, both the result of Spirit baptism. The ministry of these early Christians followed the pattern of Christ's own Spirit-anointed ministry, which was accompanied by "miracles and wonders and signs" (2:22).

The ministries of Jesus and the early Christians still provide the doctrinal basis for the signs and wonders in current Pentecostal and Charismatic churches, but at times practice fails to correspond with doctrine. There may be a subtle shift away from seeking God for miracles and experiencing the Holy Spirit in signs and wonders. Many are more comfortable with emphasizing Spirit baptism as power for witnessing rather than Spirit baptism as providing supernatural proof that Jesus is alive and God still works miracles. A number of those who have given miracles a prominent place in their ministry have been on the fringe of Pentecostalism. No doubt, the deliverance ministry has attracted its share of mavericks, charlatans and quacks. Generally, classical Pentecostals and many other believers have had their guards up against such men and women. Though there have been abuses, the promise of Pentecost that God gives gifts and power for the workings of miracles must not be neglected. Jesus said, "These signs will accompany those who have believed" (Mark 16:17). He promised those baptized in the Spirit that they would receive supernatural ability to show that Jesus is still living. This fulfillment of Jesus' promise is our inheritance as Spirit-baptized believers.

Speaking in Other Tongues

Classical Pentecostals believe that speaking in tongues is the immediate physical result of Spirit baptism. The Spirit is the source of this observable, audible manifestation that is a form of inspired speech. This manifestation is only a part of the Pentecostal experience. The initial sign points to the much larger fullness of the Spirit. Thus, speaking in tongues is not the sum total of the experience. In addition to the initial sign, Scripture indicates that there are continuing and internal evidences of being filled with the Spirit (Acts 2:44-47; Ephesians 5:15-21). These ongoing internal spiritual changes, or evidences, are as significant as the initial outward sign of speaking in tongues. But at this point we will concentrate on the implications of *glossolalia* when a believer is filled with the Spirit.

The gift of the Spirit in the Book of Acts fulfilled the promise of the Father (Luke 24:49; Acts 1–2). Christ's coming into the world, His death, His resurrection and His sending the Holy Spirit all must be understood in the context of God's redemptive work in history. The Day of Pentecost was the final event in God's implementation of the new covenant, which included both the experience of salvation and the outpouring of the Spirit (Ezekiel 36:25-27; Joel 2:28, 29). The coming of the Spirit at Pentecost was not a matter of conversion or salvation but of empowerment. The death and the resurrection of Christ—First Advent—were unrepeatable events. However, the outpouring of the Spirit occurred on the Day of Pentecost and was repeated on later occasions in Samaria (Acts 8:14ff.), Caesarea (10:44-46) and Ephesus (19:1-7). Some 25 years separate the outpouring of the Spirit in Jerusalem and the Spirit's coming in Ephesus. Therefore, the outpouring of the Spirit on believers is not limited to a particular occasion. Since the Pentecostal experience, or Spirit baptism, is not limited to any particular time or period, it is fitting to say that believers may experience "a personal Pentecost."

When Jesus' disciples received the gift of Spirit baptism on the Day of Pentecost, they "were all filled with the Spirit and began to speak with other tongues as the Spirit was giving them utterance" (Acts 2:4). According to the Book of Acts, speaking in tongues became the immediate result (sign) of being filled with the Spirit. Why did God choose *glossolalia* to accompany the experience of Spirit baptism? The answer to this question may be fourfold:

1. *Speaking in tongues revealed the supernatural presence of God.* This manifestation first occurred on the Day of Pentecost. The same kind of inspired speech resulted from later encounters with the Spirit as well (Acts 10:44-46; 19:1-7). Therefore, tongues serve as the sign from God that the Holy Spirit is "coming upon" the

believer. The content of the inspired utterance is completely determined by the Holy Spirit (2:4). A person's speaking in a language that he or she knows does not immediately offer clear evidence of a supernatural presence. However, if that person speaks in a language he or she does not know, this miraculous ability signals the presence and moving of the Holy Spirit. The utterances given by the Holy Spirit reveal the reality of the inner work of God in empowering and directing the believer. As the initial sign of Spirit baptism, tongues transform the profound encounter with God into a knowable, audible and visible event.

2. *The manifestation of tongues emphasized the mission that Christ had given to the church.* On the Day of Pentecost, the disciples spoke in foreign languages that they had never learned. Apparently their speaking in various languages served to indicate that the groups that were present needed to hear the gospel. The Holy Spirit did not equip the disciples with foreign languages to be used in preaching. Rather than preaching the gospel, they praised God for His "mighty deeds" (Acts 2:11). From the hearts of the disciples sprang praise and adoration, apparently for God's miraculous works recorded in the Old Testament and for the life and ministry of Christ. The content here was worship, just like it would be later in the household of Cornelius who was speaking in tongues and "exalting God" (10:46). The disciples' speech so caught the attention of the unbelievers at Pentecost that it created amazement. *Glossolalia* spoken in the diverse languages of the multitudes had strong implications for the proclamation of the gospel to the ends of the earth.

3. *Speaking in tongues may serve as a sign to unbelievers* (1 Corinthians 14:22). For example, tongues on the Day of Pentecost served as a sign of divine judgment to unbelievers. As Peter reminded them, Jesus had "poured forth this which you both see and hear" (Acts 2:33). On the basis of the miraculous manifestation of tongues, Peter declared, "Let all the house of Israel know for certain that God has made Him both Lord and Christ—this Jesus

whom you crucified" (v. 36). God used speaking in tongues as a means of condemning the people for the terrible crime of putting Jesus to death and for their unbelief. As a sign of God's displeasure, *glossolalia* has been instrumentally used by the Holy Spirit to bring people to repentance and to their finding salvation.

4. *In addition to being a sign, speaking in tongues may be devotional, providing a means by which believers may praise and worship God.* Paul makes reference to this personal, devotional aspect when he says that the "one who speaks in a tongue edifies himself" (1 Corinthians 14:4). This is one reason he desires that all believers speak in tongues (v. 5). The Greek tense of the verb *speak* (*lalein*) is present, suggesting the translation "to continue to speak in tongues." The practice of speaking in tongues in our devotions is understood to be a positive factor for our life in Christ. Believers, therefore, may be strengthened by this means.

The Christian community may also be spiritually built up by tongues, provided that they are accompanied by the gift of interpretation of tongues. In private, speaking in tongues edifies the one praying in tongues; but in public worship, interpreted tongues edifies the congregation. Tongues in private worship are available to all of God's people for prayer and spiritual development. Some describe *glossolalia* as a "prayer language," which calls attention to its devotional and personal nature. No doubt, Paul's admonition to "pray at all times in the Spirit" included prayer in tongues (Ephesians 6:18; cf. 1 Corinthians 14:15). Jude echoes Paul's teaching with his admonition about "building yourselves up on your most holy faith, praying in the Holy Spirit" (v. 20).

Romans 8:26, 27 likely includes what is known as "praying in the Spirit" or "praying in tongues." Paul's statement that "the Spirit Himself intercedes for us with groanings too deep for words" (v. 26) strongly suggests that the groanings are not understandable to the human mind, suggesting *glossolalia*. This interpretation is embraced by some distinguished scholars[9] who affirm the Pentecostal understanding of the passage. These verses depict the Holy Spirit's praying through believers on their behalf as they pray in tongues. The words or groanings that flow from the Spirit through the soul of the believer touch the heart of God. As God's children, we are aided by the Spirit in our weakness, that is, we are edified as the Holy Spirit prays through us in a language we do not know. At times we may not know how to pray and to praise God, but the Holy Spirit can give us the words to say. Through speaking in other tongues, we may express prayer and praise beyond the limits of our native language, interceding on behalf of circumstances that God knows, but we do not. Such an experience is a profound dimension of Pentecostal spirituality, a profound charismatic encounter with the Spirit that builds believers up in their faith and life and points them toward the return of Christ and the life of resurrection.

Holy, Christlike Living

Baptism in the Spirit has strong implications for living the Christian life and the practice of holiness. The very character of the Spirit in whom we are immersed leaves no doubt about that. The Spirit is "the Holy Spirit," and He is identified with the spiritual graces that we call "the fruit of the Spirit" (Galatians 5:22, 23). One purpose of being filled with the Spirit is to enhance the spiritual

---

[9]This interpretation of Romans 8:26, 27 is not new. The church father Origen advocated it (*De oratione* 2). Contemporary scholars such as C.K. Barrett and F.F. Bruce, in their commentaries on the Book of Romans, allow for the possibility of the phrase "groanings too deep for words" to refer to *glossolalia*. In his commentary on Romans, Ernst Käsemann argues that the phrase definitely has reference to speaking in tongues. As far as I know, none of these scholars would support the Pentecostal interpretation of Acts and have no exegetical bias in favor of Pentecostal theology.

graces in our lives, thus bringing into fuller reality a Christlike lifestyle. Spirit-filled believers should be careful not to limit Spirit baptism to speaking in tongues and evangelizing the world. Baptism in the Spirit should intensify our sensitivity to the Spirit's guidance and our dedication to the Lord—the marks of the sanctified, compassionate life.

In the Book of Acts, Luke focuses on the preaching of the gospel to the world through the power of the Holy Spirit. Consequently, his main emphasis is not the personal life of the believer. On the other hand, he does not eliminate it from the experience of being filled with the Spirit. In Acts 2, the life of the Spirit-filled community is described. There emerges what may be called "a Pentecostal lifestyle." One should not divorce individuals' encounter with the Holy Spirit from the spiritual graces manifested in their lives and community. The Christians who were present on the Day of Pentecost later devoted themselves to what the apostles had taught and to spiritual fellowship. Their harmony and love for one another were determined by their fellowship with Christ and their Pentecostal experience. They also continued "the breaking of bread," that is, the celebration of the Lord's Supper. The daily devotions of these early believers included prayer. All the individuals who had been filled with the Spirit engaged in these spiritual activities. Their experience of Pentecostal power intensified their dedication to holy living and confirmed the power and presence of the Holy Spirit (vv. 41-47).

Spirit baptism, therefore, is more than vocational in purpose and result. It is tied to righteous living as well. Believers may profess to be baptized in the Spirit, but fail to please God. It is because they do not allow their experience to bear fruit in their lives. Baptism in the Spirit should bring the spiritual graces to full fruition so that Christ may be in us "the hope of glory" (Colossians 1:27).

Sensitivity and Openness to Spiritual Manifestations

Over the years Pentecostals have seen baptism in the Spirit as "the gateway" to the flourishing of spiritual gifts.[10] The initial speaking in tongues shows that recipients have experienced something beyond the understanding of the human mind. They have obeyed God and "let go" of themselves, so as to be overwhelmingly immersed in the Spirit to the extent that their minds contribute nothing to what they say (1 Corinthians 14:14). As a result, tongues are seen as the beginning, or the gateway, to the flourishing of spiritual gifts. From that point on, the ideal is for each believer to develop a spiritual openness to all of the gifts (1 Corinthians 12:8-10, 28; Romans 12:6-8; Ephesians 4:11; 1 Peter 4:11).

Instances can be cited from Scripture where many if not all of the spiritual gifts operated in one form or another before the out-pouring of the Spirit at Pentecost. Both the Old Testament and the Gospels speak about such spiritual manifestations occurring prior to Pentecost. The disciples themselves experienced the gifts of healing the sick and casting out demons (Luke 10:9, 17; cf. Matthew 10:8; Mark 16:17). Moreover, a review of church history discloses that spiritual gifts have been manifested through Christians in all ages.[11] But the New Testament reveals that the frequency of such spiritual manifestations increased dramatically after Pentecost. Numerous examples from the Book of Acts of Spirit-filled believers' exercising spiritual gifts can be cited.

---

[10]The gateway view should not be taken to mean that those who have not experienced Spirit baptism cannot have a spiritual gift and exercise it. I do not think anyone could deny that many great non-Pentecostal evangelists have the gift of evangelism. Though believers who have not spoken in tongues may have gifts of the Spirit, it remains a fact that among Pentecostals is where gifts of the Spirit really flourish, when allowed to do so.

[11]See S.M. Burgess, "The Doctrine of the Holy Spirit: the Ancient Fathers" and "The Doctrine of the Holy Spirit: The Medieval Church," *Dictionary of Pentecostal and Charismatic Movements* (Grand Rapids: Zondervan, 1988) 417-444.

Miracles were performed by men such as Stephen (6:8) and Philip (8:7). Also, many signs and wonders took place through the apostles (2:43; 5:12). For example, the falling of Peter's shadow on the sick brought them deliverance (5:15, 16). God also performed signs and wonders through the ministry of Paul. Handkerchiefs and aprons that touched his body were used in healings and the casting out of demons (19:11, 12). Without doubt, Peter exercised the gift of faith in commanding the lame man to walk (3:1-10) as well as the gift of knowledge in exposing the sin of Ananias and Sapphira (5:1-10).

The experience of baptism in the Spirit opens up to the believer the full range of spiritual gifts. Without denying the sovereignty of the Holy Spirit, the record of history shows that it was the Pentecostal/Charismatic Movements that ushered in the revival of spiritual gifts in the 20th century. It becomes clear from observation that whenever baptism in the Spirit is confidently preached and believers are encouraged to be filled with the Spirit, spiritual gifts tend to abound and flourish. Nothing more is required than a genuine openness to the Holy Spirit. Spirit baptism, with the accompanying sign of tongues, therefore, serves as a gateway experience to the flourishing of spiritual gifts.

The Bible makes it clear that Christians who have experienced and taught Spirit baptism are open to the whole range of spiritual gifts, including those that are extraordinary in their manifestations. This is due, largely, to their belief and experience of the Spirit's fullness.[12] They have opened themselves up through that experience to the working of the Spirit; and as a result, they have an increased sensitivity and openness to His many gifts and Pentecostal-type

---

[12]Some of the opposition to Pentecostalism may be explained by the fact that secular society values public dignity and reservation, and does not give permission for public display of enthusiasm except at certain events, such as ball games and concerts.

manifestations. To them, spiritual gifts are far more than a fascination. They believe that such manifestations are the moving of the
Holy Spirit and are clear evidence of the continuation of the full
range of spiritual gifts.

At this point a word of warning against spiritual elitism in the
above matters may be in order. Pentecostals must resist the temptation of spiritual pride and feelings of superiority. The use of spiritual gifts should not be a matter of playing the "haves" against the
"have-nots." This practice creates ill will and divisiveness. It is well
to remember that an encounter with the Holy Spirit is a work of
grace—a gift God has given. God chooses when it is appropriate to
bestow the gift. We cannot know and understand completely God's
plans or His timing. To see the Pentecostal experience in the light of
a work of grace will bring about greater humility and protect us
against pride. Consequently, any experience from the gracious hand
of the Lord should enhance the quality of Christian living, resulting
in humility before the Lord and others.

CONCLUSION

Baptism in the Spirit is a profound personal experience. Through
this encounter, the Holy Spirit, who indwells all believers from the
moment of conversion, fills and empowers them for service and living. Believers are inspired by the reality of God's love and become
aware of God's power in their lives. As a result, they become bold-
er and more effective in communicating the good news of Jesus
Christ and more fervent in worship and serving the living God. This
powerful experience takes believers deeper in God and enables
them to give a bold witness for Christ and to withstand evil forces
in the world. In concluding this chapter, a few specific observations
are in order.

The condition for receiving Spirit baptism is faith. True faith
involves abiding in Christ, walking in obedience to Him and having

an ongoing trust and openness to all that God wants to do for us. Faith in Christ calls for believers to allow God to remove their doubts about the power of the Holy Spirit and to adopt a stance of openness and expectancy in regard to a second encounter with the Spirit. This is the stance of faith, or what may be described as the obedience of faith (Acts 5:32). Without this kind of response, the Holy Spirit is not free to move. In short, believers are not passive instruments of the Spirit; they can go against His will and refuse to give up their unbelief about the Pentecostal experience. Prayer is a vital element of faith in Jesus Christ, and believing and expecting prayer for the fullness of the Spirit provides the atmosphere for receiving this blessing from God.

Baptism in the Spirit is received as a conscious spiritual experience. The accompanying sign, speaking in tongues, provides evidence of the supernatural visitation of the Spirit of God. There is a greater devotion to Jesus Christ, a stronger determination to stand steadfast in the faith, a new authority in witnessing, an enlarged prayer life, and a fresh joy in walking daily with the Lord. At Pentecost, the disciples experienced a decisive encounter with the Holy Spirit and were conscious of being empowered by the presence of God. Since that time, many who have had such an encounter have testified that they knew the Holy Spirit touched all facets of their lives. Such an encounter with the Holy Spirit gives us a profound awareness of the living God and His blessings. All God's people need to seek Him for this experience, which involves a conscious awareness of the abundant life in the Spirit and power for service.

Being filled with the Spirit may occur again and again. According to Acts 2:4, all of God's children need to be baptized in the Spirit. This experience of blessing and spiritual empowerment should not be the final time that individuals have an encounter with the Spirit. Following their first empowering encounter, they will need to be renewed in the spirit continually. The experience of being refilled with the Spirit needs to occur, especially because of new opportunities for witness and service, the pressures of daily life, new challenges from Satan and the forces of evil that believers and churches face. This need for renewal calls for openness to the Spirit's moving again and again, and for new breakthroughs of the Spirit's power. The church lives from the power of the Spirit. We can never claim to possess the fullness of such power once and for all.

God encounters each believer as an individual. The situations in which baptism in the Spirit and refillings with the Spirit are experienced will vary. These encounters may occur during public or private worship. They may occur in personal prayer or during the ministry of prayer in community, such as the laying on of hands. They may occur.in large animated and emotional meetings or in small meetings among a group of friends where the atmosphere is quieter and more reserved. Emotions are involved. Some believers express their emotions more than others. Some have questioned the reality of the experience because of their observation of the expression of strong emotions. These individuals often indicate their concern that the experience is simply an emotional response rather than a spiritual one. Yet, when a person encounters God, one would expect that person to feel emotion—whether that emotion is fear, repentance, love, joy or whatever. If a person does not have an internal emotional response to God, indeed that person needs the Spirit's blessing of renewal.

To dismiss the Pentecostal experience as only emotional is a misrepresentation. There are very emotional people who are not attracted to the experience at all. In contrast, there are reserved and sedate people who actively pray for and receive this spiritual blessing. Many have been surprised because they feel as they do upon being filled with the Spirit. Regardless of the emotions involved, God works in different ways, and the outward emotional expression of an encounter with the Spirit will be unique in each person. Members of the body of Christ should not be guilty of judging an individual's encounter based on their own interpretation of an outward emotional response. Whatever the response of the individual, the heart is strangely warmed by Spirit baptism and is filled with the love of Christ. When the presence and power of the Holy Spirit are experienced, the Spirit-baptized may feel like they have been immersed into a stream of divine love and joy.

As at Pentecost, the experience of the Spirit is primarily for equipping the body of Christ, the church, for its mission in the world. In the Book of Acts, the early believers moved in the power of the Spirit to conquer cities for Christ and to plant churches across the then-known world. An evangelistic thrust of the church began on the Day of Pentecost. Before that day ended, the original 120 Spirit-anointed believers grew to about 3,000 (Acts 2:41). As these believers continued to preach the gospel, their number increased to about 5,000 (4:4). After such growth, their number swelled so much that Luke speaks of the believers simply as "the multitude [*to plethos*]" (Acts 4:32, *KJV*). This extraordinary growth was the result of their reception of the "Spirit of witness." From the Day of Pentecost to the present, part of the great work of the Holy Spirit has been to empower the church for sharing their faith and the love of Christ with others. The emphasis on power for witnessing lines up with the Great Commission (Matthew 28:18-20).

The Holy Spirit is the Spirit of witness. Believers may desire spiritual experiences for personal fulfillment. No doubt the experience of the Spirit ministers to the deep needs of the heart, but He does not come merely to fill the emotional and spiritual needs of people. He also comes to transform their lives and to equip them for effective witnessing. The primary focus of our encounter with the Holy Spirit after we become a Christian is the receiving of power to reach the lost. So what about being equipped for sacrificial service? What about the unsaved and the harvest that is ripe? The answers are found through receiving with confidence the Biblical experience of Spirit baptism, committing to similar values as our Pentecostal pioneers, being enthusiastic about serving, and exercising the gifts of the Spirit in our churches, homes and marketplace.

Pentecostal evangelism is characterized by both bold witnessing and tremendous works through signs and miracles. In the Bible, witnessing involved not only a loving, persuasive sharing of the gospel of Christ, but also supernatural demonstrations that confirmed the gospel by healings and miracles (cf. John 5:36). In the Book of Acts, again and again Pentecostal signs and wonders pushed the spread of the gospel forward. Jesus performed great miracles before He departed from the earth. He promised His disciples that He would give them power from the Holy Spirit to continue His ministry: "You will be my witnesses" (Acts 1:8, *NIV*). The signs and wonders that accompanied their ministries, as well as their anointed witnessing, fulfilled the promise.

True Pentecostal evangelism cannot exist apart from miracles within the Christian community. The occurrence of miracles should be a part of effective and diverse exercise of spiritual gifts in the local church. Where there is the powerful proclamation of the gospel with unusual manifestations of the Spirit, people will submit to Christ and their lives will be totally transformed. Miraculous healings will occur and also deliverance from afflictions, including freedom from depression and freedom from various addictions, such as drugs and alcohol.[13] Fractured marriages

---

[13]Some people are instantly freed from these problems, while others experience gradual healing. A gradual healing process, facilitated by the love and support of the Christian community, becomes a spiritual growth process for each individual, family and community involved. The fact that God chooses to heal a person through a longer process does not mean that the person lacks faith. In fact, when an individual goes through a progressive healing process, that person may experience several healings and miracles in various facets of his or her life. Many times these miracles are pleasant surprises because they are not the miracles for which the person initially prayed.

will be put back together. Whatever form signs and wonders may take, they confirm the power of the gospel.

Summary

- Spirit baptism is a spiritual blessing—a gift from God—for all Christians.

- Believers may receive on multiple occasions a spiritual blessing of empowerment for living.

- Believers who are continually empowered have a profound sense of God's presence and endeavor to love each other and others in the world without manipulation, control or pride.

- The results of Spirit baptism indicate that this blessing from God greatly enhances the Christian life and Christian service.

TABLE 6-A Reception of Spirit Baptism	
ACTS 2:39	Baptism in the Spirit is for all believers.
ACTS 2:38; 8:20; 10:45	Baptism in the Spirit is a gift of God.
LUKE 3:21, 22; 24:49-53; ACTS 1:14; 4:29, 30; 8:14-17; 9:9-11,17, 18; 10:4, 44	Prayer and praise lead to Spirit baptism.
LUKE 24:49; ACTS 2:1; 10:1ff.	God gives Spirit baptism according to His sovereign purpose.
ACTS 4:8, 29-31; 13:4-12, 52; EPHESIANS 5:18-21	One may be filled with the Spirit many times, being continually renewed and empowered for witness and service.
Notes	

TABLE 6-B

Characteristics of Being
"Full of the Spirit" or "Filled With the Spirit"

The phrases *full of the Spirit* and *filled with the Spirit* both indicate a state being in which the believer is inspired and empowered by the Holy Spirit.

LUKE 4:1; ACTS 6:3-5; 7:55; 11:24; 13:52; EPHESIANS 5:18

Filled (*pimplēmi*) With the Spirit

The phrase to be *filled with the Spirit* can mean:

- To receive the blessing of Spirit baptism.
- To receive a fresh empowerment of the Spirit to meet a specific need.
- To enjoy a continuing, ongoing, charismatic empowerment and inspiration of the Holy Spirit, the results of which are speaking to others in love and compassion and being joyful and thankful.

Full (*plērēs*) of the Spirit

The phrase to be *full of the Spirit* refers to the state of having been baptized in the Spirit and enjoying God's special blessing of empowerment for living. The word *full* suggests that the Holy Spirit is in full control of our lives, helping us develop a deeper relationship with God.

- The inner control of the Holy Spirit is demonstrated by confident witnessing.
- The inner control of the Holy Spirit is demonstrated by love for and service to others.
- The inner control of the Holy Spirit is demonstrated by a manifestation of Christian graces and virtues, such as wisdom, faith, grace, wonder and amazement.

Table 6-C
Results of Spirit Baptism

Spirit baptism empowers Christians in their use of fruit and gifts of the Spirit.

When Christians receive the blessing of Spirit baptism, the resulting spiritual empowerment has a tremendous spiritual impact on the lives of the individuals and their churches. This blessing from God helps them increase their effectiveness as they express the love of Christ through spiritual fruit and gifts.

The Spirit-filled life results in increasing humility, love and compassion for others, not a life of pride or a sense of superiority.

God bestows spiritual blessings and gifts in His timing and for His purposes. We are to receive them graciously and use them as the Holy Spirit leads—not for selfish benefit, but to express God's love in the world around us.

Profound Sense of God's Immediate Presence

Acts 2:11, 44; 4:31; 5:32; 10:44-46; Romans 5:5	Spirit baptism results in a profound awareness of God's nearness. This sense of God's daily presence gives us joy and impacts our service to others.

Power for Witnessing

Acts 1:8; 3:12; 4:7, 33; 5:19, 20; 6:8; 10:38	Spirit baptism results in receiving guidance, power and confidence to share God's saving love and grace with our families, friends, neighbors, coworkers, those in poverty, those who are afflicted, and others to whom God may lead us.

continued

TABLE 6-C (CONTINUED) **Results of Spirit Baptism**	
Power for Doing Mighty Works	
MARK 16:17, 18; LUKE 9:1, 2; 10:17; ACTS 1:8; 2:22, 43; 5:12-16; 6:5-8; 8:6, 7; 19:11, 12	The ministry of miracles and "signs and wonders" helps communicate in a physical sense the power and presence of God. Such miracles can open hearts to receiving Christ's changing love.
Speaking in Other Tongues	
LUKE 24:49; ACTS 2:4; 10:44-46; ROMANS 8:26, 27; EPHESIANS 5:15-21; cf. 1 CORINTHIANS 14:15	Speaking in a language unknown to the one speaking is an observable sign that the Holy Spirit is present and doing a work in an individual's life. The action of speaking in tongues may be an indication of one's initial baptism in the Spirit, an exercise in personal prayer and praise, a sign to unbelievers (when the tongues are spoken in an earthly language or are interpreted), or a message meant for interpretation to the Christian community.
Holy, Christlike Living	
ACTS 2:41-47; GALATIANS 5:22, 23	Spirit baptism helps one to live a more holy, Christlike life. With the help of the Holy Spirit, individuals grow spiritually, becoming more like Jesus Christ as they mature. They become more sensitive to the leading of the Holy Spirit, exhibiting spiritual graces in their lives and making changes necessary for spiritual growth and ministry in this world.

continued

Table 6-C (continued)
Results of Spirit Baptism

Sensitivity and Openness to Spiritual Manifestations	
Matthew 10:8; Mark 16:17; Luke 10:9, 17; Acts 2:43; 5:12-16; 6:8; 8:7; 19:11; 5:1-10; Romans 12:6-8; 1 Corinthians 12:8-10, 28; Ephesians 4:11; 1 Peter 4:11	The experience of Spirit baptism opens up to the believer the full range of spiritual gifts. When the Holy Spirit is invited to work freely, spiritual gifts flourish.
Notes	

CHAPTER 6—STUDY AND DISCUSSION

RECEPTION OF SPIRIT BAPTISM

Being Filled With the Spirit

1. What are some characteristics of the reception of, or the receiving of Spirit baptism? Give some examples from the Bible. (See Table 6-A.)

Definition of "Filled [*pimplēmi*] With the Holy Spirit"

2. What are three ways one might use the phrase "filled with the Spirit"? Give examples from the Bible. (See Table 6-B.)

Definition of "Full [*plērēs*] of the Holy Spirit"

3. List some characteristics of a person's life that is "full of the Spirit." Give some examples from the Bible. (See Table 6-B.)

RESULTS OF SPIRIT BAPTISM

4. When we receive the gift of Spirit baptism, what blessings and changes can we expect in our lives? Give some examples from the Bible of these spiritual blessings. (See Table 6-C.)

CONCLUSION

5. What is the condition for receiving Spirit baptism? (See Luke 11:5-13; 24:52, 53; Acts 1:14.)

6. Is Spirit baptism a conscious experience? (See Acts 2:1-4; 10:44-48.)

7. Why would a person need to be filled with the Spirit more than once? (See Acts 4:5-11, 23-31.)

8. God encounters each believer as an individual. The situations in which Spirit baptism and refillings occur vary. What

are some of the various situations in which one might encounter the Spirit?

9. When we encounter God, our emotions are affected. What are some ways you can think of that a person might express these emotions?

10. Think of a time when you really felt the presence of God. Describe your feelings.

    On this occasion, how did you express your emotions? Did you express your emotions outwardly, or did you quietly meditate on what was happening?

    At other times when you have felt God's presence, have you expressed your emotions differently? If so, how?

11. What was the primary purpose for the disciples' encounter with the Spirit on the Day of Pentecost? (See Luke 24:49; Acts 1:8.)

12. What are some simple ways that you might demonstrate and tell others about God's saving love on a daily basis? Consider the following with whom you might have direct or indirect contact:

    • family, friends, neighbors, coworkers, acquaintances, individuals you meet running your errands

    • children, teens, young adults, middle-aged adults, elderly adults

    • people in poverty, people who are ill, people who are sad or angry, people who have been traumatized

    • people who are in prison

    • people who live in other countries, foreigners who are staying in this country

    Please note: In group discussions, individuals may have

different responses, many in keeping with their own spiritual gifts. This is a wonderful opportunity to learn and grow from the expression of each person's gifts.

Part Four

Spiritual Gifts

Now there are varieties of gifts, but the same Spirit; and there are varieties of service, but the same Lord; and there are varieties of working, but it is the same God who inspires them all in every one. To each is given the manifestation of the Spirit for the common good (1 Corinthians 12:4-7, *RSV*).

7

Introduction to
Gifts of the Spirit

Spiritual gifts remind us of the diversity of the Spirit's works and power. Paul concludes a list of them with the words, "But one and the same Spirit works all these things, distributing to each one individually just as He wills" (1 Corinthians 12:11). The works of the Spirit include not only conversion and Spirit baptism, but also varied powers and activities known as "gifts of the Spirit."

Gifts of the Spirit were manifested among God's people in Old Testament times and during Jesus' life on earth as recorded in the Gospels. Following the outpouring of the Spirit at Pentecost, they began to flourish. Spiritual gifts arise more "naturally" among believers who have experienced the fullness of the Spirit. Spirit-filled believers know God as One who is ready to break into a situation, revealing gifts of healings and miracles, giving words of wisdom or prophecy, and speaking through tongues and their interpretation. The gifts of the Spirit, therefore, are concrete, intense manifestations, or public demonstrations, of God's presence and His remarkable love.

Spiritual gifts belong in the church, home and marketplace. The full range of the gifts is essential to the life and growth of the church. According to Paul, the gifts of the Spirit are marks of the church, the body of Christ (1 Corinthians 12). Such spiritual manifestations occurred in churches in Corinth, Thessalonica (1 Thessalonians 5:19-21) and Galatia (Galatians

3:5). Paul established these congregations. Although he did not establish the church in Rome, he discussed spiritual gifts in his correspondence to them (Romans 12:6-8). His comments about gifts of the Spirit to that church strongly suggested that the subject was prominent in his teaching and that of other early Christian missionaries. Charismatic manifestations were "normal" experiences for the Christians who wrote and first read the New Testament.[1] They regularly encountered the Holy Spirit through the exercise of spiritual gifts. A central feature of their experience and worship was such demonstrations.

The most extensive treatment of this subject is 1 Corinthians 12–14, where Paul observes that the Corinthians had emphasized spiritual gifts and ignored spiritual virtues. He urged the Corinthian church to concentrate on exercising a variety of gifts through love, so that they might edify the church rather than promote sensationalism and divisions among the believers. At the beginning of his extensive discussions, he told the Corinthians, "Now concerning spiritual gifts, brethren, I would not have you ignorant" (12:1, KJV). Because of their overemphasis on certain gifts and their neglect or ignorance of others, Paul wanted them to be fully informed about the nature and proper function of spiritual gifts in worship.

Spiritual gifts, however, have a broader significance for the church than merely their function in worship. The New Testament, especially the Book of Acts, teaches that in addition to providing spiritual enlightenment in the church's worship services, the *charismata* empower the church for witness and service. Through the manifestation of gifts, the body of Christ is strengthened and better equipped to fulfill its mission in the world. The church's use of spiritual gifts in sharing God's saving love is a major factor in individuals' seeking a relationship with Christ. Therefore, it

---

[1]Anthony D. Palma, *The Holy Spirit* (Springfield, MO: Gospel Publishing House, 2001) 181.

can be said that spiritual gifts are central to much of the growth that is occurring in the Pentecostal/Charismatic Movements today. Because of this, Paul's desire for the Corinthians to not be ignorant about spiritual gifts make the study of this topic desirable and profitable for God's people.

In order to achieve a more accurate understanding of spiritual gifts and a greater appreciation of them, it is necessary to examine general matters that pertain to gifts of the Spirit. The rest of this chapter will consider basic terms for the gifts, the number of gifts, the possession of gifts, the gifts and the church community, the relation between gifts and fruit of the Spirit, and the claim that the "extraordinary gifts" or "sign gifts" have ceased, known as *cessationism.*

BASIC BIBLICAL TERMS FOR SPIRITUAL GIFTS

The New Testament uses a variety of terms for the Charismatic gifts. A discussion of the more common terms should aid us in understanding the fundamental nature of spiritual gifts.

Gifts of Grace
(charismata)

The Greek word *charisma* (the singular of *charismata*) is used in the New Testament almost exclusively by Paul. It appears 17 times, and all are in Paul's letters with one exception, which is in Peter's first letter (1 Peter 4:10). The word *charismata* is intimately connected to divine grace (*charis*) and can appropriately be translated "grace-gifts." In Paul's letters, *charisma* has a variety of meanings. It can be used in both a broad and restricted sense. A number of passages illustrates the broad use. Referring to the gift of salvation, Paul says, "For the wages of sin is death, but the free gift [*charisma*] of God is eternal life in Christ Jesus our Lord" (Romans 6:23; cf. 5:15ff.). The term is used for the blessings bestowed on Israel as

God's chosen people: "For the gifts [*charismata*] and the calling of God are irrevocable" (Romans 11:29). Paul uses the same term to speak of his deliverance from mortal danger in 2 Corinthians 1:11: "The favor [*charisma*] [was] bestowed upon us through the prayers of many." We may conclude, therefore, that the word *charisma*, in a general sense, refers broadly to God's gracious forgiveness, deliverance or favor.

Charisma appears in the broad sense of God's gift of salvation in Christ or other blessings; but when it is used with restricted meaning, it refers to special spiritual gifts or endowments bestowed on believers by the Holy Spirit for Christian service. It is said that the *charismata* are the endowments of the Holy Spirit (1 Corinthians 12:11). Such endowments distinguish believers from one another and enable them to give loving service to one another and to others. Paul gave a list of nine gifts in 1 Corinthians 12:8-10, but he broadened the list of gifts in 12:28-31; Romans 12:6-8; and Ephesians 4:11. The Holy Spirit bestows a variety of gifts, and they may be as diverse as the human personality. Paul reminded the Corinthians that they did not lack any of the spiritual gifts (1 Corinthians 1:7). A little later he gave them advice on marriage and said, "Each man has his own gift from God, one in this manner, and another in that" (7:7).

In Romans 1:11 Paul wrote, "For I long to see you so that I may impart some spiritual gift to you." What exactly is meant by "some spiritual gift" he does not tell us, but we get a good idea from the lists of gifts in Romans 12:6-8 and 1 Corinthians 12:28-31. Only in Romans 1:11 does Paul place *spiritual* (*pneumatikōn*) and *gift* (*charisma*) side by side. The term *charisma* does not mean, in itself, "spiritual gift"; but through common usage it has come to mean that today. It is more accurately rendered "grace-gift." Therefore, spiritual gifts can be described as "gifts of grace." They are manifestations of God's grace in the lives of His people. As a result, they are spoken of as "gifts that differ according to the grace given to us" (Romans 12:6; cf. 1 Corinthians 1:4, 7). According to Paul, only believers receive the Spirit and can exercise spiritual gifts. Salvation is the supreme gift, and God makes available spiritual gifts to those who have received this gift. Every spiritual gift is a concrete expression of divine grace. Like the gift of eternal life, a spiritual gift has its source in God's grace (*charis*) and is a particular outworking of that grace.

A look at two related passages in Paul's letters to Timothy reveals the same emphasis. Timothy was urged, "Do not neglect the spiritual gift [*charisma*] within you, which was bestowed on you through prophetic utterance with the laying on of hands by the presbytery" (1 Timothy 4:14). Later, Paul again admonished him, "Kindle afresh the gift of God which is in you through the laying on of my hands" (2 Timothy 1:6). Like any spiritual gift, Timothy's endowment for ministry was a gift of grace (*charisma*), a gift that had its origin in God's grace. Peter affirmed the same truths when he exhorted the believers to use their gifts to serve one another "as good stewards of the manifold grace [*charis*] of God" (1 Peter 4:10). Those who follow Peter's teachings will administer divine grace in its many forms, as they exercise their various gifts.

To conclude, spiritual gifts are received as the result of God's grace and the work of the Holy Spirit in the believer. The word *gift* (*charisma*) reminds us that our spiritual gifts for ministry and service are apart from human merit. They are gifts, not rewards based on merit as though we had earned them. Flowing from God's grace, His gifts are always gracious and free. It is inappropriate, therefore, to exalt the recipients as though the gifts have been bestowed meritoriously. Nor is there any room for believers to have feelings of superiority or to be dissatisfied with their spiritual endowments. Although some gifts are less visible than others, all are vital to God's work in the church and in the world. After all, every spiritual gift is an expression of grace and comes from the Holy Spirit.

Spiritual Gifts
(*pneumatika*)

Literally, the Greek *pneumatika* means "spiritual things." At the beginning of 1 Corinthians 12, Paul uses a form of the term (*pneumatikōn*, plural genitive) that can refer to either people or to gifts. The term can be either masculine, referring to "spiritual persons," or neuter, signifying "spiritual gifts." The difference is not very significant since spiritual people normally have spiritual gifts. It seems better to understand the term *pneumatika* as a reference to spiritual gifts, especially in light of the lengthy discussion that follows in chapters 12–14.

The basic meaning of the word *pneumatikōn* is "spiritual." It appears frequently with this general meaning (1 Corinthians 2:13, 14; 3:1; Galatians 6:1), but it is linked to gift (*charisma*) only once in the New Testament (Romans 1:11). This obviously refers to spiritual gifts (*charismata*). The term stands by itself in 1 Corinthians 12–14 as a designation for the manifestations of the Spirit.

The question arises: How is the term "spiritual gifts" (*pneumatika*) related to the "gifts of grace" (*charismata*)? A look at 1 Corinthians 12 reveals that Paul uses them interchangeably. Two parallel statements indicate that they are synonyms: "Now concerning spiritual gifts [*pneumatikōn*] . . . I do not want you to be unaware" (v. 1); and "earnestly desire the greater gifts [*charismata*]" (v. 31). In each instance he refers to gifts of the Spirit, but the emphasis is different. The rendering "spiritual gifts" (*pneumatika*) shows the close connection between the gifts and the Spirit (*pneuma*). But the phrase "gifts of grace" (*charismata*) calls attention to the gracious character of the gifts. They flow from divine grace. The term "spiritual gifts" (*pneumatika*), however, emphasizes the Holy Spirit as the giver of the gifts. In His sovereign action, the Spirit breaks through and makes available to Christians His gifts. The Holy Spirit distributes to each believer as He wills (1 Corinthians 12:11). The Holy Spirit, as well as divine grace, determines the character of the gifts. Indeed, they are appropriately described as "gifts of the Holy Spirit" (Hebrews 2:4). The Spirit chooses what gift(s) will be given to each believer. As His gifts, they are individual expressions of God's free grace. They are not human or worldly in origin. They all come from the Spirit and take their character from the Spirit, who applies God's manifold grace, bestowing on His people a full range of supernatural gifts.

Manifestations of the Spirit
(phanerōsis tou pneumatos)

All the gifts are actions of the Holy Spirit, making known His presence, at times in a dramatic way. They demonstrate first and foremost the reality of His activity and presence, as the manifestation of the invisible God.[2] The Spirit reveals Himself in a variety of ways—"to each one is given the manifestation of the Spirit" (1 Corinthians 12:7). As the list of gifts in 12:8-11 indicates, spiritual gifts are not only gifts, but above all they are manifestations or indications of the Spirit's presence. The gifts are not hidden talents and abilities, but they are the working of God. They may be striking acts, such as healings and miracles, or ordinary services of exhortation and giving (Romans 12:6-8). They all reveal the action of the Holy Spirit in the service of Christ for the common good of the church.

Paul provides a model for the manifestation or use of spiritual gifts: "When you assemble, each one has a psalm, has a teaching, has a revelation, has a tongue, has an interpretation" (1 Corinthians

---

[2]Nowhere does Paul speak of "manifestations of the Spirit." Using only the singular may be due to Paul's regarding the phrase "manifestation of the Spirit" as a comprehensive term for the several ways that the Holy Spirit manifests Himself. Similarly, he seems to use the singular "fruit of the Spirit" and then gives a list of nine (Galatians 5:22, 23).

14:26). All of these must be exercised for the strengthening of the church. Three elements are vital to the manifestation of spiritual gifts: the needs of the local church, the availability of God's people, and the freedom of the Spirit to manifest gifts as He wills (12:6, 7, 11). It comes as no surprise that we have difficulty accepting this dynamic model for worship. So often our services are predictable, because we schedule each person's contribution in advance, or we develop habits of expecting and recognizing the expression of only particular spiritual gifts.

For Paul, spontaneous manifestations of the Spirit and good order in worship are compatible. At the disposal of the church is a variety of spiritual manifestations, but all the gifts are to be exercised for the building up of the church (1 Corinthians 14:26-33, 39, 40). In worship there must be freedom for the Spirit to move. A worship service may be so rigidly structured by habit or by deliberate design that it makes it difficult for the Spirit to show His presence. But structure can also aid the Spirit.

By seeking the Spirit's guidance in planning a flexible structure, worship communities can create an atmosphere where all gifts are allowed to operate. Spirit-inspired structure can also help us focus our hearts and minds, so that we are open to the move of the Spirit. With no structure, the result is confusion; and worship can become chaotic. The key to balance and order in worship is structure that allows the Holy Spirit to manifest His gifts.

Such gifts are God-given abilities demonstrated through believers by the Holy Spirit. These manifestations are evidence of the Spirit's power and show the reality of God's presence and His unfailing love. More than just being symbols of the Spirit's works, they actually demonstrate the immediate presence of the Divine Giver. Their operation is open and visible so that they can be seen and heard. Spiritual gifts, therefore, reveal that the Spirit is "on the scene" in His dynamic presence, and that He is not the "shy member of the Trinity."

Gifts

(domata)

Spiritual gifts are also spoken of in Ephesians 4. They are not called *charismata* or *pneumatika* but *domata*. Paul quotes Psalm 68:18: "He [Christ] gave gifts [*domata*] to men" (Ephesians 4:8). In verse 11, he mentions five such gifts: apostles, prophets, evangelists, pastors and teachers. No hard-and-fast distinction should be made between gifts (*domata*) and gifts of grace (*charismata*). The two terms may be regarded as equivalent to each other.

In Ephesians 4, Paul does not use the term "gifts of grace" (*charismata*), but he states, "To each one of us grace was given according to the measure of Christ's gift" (v. 7). Here, grace does not refer to saving grace, but to grace for ministry and service that is granted to believers as a portion of "Christ's gift," that is, His anointing by the Holy Spirit for ministry. The close connection of the gifts in Ephesians 4 with grace indicates that they are gifts of grace, though the term (*domata*) does not appear in 1 Corinthians 12:4 and in Romans 12:6. The attributes of all the gifts are determined by divine grace.

As Christ is the giver of the gifts in Ephesians 4, and God the Father is the giver in Romans 12, so the Holy Spirit is involved in both the gifts of Christ and the gifts of the Father. Therefore we can be confident that they are all appropriately described as "gifts of the Holy Spirit" and "gifts of grace."

Gifts, Ministries and Operations

(charismata, diakonai and energēmata)

In 1 Corinthians 12:4-6, Paul employs three terms to speak of spiritual gifts. Observe what he says: "Now there are varieties of gifts [*charismata*], but the same Spirit. And there are varieties of ministries [*diakonai*, services], and the same Lord. And there are varieties of effects [*energēmata*, operations], but the same God who works all things in all persons." The threefold reoccurrence of *varieties* (*diaireseis*) emphasizes the diversity of gifts, ministries and operations. Regardless of how manifold and diverse spiritual gifts are, it is the same Holy Spirit, the same Lord, the same God at work in all of them. The triune God—Father, Son and Holy Spirit—are at work in the great variety of spiritual gifts. Each of the Divine Persons manifests Himself in a wide range of gifts; but the unity of spiritual gifts as well as their variety are due to the triune God.

Should the three terms—*gifts, ministries* and *operations*—be distinguished from one another? Biblical research offers no support for a significant difference among these terms for a threefold classification of gifts. Paul presents three aspects rather than three types of spiritual manifestations. The first term, *gifts* (*charismata*), is a broad description of the demonstrations of the Spirit. It emphasizes the source of spiritual gifts as divine grace. Therefore they are not bestowed because of personal merit and excellence. They are given, not earned.

The second term, *ministries* (*diakonai*), emphasizes the practical usefulness of the gifts. The manifestations of the Spirit are for "the common good" (1 Corinthians 12:7), meaning for the benefit of all. The gifts are to be used in love and in service. They find their fulfillment in service that contributes to the growth and the building up of the church (14:26, 27; Ephesians 4:12).

The third term, *operations* (*energēmata*, "effects" or "workings"), draws attention to God the Father as the ultimate source of all the gifts. He is the ultimate fount of power, inspiring the operations of the gifts and working in and through all of them. To experience God through the manifestation of spiritual gifts is to encounter God's power, which stands behind all of the spiritual gifts in their rich diversity.

THE TRINITY AND THE GIFTS

It is important to note that in 1 Corinthians 12:4-6, Paul associates the three persons of the Trinity with the gifts. He does not list them in the usual order—Father, Son and Holy Spirit—but he inverts the order—"the Spirit" (v. 4), "the . . . Lord [Jesus]" (v. 5), and "God [the Father]" (v. 6). The Father, the fount of all spiritual gifts, is mentioned last (cf. Romans 12:3-8). The ascended Lord is identified in Ephesians 4 as the One who bestows the gifts: "When He ascended on high . . . He gave gifts to men" (v. 8). Nevertheless, the gifts are also distributed by the Holy Spirit (1 Corinthians 12:7, 11), and through them the Spirit manifests Himself.

Ultimately, all the gifts flow from the Father, the giver of all blessings; but they also come from the hand of the glorified Lord as much as they do from the Holy Spirit himself.[3] Spiritual gifts point us to the Holy Spirit, and the Holy Spirit leads us back to the Son. The Son points us to the Father, the ultimate donor of the gifts. Behind all spiritual gifts stand the Triune God—Father, Son and Holy Spirit. God is one, but He is also three persons and each is involved in the operation of the gifts.

The operation of the gifts heightens our sense of encounter with the Holy Spirit. But the Spirit's person and presence must not be recognized to the exclusion of the Father and the Son. None of the gifts are possible without the enabling power and presence of the Spirit, but the total operation of gifts is not of the Holy Spirit, but of the Father, Son and Holy Spirit—the triune God. Pentecost reminds us

---

[3]In Acts 2:33, we see the same Trinitarian emphasis. Jesus was anointed by the Holy Spirit for His public ministry after His baptism in water (Luke 3:21, 22; Acts 10:38). As a result He did not need to be endowed with the Spirit when He ascended into heaven, but the Father gave Jesus the Holy Spirit for distribution to the church. All that was seen and heard at Pentecost flowed from the ascended Lord. Christ continues to distribute the power of the Holy Spirit and spiritual gifts that He received from the Father. Cf. Ernst Haenchen, *The Acts of the Apostles* (Philadelphia: Westminster Press, 1971) 193.

that to be truly empowered by the Spirit is to be thoroughly Christ-centered and Trinitarian (Acts 2:33).

THE NUMBER OF SPIRITUAL GIFTS

A rich variety of gifts exists. The Spirit is manifested in many ways through the members of Christ's body; for each believer "is given the manifestation of the Spirit" (1 Corinthians 12:7). Some Pentecostals have tended to restrict spiritual gifts to the nine listed in verses 8-10. They are a word of wisdom, a word of knowledge, faith, healings, miracles, prophecy, discerning of spirits, different kinds of tongues, and the interpretation of tongues. In the same chapter a second list of *charismata* appears (vv. 28-30). A number of the items are reiterated, but the second list adds the gifts of apostles, teachers, helps and administrations.

There are three remaining lists, but they are much briefer. One mentions prophecy, serving others, teaching, exhortation, giving, ministry of spiritual guidance and discipline, and acts of mercy (Romans 12:6-8). Still another list consists of apostles, prophets, evangelists, pastors and teachers (Ephesians 4:11). The last list includes only two gifts: speaking the Word of God and serving (1 Peter 4:11).

These lists seek to give examples of various types of ministry in the church, and they all differ. Nowhere in the New Testament is there an attempt to present a definitive list of spiritual gifts. Nor do the various lists, as a whole, exhaust the possibilities of *charismata* available to the people of God. The gifts listed probably spring from the nature of the audience or group that Paul or Peter had in view. Hence, a careful examination of the various Biblical lists of spiritual gifts reveals that they are intended to be representative, not exhaustive or comprehensive. No doubt they were related in some measure to the situational needs, as well as ongoing functions, of the particular churches. In light of this, the nine gifts of 1 Corinthians 12:8-10 provide typical examples of the Spirit's manifestations. In fact, the various lists offer samples of what the Spirit can do in the life of a Christian.

The New Testament lists the specific leadership gifts as apostle, prophet, evangelist, pastor and teacher (Ephesians 4:11; 1 Corinthians 12:28). Then there are those gifts that are extraordinary in their manifestations, such as faith, healings, miracles, speaking in tongues and interpretation of tongues. But such designations as helps, service, giving and acts of mercy are general categories that could include a wide range of specific gifts. Any ministry inspired and used by the Holy Spirit—whether in intercessory prayer, ministry to children, music, art, hospitality, construction, maintenance, writing, counseling or whatever—is indeed a legitimate spiritual gift. If God has given the gift, it is good and should be used in service of God's people (1 Peter 4:10, 11).

The very nature of the Holy Spirit makes it impossible for us to limit His gifts to those that appear in the Biblical lists. He is God, and His gifts must be seen as open-ended in character. The possibilities of His operation reach beyond nine gifts. Jesus explained that the wind blows wherever it pleases (John 3:8). The Spirit works in the same manner, for He bestows not only the gifts listed by Paul and Peter, but also many others.

POSSESSION OF SPIRITUAL GIFTS

On whom are the gifts of the Spirit bestowed—on individuals or on the church? A prominent view among Pentecostals has been that spiritual gifts are given to the church and that on particular occasions the Holy Spirit dispenses the gifts through whomever He chooses at that time. The Bible clearly teaches that *charismata* are given to individual Christians. "But to *each one* is given the manifestation of the Spirit for the common good. For to one is given the word of wisdom through the Spirit, and to another the word of knowledge according to the same Spirit; to another faith by the same Spirit, and to another gifts of healing by the one Spirit, and to another the effecting of miracles, and to another prophecy, and to another the distinguishing of spirits, to another various kinds of tongues, and to another the interpretation of tongues" (1 Corinthians 12:7-10). "Each one should use whatever gift he has received to serve others" (1 Peter 4:10, *NIV*).

Both Paul and Peter teach that each Christian has received a gift. Paul also instructed the Corinthian believers not to speak in tongues unless there was an interpreter present in the worship service (1 Corinthians 14:27, 28). If spiritual gifts are not given to individuals, then one could reason that an individual would not receive the gift of interpretation for regular use in a particular congregation and that everyone would share the responsibility of interpretation. If there was not a person who was regularly used to interpret, how then could the Corinthian believers have known whether or not there was an interpreter present? Could it not be said that the individual who exercises this ministry from time to time has the gift of interpretation?

Gifts in the Church

At this point we can raise a couple of questions. Can a spiritual gift be resident in the church and not in any member of the church? Should we not understand that the gifts are resident in the Holy Spirit? Certainly the Holy Spirit is the permanent resident in the church, and the gifts are resident in the Spirit in that He is the One who dispenses them. When we say that the gifts reside in the Spirit, we really have not said anything that changes the use of gifts in the church. There remains the emphasis of Scripture—to one is given a word of knowledge, to another a word of wisdom, to another faith, to another the gifts of healings. This kind of language teaches that gifts are given to individuals; but individual believers and the church are the same. For individuals to receive gifts means that the Holy Spirit bestows gifts on the church.

Individuals' Use of Gifts

The fact that individuals do receive spiritual gifts should not be taken to mean that they can exercise their gifts whenever they wish. A real danger is to assume that a gift we possess can be used at our own whim. If that is our assumption, then the word *possession* means "I own, I control, I operate, I manipulate." Such an understanding can create division in the church. The Holy Spirit bestows *charismata* on believers according to His will (1 Corinthians 12:11). The recipient of a gift should exercise the gift only at the direction and anointing of the Spirit. The gifts should not be thought of as detached from the Holy Spirit and should always operate under His guidance.

The Biblical teaching is plain. The church is composed of individual believers, each of whom has received a particular gift. As Paul says, "To each one is given the manifestation of the Spirit" (12:7). For him, there is no such thing as an "ungifted believer." Every believer has one or more spiritual gifts, which are bestowed on the occasion of becoming a member of the body of Christ. The gifts mentioned by Paul in verses 4-11 are examples of what a person may receive at the time of conversion. The gifts, however, are not bestowed indiscriminately. The ninefold repetition of "to one" and "to another" stresses the distribution of different gifts to different believers.

The questions posed in 1 Corinthians 12:29, 30 are written in a form that indicates the anticipation of an emphatic, negative answer:[4] "All are not apostles, are they? All are not prophets, are they? All are not teachers, are they? All are not workers of miracles, are they? All do not have gifts of healings, do they? All do not speak with tongues, do they? All do not interpret, do they?" The

---

[4] The questions are introduced by the Greek *mē,* and when so used, the expectation is for the answer to be "Of course not!" Verses 29, 30 contain a plea for diversity of gifts to be manifested in the church.

expected answer is "No, they do not." No believer has all the spiritual gifts. No one is equipped or gifted to do everything in the church. The wide distribution of the gifts to every believer in the church ensures that no one is left out.

The Spirit's Distribution of Gifts

We should not understand 1 Corinthians 12:29, 30 to mean that a person may not have more than one gift of grace. For example, a person with the gift of tongues may also have the gift of interpretation (14:13). A gifted teacher would need to have an understanding of the Scriptures and insight into the life of the congregation, but that person would need also the gift of exhortation (Romans 12:8). The apostles likely possessed a variety of spiritual gifts, including healing, tongues, prophecy, teaching, and so on. A believer, therefore, need not think of himself or herself as a specialist with only one gift. No doubt, some have a mixture of gifts that enable them to serve the church. The Holy Spirit bestows a variety of gifts on individual members of the church's body so that every member is a gifted minister.

The Spirit's work is designed so that each individual's use of a spiritual gift in the church is dependent on other individuals' gifts. This pattern creates purpose and unity in the body of Christ. The Holy Spirit is sovereign in His distribution of spiritual gifts. He chooses who will receive what gift, but His wise choice that all do not receive the same gift does not set aside our personal responsibility. The Holy Spirit is the sovereign God, but He does not treat believers as puppets, not even in the distribution of spiritual gifts.

To counter that understanding, Paul urges believers to "pursue love, yet desire earnestly spiritual gifts" (1 Corinthians 14:1; cf. v. 39; 12:31). The Spirit's choice does not deny our responsibility to seek His gifts prayerfully. The verb *desire*, which is a synonym to *pursue* (*zeloō*) means "to seek" and it is durative in force, meaning "to keep on seeking." The word *pursue* fits well with Paul's advice that the one who speaks in tongues should pray for the gift of interpretation, too. As the qualities of love are to be actively pursued, so are spiritual gifts. Believers may express their desire in prayer in regard to the matter of spiritual gifts, but at the same time be receptive to whatever gifts the Spirit chooses to bestow.

SPIRITUAL GIFTS AND THE CHURCH

The Purpose of Spiritual Gifts

The New Testament places spiritual gifts in the context of the church. Paul compares the church to a physical body and speaks of it as the body of Christ. Believers are true members of the one body of Christ, and each receives a minimum of one gift; but many believers have received more. They are gifted within the church and for the benefit of the church. The gifts bestowed upon them are not for personal aggrandizement, personal satisfaction, and not even exclusively for personal ministry.

Spiritual gifts are for ministry within the body of Christ. Paul says that the manifestation of the Spirit is given to every believer "for the common good" of the church (1 Corinthians 12:7). No doubt, the gifts of the Spirit do serve other purposes as well. They authenticate the gospel and its messengers (2 Corinthians 12:12). They convict and convert unbelievers (1 Corinthians 14:21-25). But their supreme purpose is to edify the local fellowship of believers.

The mere presence of spiritual gifts in the church does not ensure the accomplishment of their ultimate purpose. Gifts only achieve their goal when they are exercised for some useful purpose. The manner in which gifts are used is crucial to the building up of the church. They are to be exercised in love, not in a spirit of divisive competition, of which the Corinthians were guilty of doing. Paul shows to the Corinthians a "more excellent way" (1 Corinthians 12:31), in which the exercise of gifts is governed by love, an attitude of joyful service and obedience to Christ. That is why he exhorts them to make love their aim (14:1).

The Spirit's bestowal of gifts calls each member of Christ's body to unselfish service and obedience to Christ as Lord. The purpose of spiritual gifts is to enable us to serve Christ and His church. None of the gifts can be fulfilled apart from service directed and guided by love. When the law of love governs the operation of spiritual gifts, the *charismata* are used for the benefit of the local fellowship of believers, especially promoting the supreme goal of its spiritual and numerical growth. All the gifts have one and the same goal: edification of the community by believers serving in love to Christ and one another. So when a prophecy is given, a word of wisdom spoken, tongues and interpretation expressed, or a miracle is effected, it is for the purpose of edifying the church.

Gifts of the Spirit and the Body of Christ

The gifts of the Spirit are bestowed only within the body of Christ and on members of that body. Three major passages in the letters of Paul deal with the gifts of the Spirit. It is significant that in each of them the body of Christ is also mentioned (Romans 12:4, 5; 1 Corinthians 12:12-28; Ephesians 4:11-16). The body of Christ may be understood to encompass all believers, the universal church (Ephesians 1:22, 23). But the church throughout the world is expressed in the local congregation. The term "temple of God," which is used by Paul also for the church, illustrates this point. Paul says, "For we are the temple of the living God" (2 Corinthians 6:16), referring to believers everywhere as the one temple of God.

But he also states, "Do you not know that you are a temple of God and that the Spirit of God dwells in you? If any man destroys the temple of God, God will destroy him, for the temple of God is holy, and that is what you are" (1 Corinthians 3:16, 17). Here, Paul is thinking of the local manifestation of God's temple, the local church in Corinth where the spirit of divisiveness threatened to destroy that fellowship of believers. It is inconceivable that the universal temple of God could be destroyed; not even the gates of hell can prevail against it (Matthew 16:18). Local churches, however, have been destroyed and have gone out of existence.[5]

The one Spirit indwells the one body of Christ with its many members. As already noted, the gifts of the Spirit are linked closely to the body of Christ, the church. The following observations show how the rich variety of gifts goes with Paul's understanding of the church as the body of Christ.

1. *The gifts are to promote the unity of the local church* (1 Corinthians 12; Romans 12:3-8; Ephesians 4:1-16). The diversity of the gifts and the fellowship of believers make it possible for the church to function in perfect harmony. Just as the proper use of our physical members make it possible for our bodies to function properly, so the manifestations of the Spirit make it possible for the local church to function properly as a whole. Strife and divisions among the Corinthian believers reflected the fact that they had not learned to live as a body. Operating properly in the congregation, gifts served to strengthen the body of believers. It is beautiful to see a Christian community in which all the gifts function as they should. Truly, edification is at its maximum, and God is magnified.

2. *The congregation as a body allows for a rich variety of gifts and ministries.* Care must be taken not to promote diversity of gifts and ministries at the expense of the unity of the body. They are deeply related to one another, but Paul always emphasizes unity first, then diversity of its members (Romans 12:4ff.; 1 Corinthians 12:4ff.; Ephesians 4:3ff.). This order is not without significance (see especially 1 Corinthians 12:27). Gifts within the community point to its diversity, but in their proper function they serve the whole body and promote unity.

---

[5]C.K. Barrett, *The First Epistle to the Corinthians* (New York: Harper and Row Publishers, 1968) 91.

3. *The wide range of distribution of the gifts makes believers dependent on one another.* Like the members of the human body, every member of the church has a service to perform and thus, an appropriate gift. The Holy Spirit distributes the gifts in wide and varied ways. Not all have the same gift. No one can do all that needs to be done in the church. A believer's spiritual gift may appear to have a greater capacity for edifying than another believer's gift, but there is no room for pride on the part of anyone (1 Corinthians 12:21-24).

Individuals should not feel inferior because others seem to be more gifted (vv. 15-17). The differences among them must not be seen in terms of natural abilities, but in terms of their spiritual gifts. Since God gives all spiritual gifts, who are we to value some and devalue others? As humans, we are unable to know the total spiritual impact that our gifts have on the church and the world. Paul states in Romans 12:6, "Since we have gifts that differ according to the grace given us, each of us is to exercise them accordingly." No member of the body and his or her gift are dispensable. In short, we all need one another, and the gifts of the Spirit are manifested not just through a few but through all.

It follows, therefore, that the church is to be charismatic in its entire life, exercising the *charismata* of the Spirit to build up its own members and to serve the world.

SPIRITUAL GIFTS AND THE FRUIT OF THE SPIRIT

Both the gifts and the fruit are central to Paul's teaching about the ministry of the Holy Spirit. Since the gifts and the fruit flow from the same Spirit, there is no ground for elevating one over the other. The fruit of the Spirit (Galatians 5:22, 23) are what the Spirit endeavors to do in us, namely to conform us to the likeness of Christ. Whereas the gifts of the Spirit are what the Spirit endeavors to do through us. The danger is to become preoccupied with either one of these so that the other is neglected. The Corinthians' basic problem was not the gifts; it was the fruit. This is why Paul wrote the great chapter on love (1 Corinthians 13). In it, he spoke eloquently about love, the crowning fruit of the Spirit. He told them they could have the gifts of tongues, knowledge and faith, but without love they were nothing.

Paul speaks of the "more excellent way" (1 Corinthians 12:31). In the context of his emphasis on love, he is dealing with the gifts of the Spirit (1 Corinthians 12–14). So the more excellent way is the more excellent way of manifesting the *charismata*. What is "the more excellent way"? It is love working through the gifts. It is not either love or gifts, but both gifts and love. Both are the working of the Holy Spirit and both are necessary. The necessity for love to operate along with spiritual gifts is evident during occasions when a person is used by the Spirit to perform a powerful spiritual manifestation. Because of the visibility of the gift, such a person may easily become proud or may be placed on a pedestal by others. The only sure corrective is the moderating quality of God's love. In love, an individual's use of any spiritual gift is an act of compassionate service to the church. The church's response is to praise God and to be gracious toward each other. Above all other graces, the Holy Spirit uses love to maintain balance in the body of Christ. Consequently, Paul sees the gifts and fruit as being complementary and vital to the Christian life.

In some circles, the fruit of the Spirit are viewed as preferable to the gifts of the Spirit, while others strongly stress the gifts of the Spirit to the neglect of the fruit and the importance of holiness (Christlike living). In his writings, Paul does not elevate the fruit over the gifts; nor does he emphasize gifts and ignore the importance of bearing the fruit of the Spirit. His teachings indicate that he was unwilling for any of the spiritual gifts to operate apart from love (1 Corinthians 13). When the gifts of the Spirit are exercised in love, the body of Christ is strengthened.

Love is patient and kind; it never seeks to divide; it is never pride-ful or boastful. Love strives to maintain unity in the bond of peace (Ephesians 4:3). Love is to express itself in the gifts; but more than that, the foremost fruit of the Spirit, love, is to be the controlling fac-tor of all the gifts. This is "the more excellent way." It is often said that love is the greatest charismatic gift, but Paul never identifies it as a spiritual gift. Love is a fruit of the Spirit, not a Charismatic gift. Love provides the climate in which gifts are to operate. The distinc-tions between the fruit of the Spirit and His gifts must not be blurred.

Similarities in Spiritual Gifts and Spiritual Fruit

To develop the relation between the gifts and the fruit of the Spirit, we will consider their similarities as well as their differences. Three basic similarities can be identified between the gifts and the fruit.

1. *They both have their origin in the Holy Spirit.* The Spirit bestows spiritual gifts and cultivates spiritual fruit in the life of the Christian who abides in Christ.

2. *The purpose of both gifts and fruit is to build up the commu-nity of believers.* Gifts are for the benefit of the church (1 Corinthians 12:7; 14:26), and likewise love, the first fruit of the Spirit, builds up (8:1). The fruit and gifts are meant to work togeth-er to strengthen the church and to bring balance in our lives.

3. *Christian growth and maturity bring about the full and mature expression of gifts and fruit.* The problem of the Corinthians was not a deficiency of gifts (1:7) but a lack of maturity in exercising them. Spiritual fruit must be developed and brought to maturity. As we practice the discipline of a dedicated life, the Spirit cultivates His fruit in our lives and Christ's own likeness is reflected in us. This is what Paul had in mind when he said that we are constantly transformed into the image of Christ (2 Corinthians 3:18).

Distinctions Between Gifts and Fruit

In addition to these three similarities, there are also four basic distinctions between gifts and fruit.

1. *A Christian should have all of the fruit of the Spirit, but God does not require a Christian to have all of the charismata.* Every Christian should earnestly desire and be receptive to spiritual gifts (1 Corinthians 12:31; 14:1). However, the Holy Spirit is sovereign in the distribution of the gifts (12:11).

2. *The fruit of the Spirit are devotional and ethical.* They produce the likeness of Christ in us. The gifts of the Spirit, on the other hand, are charismatic, enabling us to perform a particular service or ministry.

3. *While all the gifts have a vital place in the church until the kingdom of God fully comes, the fruit of the Spirit are eternal.* Paul reminds us in 1 Corinthians 13 that gifts such as prophecy and tongues will cease when God's kingdom comes in great power and glory; but faith, hope and love will continue to abide. Charismatic gifts are given to meet our temporal spiritual needs. They are given for a time and for the journey that we are on, but not for eternity. When we "know" as we are "known," there will no longer be any need for spiritual gifts. When that which is "perfect"—the eternal kingdom of God—has fully come, then spiritual gifts will cease. The full revelation of God will make them unnecessary. But in contrast, the spiritual graces of love, faith and hope are given to us for eternity.

4. *The fruit of the Spirit are broader than spiritual gifts.* The fruit provide the lifestyle in which the gifts are to be exercised. The life of the believer is characterized as walking according to the Spirit (Romans 8:4, 5) or "according to love" (14:15) or by faith (2 Corinthians 5:7). The focus is on the fruit as being the broad context in which charismatic gifts operate. Paul calls it the "more excellent way." He is not saying that the way of love overrides gifts, but that the way of love is love working through the gifts to edify the church. Without love, gifts are not useful. Neither is much of anything else in the church's life.[6]

---

[6]Gordon D. Fee, *God's Empowering Presence* (Peabody, MA: Hendrickson, 1994) 197.

Fruit and Gifts: Integral Parts of Christian Living

The gifts and the fruit of the Spirit should go hand in hand. They are integral to the work of the Spirit and to the Christian life. Normally, gifts are manifested through holy people; but, as Paul recognized, the possession of a gift does not in itself signify the possession of spiritual fruit: "If I have the gift of prophecy and can fathom all mysteries and all knowledge, and if I have a faith that can move mountains, but have not love, I am nothing" (1 Corinthians 13:2, *NIV*). Scripture stresses the fruit of the Spirit as important signs of the Christian life (John 13:34, 35; 14:15, 23; Galatians 5:19-24) and as an important test of those who manifest gifts of the Spirit (Matthew 7:15-23).

Applying the test of spiritual maturity to those who exercise gifts of the Spirit has its place, but the discernment of spiritual maturity must be tempered with the strong warnings about judging a brother or sister (Matthew 7:1-6; 14:4-12; Romans 2:1). The weaknesses of the Corinthians showed a lack of the fruit of the Spirit—a lack of spiritual maturity. So the problem of spiritual gifts being exercised by the spiritually immature is nothing new. A wide range of growth and maturity may be found among believers.

The solution to the problem does not come by abandoning the gifts of the Spirit as though they are dangerous to the church, but by the congregation's exercising its authority, which ensures the full and pure operation of spiritual gifts. There is no denying that spiritual gifts are holy since they come from the Holy Spirit, but they are more effective when exercised by holy people. A lack of dedication to God in daily life by those through whom gifts operate hinders and diminishes the gifts' positive influence. On the contrary, gifts working through holy vessels strengthen the church spiritually and numerically.

THE CONTINUATION OF SPIRITUAL GIFTS

A number of contemporary churches make little room for the spontaneous manifestation of spiritual gifts. This practice reflects a crippling misunderstanding of the Biblical doctrine of gifts of the Spirit. The extreme form of such a practice has been called *cessationism*, which teaches that the "extraordinary gifts" or "sign gifts" (tongues, interpretation of tongues, prophecies, healings and miracles) were withdrawn from the church at the end of the first century. The argument is that such gifts no longer have a legitimate place in the life of the church. A more moderate but subtle form admits the legitimacy of spiritual gifts, but in practice is suspicious of them and tends to discredit their operation. Those who outright reject spiritual gifts as having any proper place in today's church or those who have a fear of them fail to understand their nature. They see the gifts as erratic, individualistic, bizarre, showy behavior that threatens the unity of the body of Christ.

This view misrepresents what the Bible means by spiritual gifts. There is no Biblical evidence whatsoever for restricting the extraordinary gifts to the apostles. To the contrary, as *continuationism* teaches, God did not withdraw the gifts such as miracles, prophecy and tongues at the end of the apostolic age. They are just as valid and needed today as at any time. In fact, apostolic and prophetic-like ministries can and should have their place today as they did in the first century. This does not deny that the apostles and prophets had a unique role in establishing the church. Individual Christians who are spiritually gifted with authority and influence may function today as apostles or prophets serving in a similar manner as the apostle Paul did (Ephesians 4:11-13).

Cessationism

Cessationists base much of their argument on 1 Corinthians 13:8, which states that prophecies and tongues will cease and knowledge will pass away. Paul indicates that there will come a time when spiritual gifts will no longer be available, but that will happen only "when the perfect comes" (v. 10). Cessationists teach that "the perfect" refers to the completion of the New Testament, and that miraculous signs were only a temporary provision to authenticate the message of the apostles. Nothing in 1 Corinthians 13 suggests that Paul has in mind the establishment of the canon of the New Testament. That which is "the perfect" (*to teleion*) can refer to no less than the return of Jesus Christ and the blessed state that follows. The cessationists fear that a gift such as prophecy, which produces fresh revelations, would infringe on the sufficiency and the authority of Scripture.

But they have a limited understanding of prophecy. This gift not only reveals truth and exposes sin, but its primary function is to strengthen, encourage and comfort (1 Corinthians 14:3). Any prophecy that is given stands subject to the Scripture; it must agree with the teachings of the Bible. In light of this, how then can prophecy that is inspired by the Holy Spirit diminish the authority of Scripture? Prophecy exalts the Bible. Like all the other gifts, the gift of prophecy is needed until believers no longer need strengthening, encouraging and comforting. Needs of people and the church have not changed. A variety of spiritual gifts are now as vital to the life of the church and its witness to the world as they were in the first century.

A second interpretation, held by some cessationists, is that *the perfect* means "maturity." This meaning is possible in light of the definition found in Greek lexicons (cf. 1 Corinthians 2:6), and the illustration about childhood in 1 Corinthians 13:11 seems to confirm it. The word *perfect* (*teleios*) used in 1 Corinthians 2:6 is often defined as "mature" in Greek lexicons. The illustration in 1 Corinthians 13:10-12 does describe maturity; but it is an eternal maturity or perfection. The lexicons' interpretation of *perfection,* meaning earthly maturity, ignores the significance of verses 10 and 12. Moreover, Paul emphasizes the importance of all the spiritual gifts to the church. It is unlikely that he would think of excluding any of them from the most mature church. He clearly sees the gifts as strengthening the church until Christ returns (1 Corinthians 1:7).

The point of 13:11 is not that the church on the earth will become so mature that it will no longer need such gifts as prophecy, tongues and knowledge. On this earth the church needs these gifts because its knowledge remains incomplete. An accurate understanding of the idea of spiritual gifts passing away at maturity (or perfection) is this: regardless of how magnificent gifts may be, the partial knowledge they provide now must be seen as childish in comparison to the fuller knowledge that believers will possess at the return of the Lord, when their faith gives way to sight.

Continuationism

No Biblical basis exists for declaring specific gifts as invalid for today. Prophecies and tongues will cease, but not until our understanding through spiritual gifts has been replaced by a face-to-face relationship with Jesus Christ (1 Corinthians 13:12). Gifts are not forever, but all of them are needed until Christ comes the second time. For this reason, none of the *charismata* should be seen as being nonessential or culturally bound to a particular time and place. They are relevant to every time and culture, and will continue to exist in the church until Christ comes.

In Romans 12 and Ephesians 4, Paul relates the unity of the church to the diversity of the gifts. His appeal to "present your bodies a living and holy sacrifice" and "be transformed by the renewing of your mind" is followed by the appeal, "Since we have gifts that differ according to the grace given to us, each of us is to exercise them accordingly" (Romans 12:1-6). Both exhortations apply to the church today.

No one has the right to try to bind the hands of God by denying that He has the power to bestow spiritual gifts on His people. There is no solid Biblical basis for the belief that the extraordinary manifestations of the Spirit were limited to New Testament times and that the Charismatic age ceased with the death of the last apostle. Healings and other miracles confirmed the gospel in the first century, but they also accomplished much more than that. They did, and still do, minister to needs of people; and remain vital to the worship and ministry of the church. The *charismata* have not ceased, for the coming of the Lord is still ahead.

CONCLUSION

The God of salvation is ready to break in on a situation in power. He is the One who acts through spiritual gifts to bring strength and deliverance. A situation may call for a word of wisdom or discernment regarding the source of a spiritual manifestation. It may call for prayer for healing or words of encouragement. The situation may call for prophecy or tongues and their interpretation. The gifts of the Spirit are breakings-in of God's presence and His love. God works through them to minister to needs of His people and the needs in the world. None of the gifts should be seen as ornaments for display and show. In the New Testament, every gift is given for the purpose of service. I want to conclude this chapter with a few observations about the importance and scope of spiritual gifts in the church.

Believers need to take the stance of openness and expectancy. This is the stance of faith, one condition that must be met so that the Spirit is free to work and manifest His gifts. Suspicion and doubt about the validity of spiritual gifts limit the operation of the Holy Spirit. When we devalue spiritual gifts, we also devalue the Biblical understanding of the church and the Spirit-filled life. Faith in God should prompt us to accept the full range of Biblical teaching on the subject and be open to God's move through spiritual gifts in our lives. Such a response is necessary to avoid crippling the church.

The Holy Spirit gives spiritual gifts for individuals to use in Christian community. Spiritual gifts are often seen as a private matter between the individual believer and God. Today, personal fascination with spiritual gifts and manifestations is common, but the move of the Holy Spirit is not strictly a matter of the believer's private relationship to God. Again and again, Paul emphasizes that spiritual gifts are for the edification of the church. Yet, the church must not forget that the ministry and life of the church is to be the guiding context in which individuals use their spiritual gifts.

A community of believers may be enriched by the use of a gift, but the community should also serve to check and bring balance when some extreme or uncontrolled action occurs. The effort to create balance should include helping individuals to recognize and use their God-given gifts. In addition, the church should provide encouragement and support for all spiritual gifts, even those that are somewhat outside the church's usual style and comfort zone. Small Bible-study groups can be useful for building community and helping to awaken gifts and manage their operation. As a result, the whole community of believers is edified.

The gift of discernment remains crucial for distinguishing between the genuine and counterfeit exercise of various gifts. Spiritual gifts were not considered by the early Christians as infallible and on the same level as the Scriptures. A number of tests, however, can be applied to determine if the use of a spiritual gift is inspired by the Holy Spirit.

- *First, does the gift exalt Christ?* The Spirit comes to glorify Christ (John 16:14; cf. 1 Corinthians 12:5). A prophecy or a tongue does not have to mention Christ, but they or any other gift should have the aim of exalting Christ.

- *Second, does the gift edify the body of Christ?* Are the people being blessed or enlightened by the operation of the gift? Obviously we should not expect every manifestation to bless every person equally on every occasion.

- *Third, does the person who speaks or acts do it in love?* The word that comes may be strong and pronounce judgment; but God is eternally a God of love, and His gifts are manifestations of His love.

- *Fourth, is Jesus the Lord of the person's life through whom a gift operates?* The Bible warned against false prophets. No person is perfect, but Jesus said that false prophets would be known by their fruit (Matthew 7).

- *Fifth, is the person willing for mature Christians to evaluate what has been said or done?* If there is refusal to submit to godly and prayerful church leaders, such an independent spirit can cause schisms and splits in the fellowship.

- *Finally, if it is a predictive word, then is it fulfilled?* It is clear that if it does not come to pass, that word was not a word from the Lord (Deuteronomy 18:22).

Spiritual gifts go beyond the dedicated use of natural abilities and talents. They are more than merely the faithful use of native abilities; they must be understood to be literally "gifts of the Spirit." God bestows native abilities at birth, but spiritual gifts do not begin to operate in a person's life until after conversion. Often, spiritual gifts are combined with natural abilities. A person who has natural talent for teaching may, as a Christian, receive the spiritual gift of teaching and, as a result, far exceed his or her natural capacity for teaching and scholarship. The gifts of the Spirit often set on fire talent or developed abilities for serving God and are the result of the Spirit's operation in the life of the believer. As Paul says, the "Spirit works all these things, distributing to each one individually just as He wills" (1 Corinthians 12:11).

The gifts administered by the Holy Spirit identify individuals with certain ministries. Is it possible for a person's gift or mixture of gifts to shift or change? God may have equipped a person for a certain ministry; but because of the changing needs of the congregation, He may lead that person into a different ministry. Likely, the new ministry will demand other gifts, so gifts may shift in terms of need. But we can be confident that the distribution of them will be wise and appropriate. This possibility teaches us to be flexible, depending on God's direction and the circumstances in which we find ourselves. Our ministry may change because of our spiritual growth and the changing needs of the body of Christ. Maybe God has given us certain gifts, but due to new opportunities of service He will give us other gifts.

The exercise of spiritual gifts is not an experience "beyond Christ." Throughout the New Testament, the ministry of Christ and the Holy Spirit are intertwined. Spiritual gifts can be misunderstood as giving the believer the opportunity "to do his own thing," but it must not be forgotten that gifts are primarily for the benefit of the church. The manifestation of gifts is not to be determined by a personal desire for glory, but by Christ's life and ministry. As His death was for others, our use of spiritual gifts should be for the benefit of others. The proper exercise of spiritual gifts leads us not to a throne but to a cross—that is, to self-sacrificing service. Biblically, gift affirmation has its place; but so does self-denial. In fact, both go together. Gifts exercised faithfully lead us to self-giving, which in turn brings personal satisfaction and spiritual blessings. Gifts of the Spirit spell responsibility, sacrifice and service.

We are to pray for the gifts that are needed in the work of the church. The fact that spiritual gifts are gifts from the Holy Spirit does not give us license to take a passive attitude toward their distribution. Although spiritual gifts are distributed according to the Holy Spirit's discretion, Paul tells us to "earnestly desire the greater gifts" (1 Corinthians 12:31). We do not know what the "greater gifts" are—he does not tell us—but they would probably depend on the particular needs of the congregation at the time. Whatever gift or gifts were needed and were the most edifying, the Corinthians were urged to seek. They had failed to seek the greater gifts. Paul's admonition counters the attitude of folding our hands and not worrying about the manifestation of gifts. We are to seek the gifts that will make the maximum contribution to the community of believers.

The gifts of the Spirit are many. Some gifts are more conspicuous than others. Paul, however, is careful not only to include the extraordinary gifts—prophecy, miracles, healings, tongues and interpretation—but also those that are humble and simple acts of service. These gifts of practical service can be easily overlooked in the congregation. They include doing helpful deeds, teaching, encouraging, showing mercy and contributing to the needs of others. All spiritual gifts give evidence of the Spirit's presence. Therefore, caution should be taken not to limit spiritual gifts to one type of manifestation.

Summary

- Spiritual gifts are gifts of grace given to believers by the Triune God for use in ministry and service.

- God gives every believer at least one spiritual gift.

- A diversity of spiritual gifts are essential to the life and work of the church.

- God's love is expressed through the use of spiritual gifts.

TABLE 7-A
Biblical Terms for Spiritual Gifts

Gifts of Grace
Charismata; Singular *Charisma*

ROMANS 11:29; 2 CORINTHIANS 1:11	The term *gifts of grace* when used in a broad manner includes the gift of salvation in Christ and other blessings.
ROMANS 12:6-8; 1 CORINTHIANS 1:7; 12:4ff.; 1 TIMOTHY 4:14; 2 TIMOTHY 1:6; 1 PETER 4:10	The term *gifts of grace* when used in a narrower manner indicates gifts of the Holy Spirit that enable believers to give loving service to one another and to others. This term emphasizes God's grace.

Spiritual (Gifts)
Adjective: *Pneumatika*; Singular *Pneumatikon*

1 CORINTHIANS 12:1; 14:1	The term *pneumatika* when used with the word *gifts* indicates the spiritual aspects of God's gifts. It shows the close connection between the gifts and the Holy Spirit (*pneuma*)—the Holy Spirit being the One who distributes spiritual gifts.

Manifestations of the Spirit
Phanerōsis tou Pneumatos

1 CORINTHIANS 12:7	The phrase *manifestation of the Spirit* indicates that through the gifts, the Holy Spirit makes manifest, or makes known, His presence.

continued

TABLE 7-A (CONTINUED) **Biblical Terms for Spiritual Gifts**	
Gifts *Domata*	
PSALM 68:18; EPHESIANS 4:8	The word *gifts* (*domata*) is equivalent to *gifts of grace* (*charismata*). They both emphasize the grace of God.
Ministries *or* **Services** *Diakonai*	
1 CORINTHIANS 12:5	The terms *ministries* and *services* indicate the practical usefulness of spiritual gifts.
Operations *or* **Effects** *or* **Working(s)** *Energēmata*	
1 CORINTHIANS 12:6	The English terms used vary among versions of the Bible. The terms *operations*, *effects* and *working(s)* draw attention to God the Father as the ultimate source of all gifts. God's creative power stands behind all spiritual gifts.
Notes	

TABLE 7-B

The Trinity and the Gifts

"Now there are varieties of gifts, but the same Spirit. And there are varieties of ministries, and the same Lord. And there are varieties of effects, but the same God who works all things in all persons."

1 CORINTHIANS 12:4-6

God the Father

MATTHEW 7:11; JOHN 14:26; ACTS 1:4; ROMANS 12:3; 1 CORINTHIANS 12:6; HEBREWS 2:4	God the Father is the fount, or the Creator, of all spiritual gifts. He is the giver of all blessings.

The Son, the Lord Jesus Christ

LUKE 24:49-51; JOHN 14:26; ACTS 1:4; 2:33; 1 CORINTHIANS 12:5	Upon His ascension the Father gave Jesus the Holy Spirit for distribution to the church. The Lord Jesus Christ gives spiritual gifts.

The Holy Spirit

1 CORINTHIANS 12:4-11	The Holy Spirit distributes spiritual gifts, and through the gifts the Spirit manifests Himself.

- Spiritual gifts point us to the Holy Spirit.
- The Holy Spirit leads us back to the Son.
- The Son points us to the Father, the ultimate donor of spiritual gifts.

TABLE 7-C
Examples of Spiritual Gifts

God gives spiritual gifts to believers for enlightenment and the building up of the church, as well as for ministry and service in the world.

1 CORINTHIANS 12:4-7

The following are lists of various types of spiritual gifts. Nowhere in the New Testament is there a definitive list of gifts. God gives spiritual gifts as they are needed by particular believers in particular situations.

1 Corinthians 12:8-10

• Wisdom, God-given ability to speak words of wisdom or to give wise advice (word of wisdom)	• God-given ability to prophesy
• Special knowledge from God (word of knowledge)	• God-given ability to discern between the true and the false (discernings of spirits)
• God-given faith	• God-given ability to speak in tongues (other languages) for the enlightenment of the church
• God-given ability to heal the sick (healings)	
• God-given ability to perform miracles (workings of miracles)	• God-given ability to interpret what is being said in tongues

1 Corinthians 12:28-30

• Apostles	• Those who help others
• Prophets	• Those who administrate and motivate others to work together
• Teachers	
• Those who do miracles	
• Those who have the gifts of healings	• Those who speak in unknown languages

continued

TABLE 7-C (CONTINUED)
Examples of Spiritual Gifts

Romans 12:6-8	
• Prophesying • Serving • Teaching • Encouraging (exhorting)	• Contributing to the needs of others • Leading • Showing kindness and mercy

Ephesians 4:11	
• Apostles • Prophets • Evangelists	• Pastors • Teachers

1 Peter 4:11	
• Speakers • Helpers	

Notes

Table 7-D
Spiritual Gifts and the Church

"But to each one is given the manifestation of the Spirit for the common good."
1 Corinthians 12:7

"Each one should use whatever gift he has received to serve others, faithfully administering God's grace in its various forms."
1 Peter 4:10, *NIV*

The body of Christ (the church) is composed of individual believers. God has given each of these believers one or more spiritual gifts for use in the church and world.

2 Corinthians 12:12	Spiritual gifts authenticate the gospel and its messengers.
1 Corinthians 14:21-25	Spiritual gifts convict and convert unbelievers.
1 Corinthians 14:1	Spiritual gifts operate within the context of and express love.
1 Corinthians 3:16, 17; 6:19	The Holy Spirit dwells in each believer and expresses himself through our spiritual gift(s). We are His temple, and together we comprise the body of Christ (the church).
Romans 12:3-8; 1 Corinthians 12; Ephesians 4:1-16	The proper use of spiritual gifts promotes unity in the church.
Romans 12:4ff.; 1 Corinthians 12:4ff.; Ephesians 4:3ff.	The congregation as a body allows for a rich variety of gifts and ministries.
1 Corinthians 12:15-24	The wide range of distribution of the gifts makes believers dependent on one another.

	TABLE 7-E **Spiritual Gifts and Spiritual Fruit**
	Similarities
	Both spiritual gifts and spiritual fruit have their origin in the Holy Spirit.
	The purpose of both gifts and fruit is to build up the community of believers.
	Christian growth and maturity bring the full and mature expression of gifts and fruit.
	Differences
1	The gifts of the Spirit are what the Spirit endeavors to do through us (ROMANS 12:3-8; 1 CORINTHIANS 12:4-11). The fruit of the Spirit are what the Spirit endeavors to do in us, namely to conform us to the likeness of Christ (GALATIANS 5:22, 23).
2	God gives individual believers one or more gifts. He does not give any one person all of the gifts (ROMANS 12:3-8; 1 CORINTHIANS 12:7-11; 1 PETER 4:10). A Christian should have all of the fruit of the Spirit (GALATIANS 5:22, 23; 2 PETER 1:5-11).
3	The gifts enable us to perform a particular service or ministry (ROMANS 12:6-8; 1 PETER 4:10, 11). The fruit are devotional and ethical. They produce the likeness of Christ in us (GALATIANS 5:22, 23; 1 CORINTHIANS 13:4-7; 2 PETER 1:5-11).
4	The gifts have a vital place in the church until the kingdom of God fully comes (1 CORINTHIANS 13:8-13). The fruit are eternal (1 CORINTHIANS 13:8-13).
5	Spiritual gifts operate within the context of and express love (1 CORINTHIANS 13:1-13; 14:1). The fruit are broad. The fruit *love* expresses itself through various spiritual gifts (1 CORINTHIANS 13:1-13; 14:1).

TABLE 7-F **Guidelines for Using Spiritual Gifts**	
COLOSSIANS 2:5; 2 THESSALONIANS 1:3	Believers are to have faith, be open and be expectant.
1 CORINTHIANS 12:7; 1 PETER 4:10	Individuals are to use their spiritual gifts for the benefit of the Christian community.
1 CORINTHIANS 12:11; cf. 2:14; HEBREWS 5:14	The Christian community is to pray for the gift of discernment in order to distinguish between genuine and fraudulent exercise of the gifts. The godly use of a spiritual gift should meet the following criteria: • Does the gift exalt Jesus Christ? • Does the gift enlighten or encourage the Christian community? • Does the person who speaks or acts do so in love? • Is Jesus the Lord of the person's life through whom a gift operates? • Is the person willing to have mature Christians evaluate what has been said or done?
1 CORINTHIANS 12–14	We need to realize that our spiritual gifts will stretch us beyond our natural abilities and talents.
ROMANS 12:6-8	Our spiritual gifts often identify us with a particular type of service or ministry. We are to be willing for that ministry to change as God wills it to change.
1 CORINTHIANS 13	We are to use our spiritual gifts in a Christlike manner.
1 CORINTHIANS 14:1; cf. 12:7-11	We are to pray for the gifts that are needed in the work of the church, recognizing that God will distribute them as He desires.

CHAPTER 7—STUDY AND DISCUSSION

1. What is the difference between "the gift of the Spirit" and "gifts of the Spirit"? (See the Glossary.)

2. Where do spiritual gifts belong, in other words, where should they be used?

BASIC BIBLICAL TERMS FOR SPIRITUAL GIFTS

3. What are some terms the Bible uses to describe spiritual gifts? How are they used? (See Table 7-A.)

THE TRINITY AND THE GIFTS

4. What role does each Person of the Holy Trinity have in the giving and use of spiritual gifts? (See Table 7-B.)

THE NUMBER OF SPIRITUAL GIFTS

5. Since the Bible does not give a definitive list of spiritual gifts, what can we learn about the nature of spiritual gifts from those that are listed? (See Table 7-C.)

6. Who receives spiritual gifts? (See 1 Corinthians 12:7; Table 7-C.)

7. Name some of the spiritual gifts. (See Table 7-C.)

8. Think of a spiritual gift God has given you.

9. Think of ways you may have used this gift in the past, and how you can use this gift in the future to demonstrate your love for God and others.

POSSESSION OF SPIRITUAL GIFTS

10. Which of the following is a more Biblically accurate statement concerning receiving spiritual gifts? (See 1 Corinthians 12:7; Table 7-C.)

- Individuals in the body of Christ (the universal church) receive spiritual gifts for use in their local Christian communities (their local churches) and in their lives.

- The local Christian community (the local church) receives spiritual gifts, but individuals do not receive them.

11. How are spiritual gifts distributed? (See 1 Corinthians 12:11.)

SPIRITUAL GIFTS AND THE CHURCH

12. How does God use spiritual gifts to create purpose and unity in the body of Christ? (See 1 Corinthians 12:4-7; Romans 12:3-8; Table 7-D.)

13. What are some characteristics of the proper use of, or operation of, spiritual gifts in the local church? (See Table 7-D.)

SPIRITUAL GIFTS AND THE FRUIT OF THE SPIRIT

14. Read the entries for "spiritual gifts" and "spiritual fruit" in the Glossary, and give a short definition for each.

15. According to the apostle Paul, which spiritual fruit is the necessary context in which all spiritual gifts operate? (See 1 Corinthians 13.)

16. What are some similarities between spiritual gifts and spiritual fruit? (See Table 7-E.)

17. What are some differences between spiritual gifts and spiritual fruit? (See Table 7-E.)

THE CONTINUATION OF SPIRITUAL GIFTS

18. Which works of the Spirit are eternal and which are for use only until God's kingdom is fully come? (See Table 7-E.)

19. Discuss some spiritual concepts that, when followed, help the Christian community use spiritual gifts as God intends. (See Table 7-F.)

20. This week:

    • Pray for God to help you use your spiritual gifts in service for Him.

    • Encourage other believers in the use of their spiritual gifts.

Remember your leaders who first taught you the word of God. Think of all the good that has come from their lives, and trust the Lord as they do. Jesus Christ is the same yesterday, today, and forever (Hebrews 13:7, 8, *NLT*).

8

Gifts of Leadership

Within the body of Christ exists a rich variety of spiritual gifts. They can be defined as special endowments given to individuals for ministry and service in the church. Paul, however, offers no definition of the various gifts. Apparently, he assumed that his reader has gained an understanding of their nature from previous instruction and from observing the gifts at work. There is one exception—1 Corinthians 14, where Paul explains in detail the nature of prophecy and tongues. His primary purpose is not to define the nature of these two gifts, but to correct the Corinthians' understanding and use of them.

To restrain the misguided zeal of the Corinthian believers for the gifts of prophecy and tongues, Paul emphasizes the diversity of gifts by listing representative examples (1 Corinthians 12:8-10, 28-30). He also identifies common characteristics that unite them. In 1 Corinthians 12:1-7, he gives five common characteristics:

1. All the gifts are the works of God (v. 6).

2. All the gifts are opportunities for serving the Lord (v. 5).

3. All the gifts are manifestations of the Spirit (v. 7).

4. All the gifts are for the common good of the church (v. 7).

5. All the gifts are given by the Holy Spirit (v. 4).

Basic to Paul's whole discussion is that the gifts are events in which the Spirit makes manifest, or demonstrates, His presence and power. Spiritual gifts make the Spirit's work relatively clear, and at times they are extraordinary manifestations of His power. Natural talents and abilities of people are developed and honed in this world, but spiritual gifts are events in which the Spirit moves and makes His works visible.

We will now discuss briefly spiritual gifts in the context of Paul's thought, their relation to church offices, and their classification and order before dealing with the individual gifts.

SPIRITUAL GIFTS IN THE CONTEXT OF PAUL'S THOUGHT

A strong link exists between all gifts of the Spirit and the body of Christ, the church. To illustrate this point, Paul uses the human body to represent the church. For him, spiritual gifts are a significant aspect of the church. They are integral and fit together harmoniously with the life and work of the church, similar to the way various parts of the human body work together for the entire body to function. Each member of the church has a spiritual gift and a task to do for the benefit of the church. The church and the gifts are deeply interrelated to one another.[1] It comes as no surprise that in the three passages where Paul discusses the gifts of the Spirit, he speaks of the church as "the body of Christ." But it is striking how Paul develops the relationship between the church and spiritual gifts, emphasizing the need for unity and diversity in the community of believers. Now

---

[1] In Paul's understanding, there exists a profound harmony and correspondence between the church and inner nature of the ministry. Because the church has many members and each has a spiritual gift, all may take part in ministry. It means, therefore, that the church, gifts of the Spirit and ministry are deeply connected and that Paul has a unified view of the church, gifts and ministry.

we analyze briefly what Paul says to the Corinthian, Roman and Ephesian believers.

1 Corinthians 12–14

The believers in Corinth were more interested in the gifts that were more spectacular in their manifestation. Paul gives them pastoral advice on how to properly exercise spiritual gifts. He observes that all who affirm that Jesus is Lord do so by the Holy Spirit (12:3), and that the gifts of the Spirit are not limited to an inner circle of believers (vv. 7, 11), who likely thought of themselves as the "spiritual ones." The Spirit has made the believers one body, and all of them have been made to drink of the same Spirit (vv. 12-31). Comparing the church to the human body allows Paul to insist on the need of diversity in the church as well as unity. The various parts of the physical body—foot, ear, eye and hand—are indispensable. Even the weaker, less honorable and less presentable parts may receive special honor (vv. 22-24). God is able to give greater honor to the seemingly inferior parts.

Some of the Corinthians wanted to downplay certain spiritual gifts, including the leadership gifts. But Paul gives priority to them by pointing out that God set in the church first apostles, second prophets and third teachers (12:28). In the same breath, he lists *charismata* such as "helps" and "administrations" with the gifts that are more dramatic manifestations of the Spirit. What appears as ordinary services—helps and administrations—performed in the body of Christ as God's work are demonstrations of the Spirit. They are not striking acts like some of the gifts. But though such gifts may be thought of as "weak" and "less honorable" services, they demonstrate the Spirit's works and indeed are to be placed beside the other *charismata* as God's work. The implication of Paul's comments is that when each member of the church uses his or her spiritual gift, the whole body functions normally. All the gifts are needed. None of them are to be looked down upon, despised or suppressed. Every

Spirit-given part, even the weaker and less acknowledged ones, are indispensable.

Romans 12

The main point is that there is to be both unity and diversity in the one body. Using the human body as an illustration, Paul places the emphasis on the need of believers to understand the role of each person as contributing to the entire community of faith (v. 3). Among the believers at Rome were those who thought of themselves as superior to others. A corrective to this attitude was a shift in thinking that required the believers to recognize the limits and functions of their spiritual gifts. They needed to recognize that their ability to use the gifts was an expression of God's grace (*charis*, v. 6). Differences among them were not due to their own efforts in using natural abilities, but to God's gifts. No matter what gifts a person had received, all of them were essential to the life of the church. All gifts were to minister within the community of faith, whether during worship (by prophesying, teaching, serving or encouraging) or in different circumstances through helping others (by giving, providing care or showing mercy).

The gifts are necessary for the proper working of the body. God has given a gift to each believer (cf. "every man" and "to each," v. 3). The sensible estimation of one's gifts will not result in a person's being arrogant toward others, but rather will inspire an attitude of humility and service. Paul stated that the members of the body had nothing that they had not been given (1 Corinthians 4:7). The gifts that they had received equipped them for the roles of teaching, serving and leadership, as well as prophesying. They had a good mix of gifts, all for the purpose of caring for and promoting the total health of the body of Christ.

Ephesians 4

We find again the emphasis that each believer is part of the one body of Christ, and each has received an appropriate spiritual gift.

As Paul frequently does, he moves from the thought of unity to diversity within unity (vv. 3-7). He states that the foundation and the source of everything is the "one God and Father of all" (v. 6). Then Paul shifts his focus: "To each one of us grace was given" (v. 7). Rather than the saving grace of 2:8, this grace is revealed through the gifts of Christ (cf. Romans 12:3-6). The word for *gifts* in Ephesians 4:8 is *domata*, meaning essentially the same as *charismata* (grace gifts), which is used in Romans 12:6 and 1 Corinthians 12:4. Such gifts the members of Christ's body have (1 Corinthians 12:8-10; Romans 12:6-8). These spiritual gifts are in fact given to the church by the exalted Christ in heaven. Because Christ baptizes believers in the Holy Spirit (Acts 2:33-36), it stands to reason that He also is the One who bestows gifts of the Spirit on them.

To illustrate his point of Christ as the dispenser of the gifts (Ephesians 4:8), Paul appeals to Psalm 68:18. This Old Testament passage enables him to picture the conquering Christ as ascending to the throne of God and endowing the church with grace-gifts. From His exalted position as Lord of the universe, Christ bestows gifts upon the church. Then Paul shifts from discussing "each one" as the recipients of gifts, to stating that spiritually gifted persons are themselves gifts to the body of Christ (cf. 1 Corinthians 12:28). The emphasis, therefore, falls on the roles they have as gifted ministers. Paul identifies them as apostles, prophets, evangelists, pastors and teachers. Their function in the church is "the equipping of the saints" to participate in building up and serving the body of Christ (Ephesians 4:12). Those who serve in these capacities exercise teaching and leadership gifts. Their ministry agrees with Romans 12 and the ranking of church leaders in 1 Corinthians 12:28. As gifted people, those in leadership are to serve in such a way that they enable others to participate in the ministry of the church.[2] As they fulfill their mission by equipping the saints for the work of ministry, the result is

---

[2]Gordon D. Fee, *God's Empowering Presence*, 708.

"the proper working of each individual part, [that] causes the growth of the body for the building up of itself in love" (Ephesians 4:16).

God has established different leadership ministries, all of which are to equip the entire congregation to serve Christ and to promote the spiritual health of the body of believers. So everyone is to be involved in the ministry of edification. A Spirit-gifted church does not look merely to the pastor or to a few to minister to Christ's body. Every believer is expected to be involved in service and ministry through the use of his or her spiritual gifts.

SPIRITUAL GIFTS AND CHURCH OFFICES

As has become clear, every believer has been given a gift of the Spirit. The gifts of the Spirit are not limited to the leaders or office-holders of the church. All believers are gifted and are to take part in the ministry. Therefore, are gifts a matter of function or office? When we consider the list of gifts in 1 Corinthians 12:8-10, we see that a variety of functions exist in the church. In the second list in the same chapter, the first three gifts—apostles, prophets and teachers—are church offices, and the rest in the list are functions (vv. 28-30). The list in Romans 12 emphasizes functions, not offices. Paul speaks of Christians who have different functions in the body of Christ—functions that correspond to the gifts given to them. The various gifts enable believers to perform diverse functions in the church. As Paul says, "We have many members in one body and all the members do not have the same function [*praxis*]" (v. 4). In Romans, Paul identifies the gifts by listing the functions (vv. 6-8). The last list, which appears in Ephesians 4, enumerates gifted people as the gifts of the exalted Lord. Again the emphasis falls on the idea of the harmonious functioning among the members of Christ's body. The gifted people—apostles, prophets, and so forth—are seen as exercising functions, rather than being holders of offices.

In view of this understanding of spiritual gifts, the emphasis seems to be on functions such as prophesying, healing, helping, giving and caring (Romans 12:8; 1 Corinthians 12:28). Despite this emphasis, the New Testament suggests no opposition to the church's participating in Spirit-led ministry and, at the same time, having church offices and institutional leadership. In his letters, Paul does not define church polity and government as such, but it is clear that he saw charismatic functions and church offices as compatible. He himself appointed elders in the churches of Galatia (Acts 14:23). In his writings, Paul indicates that in the church in Philippi there were overseers (bishops) and deacons (Philippians 1:1).

The evidence is clear that there were church officers in Paul's day. How else should we understand the terms *apostles, prophets, teachers, evangelists* and *pastors* (1 Corinthians 12:28; Ephesians 4:11)? These kinds of ministries probably were the result of the Spirit's regularly prompting individuals to perform some kind of service. Over time, the functions became recognized by the church as established or official ministries.

It seems that Paul is more concerned about function than office, however. For example, he is more interested in the function of prophecy or teaching in the church than in the position of the prophet or the teacher. The Biblical scholar Anthony Palma sums it up very well when he observes:

> One group of ministries was not bound necessarily and permanently to an officeholder, while other ministries were exercised only as a specific function for an actual situation. But even when officebearers are mentioned, the emphasis is not so much on their ecclesiastical office as it is on the variety of functions, activities, and ministries in the church.[3]

Spiritual gifts in and of themselves are not church offices, but they should not be seen to oppose church offices or organization.

---

[3] Anthony D. Palma, *The Holy Spirit*, 204.

Paul saw his ministry as being that of an apostle and the ministry of others as being Spirit-given and Spirit-empowered (1 Corinthians 12:28). In his discussion of spiritual gifts, Paul's intent is not to define church offices, but to show that different functions are vital to the ministry of the church. His references to gifts such as administrations and leadership indicate that in the early church there were gifted believers who had special authority and positions of trust. A Biblical understanding, therefore, of spiritual gifts is that they enable us and make us competent to serve Jesus Christ.

Paul uses terms for the gifts in a broad sense, without carefully giving specific meanings for each individual gift. For this reason some matters must be left open, but one thing is clear from Paul's letters: All the members of the church were potentially "at the same time priests or officeholders, that is, instruments of the Spirit for the enactment of the Gospel in the everyday world."[4] In the churches, as in the society at large, there emerged those who were duly recognized as leaders (Acts 14:23; Philippians 1:1; 1 Timothy 3:1-13; Titus 1:5-9). The church in Corinth may appear to have been an exception. Paul urged the whole congregation to take action in dealing with the confusion and chaos in that church. It appears that the church might not have had official leaders, since no appeal is made to them for action. This lack of appeal, however, could just as well indicate that Corinth had ineffective leaders; and furthermore, that the Holy Spirit provided the basic leadership when the church gathered for worship. Obviously, the churches of Paul's day had leaders, but the emphasis is more on what they did in serving the church than on their office or title.

In conclusion, Paul sees the ministries of the church primarily as functions, though the concept of office appears in his letters. The New Testament makes it clear that the Holy Spirit can carry out His sovereign work through any believer and that some are called and

---

[4]Ernst Käsemann, *New Testament Questions of Today* (Philadelphia: Fortress, 1969) 246.

equipped for leadership functions. Hence, the gifts of the Spirit must not be seen as limited in any way to the official leaders of the church. Yet the institutional church, marked by its offices, polity and programs could not and still cannot fulfill its mission without the Spirit's power and gifts. The whole body of Christ needs the anointing and endowments of the Spirit for its own benefit and for the benefit of the world.

ORDER AND CLASSIFICATION OF SPIRITUAL GIFTS

Order

Can we attach any significance to the order in which the gifts appear? When the lists in 1 Corinthians 12, Romans 12 and Ephesians 4 are examined, it becomes clear that the specific gifts listed vary, and the order in which they are listed also differs. Apparently, Paul attached no importance to the order in which he listed them. The only possible exception to this is apostles, prophets and teachers, whom he ranks as first, second and third in 1 Corinthians 12:28. They may enjoy some priority in the church, especially the apostles and prophets, because they were special agents of divine revelation (Ephesians 3:5) and were foundation gifts to the church (2:20). A comparison of the two lists in 1 Corinthians 12 reveals that the order of "miracles" and the "gifts of healing" are reversed (vv. 8-10, 28-30). As the lists reveal, the order is fluid and may be due to the circumstances in the particular church.

Note, however, that Paul wrote, "But earnestly desire the greater gifts" (1 Corinthians 12:31). This admonition suggests that some gifts may rank higher than others. What the "greater gifts" are, Paul does not tell us; but they may be the ones the congregation needs most and that excel in blessing the church. In Corinth, such gifts could have included prophecy (1 Corinthians 14:1). But it is certain that Paul lacks interest in ranking gifts. In the second list in 1 Corinthians 12:28, he fails to include some items that are in the first list (vv. 8-10). His concern is to stress the wide range of gifts rather than giving them value in a descending order. The Christian community is to desire all the spiritual gifts. Whether greater or lesser, they are gifts of the Holy Spirit; and we need every gift that the Spirit will give us.

In 1 Corinthians 12:8-10 and 28-30, tongues and interpretation stand last in the lists of gifts. Does the order indicate that tongues are the least of the gifts and that the other gifts should be sought rather than those on the bottom? That is not likely Paul's intent. Some of the problems in Corinth centered around the excessive exercise of tongues in worship. He gives the Corinthians some guidance in the matter, but not before he addresses the need for variety in worship. The call of 1 Corinthians 12 is for diversity, using the human body as an illustration.

Later, all of 1 Corinthians 14 is devoted to the gifts of prophecy, discerning of spirits, tongues and their interpretation. An author may list the broad items of a subject and then limit the discussion to a few of the items. So often he will elaborate on the items listed last. Paul lists nine gifts of the Spirit (12:8-10), then he goes on to discuss the last four—prophecy, discerning of spirits, tongues and interpretation of tongues—at some length in chapter 14.

Classification

Now it is time to turn our attention to the classification of spiritual gifts. When we compare the lists of the *charismata* in Paul's letters, it becomes clear that no two of them are alike. No doubt, they are representative of the diversity of the Spirit's manifestations and tailored to the respective church that Paul addresses. Systematizing the gifts and establishing categories for them can be difficult, if not almost impossible. Attempts to classify them are many and varied. An easy and convenient way of grouping them is as follows:

- Gifts for the leadership of the church
  apostles, prophets, evangelists, pastors, teachers, those in administration, those who lead

- Gifts of instruction
  wisdom, knowledge
- Gifts of inspired speech
  prophecy, discernings of spirits, tongues, interpretation
- Gifts of power
  faith, healings, miracles
- Gifts for practical service
  giving, helps, service, mercy, exhortation

No grouping of the various gifts may be completely satisfactory. A number of them overlap with others. Rigid distinctions should be avoided in classifying the gifts. For example, the gift of exhortation overlaps with prophecy and functions within that gift (1 Corinthians 14:3, 31). Another example is the "word of wisdom" and the "word of knowledge." They are different, distinct gifts that both overlap with the gifts of prophecy and teaching. Moreover, the apostles, prophets and evangelists are mentioned separately in Ephesians 4:11, but pastors and teachers are so closely linked together by the Greek (only one definite article for both) that they may refer to the same persons. Furthermore, the gift of helping (1 Corinthians 12:28) has much in common with the gifts of serving, giving and showing mercy (Romans 12:7, 8). The gifts may be grouped under five major headings:

- Leadership
- Practical Service
- Power
- Revelation
- Worship

I propose this division of the gifts for convenience and greater ease in discussing the great diversity of the manifestations of the Spirit.

GIFTS OF LEADERSHIP

A thread running throughout Paul's discussion of the *charismata* is the building up of the church and each individual member of it. The whole range of gifts plays a significant role toward this end, but a striking feature of the list in 1 Corinthians 12:28-30 is that Paul mentions persons (apostles, prophets and teachers) and ranks them. There can be little doubt that those who served in these three ministries had a special role in the establishing and strengthening of the body of Christ. Because of this role, they enjoyed a measure of importance and authority over the other gifts. Even so, the emphasis is more on function of gifts than position and status of persons. Probably the best way to understand their positions and functions is to see them as the result of spiritual gifts. God has given, and still gives, gifted spiritual leaders for the edification of the church.

Apostles

As gifted leaders of the church, apostles stand first in two of the lists of spiritual gifts. The word *apostle* (*apostolos*) literally means "the sent one," and refers to any messenger appointed and sent on a special mission. The term was used to describe Christ (Hebrews 3:1), the 12 disciples (Matthew 10:2), Paul (Romans 1:1; 2 Corinthians 1:1; Galatians 1:1), and others (Acts 14:4, 14; Romans 16:7; Galatians 1:19; 1 Thessalonians 2:6, 7). In a broad sense, *apostle* referred to messengers or delegates sent out by churches. The congregation in Philippi had sent Epaproditus as their apostle, or "messenger" (Philippians 2:25). Paul designated individuals that he sent to Corinth as "messengers [literally, apostles] of the churches" (2 Corinthians 8:23). These people had been personally appointed by the churches as delegates to assist Paul in carrying the offering to the poor Christians in Jerusalem. So the general meaning of *apostles* in the New Testament included people who had been commissioned and sent by local churches as missionaries, or sent with other special responsibilities (Acts 14:4, 14; Romans 16:7). They were believers whom God used in a powerful and effective way. As a result, they demonstrated remarkable spiritual leadership. They were anointed by the Spirit to confront directly the powers of Satan and darkness, and to confirm the gospel with mighty signs and wonders. They were also dedicated to establishing churches. They traveled extensively, preaching Jesus as Lord and risking their lives for the sake of His name (Acts 11:21-26; 13:50; 14:19-22; 15:25, 26). They were Spirit-filled people of faith and of prayer, and were committed to apostolic truth and purity (11:23, 24; 13:2-5; 14:1-7).

In the New Testament, the word *apostle* is also used with a more restricted meaning. The Twelve are designated as apostles in a special sense (Luke 9:10). They were given authority and commissioned by Jesus to proclaim the presence of God's kingdom and to cast out demons and to heal the sick (vv. 1, 2). The Twelve served as representatives of Jesus, a function shared by others (10:1, 17).[5] Their designation as apostles, therefore, refers to their function rather than their status. They were chosen from a larger group of disciples (6:12-16). By the end of Jesus' earthly ministry, the Twelve formed a special group (cf. 1 Corinthians 15:5). God gave them charismatic gifts, and they were recognized as having special ministry and a place of leadership (Acts 1:20, 25, 26).

A major task of the Twelve was the preaching of the Word of God, accompanied by signs and wonders. At the center of their preaching was their telling about Jesus' resurrection (v. 22). As the Book of Acts makes clear, after the tragic end of Judas, the replacement for him had to meet two requirements: (1) the man must have been a traveling companion of Jesus throughout His earthly ministry, and (2) he must have seen Jesus after His resurrection, the essential qualification (vv. 21, 22). Matthias became the replacement for Judas, but after that no one replaced any of the Twelve as

---

[5]The 70 missionaries had the same authority, power and commission given to them by Jesus (Luke 10:1-12). At that time charismatic authority and ministry were not limited to the Twelve.

they passed away because of martyrdom and natural death. They were, therefore, a limited group and had a special ministry in preaching, teaching and establishing churches, as well as baptizing converts and proclaiming Christ's resurrection. They had a vital role in laying the foundation of the Christian church (Luke 9:1, 2; Mark 3:14, 15; Acts 8:14, 15; 15:2ff.).

Paul uses the word *apostle* in the broad sense of messenger or representative (Romans 16:7; 2 Corinthians 8:23; Philippians 2:23-25). His broad use of the word made it possible for him to speak of false apostles, who disguised themselves as apostles of Christ and servants of righteousness but who, in reality, were agents of Satan (2 Corinthians 11:12-15). However, Paul usually uses *apostle* in a more restricted sense to refer to the witnesses who had seen the risen Lord and were commissioned by Him (Galatians 1:17-19). This group included more than the Twelve. Among them were James the Lord's brother (Acts 15:13-21), Paul himself (Acts 9:1ff.; 1 Corinthians 9:1), and others.

Paul never identified himself as one of the Twelve, but he insisted that he was an apostle. Supporting Paul's apostleship was the fact that like the original apostles, he had received a direct, divine calling and had seen the risen Lord. But there were other indicators that he was an apostle: (1) his success in preaching the good news of God's saving love, (2) his founding of churches, and (3) the signs and wonders that verified his ministry (Romans 15:18, 19; 2 Corinthians 12:11, 12).

In a restrictive sense, apostles were those who had an unrepeatable ministry. That is, they engaged in a type of Christian service that was unique to their time in history (Ephesians 2:20; 3:4, 5). One of the tasks of those apostles (thought to be the Twelve and Paul) was to lay the spiritual foundation of the churches. Portions of the apostles' ministry, such as telling the good news of Christ and guiding believers, have expanded over time and have continued until today. This broader aspect of apostolic ministries is not limited by time, nor is there a special requirement, such as having witnessed the resurrection of

Christ, in order to engage in such ministries. Since the ministry of an apostle is not limited to a specific time, Paul affirms that God has appointed apostles in the churches (1 Corinthians 12:28). Using the same kind of language, he makes the comparison that God has placed members such as the foot, hand and eye in the human body. As these members are necessary for the proper functioning of the physical body, so the gift of apostle and the other gifts remain vital to the proper function of the body of Christ (vv. 15-18). The dynamic, spiritual nature of the church demands a Spirit-guided, charismatic ministry if the church is to function as it should.

God set in the church apostles, prophets and teachers (1 Corinthians 12:28). These leaders and others received Spirit-given authority. Probably the most distinctive feature of the apostles is that they traveled—preaching, establishing churches and building up the body of Christ. Their ministry was not just to the local church, but also to the church-at-large. In this broad sense, the ministry of the apostles continues today, especially the aspects of itinerant preaching and the establishing of churches. God still equips people for apostolic ministry. As Bible scholar Arnold Bittlinger says, "The New Testament nowhere suggests that the apostolic ministry was intended only for first-generation Christians. On the contrary, we constantly encounter people in church history whom we designate as apostles."[6]

The original apostles laid the foundation of the church, and we rely on their message as the Word of God. In that regard, their ministry was unique, and they have no successors. Yet, the apostolic ministry has continued throughout the history of the church and is still needed as much as ever. The apostles evangelized, planted churches, built up the churches in the faith, and organized them with elders and deacons. These kinds of spiritual leaders are called for today. The church needs people who are spiritually equipped and committed to doing the work of an apostle.

---

[6]Arnold Bittlinger, *Gifts and Ministries* (Grand Rapids: Eerdmans, 1973) 77.

Prophets

In the New Testament churches, a prophet (*prophētēs*) had an important Spirit-anointed ministry. Paul listed them as second only to apostles (1 Corinthians 12:28). They appear in the major lists of the gifts of the Spirit (1 Corinthians 12:8-10, 28-30; Romans 12:6-8; Ephesians 4:16). Like the word *apostle,* the term *prophētēs* is used in both a broad and a narrow sense. When used broadly, it refers to any believer whom the Spirit has moved to prophesy. Acts 2 illustrates the breadth of prophecy. On the occasion of the outpouring of the Spirit, Peter understood that the disciples' speaking in tongues fulfilled Joel's promise: "Your sons and daughters will prophesy" (v. 17, *NIV*). The manifestation was, therefore, a form of prophetic speech.

On the other hand, in the narrow meaning the term *prophet* refers to a distinct group in the church. For the most part, this is the way Paul appears to use it. The gift of prophecy can be given to any believer, indicated by Paul when he says, "You can all prophesy one by one"[7] (1 Corinthians 14:31; cf. vv. 1, 5, 39). Since believers are indwelt by the Holy Spirit, none of them are excluded from the possibility of prophesying. They all are potential prophets, but God does not bestow any one gift on all believers (1 Corinthians 12:14-30). Only some people receive this gift in the body of Christ. The anticipated answer to the question of verse 29, "All are not prophets, are they?" is "No." This observation underscores the fact that no single gift can be exercised by all.

Apparently those who were called prophets were individuals who frequently gave prophecies. Paul's letters indicate that prophets were present in the local Christian communities. In contrast to the apostles, many prophets appear to have served in the

---

[7]Paul may have had in mind only the prophets, especially since he offers guidelines for prophetic utterances (1 Corinthians 14:29-33).

local areas where they resided, such as Antioch of Syria (Acts 13:1) and Caesarea of Judea (21:9). There are also indications that some prophets did move about and had an itinerant ministry (Matthew 10:41; 23:34; Acts 11:27, 28; 21:10). Paul recognized that in Corinth prophets were active participants in the church's worship (1 Corinthians 14:29-32). There and elsewhere, prophets were members of a local congregation. Their prophetic gift gave them recognition as spiritual leaders.

A characteristic of prophets is that they spontaneously speak divinely given revelation (*apocalypsis*). What they declare is a Spirit-inspired message for a situation or occasion. It is a message from the Lord, revealed directly to the prophet by the Holy Spirit and proclaimed spontaneously by him or her for the enlightenment or encouragement of the church. The message given to the prophet directly by the Spirit may come in a thought, vision or dream. The prophet may receive the message of revelation during worship (1 Corinthians 14:30). This person may feel compelled to speak; but if he or she does, this prophet must be sufficiently aware of what is going on, so that the message may be effectively communicated and brought to a timely conclusion. The prophet is to be in control of his or her speech and behavior so that when another prophet receives a fresh truth, that person will have opportunity to speak. Though inspired by the Spirit, the prophet can stop speaking if there is a need for silence. No one has a monopoly on the gift of prophecy. Another prophet may also receive a revelation.

In the New Testament, the prophets addressed a wide range of situations and concerns. Some prophets predicted the future. The prophet Agabus gave an inspired prediction of a famine that was to extend over the Roman world (Acts 11:28, 29). His prophetic words inspired the Christians at Antioch to send money to the mother church in Jerusalem to aid in the coming crisis. As Paul made his way to Jerusalem for the final time, the Spirit used prophets in several cities to warn him of imprisonment and hardships that would befall him (20:23). Later, Agabus confirmed the personal fate of Paul and announced that the Jews would hand Paul over to the Gentiles (21:10, 11).

In addition to predicting the future, a prophet may offer a message as a solution to disputes or as specific guidance and assurance regarding particular circumstances. Judas and Silas, both described as prophets, must have had a strong influence on the leaders of the Jerusalem church by addressing the question of whether circumcision should be required for admission into the Christian church (Acts 15:28, 32). At times prophets gave direction to churches in choosing people for a special work. The Holy Spirit directed the church in Antioch to "set apart for Me Barnabas and Saul for the work to which I have called them" (13:2). This message apparently was communicated by one or more of the prophets. Prophecy may have a predictive element, but its primary function is to help believers in their Christian walk. The major passage on prophecy (1 Corinthians 14) does not refer to the predictive element at all.

Each of the examples above show that the Holy Spirit reveals particular knowledge through His prophets. The prophets, therefore, receive supernatural insight and speak inspired messages that apply directly to the situation. In 1 Corinthians 14:24, 25, Paul mentioned an unbeliever who was present in the worship of the church. Through a word of prophecy, the secrets of the unbeliever's heart were revealed. Because of the personal information disclosed about him, the unbeliever was convinced that only God could have revealed it, and fell on his face worshiping God. The experience of the Samaritan woman is another example (John 4:16ff.). Jesus disclosed a startling revelation about her marital status. She could not deny that it was true; she responded, "Sir, I perceive that You are a prophet."

Because prophecy communicates divine revelation and may include certain facts that expose a person's spiritual condition, it may be an instrument of conversion. However, this does not seem to be the primary purpose for prophecy (1 Corinthians 14:3). First and foremost, the audience of the prophet are usually believers. Today, many spiritually-minded believers seek God's guidance on matters that may not be specifically addressed in the Bible or for which no course of action is immediately clear. They pray to receive a direct communication—a "word from the Lord"—on the matter. When such an encounter is experienced, we have the dynamics of what the New Testament calls "prophecy." The Holy Spirit gives a direct, inspired message to an individual, and a prophet tells it to those for whom God intends it. The Spirit speaks directly and spontaneously to God's people through His prophets. This kind of prophetic breaking-in by the Holy Spirit has a significant place in Pentecostal and Charismatic worship services, but prophecy must not be confused with preaching.

A prophetic message given in the local assembly of believers should not be identified with what we call a sermon. The sermon is prepared through the conventional means of study and prayer, but the substance of a prophecy is based on revelation from the Lord and the result of the immediate inspiration of the Holy Spirit. From time to time, we hear that preaching is the same as prophecy. This view fails to find support in the Scriptures. In 1 Corinthians 14, Paul gives an extended treatment of the gift of prophecy. In that passage, he does not use the common words for preaching such as *proclaim* (*kērussō*), *announce* (*angellō*) or *to preach good news* (*euangelizomai*). The absence of these terms implies that Paul does not see preaching and prophecy as the same.

Preaching involves *proclamation* (*kērugma*). The mighty saving work of Christ is proclaimed, and people are assured of what will be done for those who hear and receive the "good news." The message may be for unbelievers or believers. On the other hand, prophecy is the declaration of a message that is received directly from the Holy Spirit. It is primarily for God's people and frequently is concerned with special needs or a crisis. A pastor may prepare to preach with a keen sense of dependence on the Holy Spirit, and may preach under the anointing of the Spirit. The message of the preacher is based on consideration of the Scriptures and is not the same as a message directly from God. Nevertheless, the prophetic gift may operate through preaching, song, testimony, teaching or prayer when the speaker is inspired by the Holy Spirit to declare a fresh word from the Lord.

The gift of prophecy is not intended to replace preaching or to be considered the same as preaching. Prophecy and preaching make distinct and vital contributions to the life of God's people. Spirit-anointed worship allows for preaching *and* for the Spirit to speak directly to God's people through a godly prophet. The gift of prophecy, therefore, is important, yet preaching receives priority. Christ sent the apostles to preach the gospel. Because of the association of preaching with the apostles, preaching is given priority over the other gifts (1 Corinthians 12:28). Preaching of the gospel brings sinners to salvation, may offer guidance to believers, and has the place of honor.[8] Prophecy speaks to a wide range of needs among God's people in the congregation. Consequently, only in a secondary way does prophecy function to convict unbelievers and outsiders of their wrongdoings and need for God. Prophecy may be instrumental in the conversion of unbelievers; yet the primary function of the prophet is to speak to the needs of the congregation.

Prophecy must have been one of the "greater gifts," that Paul urged the Corinthians to seek earnestly (1 Corinthians 12:31; cf. 14:1, 39). Such gifts are greater because of their ability to build up the church. As 1 Corinthians 14 makes clear, the gift of prophecy accomplishes that goal more than tongues unaccompanied by interpretation. Moreover, the significance of the prophetic gift is indicated by the close association of prophets with apostles on a number of

---

[8]Anthony D. Palma, *The Holy Spirit*, 210-11.

occasions. This gift's importance is further affirmed by its appearance in each list of the gifts (Romans 12:6-8; 1 Corinthians 12:8-10, 28-30; Ephesians 4:11). Should an attempt be made to rank the gifts of the Spirit, we would not be in error to consider prophecy as one of the most important.

Teachers

Among the gifts of the Spirit, Paul ranks teachers third, taking a lower place only to apostles and prophets (1 Corinthians 12:28). In the same breath, he mentions teachers with pastors in Ephesians 4:11. Teaching is also referred to as a gift in Romans 12:7. In the Pastoral Epistles, elders have the responsibility of teaching (1 Timothy 3:2). The elders "who labor in the word and doctrine" are singled out for special recognition (5:17, *NKJV*). Certain elders had the gift of teaching, which was necessary for correctly explaining the Word of Truth and instructing the flock in the faith. Paul indicated that he himself had the gift of teaching (1 Corinthians 4:17) and the gift of prophecy as well (14:6).

Teaching is recognized as a definite ministry in the church, and those who have this gift exercise leadership in the body of Christ (1 Thessalonians 5:12, 13; Galatians 6:6). Such people have a special God-given gift that enables them to explain, expound and proclaim the Word of God with power for the purpose of enlightening and building up the fellowship of believers (Ephesians 4:12). Endowed by the Spirit for the task of teaching, they are able to relate Scripture to the immediate needs of the congregation. This task requires them to hold on to the faithful Word so that they can give instruction in sound doctrine and offer an effective defense for their beliefs (Titus 1:9).

It is no simple matter to distinguish among the ministries of teachers, pastors and prophets. For example, pastors and teachers are understood to stand in a very close relationship in Ephesians 4:11.

295

Are they the same individuals? Biblical scholars are divided. If we assume that the terms *pastors* and *teachers* refer to the same persons, then the terms could be translated "teaching pastors." Such translation strongly indicates that pastors also normally have a teaching function. Even so, the evidence seems to be clear in the New Testament that teachers were a distinct group of ministers, though pastors and elders could function as teachers, giving their ministry a broader scope. Teachers are identified as a separate group in the church, as were apostles and prophets (Acts 13:1; 1 Corinthians 12:28). In the local Christian communities, there were those who regularly exercised the gift of teaching. These individuals, known as "teachers," were considered to be mature Christians. They based their instruction on the Old Testament and the teaching of the apostles, with an emphasis on God's mighty saving work in Christ. Gifted to instruct others, their ministry was to teach doctrine and explain the Word of God so that the people would be strengthened in their faith and grounded in the truth.

Furthermore, how should we understand teaching in relation to prophecy? Both teaching and prophecy are spiritual gifts, and both are ministries of God's Word. What distinguishes teaching and prophecy from each other is the way individuals exercise these gifts. In Biblical times, the prophet, upon receiving direct revelation, spoke as a result of the inspiration of the Holy Spirit. Normally, the prophet gave a specific message for a specific situation; whereas teachers related Scripture and doctrine to the immediate needs of the congregation. God revealed directly to the prophets their message, but the teachers derived their instruction through the study of Scripture. As it has been said, prophecy appeals more to the heart, while teaching appeals more to the understanding. But it would be inaccurate to see prophecy as Spirit-inspired and teaching as lacking the inspiration of the Spirit. Both are gifts of the Spirit. The teachers, as well as the prophets, need the direct inspiration of the Holy Spirit.

New issues and challenges are now facing the church. The world is constantly changing, and there are new human ideas and religious teachings that are contrary to the clear teaching of Scripture. The situation calls for godly teachers who accept the Spirit-inspired Word of God as the standard for faith and practice and who are gifted by the Holy Spirit to teach and guide the church. The Holy Spirit is the Great Teacher (John 14:26; 15:26; 16:13-15; 1 Corinthians 2:12), and He equips some of God's people with the gift of teaching so that they may defend the truth against error and may build up the church.

Pastors

The word for *pastor* literally means "shepherd" (*poimēn*). Pastoral language is used a number of times to describe Jesus Christ (Hebrews 13:20; 1 Peter 2:25). John 10 indicates that Jesus is the Good Shepherd who knows His sheep, leads them, cares for them, and even lays down His life for them (vv. 11-18). The life and ministry of Jesus is the supreme example for those who serve the church as pastors.

Only once, however, are church leaders spoken of as "pastors" in the New Testament (Ephesians 4:11). In this passage, they are listed as one of the spiritual gifts, and their ministry seems to be closely related to that of the teachers. The pastors mentioned in Ephesians functioned as shepherds of God's people, exercising the spiritual gift of pastors and thereby feeding the flock of God. The idea of leaders shepherding the sheep occurs in several passages. Jesus' command to Peter to feed His sheep (John 21:15-17) is similar to Paul's charge to the elders in Ephesus "to shepherd the church of God" (Acts 20:28; cf. 1 Peter 5:2). The feeding of the sheep refers to the pastor's nurture of the church through the teaching of God's Word, especially the teaching of sound doctrine and refuting false teachings (Titus 1:9-11).

In the early church, the ministry of the overseer (*episkopos*, bishop) and of the elder (*presbuteros*) corresponded with that of the pastor. They functioned as pastors, with the responsibility of caring for and having spiritual oversight of God's people. An elder (*presbuteros*) was a respected and likely older man in the congregation. The terms *elder* and *overseer* describe the same spiritual leaders, but one describes the person of the leader and the other the function.[9] In Miletus, Paul sent for the elders (*presbuteros*) of the church in Ephesus and reminded them that the Holy Spirit appointed them as overseers (*episkopos*) over the church of God (Acts 20:28). Their appointment as pastors is attributed directly to the Holy Spirit, meaning that He had given them spiritual gifts and equipped them to serve as shepherds. Leaders like those at Ephesus were qualified by the Holy Spirit to discharge their pastoral duties, which involved nurturing, encouraging, strengthening and training. As pastors, they were responsible for the general guidance, especially the preaching and teaching of the Word (1 Timothy 5:17; 2 Timothy 4:1-5).

From a Biblical perspective, pastors are not masters but servants of the church (Mark 10:42-45). They are gifted by the Holy Spirit to serve the people of God. Christ is the supreme model for the pastoral ministry.

Evangelists

The word for *evangelist* (Greek, *euangelistēs*) appears only three times in the New Testament (Acts 21:8; Ephesians 4:11; 2 Timothy 4:5). The literal meaning of the Greek term is "one who proclaims the gospel (good news)." The corresponding verb *euangelizomai* means "to evangelize by bringing good news to someone." As a

---

[9]From the New Testament, it is clear that the terms *elder* and *bishop* were used interchangeably and their ministry was confined to local churches. In time, however, the *bishop* became the supreme pastor of several churches and the *elder*s served as the bishop's assistants.

spiritual gift, we find *evangelist* only in Ephesians 4:11, where it is mentioned along with apostles, prophets, pastors and teachers. The other two places where the term *evangelist* occurs involve Philip and Timothy. After Philip was chosen as one of the seven to relieve the apostles from the task of the distribution of food, he became known as an "evangelist" (Acts 21:8). Paul urged Timothy to do the work of an "evangelist" (2 Timothy 4:5).

The number of evangelists perhaps exceeded what the sparing use of the name would suggest. Philip is a good model of an evangelist. He took the message of the gospel to the people in Samaria. In that city, he proclaimed Jesus Christ. Many of the Samaritans, observing great miracles that accompanied Philip's ministry, believed and were baptized (Acts 8:4ff.). From there, Philip was sent to share the gospel with a single individual, an Ethiopian, on the road from Jerusalem to Gaza (v. 26ff.). Later, he preached about God's saving love from Azotus to Caesarea (v. 40). Similar to Philip, the evangelists were itinerant preachers. Their ministry was not primarily to the churches, but to where the unbelievers were. So the evangelists were gifted to preach the gospel to the unsaved and to establish new churches, similar to the ministry of apostles.

In contrast to the pastors, whose ministry was primarily to explain the Word of God to believers, the evangelists' chief concern was the conversion of unbelievers to the gospel. Of course, this does not prohibit a pastor from preaching evangelistically (cf. 2 Timothy 4:5). All of God's people are to be witnesses, sharing their stories of personal encounters with God, but some have a special gift of evangelism. These people are particularly effective and inspirational in their telling of the story of God's love, moving others to commit their lives to Christ.

Those Who Lead

This gift ("he who leads") occurs in the list of Romans 12:6-8 and stands in the final grouping of three in the passage. The Greek verb *proistēmi* used in verse 8 means "to set before," "to set," "to manage" or "to lead," and points to those who give leadership in the church. For example, Paul speaks of those who "have charge over you in the Lord" (1 Thessalonians 5:12). He states in 1 Timothy that the overseer (elder) "must be one who manages his own household well" (1 Timothy 3:4). Still another example: "The elders who rule well are to be considered worthy of double honor" (1 Timothy 5:17). Thus, the term is definitely connected to the work of the elder.

The word *proistēmi* was not only used to describe leadership, but a second meaning was "to care for" or "to give aid." It is not necessary to choose one meaning and exclude the other. The two meanings are not mutually exclusive. In Romans 12:8, the phrase "he who leads" appears between "he who gives" and "he who shows mercy." Because of this, it seems best to think in terms of the giving of care and assistance as part of leadership. God has given leaders to the church. They are gifted by the Holy Spirit to care for various needs that individuals in the Christian community and others in the world might have. According to Paul, the gift of leadership is to be exercised "with diligence" (v. 8). Gifts of the Spirit are always to be works of love.

Administrations

The gift of administrations (*kubernēseis*, 1 Corinthians 12:28) has been described as the gift of direction or guidance. The word *administration* is used to describe a steerman or pilot of a ship, suggesting the idea of one who serves as a guide (cf. Acts 27:11; Revelation 18:17). The person who has this spiritual gift is enabled by the Holy Spirit to direct the congregation and to see that things are in good order and go well. Very likely the functions of administration foreshadow the ministry of the bishops, provided the term *bishop* is understood to be the same as *elder* or *pastor*. Equipped with the gift of administrations, a person can provide spiritual leadership, give wise counsel and manage the affairs of the congregation.

Helps

The word *helps* (*antilēmpseis*, 1 Corinthians 12:28) conveys the meaning of coming to the assistance of someone. In the plural, it is appropriately translated "helpful deeds" and is identified as one of the spiritual gifts. The Holy Spirit has endowed some individuals with a great capacity to be helpers. The precise scope of their ministry is not indicated, but apparently in New Testament times it was quite broad, including helping the weak, sharing of resources with others, serving the church, and doing deeds of kindness and mercy.

The ministry of helps must have had prominence in the work of the deacons (Philippians 1:1; 1 Timothy 3:8-13). The same holds true for the seven men who were chosen in Acts 6:3-6. They were equipped by the Spirit to devote themselves to the care of the widows. Indeed, their ministry was a charismatic ministry in which they exercised the gifts of helps to meet pressing needs in the community of believers.

CONCLUSION

Today, great confusion exists around the Biblical doctrine of spiritual gifts. The modern church is often crippled by a misunderstanding of the Spirit's gifts. Some church traditions implicitly, if not explicitly, deny the relevance of Paul's comments in Romans, 1 Corinthians and Ephesians on the gifts of the Spirit. When the model for the church is institutional rather than charismatic, there is a strong temptation to rely on ourselves, replacing reliance on the Spirit with our native abilities, education and personal skills. Without question, all of these have their place in the life and ministry of the church. None of them, however, are adequate replacements for gifts of the Spirit. Activities of the occult and other counterfeits of the divine flourish today. Never has there been a greater need for the breaking-in of God and the exercise of God's spiritual gifts. Now for a few specific observations.

The gifts of the Spirit enable and make us competent to serve Christ and the church. When spiritual gifts are seen as serving Christ, we understand their unifying nature. We understand that they are not individualistic and eccentric manifestations that disturb the unity of the body of Christ and create disorder, envy and rivalry. Selfish use of the gifts is contrary to God's intention. The proper exercise of the gifts is for the edification of the church. Without this emphasis, they lose their significance. The individual's gift is balanced with community responsibility and service. When there is this kind of proper balance, extremes are discouraged and the use of spiritual gifts contributes to the building of community.

Regardless of their gifts, believers are not to think too highly of themselves. Paul never implies that the special ministry of the apostles, prophets and teachers elevated them above others in the church (Romans 12:3-8; 1 Corinthians 12:25-28; Ephesians 4:11). Their gifts were for performing a definite ministry in the church.

At the Jerusalem Council, no special preeminence or supremacy was given to leaders. Judas and Silas, both prophets, were present, but they are only mentioned as the men who would accompany Paul and Barnabas back to Antioch with the official letter that announced the decision of the Council (Acts 15:22). The Book of Acts consistently portrays the character of church leadership as leadership that includes the sharing of authority among colleagues. An example of this shared authority is the leadership of Paul and Barnabas. Together they shared leadership with other prophets and teachers in the church in Antioch. The congregation recognized that

Paul and Barnabas had received a divine call. In a solemn service, they commissioned Paul and Barnabas as missionaries and committed them to the care of the Lord (13:1-4; cf. 1:13-26; 6:2ff.; 8:14ff.; 11:1ff.). These prophets and teachers continued to minister in the local church, while Paul and Barnabas traveled and ministered in other cities.

God has gifted certain individuals to serve as leaders in the church, but none of these individuals or any group in the church should think of themselves as superior to others. The ministry of apostle, prophet or teacher is not due to personal merit, but to gifts of the Spirit. Believers' opinions of themselves should not be based primarily on their natural abilities, but on what God has gifted them to do. God may have called a person to be a prophet or an evangelist, but never should that person be boastful or arrogant. All gifts and abilities come from God; they are not a result of merit or superiority.

In addition to being humble, Christians should be grateful and content with the spiritual gifts that God chooses to give them. I have known of believers who had a special gift for edifying the congregation, but they were unsatisfied with the gift they had received. A number of them wanted a gift of leadership that would give them a more public ministry, or a gift that has a dramatic manifestation. This attitude is unfortunate. Each gift is important, and every believer's gift should be affirmed. Inaccurate understanding of the ranking of gifts as in Corinth sometimes leads to an attitude of superiority and arrogance (1 Corinthians 12–14) on the part of an individual or congregation. There is no place for superiority complexes in the body of Christ. On the other hand, neither should there be inferiority complexes. According to Paul, no matter what a person's gift may be, that person is vital to the life of the church (12:12-31). Therefore the wise course of action is to exercise whatever gift the Spirit has given us. God will be glorified.

Summary

- All gifts and all believers are valuable and essential to the health and function of the body of Christ.

- God gives gifted spiritual leaders for the building up of the church.

- God's gifts of leadership include: apostles, prophets, teachers, pastors, evangelists, those who lead, administrations, and helps.

TABLE 8-A

Spiritual Gifts in the Context of Paul's Thought

1 Corinthians 12–14

Corinthian believers were too interested in the more spectacular gifts, so Paul gave them pastoral advice as to how to properly think of and exercise these gifts.

All who affirm that Jesus is Lord do so by the Holy Spirit (12:3).

The gifts of the Holy Spirit are for all believers (vv. 7-11).

As parts of Christ's body, we are all needed (vv. 22-24).

God is able to give honor to seemingly inferior parts. Although we may think of certain gifts as weak or less honorable, they demonstrate the Spirit's work and are valuable to the body of Christ (vv. 18-27).

First, God places apostles; secondly, prophets; and thirdly, teachers. Then, He gives gifts of helps, administrations, and so forth (vv. 28-30).

Romans 12

Paul emphasizes unity and diversity in the body of Christ.

Each person has received a gift, in order to contribute to the health and work of the entire community of faith (v. 3).

In the body of Christ, no individuals are dispensable; but all are necessary (vv. 3-5).

All individuals' gifts and abilities are results of God's grace (v. 6).

God has given a spiritual gift to each believer (v. 3).

---

continued

TABLE 8-A (CONTINUED)
Spiritual Gifts in the Context of Paul's Thought

Ephesians 4

Paul emphasizes that each believer is part of the one body of Christ, and each has received a spiritual gift. He moves from the thought of unity to diversity within unity.

The foundation and the source of everything is "one God and Father" (v. 6).

Jesus Christ gives grace, in the form of spiritual gifts, to each of us (vv. 7, 8; Psalm 68:18).

Each person is a gift of God to the body of Christ (vv. 11-13; 1 Corinthians 12:28).

God gives leaders so that the body of Christ is equipped for service. The proper use of leadership gifts in the church helps believers to mature and to use their God-given gifts to build up the body of Christ (vv. 12, 13).

Notes

TABLE 8-B
Spiritual Gifts and Church Offices

Every believer has been given a spiritual gift. The gifts of the Spirit are not limited to leaders or officeholders of the church.

Biblical Description	
1 CORINTHIANS 12:8-10	Spiritual gifts are listed by *function*.
1 CORINTHIANS 12:28-30	Spiritual gifts are listed by *office and function*.
ROMANS 12:6-8	Spiritual gifts are listed by *function*.
EPHESIANS 4:11	Spiritual gifts are described as being *people*, who are gifts of God.

Diversity	
ROMANS 12:4-8	The various gifts enable believers to perform diverse functions in the church.

Compatibility	
ACTS 14:23; 1 CORINTHIANS 12:28; EPHESIANS 4:11; PHILIPPIANS 1:1	Church offices and the functions of spiritual gifts are compatible.

Function vs. Office	
ROMANS 12:6-8; 1 CORINTHIANS 12:28-30	The use of spiritual gifts is more a matter of function than of office. Individuals may serve the body of Christ through the use of their spiritual gift(s) and hold no appointed, elected or paid position.

TABLE 8-C
Order of Spiritual Gifts

There is a wide range of gifts, and all are essential in the body of Christ.

ROMANS 12; 1 CORINTHIANS 12; EPHESIANS 4	Paul stresses a wide range of gifts rather than provide a ranking of the importance of the gifts.
1 CORINTHIANS 12:28; EPHESIANS 2:20; 3:5	Paul gives priority to apostles, prophets and teachers, perhaps because these gifts are essential to the spiritual foundation of the church. The use of other spiritual gifts often flows out of believers' being enlightened and inspired by the humble use of apostolic, prophetic and teaching gifts.
1 CORINTHIANS 12:31	Paul tells the Corinthians to desire the "greater gifts," which most likely means that believers are to pray for those gifts needed most in their particular Christian communities.

Notes

TABLE 8-D
Classification of Spiritual Gifts

Each spiritual gift is unique.
The apostle Paul's lists of gifts show the wide variety of gifts and how God customizes them to the particular needs of a faith community.

Classifying gifts is difficult.
Due to their uniqueness in each situation and community and the overlap in their use, rigid distinctions should be avoided in classifying spiritual gifts.

Classification Method #1

Leadership	Apostles, prophets, evangelists, pastors, teachers, administrations, those who lead
Instruction	Wisdom, knowledge
Inspired Speech	Prophecy, discernings of spirits, tongues, interpretation of tongues
Power	Faith, healings, miracles
Practical Service	Giving, helps, service, mercy, exhortation

Classification Method #2 (used in this book)

Leadership	Apostles, prophets, teachers, pastors, evangelists, those who lead, administrations, helps
Practical Service	Service, exhortation, giving, showing mercy
Power	Faith, healings, miracles
Revelation	Wisdom, knowledge
Worship	Prophecy, discernings of spirits, speaking in tongues, interpretation of tongues

---

TABLE 8-E

Gifts of Leadership

God gives gifted spiritual leaders for the building up of the church.

Apostles

First, God appoints apostles to share the good news about Christ and to establish local churches.
>   MATTHEW 10:1-15; ACTS 13:50; 14:19-22; 15:25, 26
>   *Paul*—ROMANS 1:1; 2 CORINTHIANS 1:1; GALATIANS 1:1
>   *Others*—ACTS 14:4, 14; ROMANS 16:7; GALATIANS 1:19; 1 THESSALONIANS 2:6, 7

Prophets

Second, God appoints prophets to build up, encourage, inspire and comfort the church.
>   ACTS 13:1, 2; 15:32; 1 CORINTHIANS 14:3, 24, 25, 29-33

Teachers

Third, God appoints teachers to explain His Word to believers. Their work builds on the work of apostles and prophets.
>   ROMANS 12:7; 1 CORINTHIANS 12:28; EPHESIANS 4:11, 12

Pastors

God appoints pastors (shepherds) to feed and lead His flock, the church. Their work is closely related to that of teachers.
>   JOHN 21:15-17; ACTS 20:28; cf. 1 PETER 5:2;
>   1 TIMOTHY 5:17; 2 TIMOTHY 4:1-5; TITUS 1:9-11

Evangelists

God calls evangelists to proclaim the good news about Jesus Christ.
>   ACTS 8:4-13, 26-40; 21:8; EPHESIANS 4:11; 2 TIMOTHY 4:5

---

continued

TABLE 8-E (CONTINUED) **Gifts of Leadership**
Those Who Lead
God calls "those who lead" to lead, manage and care for the church.   ROMANS 12:8; 1 THESSALONIANS 5:12; 1 TIMOTHY 3:4, 5; 5:17
Administrations
God calls particular individuals to serve through "administrations"; that is, to help organize and guide the daily life of the church and to provide leadership in other ministries.   1 CORINTHIANS 12:28; cf. ACTS 27:11; REVELATION 18:17
Helps
God calls helpers to lead in providing assistance to individuals, families and the church.   ACTS 6:3-6; 1 CORINTHIANS 12:28; PHILIPPIANS 1:1; 1 TIMOTHY 3:8-13
Notes

TABLE 8-F
Gifts of Leadership in Action

Apostles

Church Offices	Examples of church offices in which apostles often minister: • Church planter • Missionary • Itinerant evangelist

Prophets

Church Offices	Examples of church offices in which prophets often minister: • Prophet • Pastor • Missionary • Itinerant evangelist
Ministry	Prophets regularly use the gift of prophecy to deliver messages from God to the congregation or to individuals. The messages: • Always enlighten or encourage the church • May predict the future • May provide a solution to a problem • May provide guidance or assurance for a situation • May lead an individual to realize his or her spiritual condition, inspiring that person to turn to God

Teachers

Church Offices	Examples of church offices in which teachers often minister: • Sunday school teacher • Teaching pastor • Spiritual director • Counselor

continued

TABLE 8-F (CONTINUED)
Gifts of Leadership in Action

Teachers (continued)	
Other Types of Ministry	Examples of ways that one might use the gift of teaching: • A teen's or adult's serving as a mentor to a younger person • A parent's teaching his or her children during family devotions • A scout leader's explaining and modeling Biblical values and truths to children • A schoolteacher's working closely with parents to help them guide their children • A playwright's teaching Christian truths through drama • A person's writing letters to the local newspaper, sharing with the community Christian viewpoints on issues
Pastors	
Church Offices	Examples of church offices in which pastors often minister: • Pastor • Children's or youth minister • Hospital, military, workplace, or prison chaplain
Other Types of Ministry	Examples of ways that one might use the gift of pastoring: • A neighborhood Bible study leader's providing pastoral leadership and guidance • A person's providing guidance to coworkers • Parents' providing spiritual guidance in the home

continued

TABLE 8-F (CONTINUED) Gifts of Leadership in Action
Evangelists

Church Offices	Examples of church offices in which evangelists often minister: • Itinerant evangelist • Short-term or long-term foreign missionary • Home missionary • Participant in evangelism or visitation ministry
Other Types of Ministry	Examples of ways that one might use the gift of evangelism: • Sharing the good news of Jesus Christ with neighbors • Holding a workplace or home-based Bible study • Using face painting and storytelling to share the love of Christ with children

Those Who Lead

Church Offices	Examples of church offices in which "those who lead" often minister: • Church council member, board member, committee chairperson • President or vice-president of a particular ministry, such as women's or men's ministry president • Deacon, deaconess • Church administrator, administrative pastor, program director, director of ministries

continued

314

TABLE 8-F (CONTINUED)
Gifts of Leadership in Action

Those Who Lead (continued)

Other Types of Ministry	Those who lead in the church are often wise, mature Christians to whom members of the congregation turn for guidance. Examples of ways that one might use a gift of leadership: • A teenager's using his or her leadership gift in a youth group • An elderly person's providing wisdom and guidance in the life of the church

Administrations

Church Offices	Examples of church offices in which those with the gift of administrations often minister: • Bishop • Elder • Pastor • Church administrator, administrative pastor, program director, director of ministries
Other Types of Ministry	Examples of ways that one might use the gift of administrations: • Organizing a church ministry event • Proposing and helping plan a new ministry in the local church • Organizing a Sunday school class • Planning a gathering for one's family or neighborhood

continued

TABLE 8-F (CONTINUED)
Gifts of Leadership in Action

Helps

Church Offices	Examples of church offices in which those with the leadership gift of helps often minister: • Deacon, deaconess • Chaplain • Lay minister to the sick or bereaved • Lay minister to the poor
Other Types of Ministry	Examples of ways one might use the leadership gift of helps: • Organizing a sewing circle to make quilts for the homeless • Seeing a need in the church or community and contacting people who have the needed spiritual gifts or resources to help
Notes	

CHAPTER 8—STUDY AND DISCUSSION

SPIRITUAL GIFTS IN THE CONTEXT OF PAUL'S THOUGHT

1. What major aspects of the gifts of the Spirit does the apostle Paul emphasize in his writings? (See Table 8-A.)

2. Why does God give gifts of leadership? (See Table 8-E; Ephesians 4:14-16.)

SPIRITUAL GIFTS AND CHURCH OFFICES

3. Are spiritual gifts a matter of function or office? (See Table 8-B.)

4. Must a person hold an office in the church in order to use a spiritual gift? (See Table 8-B; 1 Corinthians 12:28.)

ORDER AND CLASSIFICATION OF SPIRITUAL GIFTS

5. Instead of providing a ranking of spiritual gifts, what does the apostle Paul emphasize? (See Table 8-C.)

6. What is the most likely reason the apostle Paul stated that God gives to "the church, first apostles, second prophets, third teachers"? (See Table 8-C; 1 Corinthians 12:28.)

7. What does the apostle Paul most likely mean when he says that we should desire the "greater gifts"? (See Table 8-C; 1 Corinthians 12:31.)

8. Why is it difficult to classify spiritual gifts? (See Table 8-D.)

GIFTS OF LEADERSHIP

Discussion suggestion for study groups: Break into smaller groups and divide these questions among the groups. After a few minutes, each smaller group may summarize its discussion for the larger group.

9. What are the gifts of leadership? (See Table 8-E.)

Apostles

10. Describe what an apostle does. (See Table 8-E and the Glossary.)

11. In his writings, Paul uses the word *apostle* in a broad sense and a restricted sense. In your own words, describe the difference.

    Broad sense (See Romans 16:7; 1 Corinthians 12:28; 2 Corinthians 8:23; 11:12-15; Philippians 2:23-25.) *Restricted sense* (See Acts 15:2, 4, 22, 23; 1 Corinthians 9:1; 2 Corinthians 12:11, 12; Galatians 1:17-19; Ephesians 2:20; 3:4, 5.)

12. What are some types of ministry that apostles might do today? (See Table 8-F.)

13. Do you know any apostles? Describe their acts of service.

Prophets

14. Describe what a prophet does. (See Table 8-E and the Glossary.)

15. In his writings, Paul uses the word *prophet* in a broad sense and a restricted sense. In your own words, describe the difference.

    Broad sense (See Acts 2.) *Restricted sense* (See 1 Corinthians 14:29-32.)

16. What are some types of ministry that prophets might do today? (See Table 8-F.)

17. Do you know any prophets? Describe their acts of service.

18. How should prophets conduct themselves when sharing a message of prophecy during worship? (See 1 Corinthians 14:30.)

Teachers

19. Describe what a teacher does. (See Table 8-E and the Glossary.)

20. Describe how teachers and pastors are closely related. (See Ephesians 4:11.)

21. What are some types of ministry that teachers might do today? (See Table 8-F.)

22. Think of a teacher who has had a major impact on you or a member of your family. Describe that teacher's acts of service.

Pastors

23. What does the word *pastor* mean? (See Table 8-E.)

24. Describe what a pastor does. (See Table 8-E and the Glossary.)

25. Who is our supreme example of a pastor? (See John 10:11-18; Hebrews 13:20; 1 Peter 2:25.)

26. What are some examples of pastoral service in the Bible? (See John 21:15-17; Acts 20:28; Ephesians 4:2-13; 1 Peter 5:2; Titus 1:9-11.)

27. What are some types of ministry that pastors might do today? (See Table 8-F.)

28. Describe your pastor's acts of service.

Evangelists

29. Describe what an evangelist does. (See Table 8-E and the Glossary.)

30. Philip was an evangelist. Where did he carry the "good news"? (See Acts 8:4, 26, 40.)

31. What are some types of ministry that evangelists might do today? (See Table 8-F.)

32. Do you know any evangelists? Describe their acts of service.

Those Who Lead

33. Describe what "one who leads" does. (See Table 8-E and the Glossary.)

34. How should we treat our spiritual leaders? (See 1 Timothy 5:17).

35. What are some types of ministry that those who lead might do today? (See Table 8-F.)

36. Think of some spiritual leaders in your Christian community. Describe their acts of service.

Administrations

37. What does the term *administrations* (*kubernēseis*) mean? (See 1 Corinthians 12:28; cf. Acts 27:11; Revelation 18:17.)

38. Describe what one who serves through "administrations" does. (See Table 8-E and the Glossary under "Gift of Administrations.")

39. What are some types of ministry that persons with the gift of administrations might do today? (See Table 8-F.)

40. Do you know someone who serves God through the gift of administrations? Describe that person's acts of service.

Helps

41. What type of leadership do persons who have the gift of helps provide? (See Table 8-E and the Glossary.)

42. What are some types of ministry that persons with the leadership gift of helps might do today? (See Table 8-F.)

43. Do you know someone who serves God through his or her gift of helps? Describe that person's acts of service.

CONCLUSION

44. What should our attitude be regarding the spiritual gifts that God has given us?

*And all of you, serve each other in humility, for "God
sets himself against the proud, but he shows favor to
the humble." So humble yourselves under the mighty
power of God, and in his good time he will honor you*
(1 Peter 5:5, 6, *NLT*).

9

Gifts of Service, Power, Revelation and Worship

Christian service that is offered through our use of spiritual gifts exceeds service that can be accomplished only through our natural talents and abilities. God intends for all of the gifts to be used for serving Christ and the members of His body. Some of these gifts are not as dramatic in their manifestation as others are. Whether spectacular or not, they are all very special. In Romans 12:6-8, Paul mentions seven spiritual gifts. Four of these—serving, giving, giving assistance[1] and showing mercy— emphasize forms of practical service, not miracles or inspired speech. The Holy Spirit has especially equipped some believers to be of service to members of the congregation and others who are in need of assistance, compassion and understanding.

GIFTS FOR PRACTICAL SERVICE
Service

It may come as a surprise to some that *service* (Greek, *diakonia*) is also a spiritual gift (Romans 12:7). Our word *deacon* is derived from this Greek word. The first step toward the establishing of the office of deacon in the church seems to have been

---

[1]In the preceding chapter, we have discussed this gift. See the subheading "He who leads," under which is noted that the verb *proistēmi* has the meaning of "giving assistance."

the appointment of seven Spirit-filled men (Acts 6:2-6). Their duty was to provide care for the widows in Jerusalem so that the apostles could devote their time to prayer and to preaching about the good news of salvation. No doubt, the word *service* is associated with the ministry of deacons. Does Paul use the term in a narrower sense to refer to "acts of service," which came to be seen as relating only to the ministry of the deacons? Or does he use the term in a broader sense including, in a general way, every deed of service? It is best to take the word *service* in the broader sense, understanding that the gift of service encompasses various kinds of spiritual service such as ministry to the poor, preparing of meals, assisting the disabled, and providing other practical services as opportunities present themselves.

Paul says that the one who has the charismatic gift of service is to exercise it by serving (Romans 12:6, 7). Believers with this gift are to function in the community of faith by serving, just as a gifted teacher functions by teaching. Those who have this spiritual capacity, the gift of providing practical assistance, are to devote themselves wholeheartedly to showing the love of Christ in their acts of service to others.

Exhortation

A function of the gift of prophecy is that of "exhortation." This means to offer encouragement, inspiration or advice (1 Corinthians 14:3); but Paul identifies exhortation (*paraklēsis*) as a distinct gift of the Spirit (Romans 12:8). The gift of exhortation is a special ability given by the Holy Spirit to certain believers, which enables them to minister words of comfort and encouragement to other believers. Those who have this gift are able to speak wisely and provide consolation to the lonely, discouraged and weak. No doubt, the gift of exhortation was greatly needed in the early church. Many of the believers probably lived a difficult life, tested and tried by Satan and the world. Some might not have found Christianity to be all that they expected it to be. As a result, they were in need of a gifted person to give wise counsel and to speak words of comfort and encouragement. Today, many have the same need to be encouraged to remain faithful to God. The Holy Spirit is able to break into a situation through the gift of exhortation and bring a message that strengthens and builds up believers in the faith.

Giving

"He who gives" (Romans 12:8) implies a God-given capacity to share with others one's personal possessions. The expression of this gift may include the giving of either finances or other items that are needed. Therefore, *giving* is the sharing of our possessions, whether money, food, clothing or shelter, for the benefit of others. It probably does not involve only the giving of time, since the use of any of the spiritual gifts requires an investment of time and energy. The proper way to exercise this gift is "with liberality" (*aplotēs*), that is, generously and sincerely, without any motive of personal gain. It refers to the kind of sharing that is "open-handed and open-hearted giving out of compassion and singleness of purpose, not from ambition."[2]

A magnificent example in the Bible of the gift of giving was Barnabas (Acts 4:36, 37). He sold a tract of land, and this Spirit-filled man voluntarily gave the proceeds to a fund from which assistance was distributed to the needy. He was prompted by sincere concerns without the hope of personal gain. Ananias and Sapphira, on the other hand, stand in bold contrast as being people who gave out of mixed motives (4:36–5:11). They, too, sold a piece of land, but unlike Barnabas, they kept some of the proceeds for themselves. They then pretended to give all of the money to the church. Ananias and Sapphira gave in order to gain a reputation for generosity, not

---

[2]Fritz Rienecker, *A Linguistic Key to the Greek New Testament* (Grand Rapids: Zondervan, 1980) 2:30.

because they were concerned for the needy. Giving should always be motivated by sincerity, not out of self-interest and selfishness.

Showing Mercy

The gift of "he who gives," which we have just discussed, is closely linked to "he who shows mercy" (Romans 12:8). The one who gives to the needy with the proper motives performs an act of mercy. But in his use of the phrase "he who shows mercy," Paul may have something more specific in mind, since he has already mentioned the gift of giving. In the Old Testament, *mercy* expressed God's goodness, especially toward those in trouble (Genesis 43:14; Exodus 34:6). Those who exercise the gift of mercy extend mercy to those in need and trouble. It is what we could describe as "empathy in action." This action can take a number of concrete forms, such as giving to the homeless; caring for the sick, the aged and the disabled; and visiting shut-ins and prisoners. *Mercy* is a broad term and is used to describe the Samaritan's act of compassion in the well-known parable commonly titled "The Good Samaritan" (Luke 10:30-37).

Indeed, the gift of showing mercy manifests itself in caring for others in need, and it takes this gift to minister in this manner. Such kindness is to be done with cheerfulness. It is not a matter of duty but of delight and gladness. Service through the gift of mercy flows from a joyful heart.

GIFTS OF POWER

Gifts of supernatural power demonstrate the immediate effect of God's hand. Spiritual gifts, especially the gifts of faith, healings and miracles, bring people face-to-face with the reality of the invisible God. Gifts of power are concrete manifestations of the sovereign action of the Holy Spirit and are divine breakthroughs of miraculous power. The operation of the "power gifts" results in a profound encounter with the Spirit. These extraordinary works of the Spirit are not theatrical in nature; that is, they are not for the purpose of showmanship. Miracles are for the purpose of demonstrating the power of the Holy Spirit and of meeting the needs of God's people.

Faith

The spiritual "gift of faith" (*pistis*) calls attention to a particular gift of the Spirit. All believers have saving faith, but all do not have the spiritual "gift of faith." When speaking of the "gift of faith" in the context of the distribution of the gifts, Paul writes, "To another [is given] faith" (1 Corinthians 12:9). This gift is the supernatural endowment by the Spirit that enables a believer to trust God for extraordinary demonstrations of His power.

Scripture provides a basis for distinguishing among *saving* faith, *fruit* of faith, and the spiritual *gift* of faith.

Saving Faith

Throughout Scripture, *saving faith*—sometimes called *justifying faith*—is discussed as a requirement for salvation. Paul wrote of being justified through faith in the blood of Christ (Romans 3:24, 25). Saving faith is the means by which we enter into a right relationship with God and is the basis of our entire relationship with Him.

Fruit of Faith

On the other hand, the *fruit* of faith can also be distinguished from the *gift* of faith. Faith as a fruit is more accurately translated "faithfulness" (see Galatians 5:22). A believer may manifest the devotion of faithfulness, but not have the gift of faith.

Gift of Faith

The word *faith* as it is used in 1 Corinthians 12:9 is neither saving faith nor the fruit of faith. It is a supernatural ability bestowed by the Holy Spirit for extraordinary works. This gift is a miracle-working faith. As we may say, it is a mountain-moving faith (Matthew 17:20; 21:21; 1 Corinthians 13:2). No human has the power through speech alone to remove a mountain, but when an individual has the gift of faith, that person's basic faith relationship with God is intensified so that he or she can believe God for the humanly impossible. Therefore, through the gift of faith, the Holy Spirit increases the believer's faith so that this person has great confidence that God will grant healings, miracles and other mighty works. There are many examples of this special faith in both the Old and the New Testament (1 Kings 18:20-39; Daniel 6:19-22; Acts 3:3-11; 14:8-10). Each of these passages points to a special God-given faith.

The power to accomplish the extraordinary always resides in God and in the faith that He grants as a gift. True faith does not attempt to coerce God, but is submissive to Him and is based on accepting His Word. There is no evidence that the apostles or anyone else were able to perform signs and wonders without the prompting of the Holy Spirit. Where the gift of faith is recognized and is exercised, God manifests His power in remarkable ways. God is glorified and His people are edified through the operation of the gift of faith.

Healings

In 1 Corinthians 12:9, 28, the "gifts of healings" are distinguished from the "gift of faith." No doubt, healing the sick is part of exercising the gift of faith. The gift of faith, however, seems to be broader, bringing about other miracles in addition to extraordinary healings. Notice that this manifestation of the Spirit is spoken of with a double plural in the Greek—"gifts of healings" (*charismata iamatōn*). The use of the plural *gifts* here possibly implies, as some Biblical scholars have suggested, that no single gift of healing

328

is effective in curing all illnesses. Normally, each kind of illness is unique and requires a particular cure or healing treatment. Therefore, a special gift would be needed to address each type of condition. So rather than one, there would be many gifts of healings.

Of course, several gifts of healings may operate through the same person and cure many different kinds of sicknesses. Jesus' own ministry is summed up in the words that He went about "proclaiming the gospel of the kingdom, and healing every kind of disease and every kind of sickness among the people" (Matthew 4:23; cf. Acts 10:38). In light of Jesus' ministry, questions have been raised about the claim that some make regarding having a healing gift for only certain disorders. More likely, "gifts of healings" indicate that there are a variety of forms of this gift; and the plural words call attention to different types of healing that are involved in the supernatural restoration of health to the body, soul and spirit.

It has been suggested that the gifts of healings are not given to a believer who is used by God to heal, but to the one who is healed. There can be no doubt that a person who is healed receives the miracle of healing, but God uses the individual with the gifts of healings to heal others. First Corinthians 12:7-10 focuses on the fact that each Christian receives a spiritual gift for the purpose of exercising it. Therefore, to be accurate, it is better to say that the spiritual gift is given to a person for the healing of another person.

The Holy Spirit may provide healing for the mind and soul, as well as for the body. Perhaps the second plural, *healings*, calls attention to different types of healing that are necessary for the restoration of the whole person. Scripture affirms that Jesus was responsible for healing every kind of disorder. Peter says that Jesus healed "all who were oppressed by the devil" (Acts 10:38). He healed the mentally ill as well as the blind and the lame. Furthermore, He sent out the 12 disciples "to heal every kind of disease and every kind of sickness" (Matthew 10:1). God is unlimited in what He is able to do, and can heal the entire person—body, soul and spirit. Through the gifts of healings, God heals all kinds of physical, mental, emotional and spiritual disorders. Like other kinds of miracles, healings are signs of the extraordinary power of the Holy Spirit and of freedom from all suffering and infirmities in the life to come. They do not, however, indicate an end to sickness, suffering and death in this present life. The reality is that perfect health will be enjoyed only in the world to come. At the return of Christ, a final result of salvation will be "the redemption of our body" (Romans 8:23). Nevertheless, God has made provision even today through the gifts of healings for deliverance from sickness and disease.[3]

Workings of Miracles

Again we have two plural nouns—"the workings of miracles" (*energēmata dunameōn*, 1 Corinthians 12:10, 29). The plural forms emphasize variety in the manifestations of this spiritual gift. In addition to healing, many different kinds of miracles occur. The

[3]Scripture makes a connection between God's provision of healing and the redemptive work of Christ. Isaiah 53:4 speaks to this point, clearly indicating that the Messiah would die for the sins and sicknesses of God's people. That same passage is cited in Matthew 8:17 where, after recounting a number of healings and the casting out of demons, Matthew explains, "in order that what was spoken through Isaiah the prophet might be fulfilled, saying 'He Himself took our infirmities and carried away our diseases.'" Included in the Atonement is not only salvation for the soul but also healing for the body. Scripture teaches a holistic concept of salvation. Therefore, miraculous healings are the result of the atoning work of Christ, but at best such healings are only temporary since all must die. For believers, there remains the redemption of their bodies, which will be the result of resurrection and transformation. Never again will they be subject to suffering, sickness and death. But until that time, Christians will not enjoy all the benefits of the Atonement, and therefore in this life should not expect to have perfect health. See Terry Cross' excellent treatment of the doctrine of healing (Yung Chul Han, ed., *Transforming Power*, 179-231).

term *miracles* (*dunameis*, powers) refers to extraordinary manifestations and can include healings. Usually, the "workings of miracles" is associated with God's mighty works apart from miracles of healing. Paul listed the gifts of healings as a distinct gift from the workings of miracles, which covers a wide range of supernatural manifestations, as suggested by the phrase "signs and wonders" (Hebrews 2:4; Galatians 3:5).

Miracles are associated with power. This gift to do powerful deeds far exceeds human power. It is a profound encounter with God's sovereign action and the Spirit's power to do supernatural works. The workings of miracles are an invasion against the kingdom of Satan and a sign of the breaking-in of God's kingdom into this present world. The manifestation of this gift includes the resistance and the casting out of demons (Matthew 12:28). It could just as well include events such as Paul's afflicting Elymas, a magician, with blindness (Acts 13:4-12) and bringing the physically dead back to life (9:36-42; 20:9-12). The Holy Spirit does break through in this human world and does the unusual, the extraordinary. At times, He moves through individuals and gives them the ability to work miracles.

GIFTS OF REVELATION

The Holy Spirit is called "the Spirit of truth" because He is the great revealer of truth (John 14:26). He takes the things of Christ and makes them known to believers (16:13-15). Paul said, "Now we have received . . . the Spirit . . . that we might know the things freely given to us by God" (1 Corinthians 2:12). As God's agent of revelation, the Spirit makes known to us the deep things of God. Listed among the spiritual manifestations are "a word of wisdom" and "a word of knowledge," through which the Holy Spirit gives spiritual insight into God's plan or will. It is difficult, if not impossible, to make a rigid distinction between these particular gifts. For the Corinthians, the use of both of these gifts probably occurred frequently, and the differences were clear to them. Because of the overlapping between the gifts of wisdom and knowledge, it may be wise not to spend a great deal of time trying to determine the differences between the two. What is important is to observe that both gifts involve the mind and speech, and they both stem from revelation and enlightenment given by the Holy Spirit. In the following discussion, we will examine the characteristics of each of these gifts, so that we can better understand how they function.

A Word of Wisdom

Among the Corinthian believers was a love of wisdom. They understood wisdom as eloquence, persuasion, and speculations about life and salvation (1 Corinthians 1:17, 22-24; 2:4). They judged the story of Jesus Christ's being the Messiah by the human standards and values of their age, or what can be called the "wisdom of the world" (1:20, 21; 2:6, 13). To clear up their misconceptions of wisdom, Paul explained the "wisdom of God," which is God's plan of salvation achieved through the cross of Christ. All believers have experienced the wisdom of God through faith in the story of His love, which centers on the Cross. But there is a special gift of wisdom—a word of wisdom—that God bestows on some of His people.

The term *word* (*logos*) may be translated "utterance" or "message." A "word of wisdom" is, therefore, an utterance or a message of wisdom revealed by the Spirit. It is the result of enlightenment from the Holy Spirit. Out of such revelation comes new light and fresh insight. This new insight provides the basis for speaking "a word" or a message full of wisdom.

Biblical scholar Arnold Bittlinger observes, "In a different or dangerous situation a word of wisdom may be given which resolves the difficulty or silences the opponent."[4] We have examples in Scripture

---

[4] Arnold Bittlinger, *Gifts and Graces* (Grand Rapids: Eerdmans, 1967) 29.

where a message of wisdom takes the form of silencing opponents or providing spiritual guidance in difficult circumstances. When Jesus' opponents set a trap for Him by asking if Jews should pay taxes to the Roman government, they hoped for a "yes" or "no" answer. But speaking wisely, He answered in these words: "Render to Caesar the things that are Caesar's, and to God the things that are God's" (Luke 20:20-26). Jesus assured His disciples that they too would have similar ability to face opponents. He promised them that when they were brought before rulers and authorities, "the Holy Spirit will teach you in that very hour what you ought to say" (12:11, 12). God fulfilled this promise to Peter when he was brought before the Jerusalem authorities. "Filled with the Holy Spirit," Peter spoke to them and his defense caused them to marvel (Acts 4:8-13). Another example is James' speech to the Jerusalem Council (15:13-21). His Spirit-inspired words provided a fuller understanding of God's plan for the salvation of the Gentiles and inspired the church to make the decision to open its doors to Gentiles. Such an utterance was, therefore, a "word of wisdom," as were the brilliant statements of defense that Paul delivered before the rulers and authorities (Acts 21–26).

A message of wisdom will normally be spoken by the believer who has been granted "a spirit of wisdom and revelation" (Ephesians 1:17). From such revelation comes a message of wisdom for challenging situations. But at times God may not intend for words or insights of knowledge or wisdom to be spoken. The Holy Spirit may give a word of wisdom or knowledge for an individual's personal guidance. He or she is not expected to share it with others.[5] Although not shared verbally, this individual's new knowledge or wisdom, when embraced and put into action, will also contribute indirectly to the rest of the body of Christ. As always, spiritual gifts should build up the Christian community.

---

[5]Anthony D. Palma, *The Holy Spirit*, 223.

A Word of Knowledge

This manifestation of the Spirit is another gift of utterance, or speech. The term *word* corresponds with its use in the phrase "word of wisdom." "A word of knowledge" is a Spirit-given capacity to express knowledge through language. It is more than knowledge derived from the study of Scripture and reflection. This special knowledge or insight is obtained only by revelation from the Holy Spirit. This conclusion is suggested by its position between "revelation" and "prophecy" in 1 Corinthians 14:6. A revelation of knowledge may give a believer deeper knowledge and insight of Scripture, beyond natural capacity. Another manifestation of this gift may be having knowledge of facts or a situation, information that could not be acquired by a believer except through the Holy Spirit.

The Spirit-anointed Jesus exercised the spiritual gift of knowledge. Without being told by anyone, He knew the name, character and prior location of Nathanael (John 1:44-49). Peter's knowledge of the dishonesty and hypocrisy of Ananias and Sapphira also provides a good example of this gift in action (Acts 5:1-11). The entire passage portrays Peter as one who knows. His knowledge of their deception was not the result of human ability, but insight imparted by the Holy Spirit. It was the Holy Spirit who unmasked what the couple had done. Their encounter with the Holy Spirit had serious consequences.

Revelation is critical to both the gifts of knowledge and wisdom. Both gifts involve messages given by the Holy Spirit in order to make the things of God understandable to His people. The Holy Spirit enables a believer to declare truth that is beyond his or her natural capacity.

GIFTS FOR WORSHIP

Pentecostal and Charismatic Christians enjoy a remarkable intensity and quality in their worship and praise of God. In their worship services, they open up to the presence of God, expecting to encounter the Holy Spirit in a fresh way. The gifts of the Spirit seem to arise naturally out of their deep awareness of God's presence and His love. This expectation and awareness appear to be the essential elements in Spirit-inspired worship rather than the form of worship, the style of music or the types of musical instruments played. When the Spirit is allowed to guide, many of the spiritual gifts may be exercised in Pentecostal and Charismatic worship, but certain manifestations of the Spirit are associated more closely with worship than others.

Prophecy[6]

The importance of this gift is emphasized by Paul: "Desire earnestly spiritual gifts, but especially that you may prophesy" (1 Corinthians 14:1). Of all the gifts, prophecy must have occurred most frequently in the Pauline churches. It is the gift Paul mentions the most in his letters (Romans 12:6; 1 Corinthians 11:4, 5; 12–14; Ephesians 2:20; 3:5; 4:11; 1 Thessalonians 5:20; 1 Timothy 1:18; 4:14). A prophet speaks to God's people through the inspiration of the Spirit. The Holy Spirit gives to him a message directly from the Lord. What the prophet speaks is a divinely given revelation that may be received during worship (1 Corinthians 14:30).

Prophecy, therefore, provides a message of fresh insight from the Spirit. The primary focus of prophecy is not on the future, but on a more immediate concern—the edification, exhortation and consolation of the congregation (1 Corinthians 14:3). For unbelievers, prophecy functions to expose their spiritual condition (vv. 24, 25). For believers, the manifestation of this gift serves as a "sign" of blessing, demonstrating that God is with them (v. 22). As an inspired utterance, prophecy speaks to the needs of God's people and offers

---

[6]We have already discussed the prophet and in some measure the nature of the prophetic message under the category of "leadership gifts."

them edification, exhortation and consolation. These three terms overlap in their meaning, but the emphasis of 1 Corinthians 14 falls on *edification*.

A prophetic message may offer comfort to the discouraged. In 1 Thessalonians 4:13-18, Paul passed on a word of prophecy that comforted believers regarding their Christian loved ones who had already died. In this prophecy, he also gave an explanation about the coming of Christ. It was a "word of the Lord" (v. 15), that is, a prophetic message that the Holy Spirit had given directly to Paul to comfort those Christians.

In addition to being a message of sympathy and compassion, prophecy may take the form of exhortation and rebuke for carnal and divisive activities. Paul exhorted, or encouraged, believers in Corinth not to allow divisions to exist among them (1 Corinthians 1:10; 2 Corinthians 10:1-6; cf. Philippians 4:2). Whether a prophetic message communicates words of comfort or exhortation, the divine intent is to build up believers and to minister to the needs of their hearts. The gift of prophecy functions as an edifying gift. It assures God's people that He knows them intimately and is aware of the dangers they are facing. He has them in His hand, leading and encouraging them. Paul, therefore, states that the purpose of prophecy is that everyone may learn and be encouraged (1 Corinthians 14:31).

Spirit-inspired prophecies have great value for the church, but they must be evaluated before they are accepted as true. The task of evaluating them falls on the local congregation. Paul told the Thessalonians not to despise prophecies. He said that they should test all things and hold on to what is good (1 Thessalonians 5:20, 21; 1 Corinthians 14:29). A prophetic word can have a mixed quality, making it necessary to determine the significance and truth of what is said. A prophet may receive a genuine word from the Lord, but his understanding of it may be only partial. While seeing "in a mirror dimly"(1 Corinthians 13:12), he may be prone to give a wrong interpretation.

Because a prophet may not be able to represent accurately the revelation he has received, prophecies need to be tested. Paul urges the community of believers to test everything, including prophecies. Once this has been done, they are told to hold on to the good, separating the wheat from the chaff (1 Thessalonians 5:20, 21).[7] The danger is to see this approach as unspiritual, or to take the other extreme and discount every manifestation of the Spirit. A healthy and balanced church is not necessarily completely free of inappropriate exercise of spiritual gifts. Where prophecy is out of line, it may be that the individual has the gift, but needs wise counsel in exercising it.

The manifestation of the gift of prophecy has limitations. Paul does not assign it the same level of authority as Scripture. He clearly subordinates the authority of the prophets in Corinth, not permitting them to control the agenda for worship, and he urges the congregation to evaluate their prophecies (1 Corinthians 14:29-33). The prophet, therefore, does not stand above the community and is subject to the wisdom and guidance of fellow believers. Even so, Paul warns the Thessalonians not to "quench the Spirit" (1 Thessalonians 5:19)—that is, stifle or suppress the moving of the Holy Spirit. Rather than putting out the fire of the Spirit, the church is to discern what is valid in a prophetic message. A prophet may knowingly or unknowingly include his thoughts.

If the congregation determines a prophecy is basically in keeping

---

[7]There are three means of evaluating the truth of a prophecy. The first means is the Word of God. If prophecies are consistent with the inspired writings of the prophets and apostles, they are to be accepted. The second means is discernment. The gift of discerning of spirits is closely linked to the gift of prophecy (1 Corinthians 12:10; 1 Thessalonians 5:19-21). Discernment enables the believer to know whether a spiritual manifestation is genuine or counterfeit. The third means is the character of the prophet. A true prophet will give evidence in his life of genuine godliness and holiness and show respect for the teaching of Scripture (Matthew 7:15-20; 1 John 4:1-6).

with the Bible and has been delivered in good faith, although every single word is not spoken from spiritual revelation, minor points may be passed over with little comment. The church is to hold on to whatever is true and helpful. Prophecy promoting concepts that contradict the Word of God should be dealt with by the congregation and its leaders (1 Thessalonians 5:20, 21; 1 Corinthians 14:29-33; 1 John 4:1-6). When a prophetic message does come from the Lord, it has substantial authority (although not absolute authority) and fulfills the role expressed in 1 Corinthians 14:3 of edification, exhortation and consolation. When this happens, God has broken in by speaking directly to His people through a Spirit-inspired servant.

Discernings (Distinguishings) of Spirits

Both nouns in the phrase "discernings of spirits" (*NKJV*) are plural in the Greek (*diakriseis pneumatōn*). We find this phrase only in 1 Corinthians 12:10, where "distinguishing of spirits" is listed as one of the spiritual gifts. This gift is listed immediately after prophecy, suggesting a close link between the two gifts. The connection between these two gifts is evident in 1 Corinthians 14:29, which reads, "Let two or three prophets speak, and let the others[8] pass judgment" (*diakrinō*, "to separate, to make a distinction, to pass judgment"). The gift of interpretation is the companion gift to speaking in tongues, and a gift of discernment is the companion gift

---

[8]The debate continues as to what "others" (*alloi*) refers. Some contend that it refers to the prophets who were present; that is, they are the ones who were to evaluate prophetic messages. In 1 Thessalonians 5:19-21 and 1 John 4:1, it is the congregation that is to test prophecies. Likewise, "the others" of 1 Corinthians 14:29 must refer to the congregation as a whole. Nowhere in the New Testament is there an indication that only persons who are themselves prophets may evaluate and test prophecy. Prophecy is a gift to the church and it is the responsibility of the church to evaluate prophetic utterances. The prophet is subject to the judgment of the community of faith.

to prophecy. Interpretation should immediately follow tongues. The same pattern holds true for prophecy and discernment.

The gift of discernings of spirits, however, has other functions besides the testing of the truth and genuineness of prophecy. These other functions may explain the plural: *discernings*. In addition to working in respect to prophecy, this gift may determine in other areas what is from God and what is not. It can be linked with such gifts as tongues and interpretation, a word of knowledge and a word of wisdom. The authority of these gifts should not be accepted without sufficient discernment as to what comes from the Holy Spirit, and they are true breakings-in of God. Furthermore, the gift of discernment has application in the area of demon-possession. Jesus himself exercised this gift when He encountered a man with an evil spirit (Mark 1:23-28). Jesus discerned that a demon was speaking through the man. He, therefore, rejected the man's testimony about Himself, even though the man was telling the truth. As this account demonstrates, demons may speak the truth, trying to use it for their own purposes.

Another example of demon-possession is the slave girl who followed Paul and Silas, crying, "These men are the bondservants of the Most High God, who are proclaiming to you the way of salvation" (Acts 16:17). Through the gift of discernment, Paul knew that the girl spoke under the inspiration of an evil spirit. As is well known, demon-possession may manifest many symptoms of a physical sickness. By exercising the gift of discernment, a believer can know whether to pray for physical healing or to prepare to cast out demons.

The discernings of spirits should not be limited to the examples cited above. Notice the plural *spirits*, which must have a broad meaning and likely includes three possible sources: the Holy Spirit (Romans 8:32), the human spirit (1 Thessalonians 5:23) and evil spirits (Mark 5:2-16). The gift of discernment is the God-given power to distinguish what comes from the Spirit of Truth and what comes from other possible sources. A whole range of spiritual forces may be involved in a situation. This gift enables individuals in a Christian community to know intuitively the source of a manifestation. Outwardly, there may appear no distinction between a Spirit-inspired, a demon-inspired or a human-inspired manifestation. Through intense illumination, the Spirit enables the believer to discern what is in the human heart and what is truly from the Holy Spirit.

Jesus exercised the gift of discernment by looking deep into the hearts of people (Matthew 22:18; Mark 2:8; Luke 20:23). Peter perceived the deception of Ananias and Sapphira when they claimed to have given all that they received for a piece of land. Through the gift of discernment he asked, "Ananias, why has Satan filled your heart to lie to the Holy Spirit and to keep back some of the price of the land?" (Acts 5:3). On that occasion the Holy Spirit gave him the ability to discern the motivations in the human heart (cf. Acts 13:9, 10).

The importance of the gift of discernment can hardly be overstated. A believer, illuminated specially by the Holy Spirit, may discern the inner spirit of a person that could be gripped by a spirit of depression, jealousy, bitterness, pride or unforgiveness. He or she may then receive direction from the Holy Spirit as to how to best minister to the spiritual needs of the individual. At other times, the Holy Spirit may instruct a person to pray or to be cautious about a situation, rather than to be an agent in the solving of the problem.

Another important aspect of the gift of discernment is its use in worship. The gifts of the Spirit such as prophecy and tongues can be counterfeited by Satan. Undiscerning acceptance of Satan-inspired utterances in some instances has had serious consequences for the local congregation. It is only through the illumination of an individual believer by the Holy Spirit that spiritual forces at work can be perceived. The operation of the gift of discernment is for the common good of the Christian community and serves to discern if a manifestation is from the Holy Spirit or to reveal the true motives or conditions of people.

Speaking in Tongues

The evidence clearly indicates that *glossolalia* was a common experience among the early Christians (Acts 2:4; 10:46; 19:6). In 1 Corinthians 12–14, the manner in which Paul speaks about this manifestation is striking. Here he describes *glossolalia* as speaking or praying in tongues and speaking in the "tongues of men and of angels" (13:1). Paul identifies *glossolalia* as one of the spiritual gifts and refers to it as "various kinds of tongues" (*genē glōssōn*, 12:10), suggesting that different kinds of tongues spoken either on the earth or in heaven may be uttered. To put it another way, tongues are languages given by the Holy Spirit and may be either human or angelic. If the language is an earthly one, usually individuals listening to the gifted person do not understand what is being said. However, sometimes individuals who speak a different language than the speaker may hear their own native tongue. On the Day of Pentecost, the audience heard the manifestation of tongues in their own languages (Acts 2:11).[9] Whether tongues are languages of men or angels, they involve a profound encounter with the Holy Spirit. The Spirit gives the utterance as believers allow the Spirit to use their lips and tongues.

Purposes for the Gift of Tongues

An examination of 1 Corinthians 14 indicates three ways in which the gift of tongues functions:

1. *For the Building Up of the Church.* Paul leaves no doubt that the

---

[9]In the Book of Acts, the primary function of speaking in tongues is as the sign of Spirit baptism, but in 1 Corinthians there is no teaching on tongues as the initial sign of the Spirit's fullness. Writing to the Corinthians, Paul emphasizes tongues as one of the spiritual gifts. When the manifestation of tongues is accompanied by the gift of interpretation, it edifies the congregation. Both as a sign of Spirit baptism and as a gift of the Spirit for edification of the local church, tongues are the same kind of inspired speech, but the fundamental difference is in the function.

gift of tongues is designed for the common good of believers gathered together in worship. This gift accompanied by interpretation is just as useful in building up the congregation as prophecy is (1 Corinthians 14:5). Paul is not critical of tongues as such, and exercises the gift himself. Being thankful for the gift (v. 18), he encourages it (v. 5). What he does criticize is uninterpreted tongues dominating the worship services in Corinth. So Paul urges the believer with the gift of tongues to pray for the gift of interpretation. If tongues are uninterpreted in public worship, tongues are inferior to prophecy and edify only the person who speaks in tongues (v. 4). But for Paul, tongues plus interpretation equal prophecy: "Greater is one who prophesies than one who speaks in tongues, unless he interprets, so that the church may receive edifying" (v. 5). No doubt, the enlightenment and encouragement of the church are the main purposes for the gift of tongues in public worship. Tongues do not only edify the individual but also the congregation, provided someone gives the interpretation.

It was, therefore, not Paul's purpose to discourage the exercise of the gift of *glossolalia* among believers, but to avoid disorder and confusion as the Spirit manifested His gifts. The burden of chapter 14 is not suppression or prohibition, but regulation, which legitimizes the gifts.

2. *For a Sign to Unbelievers.* Paul writes, "So then tongues are for a sign, not to those who believe but to unbelievers" (v. 22). *Glossolalia* is a sign, a mark of God's presence, and may arrest the attention of unbelievers. To the contrary, prophecy is a sign of God's presence not to unbelievers, but to believers. Both tongues and prophecy function as signs, but tongues can be a sign of God's disapproval and judgment of unbelievers' wrongdoings. That is, it functions as an evangelistic sign; but even then, interpretation is usually necessary.[10]

---

[10]It is possible that where no interpretation is necessary, tongues can also have "sign value" for unbelievers (see Acts 2:6-13). Paul, however, emphasizes the importance of the ministry of tongues in public worship when they are accompanied by interpretation, so that the congregation can know what the Spirit is saying to the church.

As Paul notes, if unbelievers are present in the worship service, they will not understand the manifestation of tongues unless interpretation follows. Under the conditions where no interpretation is given, unbelievers could charge believers with "madness," especially when they speak in tongues at the same time or in rapid succession (v. 23). As a result, no interpretation could be given and they could be thought to be out of their minds. Interpretation is, therefore, usually essential for tongues to function as an aid to evangelism. Otherwise, unbelievers will not understand and will pass off the manifestation of tongues as madness. Unbelievers should be able to understand what is said in the worship service, in order to be convinced and come to faith. The manifestation of this gift with interpretation does not ensure that they will believe. Unfortunately, they may reject the significance of the sign and increase their guilt.

3. *For an Aid to Private Prayer and Devotion.* God may use the gift of tongues privately to build up the individual. This function of the gift edifies the receiver directly and the church indirectly. Of course, other gifts can be understood to build up the spiritually gifted person as well. For public worship, tongues are inappropriate without interpretation, but in private devotions they are a genuine conversation with God (1 Corinthians 14:2, 28). In public worship, if no one is present to interpret a person's *glossolalia*, that person should remain silent and "speak to himself and to God" (v. 28). That is, he or she is to speak quietly so as not to disturb other worshipers. The exercise of tongues has an appropriate place in private devotions. Paul encourages believers to pray and to sing in the Spirit, which refers to the private use of tongues (vv. 14, 15).

Devotional tongues are not directed to the church but only to God. The believer may be caught up in private worship. Inspired by the Spirit, the believer may exceed the ordinary human level of communication and may be able to praise God with a profound depth. Through the exercise of tongues in devotions, individuals have found themselves free in the Spirit to adore and praise God, and to involve themselves in some of the most soul-satisfying worship.

To summarize the purpose of the gift of tongues, the Biblical pattern provides for the manifestation of a variety of gifts in the local congregation. One gift is tongues, and the use of it in public worship is to edify the assembled body of believers. Not all Spirit-filled believers have this gift for ministry in public worship (1 Corinthians 12:30). Like the other gifts, the Holy Spirit bestows the gift of tongues on certain individuals. In Corinth, the abusive use of tongues had created confusion in public worship.

Using Tongues in Public Worship

In the interest of good order, Paul placed three restrictions on the gift in public worship:

1. *The number of messages should not exceed three in a single worship service* (1 Corinthians 14:27). This restriction should not be pressed in a legalistic spirit. Paul's concern is proper order, but not necessarily the exact number of utterances.

2. *The inspired utterances must be given one after the other, avoiding, therefore, two or more speaking at the same time* (v. 23).

3. *Tongues in public worship must be interpreted* (v. 28). Tongues, along with other spiritual gifts, have their proper place and use in the worship of God's people.

Interpretation of Tongues

The last of the spiritual gifts listed in 1 Corinthians 12:8-10 and 28-30 is interpretation of tongues (*hermēneia glōssōn*). The word *interpretation* (*hermēneia*) comes from the verb *hermēneuō*, which means "to explain, to expound or to interpret." The word *interpretation*, therefore, should not be taken to mean a word-for-word translation. The exercise of this grace gift is not an exact translation of an utterance in tongues, but a clarification or exposition of its meaning and significance. The issue at stake in Corinth was the edification of the church. Because interpretation is the companion gift of speaking in tongues, the congregation's understanding should have been no problem, but it was. In their enthusiasm, the Corinthian believers neither desired interpretations nor did they allow room for such in worship.

Tongues and interpretation are two separate manifestations, and in a public meeting they are to operate together in harmony. Otherwise, the assembly of believers will not understand what the Spirit is saying through the tongues. The interpreter does not necessarily understand the message in tongues, but the Spirit prompts that person to give the significance and application of it. Through interpretation, tongues touch the minds and spirits of those who are present. No two gifts illustrate better the importance of dependency and cooperation than do the gifts of tongues and interpretation. The gift of interpretation must be distinguished from other kinds of interpretation, such as interpretation of Scripture, of dreams and of the signs of the time. This spiritual gift functions only in relation to the gift of tongues. Likewise, the gift of discernment is related specifically to prophecy, but it may operate in other directions such as the discerning of demonic spirits and whether an illness is physical or mental. But the gift of interpretation has only one application—namely, to tongues.[11]

A couple of observations are in order here.

First, the one who speaks in tongues speaks mysteries (1 Corinthians 14:2). The word *mysteries* refers to hidden truths that lie outside of the human mind and can only be disclosed by the Holy Spirit. These truths are not those revealed in the Gospels (see Romans 11:25, 26; 1 Corinthians 15:51; 1 Timothy 3:16), but they are heavenly truths not yet revealed. Those hidden truths revealed

---

[11]T.W. Harpur, "The Gift of Tongues and Interpretation," *Canadian Journal of Theology*, vol. 12 (1966) 168.

through tongues may have to do with God's redemptive plans and involve fresh application of them in the form of exhortation and comfort, but such revelations will not contradict the teachings of the Bible if they are truly from the Holy Spirit. So as the Spirit works, the speaker utters mysteries in tongues, and through an interpreter, God makes them known to those present.

Second, Paul speaks about praying in tongues, that is, praying "with the spirit," singing "with the spirit," and blessing "with the spirit" (1 Corinthians 14:14-16). Such prayer and praise are directed to God, but without interpretation the uninformed person present will not say "Amen at your giving of thanks, since he does not know what you are saying" (v. 16). When accompanied by interpretation, tongues of praise and thanksgiving have meaning for the whole congregation and the people are enabled to say "Amen." Interpretation converts an inspired utterance given in tongues to a message that builds up the congregation and makes it possible for the church to hear what the Spirit says.

CONCLUSION

Genuine worship allows a person to encounter the Holy Spirit through conversion, baptism in the Spirit, and the exercise of spiritual gifts and fruit. In the early church, there were numerous and varied elements of worship. Paul knew as well as anyone that spiritual wealth can be misunderstood and abused when the attitude is for each Christian to do what he or she wants to do, forgetting about building up the body of Christ and about the needs of the world. To address this problem, Paul approached the whole subject of spiritual gifts with great wisdom and balance. He recognized the dangers of allowing free spiritual expression, knowing that emotions could override reason, love could be replaced by rivalry, and self-interests could diminish concern for the Christian community.

At the same time, he was determined to preserve the freedom of the Spirit during worship, to protect the variety of worship "in the Spirit," and to ensure the free operation of spiritual gifts within the limits of good order. Paul wanted structured, not over-structured, worship. Flexible order in worship serves as a safeguard for the Holy Spirit to work freely and for a variety of individuals to participate. Otherwise, the life and worship of the church will be impoverished. So what conclusions can we draw?

God has given the church a great variety of spiritual gifts. These gifts have been available to God's people since the first century. Some have taken a dim view of the gifts and have taught that they were limited to the age of the apostles. As a result, many have lost touch with the continuing work of the Spirit in the life of the church and have been willing to settle for the ordinary without fresh encounters with God. But the Holy Spirit cannot be bound, and we hear today of breakthroughs of the Spirit, who refuses to be limited to the ordinary and the familiar. Our lives are to be mainly guided by the inspired written Word, while being open and sensitive to the manifestations of the Spirit and to the help and guidance that the Holy Spirit provides through His gifts. Spiritual gifts are the mighty works of the Spirit, but they are also gentle things—gifts of grace that transform love into deeds.

Regulation of spiritual gifts, especially prophecy and tongues manifested in worship, is in the interest of edification and serves to legitimize their operation. To place any restrictions on spiritual manifestations has been seen as "unspiritual," quenching or putting out the fire of the Spirit. The church, however, cannot afford to say "yes" to everything that claims to be spiritual. Likewise, it cannot afford to allow a small group in authority to dictate the spirituality of the congregation, or to allow individuals to improperly take the liberty to embarrass and reveal openly the sins and mistakes of others in the congregation.

The primary function of spiritual gifts in worship, particularly the gift of prophecy, is that of edification, exhortation and consolation. Convinced of this, Paul insisted that a prophet is answerable to the congregation, and the congregation is to judge the character of the prophetic message. When this is the practice, the individual's exercise of a spiritual gift in worship is balanced by community responsibility and discernment. The church is to function as a check and balance to prevent extremes, as well as function to awaken the gifts that may be asleep in the community of believers. Allowing extremes to prevail in worship will eventually extinguish the fires of the Spirit just as suppressing His manifestations will.

Every true Christian has a minimum of one spiritual gift, but some have more. Many of God's people are drawn to the gifts that are more spectacular in their operation. Such gifts as miracles, tongues and prophecy easily capture our attention. Scripture teaches that these gifts are needed and have their place in the ministry of the church. But it also teaches that the church and world need the less spectacular gifts, such as helps, administrations, teaching, giving, showing mercy, intercessory prayer, hospitality, and the like. None of the gifts are to be theatrical in nature. They all show God's power, love and compassion. Take a word of wisdom as an example. This gift enables a believer to express the Lord's direction regarding what to do in an unclear or difficult situation. The gift of wisdom involves something other than the reciting of the gospel story; it is revelation from the Lord to meet a present need in the local congregation. The message of wisdom shows the leading of the Lord and His concern in advancing the church. In one way or another, all of the gifts are to serve this purpose.

A danger has been to overemphasize certain gifts and to ignore others. It is wrong to do either. The reaction to this problem should not be to minimize the importance of spiritual gifts or to forget them. The gifts are manifestations of the Holy Spirit, the power of God in operation. To disregard any of them is to miss out on the dynamic reality of the Spirit's manifestations and to fail to edify fellow believers and deepen their faith. For God's people spiritual gifts are no minor thing. Without them there is a spiritual drought and the absence of real spiritual breakthroughs. Our desire should not be for fakery, hysteria or showmanship. It should be a desire for real moves of the Holy Spirit, for a wide range of operations of the Spirit (including both the spectacular and less spectacular), and for a spirituality with signs and wonders and devotion to holy, Christlike living.

Every believer needs to be alerted as to what is at stake when it comes to the gifts of the Spirit. Through the gifts, we encounter the action of the loving God, who builds up the community of believers for ministry in the church and world. No theology of spiritual gifts can adequately describe what God does. Paul must have known this when he wrote, "Oh, the depth of the riches both of the wisdom and knowledge of God! How unsearchable are His judgments and unfathomable His ways!" (Romans 11:33). Indeed, an extraordinary fact is that human beings, frail men and women, become the channels for the Spirit's manifestations and through those manifestations encounter the living God.

Summary

- All gifts and all believers are valuable and essential to the health and function of the body of Christ.

- God's gifts for *practical service* include gifts of service, exhortation, giving, and showing mercy.

- God's gifts of *power* include gifts of faith, healings, and workings of miracles.

- God's gifts of revelation include gifts of wisdom and knowledge.

- God's gifts for *worship* include gifts of prophecy, discernings of spirits, speaking in tongues, and interpretation of tongues.

TABLE 9-A **Gifts for Practical Service**
Gifts for practical service are valuable and essential to the health and function of the body of Christ.
Service
The gift of service includes various types of spiritual service, such as ministry to the poor, preparing of meals, assisting the disabled, and providing other practical services as opportunities present themselves. ACTS 6:2-6; ROMANS 12:6, 7
Exhortation
The gift of exhortation is sometimes referred to as the "gift of encouragement." This spiritual gift includes offering encouragement, inspiration or advice. ROMANS 12:8; 1 CORINTHIANS 14:3
Giving
The phrase "he who gives" is used to describe this gift, indicating a God-given capacity to share one's personal possessions with others. The expression of this gift may include the giving of either finances or other items that are needed. ACTS 4:36, 37; ROMANS 12:8
Showing Mercy
The phrase "he who shows mercy" is used to describe this gift and indicates the expression of God's goodness to those who are in need or trouble. GENESIS 43:14ff.; EXODUS 34:6; LUKE 10:37; ROMANS 12:8

TABLE 9-B **Gifts for Practical Service in Action**
Service
Church Offices Examples of church offices in which people with the gift of service often minister: • Deacon, deaconess • Church secretary • Custodian, grounds worker • Van driver • Sound engineer • Usher, greeter, parking lot attendant • Musician • Cook • Nursery worker • Translator for the deaf • Worship banner designer • Helper for a children's Sunday school teacher
Other Types of Ministry Examples of ways that one might use the gift of service: • Making preparations for church events • Compiling the weekly church bulletin • Helping put up and take down church bulletin boards • Collecting and taking church recyclables to the community collection site • Organizing materials in the church library • Repairing the plumbing in the church • Maintaining the church's computers • Maintaining and repairing widows' cars • Building a wheelchair ramp • Driving in a neighborhood carpool • Cooking, cleaning and maintaining one's home in service to family

continued

TABLE 9-B (CONTINUED) **Gifts for Practical Service in Action**	
Exhortation (Encouragement)	
Church Offices	Examples of church offices in which people with the gift of exhortation often serve: • Counselor • Support group leader • Visitation worker • Greeter • Teacher • Mentor • Coach • Singer
Other Types of Ministry	Examples of ways that one might use the gift of exhortation: • Encouraging other people in the use of their spiritual gifts • Listening and encouraging others when they are lonely or discouraged • Painting uplifting artwork for the church and community • Singing or playing a spiritually inspiring song • Writing notes of encouragement to friends and family • Spending time playing with the neighborhood children • Listening to one's spouse tell about his or her day

continued

Table 9-B (continued) Gifts for Practical Service in Action

Giving

Church Offices	Examples of church offices in which people with the gift of giving often serve: • Mercy ministry worker • Deacon, deaconess • Christian charity fund-raiser
Other Types of Ministry	Examples of ways that one might use the gift of giving: • Giving finances to the church's ministries and to missions • Preparing and giving food for church and ministry events • Giving food, clothing, furniture or school supplies to those in need • Donating money to pay for a teenager's church activities • Assisting someone with college tuition costs • Sponsoring a child in another country • Loaning one's tools to a neighbor • Helping out a family member or friend in a medical financial crisis

Showing Mercy

Church Offices	Examples of church offices in which people with the gift of showing mercy often serve: • Mercy ministry worker • Deacon, deaconess • Hospital chaplain • Counselor • Support group leader • Visitation worker

continued

TABLE 9-B (CONTINUED)
Gifts for Practical Service in Action

Showing Mercy (continued)	
Other Types of Ministry	Examples of ways that one might use the gift of showing mercy: • Preparing food for families who have experienced the death of someone they love • Driving someone to the hospital for medical treatments • Volunteering in a shelter for battered women • Joining the volunteer fire department • Calling and encouraging someone going through a divorce • Inviting neighbors to stay in one's home when their electricity goes out • Hugging a child when he or she tells about problems with friends at school
Notes	

TABLE 9-C
Gifts of Power

Gifts of supernatural power demonstrate the immediate effect of God's work in our lives and in the lives of others.

Faith

The gift of faith is a supernatural endowment by the Spirit that enables a believer to trust God for the extraordinary.

1 KINGS 18:20-39; DANIEL 6:19-22;
ACTS 3:3-11; 14:8-10; 1 CORINTHIANS 12:9; 13:2

Types of faith in the life of the church include: saving faith, fruit of faith and the gift of faith.

MATTHEW 17:20; 21:21; ROMANS 3:24, 25; GALATIANS 5:22

Healings

The "gifts of healings" are given to individuals, empowering them to pray for the healing of mental, spiritual and physical illnesses and disabilities.

MATTHEW 4:23; 10:1; ACTS 10:38; 1 CORINTHIANS 12:9, 28

Workings of Miracles

The phrase "the workings of miracles" is used to describe the spiritual gift of performing "signs and wonders." Through this gift, God performs supernatural miracles that may be outside of natural laws or laws of probability.

MATTHEW 12:28; ACTS 9:36-42; 13:4-12; 20:9-12;
1 CORINTHIANS 12:10, 29; GALATIANS 3:5; HEBREWS 2:4

TABLE 9-D **Gifts of Power in Action**	
Faith	
Church Offices	Examples of church offices in which people with the gift of faith often serve: • Prayer meeting leader • Prayer chain member • Prayer partner • Altar assistant • Visitation worker
Other Types of Ministry	Examples of ways that one might use the gift of faith: • Trusting God for supernatural miracles • Recognizing that God-given miracles are indeed signs from God • Praying for God to provide for those in need and trusting that He will • Trusting that God will provide the answer to a problem, even when no solution is evident • Trusting that God will bring good out of difficult circumstances • Praying and trusting that God will work in the course of events in one's family, church, community, country and world
Healings	
Church Offices	Examples of church offices in which people with the gifts of healings often serve: • Prayer meeting leader • Prayer chain member • Altar assistant • Visitation worker

continued

TABLE 9-D (CONTINUED)
Gifts of Power in Action

Healings (continued)	
Church Offices (continued)	• Hospital chaplain • Counselor • Medical missionary • Parish nurse
Other Types of Ministry	Examples of ways that one might use the gifts of healings: • Praying for someone who is physically, mentally or spiritually ill • Praying for someone who is depressed • Being a calming presence with someone who is suffering from stress, so that the person can allow God to minister to and to heal him or her • Communicating knowledge and wisdom regarding steps an individual needs to take in order to receive God's healing • A health care professional's treating patients, while being guided by the Holy Spirit

Workings of Miracles	
Church Offices	Examples of church offices in which people with the gift of workings of miracles often serve: • Prayer meeting leader • Prayer chain member • Altar assistant • Visitation worker • Evangelist • Missionary • Prison ministry worker • Inner-city minister

continued

TABLE 9-D (CONTINUED) Gifts of Power in Action	
Workings of Miracles (continued)	
Other Types of Ministry	Examples of ways that one might use the gift of workings of miracles: • Praying for visible or audible signs of God's presence • Casting out demons • Praying for natural laws to be suspended as a sign to believers or unbelievers • Praying to bring someone back to life as a sign to unbelievers • Praying for God's extraordinary intervention in everyday life
Notes	

TABLE 9-E
Gifts of Revelation

The Holy Spirit is called "the Spirit of truth" because He is the great revealer of truth. JOHN 14:17; 16:13-15; 1 CORINTHIANS 2:6-16
A Word of Wisdom
The gift of "a word of wisdom" is a message of wisdom and insight revealed to an individual by the Holy Spirit. LUKE 12:11, 12; 20:20-26; ACTS 4:8-13; 15:13-21; 1 CORINTHIANS 12:8
A Word of Knowledge
The gift of "a word of knowledge" is information revealed to an individual by the Holy Spirit, along with the capacity to express the knowledge through language. JOHN 1:44-49; ACTS 5:1-11; 1 CORINTHIANS 12:8; 14:6
Notes

TABLE 9-F	
Gifts of Revelation in Action	
A Word of Wisdom	
Church Offices	Examples of church offices in which people with the gift of wisdom often serve: • Prophet • Pastor • Elder • Spiritual director • Counselor • Mentor • Visitation worker
Other Types of Ministry	Examples of ways that one might use the gift of wisdom: • Sharing a Spirit-inspired message of wisdom during a worship gathering • Sharing with a person a message of wisdom and guidance for his or her life • Having a dream that confirms or clarifies a course of action in the church or in one's own life • Sharing with one's community words of wisdom regarding political or community issues • Receiving special wisdom for addressing problems and taking action in one's personal or family life

continued

TABLE 9-F (CONTINUED) **Gifts of Revelation in Action**	
A Word of Knowledge	
Church Offices	Examples of church offices in which people with the gift of knowledge often serve: • Prophet • Prayer warrior • Spiritual director • Counselor • Mentor • Youth worker
Other Types of Ministry	Examples of ways that one might use the gift of knowledge: • Sharing a Spirit-inspired message of knowledge during a worship gathering • Offering encouragement regarding future events • Giving a warning regarding future events • Sharing with an individual some insight regarding that person's circumstances or spiritual condition, so that he or she will realize the reality of Christ's love and will be drawn to Him • Receiving insight regarding a person's circumstances or spiritual condition, and using this insight to pray, counsel or minister in other ways to the individual • Having a gut feeling that something is wrong, and using that knowledge to pray and to avoid danger

TABLE 9-G
Gifts for Worship

The gifts of the Spirit bring a remarkable intensity and richness to our worship and praise of God.

Prophecy

Prophecy is a message directly from God, in which the Holy Spirit provides fresh insight into a spiritual matter. The message may be shared with others during a worship gathering. A prophecy will always edify, exhort or console the church.

ROMANS 12:6; 1 CORINTHIANS 11:4, 5; 12–14; EPHESIANS 2:20; 3:5; 4:11; 1 THESSALONIANS 4:13-18; 5:20; 1 TIMOTHY 1:18; 4:14

Individuals who hear prophecies should evaluate them against the teachings of the Bible in order to determine their truthfulness.

1 CORINTHIANS 13:9-12; 14:29; 1 THESSALONIANS 5:20, 21

See also chapter 8: "Gifts of Leadership" and Tables 8-E and 8-F.

Discernings of Spirits

The gift of "discernings of spirits" is often referred to as "the gift of discernment." This gift may be used to determine if a prophecy is true, or to distinguish between what is from God and what is not.

MATTHEW 22:18; MARK 1:23-28; 5:2-16; 1 CORINTHIANS 12:10; 14:29

continued

TABLE 9-G (CONTINUED)
Gifts for Worship

Speaking in Tongues

"Speaking in tongues" refers to the gift that enables someone, under the inspiration of the Spirit, to speak in a language—either human or angelic—that is unknown by the speaker. A person may use this gift during public or private worship. As a gift for public worship, tongues should be accompanied by interpretation for the edification of the congregation.

The gift of speaking in tongues may serve to build up the church, as a sign to unbelievers, or as an aid in private prayer and devotion.

ACTS 2:4, 11; 10:46; 19:6; ROMANS 8:26, 27; 1 CORINTHIANS 12–14

Interpretation of Tongues

The gift of "interpretation of tongues" is the Spirit-given ability to interpret or explain the meaning of a message in other tongues in order to build up the church.

1 CORINTHIANS 12:10, 30; 14:2ff.

Notes

TABLE 9-H Gifts for Worship in Action	
Prophecy	
Church Offices	Examples of church offices in which people with the gift of prophecy often serve: • Prophet • Pastor • Teacher • Spiritual director • Counselor • Chaplain
Other Types of Ministry	Examples of ways that one might use the gift of prophecy: • Sharing a Spirit-inspired message of prophecy during a worship gathering • Speaking a message of wisdom and guidance that addresses current circumstances • Communicating a message of comfort • Communicating a message of encouragement • Communicating a message of rebuke for divisive activities and wrongdoings in the church • Communicating a message that reminds people how much God loves and cares for them
Discernings of Spirits	
Church Offices	Examples of church offices in which people with the gift of discernings of spirits often serve: • Apostle • Evangelist • Missionary • Altar assistant • Prison ministry worker • Community chaplain, street ministry worker

continued

TABLE 9-H (CONTINUED)
Gifts for Worship in Action

	Discernings of Spirits (continued)
Other Types of Ministry	Examples of ways that one might use the gift of discernings of spirits: • Determining whether a prophecy is inspired by God, by an individual's personal emotions, or by an evil spirit • Sensing that a person has evil intentions or motives • Sensing the presence of danger and changing one's course of action
	Speaking in Tongues
Church Offices	People who have the gift of speaking in tongues do not necessarily gravitate toward any particular church offices.
Other Types of Ministry	Examples of ways that one might use the gift of speaking in tongues: • Speaking a message in tongues which, when interpreted, communicates a message of knowledge, wisdom or encouragement to those who are gathered worshiping God • Speaking a message in tongues that is a human language and that is the native language of someone present • Speaking in other languages in private prayer and worship

continued

TABLE 9-H (CONTINUED) **Gifts for Worship in Action**	
Interpretation of Tongues	
Church Offices	People who have the gift of interpretation of tongues do not necessarily gravitate toward any particular church offices.
Other Types of Ministry	Examples of ways that one might use the gift of interpretation: • Interpreting a message in tongues that has been spoken in a worship gathering • Confirming another person's interpretation of a message in tongues in a worship gathering
Notes	

Chapter 9—Study and Discussion

Discussion suggestion for study groups: Break into smaller groups and divide these questions among the groups. After a few minutes, each smaller group may summarize its discussion for the larger group.

Gifts for Practical Service

1. What are gifts for practical service? (See Table 9-A and the Glossary.)

Service

2. Describe the gift of service. (See Table 9-A and the Glossary.)

3. What word do we have today that is derived from *diakonia*, the Greek word for "service"? (See Romans 12:7; Acts 6:2-6.)

4. What is an example of the gift of service in the Bible? (See Table 9-A.)

5. What are some types of ministry that a person with the gift of service might do today? (See Table 9-B.)

6. Think of an individual in your church who has the gift of service. Describe that person's acts of service, and what he or she has meant to the life of the church.

Exhortation

7. Describe the gift of exhortation. (See Table 9-A and the Glossary.

8. What is an example of the gift of exhortation in the Bible? (See Table 9-A.)

9. What are some types of ministry that a person with the gift of exhortation might do today? (See Table 9-B.)

10. Think of an individual in your church who has the gift of exhortation. Describe that person's acts of service and what he or she has meant to the life of the church.

Giving

11. Describe the gift of giving. (See Table 9-A and the Glossary.)

12. What is an example of the gift of giving in the Bible? (See Table 9-A.)

13. What are some types of ministry that a person with the gift of giving might do today? (See Table 9-B.)

14. Think of an individual in your church who has the gift of giving. Describe that person's acts of service and what he or she has meant to the life of the church.

Showing Mercy

15. Describe the gift of showing mercy. (See Table 9-A and the Glossary.)

16. What is an example of the gift of showing mercy in the Bible? (See Table 9-A.)

17. What are some types of ministry that a person with the gift of showing mercy might do today? (See Table 9-B.)

18. Think of an individual in your church who has the gift of showing mercy. Describe that person's acts of service and what he or she has meant to the life of the church.

GIFTS OF POWER

19. What are gifts of power? (See Table 9-C and the Glossary.)

Faith

20. Describe the gift of faith. (See Table 9-C and the Glossary.)

21. What is an example of the gift of faith in the Bible? (See Table 9-C.)

22. What are the various types of faith in the Christian experience and life of the church? (See Table 9-C.)

23. What are some types of ministry that a person with the gift of faith might do today? (See Table 9-D.)

24. Do you know someone who has the gift of faith? Describe that person's acts of service, and what he or she has meant to the life of the church.

Healings

25. Describe the gift of healings. (See Table 9-C and the Glossary.)

26. What is an example of the gift of healings in the Bible? (See Table 9-C.)

27. What types of ailments and disorders does God heal? (See Table 9-C.)

28. What are some types of ministry that a person with the gift of healings might do today? (See Table 9-D.)

29. Do you know someone who has the gift of healings? Describe that person's acts of service and what he or she has meant to the life of the church.

Workings of Miracles

30. Describe the gift of workings of miracles. (Table 9-C and the Glossary.)

31. What is an example of the gift of workings of miracles in the Bible? (See Table 9-C.)

32. What are some types of ministry that a person with the gift of workings of miracles might do today? (See Table 9-D.)

33. Do you know someone who has the gift of workings of miracles? Describe that person's acts of service, and what he or she has meant to the life of the church.

GIFTS OF REVELATION

34. What are gifts of revelation? (See Table 9-E and the Glossary.)

A Word of Wisdom

35. Describe the gift of a "word of wisdom." (See Table 9-E and the Glossary.)

36. What is an example of the gift of wisdom in the Bible? (See Table 9-E.)

37. What are some types of ministry that a person with the gift of wisdom might do today? (See Table 9-F.)

38. Do you know someone who has the gift of wisdom? Describe that person's acts of service, and what he or she has meant to the life of the church.

A Word of Knowledge

39. Describe the gift of a "word of knowledge." (See Table 9-E and the Glossary.)

40. What is an example of the gift of knowledge in the Bible? (See Table 9-E.)

41. What are some types of ministry that a person with the gift of knowledge might do today? (See Table 9-F.)

42. Do you know someone who has the gift of knowledge? Describe that person's acts of service and what he or she has meant to the life of the church.

GIFTS FOR WORSHIP

43. What benefit are the gifts of the Spirit to our worship of God? (See Table 9-G.)

Prophecy

44. Describe the gift of prophecy. (See Table 9-G and the Glossary.)

45. What is an example of the gift of prophecy in the Bible? (See Table 9-G.)

46. What are some types of ministry that a person with the gift of prophecy might do today? (See Table 9-H.)

47. Do you know someone who has the gift of prophecy? Describe that person's acts of service and what he or she has meant to the life of the church.

Discernings (Distinguishings) of Spirits

48. Describe the gift of discernings of spirits. (See Table 9-G and the Glossary.)

49. What is an example of the gift of discernings of spirits in the Bible? (See Table 9-G.)

50. What are some types of ministry that a person with the gift of discernings of spirits might do today? (See Table 9-H.)

51. Do you know someone who has the gift of discernment? Describe that person's acts of service and what he or she has meant to the life of the church.

Speaking in Tongues

52. Describe the gift of speaking in tongues. (See Table 9-G and the Glossary under "Gift of Tongues.")

53. What is an example of the gift of tongues in the Bible? (See Table 9-G.)

54. What are some examples of incidents in which persons might use the gift of tongues today? (See Table 9-H.)

55. Do you know someone who has the gift of tongues? Describe a time when you have heard that person use this gift and what this ministry has meant to the life of the church.

Interpretation of Tongues

56. Describe the gift of interpretation of tongues. (See Table 9-G and the Glossary.)

57. What is an example of the gift of interpretation in the Bible? (See Table 9-G.)

58. What are some examples of incidents in which persons might use the gift of interpretation today? (See Table 9-H.)

59. Do you know someone who has the gift of interpretation? Describe a time when you have heard that person use this gift and what this ministry has meant to the life of the church.

CONCLUSION

60. All believers are given one or more spiritual gifts to use to build up and encourage the body of Christ.

- Try to think what your spiritual gift(s) might be.

- Think of ways that you may have already used your gift(s) in your church, home, work, neighborhood, city and world.

- Think of new ways you might incorporate your gift into your daily routine, expressing the love of Christ to the world around you.

61. Now, think of how your gift(s) relate to other gifts in the church. What other gifts complement yours?

62. Discuss how you and others in the church might work together to minister in a balanced way, using your gifts to serve each other and the world in such a manner that:

- everyone is allowed to express his or her gift,

- each person is honored for his or her contribution to Christ's work, whether it seems big or small, or whether the service occurs in the church, home, or community,

- there are allowances for weaknesses and imperfections,

- there is time to listen to God, and

- there is time for rest and rejuvenation.

Part Five

Spiritual Challenges

You are the light of the world—like a city on a mountain, glowing in the night for all to see (Matthew 5:14, *NLT*).

10

Challenges for the Spirit-Led Church Today

One of the most exciting trends in Christianity in the last century has been a new wave of desire for things of the Spirit. Coming from humble and unexpected beginnings, the Pentecostal and Charismatic Movements have greatly impacted the world through the Spirit-led lives of their people. Their sharing of Christ's love, their enthusiasm for worship, and their passion for serving others through the power of the Holy Spirit have profoundly affected the world around them. From underground churches in communist lands, to small storefront and house churches in urban neighborhoods, to large modern churches in the suburbs, Spirit-filled Christians have enthusiastically told about and have compassionately demonstrated Christ's love to others. Their dedication to being led by the Holy Spirit has impacted both secular and religious society and has had a major effect on the Christian church around the world.

Christians who have encountered the Holy Spirit in a powerful way include people from a wide variety of backgrounds and walks of life. They include new converts as well as individuals from various religious traditions, such as fundamental, Evangelical, Catholic and mainline Christian traditions. Many Christians from these traditions have noted that the Spirit's move in their lives and in their worship has empowered them to be more effective in sharing the good news within their denominations and the world.

In recent years, the Christian community has experienced a rapid increase in the number of people who desire to be empowered by the Holy Spirit. Modern advances—such as financial prosperity in the developed world, modern communication systems, faster transportation, computer technology, and a global economy—have contributed greatly to the spread of the Pentecostal/Charismatic Movements. This growth has accelerated as the speed of our society has accelerated. Such rapid growth, while exciting, has created some special challenges for Spirit-led believers. In the face of such change, Christians are confronted with the question of how to best apply their faith to their lives in today's world. They are faced with the challenge of integrating their desire to be relevant in our modern society with teachings in the Bible and their Charismatic or Pentecostal heritage.

In this chapter, we will look at some of the issues facing the church today. The hope is that by introducing these issues, churches will be inspired to begin a dialogue, thinking creatively and discussing how they might address the challenges before them. The goal of such a process is to bring into clearer focus ways in which we, the body of Christ, might grow spiritually and serve others in the world. There are no easy formulas for expressing our faith in such changing times. For this reason, the church today needs the Holy Spirit's guidance more than ever.

UNDERSTANDING AND COMMUNICATING THE TEACHINGS OF THE BIBLE

The Question

How should we view and understand the teachings of God's Word and effectively communicate those teachings to others?

Background

The Holy Spirit calls each believer to worship and participate in the community of faith. This worship and fellowship of the church provide the context in which Pentecostals interpret the Scriptures. Pentecostals strive to hear what the voice of the Holy Spirit says through the Bible. For them, the truth and authority of Scripture must be spiritually discerned. This method of interpretation demands more than a detailed analysis of the Biblical text and the application of principles of interpretation. It also demands sensitivity to the Spirit's guidance, especially in the fellowship of the church, which is empowered by the gifts of the Spirit and by the anointed preaching of the gospel. Interpreting Scripture becomes an encounter with the Holy Spirit in which people are transformed as they experience the truth revealed in the Bible. What happened for the prophets and apostles in the past happens now for those who take to heart God's Word.

Observations

Pentecostal scholarship has made great strides in the last three decades. Many Pentecostal pastors have received graduate degrees, and many members of Pentecostal denominations have become more knowledgeable about the Bible. Today, Spirit-filled scholars write and produce materials that are acclaimed throughout the academic community. It is commendable that so many Pentecostal scholars have dedicated their lives to learning in-depth about God's teachings. Also, it is admirable that they continue to communicate this knowledge to the world and to challenge Spirit-led Christians to have the courage to resist trendiness and to embrace God's eternal truths, allowing the Spirit to lead and empower them.

Pentecostal teachings have become more mainstream. As a result, we must be cautious as we live and move in the world and communicate the teachings of the Bible. In our enthusiastic efforts to be functioning parts of our academic communities and our local communities, we can sometimes unintentionally depart from the original purpose of the writers of the Bible. As students of God's Word, we must continue to make valiant efforts to communicate our knowledge of God's ways in a manner that the world can understand. As we do, we want to remain true to the teachings of the Bible while accurately applying God's truths to the world in which we live.

God's Word

"All Scripture is inspired by God and profitable for teaching, for reproof, for correction, for training in righteousness" (2 Timothy 3:16).

Additional Scripture: Matthew 5:17, 18; 2 Peter 1:20, 21

For Consideration

In our efforts to remain true to God's teachings, put them into practice in our lives, and communicate to others that God's Word is still real and true today, we might consider the following aspects of understanding the Bible and communicating its truths.

1. *In our efforts to fit in and be relevant within our communities, we want to be careful not to add to or take away from teachings of the Bible when those teachings make us feel uncomfortable.* Our efforts for relevancy may include our scholarship in the academic community, our teaching in the church pulpit or classroom, our participation with churches of different denominations, and the sharing of our faith within a religiously diverse world.

2. *We want the Pentecostal Movement to continue to contribute scholarly works about the Holy Spirit within the Christian church, as well as to make valuable contributions to scholarship on other Christian topics.* If we adopt a position that fails to support the authority and integrity of Scripture, then the foundations upon which we, as Spirit-led people, have defined and built our very lives could begin to crumble.

3. *In our local churches, we want to believe that encounters with the Holy Spirit are real, because the Bible presents them as being a*

reality in the life of believers. As the body of Christ, we want to hear the living voice of the Spirit and follow His lead, while at the same time, being faithful to the teachings and directives of Scripture. We want to treasure the Bible as God's very Word.

If we do not rely on the Bible as our guide for living, we may interpret God's teachings in more figurative ways. We may mistakenly come to see events recorded in the Bible as only being stories from a particular culture, rather than being lessons for us today; or we may come to think that God moved in Biblical times one way but no longer moves that way today. Such understandings of the Bible may cause some people to question the very reality of God, the saving power of Jesus Christ and encounters with the Holy Spirit.

We need to be very careful to embrace the full truth of the Bible, that is, the truth that God works through His Holy Spirit . . .

- To create us and our world
- To move us to be repentant about our wrongdoings
- To inspire us to accept Christ's love and forgiveness in our lives
- To give us spiritual graces and gifts, helping us to express them in our world
- To baptize us in His Spirit, giving us spiritual empowerment to share our faith with others
- To give us wisdom and power to live an incredible life dedicated to God
- To perform miracles in our lives and in our world.

4. *We want to see the Holy Spirit's work as enhancing Scripture, not as being a rival to or a substitute for God's written Word.* The Word of God is "the sword of the Spirit" (Ephesians 6:17). The bond between the Holy Spirit and the Scriptures is strong. The Scriptures are the instrument of the Spirit, and they are effective as the Spirit uses them. Without the Holy Spirit, the

Scriptures would be words without light and power. Through His powerful inward ministry in our hearts, the Spirit works with the writers' words and illuminates the truth of the gospel and God's will. The Spirit may bring divine truth to us in song, in testimony, in sermon or through spiritual gifts; however, all such means take us back to the written Word. God's Word will not return empty, for the Holy Spirit illuminates it and makes it powerful (Isaiah 55:11; Hebrews 4:12).

The Challenge

May we embrace the Bible as God's Word, be diligent in our study of His teachings, rely on the Holy Spirit for understanding and wisdom, and accurately communicate His truths to the world.

BEING AMBASSADORS FOR CHRIST IN TODAY'S WORLD

The Question

As individuals and as a church, how can we function as members of our modern society while living Spirit-filled lives that are true to our spiritual values?

Background

The mark of a true believer is submission to the Spirit. Walking in submission to the Spirit involves allowing Him to nurture both spiritual gifts and spiritual graces (fruit) in our lives. The Spirit's power in the life of the Christian should be demonstrated not only through ministry and service, but also through personal integrity and holiness. The Christian life calls for commitment in daily living to practice the presence of God.

Observations

Because we live in a world in which we are continually exposed to values in our work, our relationships and our media that are contrary to God's teachings, Christians often feel pressure to conform. This constant pressure may hinder them from living a lifestyle that is led by the Holy Spirit.

In its beginnings, the Pentecostal Movement often saw itself as a protest movement—a protest against individuals' observing Christian worship rituals without considering their meaning; a protest against spiritual apathy in worship; a protest against the church's becoming sterile and powerless in the world; and a protest against arrogance, pride, ungodliness, and evil in the church and the world.

Today in many countries, Pentecostals and Charismatics enjoy more widespread acceptance within the Christian community and in the general public. They are often more financially affluent and have more prominent positions in society than they did in the past. No doubt this has prompted them to play down some of the more controversial aspects of their Pentecostal beliefs. If we are not careful, our success, status and affluence may breed complacency and make us less aware of our conformity to the world. The real danger for us is that of blending in and losing the cutting edge of the original message, which is that Jesus Christ is our Savior and that the Holy Spirit will empower every believer. If we are not able to offer people in this world a new life, a new family and a new culture in the Christian church, then what do we have to give them?

God's Word

"Love the Lord your God with all your heart and with all your soul and with all your mind and with all your strength" (Mark 12:30, *NIV*).

"Don't copy the behavior and customs of this world, but let God transform you into a new person by changing the way you think. Then you will know what God wants you to do, and you will know how good and pleasing and perfect his will really is" (Romans 12:2, *NLT*).

"Peace I leave with you; my peace I give you. I do not give to you as the world gives. Do not let your hearts be troubled and do not be afraid" (John 14:27, *NIV*).

For Consideration

1. *We want our lives to encompass a balance of both holiness and love.* As Spirit-filled Christians, we need to take a fresh look at the holiness of God in the Old Testament and the love of the Savior Jesus Christ in the Gospels. Jesus gave His life in order to purchase our salvation and to conquer the Evil One.

2. *We want to remember and to benefit from the heritage of our Pentecostal and Charismatic Movements' founders.* We need to embrace their passion for being committed to follow the Spirit in our everyday walk in the world, being honest, living with integrity and following God's laws.

3. *We want to pray for the Holy Spirit to rekindle and revitalize our spiritual ardor so that we hunger for more of God, long for His holiness and enjoy a vibrant life in the Spirit.*

The Challenge

With the Holy Spirit's guidance, may we not give into temptation to conform to the morals and values of the world, but to be courageous—patterning our lives after Christ and being His ambassadors, shining the light of hope to the world.

RECEIVING THE SPIRIT'S EMPOWERMENT

The Question

How are Spirit baptism and speaking in other tongues relevant to each of our lives and to the worship life of our churches?

Background

The most defining characteristic of Pentecostalism within the Christian community is belief in Spirit baptism and speaking in other tongues. Many other beliefs embraced by Pentecostals are equally or even more important to the group's identity, such as salvation through faith in Christ, Christlike living, sharing the good news, prayer for the sick, and so forth. However, speaking in tongues remains the distinguishing belief that sets Pentecostals apart from other Christian groups and movements that have similar beliefs.

Observations

Today, some Pentecostals have de-emphasized speaking in tongues. Crucial to the early life of the Movement, this experience served as verification of one's being baptized in the Spirit. When one received Spirit baptism in public worship, speaking in tongues announced to those present that the recipient was receiving empowerment for Christian service. It signified that he or she was a potential candidate for spiritual leadership and empowered ministry. Baptism in the Holy Spirit was not generally perceived by Pentecostals as being equal to or essential for salvation. They did, however, consider it to be essential to empowered Christian living, because Jesus Christ had commanded His disciples to be baptized in the Holy Spirit.

As the initial physical sign of Spirit baptism, speaking in tongues has been a controversial and highly debated belief. The subject has been debated even among Pentecostals themselves, and sometimes this discussion has become a major issue of controversy within some Pentecostal denominations. Frequently, the debate focuses only on Biblical and theological issues, overlooking the purpose that speaking in tongues has served throughout the Pentecostal Movement's existence. Speaking in tongues has proven to be a verifiable experience that provided validity and promoted a unifying cohesion that has been essential in sustaining Pentecostalism.

God's Word

"And everyone present was filled with the Holy Spirit and began speaking in other languages, as the Holy Spirit gave them this ability" (Acts 2:4, *NLT*).

"But when the Holy Spirit has come upon you, you will receive power and will tell people about me everywhere—in Jerusalem, throughout Judea, in Samaria, and to the ends of the earth" (Acts 1:8, *NLT*).

Additional Scripture: Acts 2:33; 11:15

For Consideration

Perhaps the central issue for discussion regarding speaking in other tongues should be this: Can Pentecostalism remain Pentecostal if churches give up speaking in tongues as the initial physical sign of Spirit baptism? This question concerns more than just mere definitions of Spirit baptism; it also includes the Pentecostal Movement's ability to retain the distinguishing and admirable features that have characterized it. Some of these features are a passion for God, fervent evangelism, childlike faith, empowerment of the poor, unity of faith, avoidance of worldliness, Charismatic expressions in worship and the importance of the gifts of the Spirit.

Granted, these characteristics do not rely on just one doctrine, such as speaking in tongues. Since many Evangelical groups exhibit a number of these same traits, some people contend that speaking in tongues does not contribute to the important aspects of Pentecostalism. However, such an opinion fails to consider the unique role that speaking in tongues has played in the Pentecostal Movement.

1. *Removing speaking in tongues from the Movement's teachings may bring into question other related teachings.* Since belief of tongues has been an outcome from, and in some cases a catalyst for, other Pentecostal beliefs, to give up speaking in tongues may affect other basic beliefs of the Movement. For example, just as early Pentecostal groups understood that Scripture supported their belief in Spirit baptism and speaking in tongues, they also took all aspects of Scripture to be the very Word of God.

Thus, most of Pentecostalism's teachings and practices were based on the facts and application of Scripture. If Pentecostals no longer embrace speaking in tongues, they then bring into question the entire concept of understanding the Bible as being instructions for our lives today.

2. *If Pentecostal groups give up their belief in speaking in tongues as the initial physical sign of being baptized in the Spirit, they will no longer have concrete evidence of Spirit baptism.* Such a position could lead fewer people to seek Spirit baptism, because there would not be verifiable evidence to encourage seekers. As fewer people experience speaking in tongues, eventually this shift could lead to questions concerning the validity of Spirit baptism as an experience that follows salvation. As speaking in tongues becomes less significant to Pentecostals, Pentecostalism actually could cease to be Pentecostal. That is, the Pentecostal Movement would no longer be a spiritual movement that emphasizes believers' ability to receive the gift of supernatural empowerment like the apostles did on the Day of Pentecost.

3. *Speaking in tongues has served Pentecostalism well.* It has provided evangelistic vitality to Pentecostal groups as they have experienced Spirit baptism in the same manner as portrayed in the Book of Acts. Also, the experience has contributed to the cohesion of the group, providing easy identification of like-minded believers. To diminish belief in such a central aspect of the Pentecostal Movement's existence is to remove a key component of the identity of the Movement. Before a Pentecostal group changes its position on the initial physical evidence of Spirit baptism, they may need to ask the question: Do we want to retain our identity as a Pentecostal organization?

The Challenge

May we always be open to miraculous, life-changing encounters with the Holy Spirit. May we invite Him to fill us with His presence, submitting to His guidance, and allowing Him to speak through us.

EMBRACING THE MOVE OF THE SPIRIT IN OUR LIVES

The Question

How does the Holy Spirit move in our lives?

Background

The Holy Spirit's work in our lives is very multifaceted. The Bible tells of many ways that we can recognize the Spirit's work:

- He works in the events of history.
- He plays a vital role in our conversion and spiritual growth.
- He develops spiritual graces in us and in our relationships with others.
- He blesses us with strength and courage for daily living.
- He guides us in both large and small matters.
- He takes the small daily tasks of our lives and gives them eternal significance.
- He takes our weaknesses and uses them to accomplish God's purposes.
- He speaks to us through supernatural signs.
- He speaks to us in the silence.
- He speaks to us through spiritually gifted people.
- He speaks to us through the beauty of God's creation.
- He speaks to us through human history.
- He speaks through us, allowing us to encourage, enlighten and empower others.
- He gives us the ability to love.
- He gives us the ability to do special work for God.

Observations

The Holy Spirit's work permeates every aspect of the Christian life. His work on earth is multidimensional and balanced in its expression. Among the Spirit's works in our lives are His manifestations of His presence and power through demonstrative worship and spectacular, visible spiritual gifts. He is also very present in silence, in our use of less dramatic gifts of service, and in the quiet graces of the daily Christian life.

As individuals with particular personalities and spiritual gifts, we are generally drawn to aspects of the Holy Spirit's work with which we are most familiar and comfortable. If we are more outgoing and emotive, then we may be drawn to the Holy Spirit's more demonstrative manifestations in worship and spiritual gifts. If we are more reserved and analytical, we may be drawn to quiet moves of the Spirit and more structured and reflective styles of worship. In local churches, we also tend to gravitate toward other people with similar personalities and worship styles. As a result, individual congregations often focus on particular worship practices and works of the Spirit. This becomes evident in their internal life, as well as in their external presence in the world. One of the challenges, then, for individuals and churches is to allow the Holy Spirit to move in all areas of life and in any manner He chooses.

God's Word

"But when the Holy Spirit controls our lives, He will produce this kind of fruit in us: love, joy, peace, patience, kindness, goodness, faithfulness, gentleness, and self-control" (Galatians 5:22, 23, *NLT*).

"If we are living now by the Holy Spirit, let us follow the Holy Spirit's leading in every part of our lives. Let us not become conceited, or irritate one another, or be jealous of one another" (Galatians 5:25, 26, *NLT*).

"May God, who gives this patience and encouragement, help

you live in complete harmony with each other—each with the attitude of Christ Jesus toward the other. Then all of you can join together with one voice, giving praise and glory to God, the Father of our Lord Jesus Christ. So accept each other just as Christ has accepted you; then God will be glorified" (Romans 15:5-7, *NLT*).

Additional Scripture: 1 Corinthians 3:16; Ephesians 5:19, 20

For Consideration

Each individual and each local church tend to be drawn automatically to particular aspects of the Spirit's work and to particular styles of ministry and worship. Therefore, it is desirable for all Christians who want to follow the Spirit's lead in every aspect of life to consider the following questions:

- How can we as individuals with different personalities, lifestyles and abilities recognize the move of the Holy Spirit in our lives?

- How can we invite the Holy Spirit to move in our worship, reflecting many aspects of His work?

- How can we welcome each person into our church family and invite the Holy Spirit to move through that person's gifts in the life of the church?

To begin to answer these questions, we can start with the Holy Spirit himself. The Spirit's work and gifts are varied, and He does not work alone. He works in community with God the Father and the Son. Each person of the Trinity is unique and has particular roles that are dependent on the other persons of the Godhead. Our lives are to be conducted similarly—with each person fulfilling a unique call, contributing to and working with the rest of the body of Christ (the church). Consider the questions we have raised above in light of the community structure that God has created.

1. *How can we as individuals with different personalities, lifestyles and abilities recognize the move of the Holy Spirit in our*

lives? We know that God creates us all as unique individuals with unique personalities and talents, and that the Holy Spirit gives us particular spiritual gifts that are in harmony with our personality and our life circumstances. We can conclude, then, that wherever we are is where the Spirit will use us. We do not have to try to pursue a spectacular ministry or try to copy others' gifts in order to experience the move of the Spirit and be used by Him in the church and the world. We need only to start where we are in our daily lives.

We may sometimes mistakenly think that the Holy Spirit is only present when we have overwhelming emotional feelings or when we experience a supernatural miracle or sign from God. However, the Holy Spirit is always with us. He works through us in the spectacular, but He is also there working in activities we might consider mundane. He gives us daily strength and power to do our work, to care for our families and homes, to be a friend to others, and to tend to our physical needs. When we begin to see the Spirit's work this way, we start to see God everywhere we turn. We see all of our actions as offerings to God.

We begin to find true peace—peace with others, peace with ourselves and peace with God. We start to accept His unique call in our lives and stop comparing ourselves to others and being envious of them. We realize that God is turning our small acts of service into work that has eternal dimensions. We become grateful for what we have and where God has placed us. We stop thinking, out of a sense of worthlessness, that we have to go searching for our true ministries. We begin to see families, neighbors, coworkers and people who pass us on the street as those whom God has placed in our path that day. We develop the ability to hear the Spirit speak to us, as He guides us in our daily activities and when He directs us toward new experiences and new ministry. We begin to thoroughly enjoy the Holy Spirit in our lives and to celebrate His call, His empowerment and His presence moment to moment!

2. *How can we invite the Holy Spirit to move in our worship,*

reflecting many aspects of His work? Since the Holy Spirit works in a wide variety of ways in this world, it is realistic to conclude that He also manifests Himself in different ways in worship. Because we are drawn to worship styles that suit our personalities or our emotional needs, we may inadvertently neglect other aspects of worship. For example, we may be drawn to worship in which there are spectacular demonstrations of the Spirit's power. This inclination may come from a sincere desire to follow the Spirit, a belief that the Spirit is only present when there are demonstrative manifestations, or a desire to be in a constant happy, excited spiritual state. If this is our natural inclination, we may unwittingly overlook the Spirit's presence in teaching, preaching, service and quiet prayer. We may think that God is not with us when we cannot emotionally feel His presence. Therefore, we may then miss some of the blessings that the Holy Spirit wants to give us in our worship.

We all have our own personal inclinations, we are naturally prone to habit, and we are resistant to things that are strange to us. So in order for the Holy Spirit to work and move freely in our worship, we must make a conscious effort to invite Him to do so. This means asking His help with our fears and our habits, and beginning to examine our worship routines and use of our spiritual gifts. As we do so, we might consider the following:

- The ways in which the Spirit moves in our worship

- Whether or not we are allowing the Holy Spirit to help us plan worship that leaves space and flexibility for the spontaneous move of the Spirit

- Whether or not our worship is balanced, consisting of all aspects of the Spirit's work, such as preaching, teaching, exuberant praise, quiet prayer, spectacular gifts and the less visible gifts of service

3. *How can we welcome each person into our church family and invite the Holy Spirit to move through that person's gifts in*

the life of the church? Since each local church has its own worship and ministry focus, one of our challenges is to help people with spiritual gifts different from ours to feel welcome and to become functioning members of our local church family. According to the apostle Paul, we are all members of one body, the body of Christ. As parts of His body, God intends each of us to have a special role in His work. Within the church, we are to use our particular abilities and spiritual gifts to work together in harmony in matters of worship, spiritual growth and service.

Because of our fragmented society and its narrow view of success, peoples' gifts and contributions are often overlooked in the world. Therefore, many individuals come to Christian churches in search of acceptance, affirmation, a new family, real friends and a community in which they can express themselves. This offers the church an opportunity to serve and minister. As the family of God, we want to love people regardless of their culture, ethnic background, education or socioeconomic level. When it comes to their God-given abilities or spiritual gifts, we do not want to reject them or to pressure them to change just because we would be more comfortable if they were more like us.[1] We want to be the body of Christ, realizing, as Paul suggests, that God created all parts, even the apparently weaker ones. All parts are gifts to be cherished and loved.

When the Spirit sends someone to our fellowship who is different from us, we can begin by thanking God for that person and by asking the Spirit to guide us. With the Holy Spirit's guidance, we will find ourselves incorporating each new person's gifts into our worship and ministry. We will begin to celebrate our differences and our similarities as they contribute to God's work. When we have done so, we will see the Spirit move through individuals, and we will

---

[1]Of course, when we meet new people, if the Holy Spirit reveals that they are dangerous or evil, we should follow the Spirit's lead in being cautious.

experience empowerment in the life of the church. We will have peace and joy, knowing that we are indeed being led by the Spirit.

The Challenge

May we always be open to the Holy Spirit and embrace His work in our lives. May we look for Him in spectacular miracles, in ordinary daily routines, in exuberant worship, in quiet contemplation and in our relationships with others.

SHARING THE SAVING LOVE OF CHRIST WITH OTHERS

The Question

What should be the focus of our ministry to the world?

Background

Sharing the good news of salvation, commonly referred to as "evangelism," has been at the heart of Pentecostalism. In the early days of the Movement, Pentecostals felt compelled to share their faith and experiences with other people. They would testify (or witness) to family, friends or even strangers at the grocery store—on the job, at home or almost anywhere. Without formal evangelistic training or programs, Pentecostalism grew rapidly because people who came to have a relationship with Christ shared their faith in a spontaneous fashion.

Observations

Evangelism is still an important aspect of Pentecostal and Charismatic ministry today. Most Pentecostal organizations emphasize it as one of the highest priorities of their group, and most of the laity would consider evangelism to be crucial to the life of the church. In some communities, however, believers are no longer as committed to telling others about Christ's love. We want to examine why this is the case and what we can do to rekindle our desire for Christian service.

God's Word

"For I am not ashamed of this Good News about Christ. It is the power of God at work, saving everyone who believes" (Romans 1:16, *NLT*).

"When I am with those who are oppressed, I share their oppression so that I might bring them to Christ. Yes, I try to find common ground with everyone so that I might bring them to Christ. I do all this to spread the Good News, and in doing so I enjoy its blessings" (1 Corinthians 9:22, 23, *NLT*).

Additional Scripture: Acts 1:8; 20:24; Romans 1:9

For Consideration

1. *In our churches we want to allocate funds in order to ensure that human and financial resources are adequate to support evangelism.* As institutionalization has occurred, more denominational resources and energies have been focused on administration of the organization and internal ministry. Making evangelism a financial priority is crucial to God's work and the vitality of the denominations. It is an area of ministry that many people in the local churches will support.

2. *We want to guard against treating Spirit baptism and other encounters with the Spirit as ends in themselves rather than as their being empowerment for carrying out the Great Commission.* From the perspective of the New Testament and that of the early Pentecostals, baptism in the Spirit was primarily to equip the church for mission. Spirit baptism is more than speaking in tongues; it is power divinely sent for witnessing and sharing the good news of salvation. The testimonies of Pentecostals years ago often reflected their involvement as soulwinners. The theme of power for service is still found in Pentecostal journals, but does it still have the significance for Pentecostals today that it once did?

As the result of the outpouring of the Holy Spirit at Pentecost, Jesus' disciples moved in the power of the Spirit to take their cities for Christ and to evangelize their world. The same held true for those who received Spirit baptism at the beginning of the 20th century. Today, many Pentecostals around the world still actively share their faith, especially in the developing countries. Yet, in many places the fires of evangelism and commitment to soul-winning have been gradually dying among Pentecostal believers. This often results in a decline in the planting of churches as well. We want to renew our vision of Spirit baptism and see it as a special anointing of power for witnessing about the saving grace of Christ.

3. *An emphasis on the doctrine of Spirit baptism must include bringing people to Jesus as their Lord and Savior in faith, repentance, and the new birth.* Christians often seek an encounter with the Spirit more out of a desire for personal fulfillment than they do for being equipped for sacrificial service. The Holy Spirit does not break in just to satisfy emotional needs and to fill spiritual voids in our lives; He also wants to equip us as witnesses to Christ.

The purpose of Luke's emphasis on the coming of the Spirit on the Day of Pentecost was to draw people to Jesus Christ. On that occasion, Peter's sermon pointed to the harvest of souls anticipated by the prophet Joel. The church in the Book of Acts moved in the power of the Spirit to evangelize their towns, cities and the known world. They became soulwinners as a result of a definite encounter with the Holy Spirit at Pentecost. A Pentecostal is, therefore, a soul-winner. Acts 1:8 is more than a memory verse. It is a mark of a Pentecostal: "You will receive power when the Holy Spirit comes on you; and you will be my witnesses" (*NIV*).

The Challenge

May we pray for the Spirit to inspire, empower and guide us as we share the good news of Christ's saving love and forgiveness in a world that so desperately needs Him.

Encouraging the Use of Spiritual Gifts

The Question

How can we encourage and empower individuals and churches to embrace God's call in their lives and, through their spiritual gifts, to express God's love within the body of Christ and the world?

Background

God makes every person unique and gives everyone a spiritual gift for ministry. He also makes each church unique, equipping each one with spiritual gifts for ministry in the world. No two individuals' or churches' ministries are exactly alike or have the same impact on the world. God has specially gifted each for their particular circumstances. This fact makes every spiritual gift, every person, every ministry and every church important to God's work on earth.

God gives His spiritual gifts to function in community with other spiritual gifts. We see His divine design for community in . . .

- The communal structure of the Trinity—the Father, Son and Holy Spirit, each person with His own roles but all working together as one God

- God's creation of the universe—a system of planets, elements, life forms and processes that nourish and are dependent on each other in order to produce and maintain life

- God's creation of the human body—a system of organs, tissues and processes that are all dependent on each other for the body to function properly

- God's creation of Adam and Eve—the first family community, each person having specific roles that are essential to the survival as well as the physical, mental and spiritual health of the human race

- God's creation of the universal church—the body of Christ, the family of God, working together expressing God's love and grace throughout the world

- God's creation of the local church—a part of the universal church, the cooperative community through which the Spirit expresses His gifts of leadership, practical service, power, revelation, and worship among believers and in their communities and world

Observations

The basis for defining our roles as Christians within the church and other communities is our faith in Jesus Christ. When we believed in Christ and invited Him to be the Savior of our lives, we were automatically adopted into God's family. God loves His adopted children and gives them eternal life—a life of joy in relationship with Him. Through Jesus Christ, He also gives His children His Holy Spirit, along with spiritual graces and spiritual gifts.

If we embrace the fact that we are now children of God and members of His family, we have begun to realize our true purpose in life. As a member of God's family, we have brothers and sisters around the world, who are all essential to the function of our family. We interact with each other through the Spirit's graces and gifts, expressing God's love and serving each other. As the body of Christ and the family of God, we are to encourage each other in our spiritual growth and in the use of our spiritual gifts.

God's Word

"When you meet, one will sing, another will teach, another will tell some special revelation God has given, one will speak in an unknown language, while another will interpret what is said. But everything that is done must be useful to all and build them up in the Lord" (1 Corinthians 14:26, *NLT*).

"Just as our bodies have many parts and each part has a special function, so it is with Christ's body. We are all parts of his one body, and each of us has different work to do. And since we are all one body in Christ, we belong to each other, and each of us needs all the others" (Romans 12:4, 5, *NLT*).

Additional Scripture: Romans 12:6-8; 1 Corinthians 12

For Consideration

One of the major tasks of faith communities—that is, families, local congregations, parachurch organizations, denominations, and local churches that work together within the community—is to determine how best to encourage and nurture spiritual gifts in the body of Christ.

Churches often approach this challenge by encouraging believers to become involved in church activities or church offices, such as being a teacher, choir member, usher, and so forth. This is a good practice since the Holy Spirit calls many people to serve in this manner, and many spiritual gifts are well suited for church offices. While the Spirit leads many to use their gifts by serving in church offices, He also leads other believers to use their gifts in other ways. There is such a wide variety of work to be done in the church and in the world; therefore, a wide variety of gifts and ways of using those gifts are needed to accomplish God's work. So in addition to working through church offices, the Spirit often uses individuals' gifts in more informal ways in their churches, families, neighborhoods, workplaces and communities. Churches want to be receptive to the Spirit and allow individuals to pursue what God calls them to do. At the same time, churches desire to keep their ministries alive and functioning. The dilemma, then, is how to accomplish both.

Here are some ideas and issues regarding encouraging and using spiritual gifts in the church and world.

1. *Prayer must be the starting point for us to determine the best ways to use our spiritual gifts and to encourage others in using theirs.* There are many ministry jobs in which we can use our gifts; however, each person and each church has limited resources and

time and cannot do everything. We need the Holy Spirit's guidance in choosing ministry, making ministry plans, setting priorities and following God's will daily. If we pray to the Holy Spirit for guidance regarding how to nurture and use His gifts, we will see answers and guidance come in creative ways. Since our gifts are expressed within community, we will see God begin to build bridges in unusual places, helping us work together in harmony to accomplish the Holy Spirit's purposes.

- *We should always start our Christian service to God with prayer, asking the Holy Spirit to reveal what our spiritual gifts are, what our calls are and what our priorities should be.* If we do not pray for guidance and listen to the Holy Spirit, our enthusiasm may cause us to commit to ministry to which God has not called us, or to participate in such a manner that we become overextended. For example, a church may try to do more work than the church's finances can support. Individuals may commit too much of their time to church ministry activities, causing them to neglect other work that God has called them to do, such as caring for their families. Such mistakes in using spiritual gifts can cause believers to become overstressed and discouraged, affecting their relationship with God, their marriages, their family lives and their health. Overextension may lead to ministry burnout. It is much better for us to consult the Holy Spirit and to trust that He will call others to do what we cannot.

- *Whenever there is a particular ministry need in the church, it is good for the church to pray to the Holy Spirit for help and guidance.* The church can ask the Spirit how it should go about accomplishing His work and invite Him to give the spiritual gifts that are needed. The Holy Spirit may answer a prayer for a spiritual gift by sending a new person who has the needed gift; by prompting someone already in the church who has the needed gift to step forward; by revealing a person who has the needed gift, so that the church may invite him or her to serve; or by inspiring the church to help someone develop his or her gifts in the particular area of need. However, the Holy Spirit may not always answer our prayers according to our agendas. He might have other ideas and plans for ministry. Instead of sending a gifted person to fill a ministry vacancy, He may lead the church to delay filling an office, so that other people can develop their gifts. He may lead the church to restructure the ministry. He may lead to the church to shift their resources and start a different ministry.

- *When making any ministry decision in the church, we need to pray that God will help us to listen and not let anything get in the way of our hearing what the Spirit has to say to us.* We do not want our enthusiasm, our love of meaningful church traditions, or our passion for wanting the church's ministry to be relevant to distract us from following the will of God. Decisions regarding ministry, spiritual gifts, and people need to be a result of the Spirit's guidance. It is important for us to consult the Holy Spirit and trust Him to lead us and provide everything that we need to accomplish God's purpose.

2. *We want to allow the Holy Spirit to teach us to value all of His spiritual gifts.* In the body of Christ, every spiritual gift is essential. It is through all of the Spirit's gifts that the church expresses its faith and service to God. In order to be effective in our service to God, the church must value all gifts and all believers, each of whom God has given a spiritual gift.

God gives a wide variety of gifts. Some are expressed in church offices and others more informally. We do not want to make the mistake of thinking that if we do not hold a church office, we are not spiritually gifted. The church is not to be like corporate society, which emphasizes one's title and job description. We, as Christians, are to value every person and his or her gift(s), regardless of the person's prestige or position. It is extremely important that the church values every spiritual gift.

3. *We can encourage a wide variety of gifts and uses of those gifts by creating a church environment that celebrates the gifts of the Spirit.* Here are some ways churches might create a positive environment in which spiritual gifts can thrive:

- We can gather for prayer, expressing our thanks to the Holy Spirit for His spiritual gifts and asking Him to give the church particular gifts that are needed.

- We can recognize publicly in worship gatherings that there are a variety of gifts that are a part of our worship, including gifts of leadership, practical service, power and revelation.

- We can express our appreciation to individual believers and to other churches in our community for using their spiritual gifts. We can let them know the difference that they are making in our lives and in the world.

When we begin to acknowledge and appreciate the Holy Spirit's work in our churches through His gifts, we will begin to see the church's excitement grow and the use of spiritual gifts flourish.

Once we have asked the Spirit for guidance and have followed His lead in celebrating all of His gifts, our next task is to encourage others.

4. *We can encourage individuals in the use of their spiritual gifts through our relationships with them.* We must get to know people before we can truly encourage them. We can compliment talents and abilities when we see them. But to encourage each other and work together to use our spiritual gifts in the body of Christ, we must be in relationship to each other and to Christ.

One of the greatest ways the Christian church can serve people today is to help them form relationships. It is in relationships that we express our love for one another through spiritual graces and gifts. In today's society, relationships often are secondary to busy schedules, entertainment, work, education and sometimes ministry endeavors. Many of us have become very compartmentalized in our living, playing one role in one place and another role in another place. We feel like we barely have time to meet our obligations, let alone work to establish relationships. This is one area in which the church must be different from the rest of the world.

Churches can assist individuals in developing true Christian relationships and building communities that foster spiritual growth and use of spiritual gifts. Here are some ways the church might go about doing this:

- *The church can provide opportunities for participation in small groups.* Small groups allow individuals to have regular interaction, helping them get to know each other more quickly and on a more intimate level. It is best if churches can provide (1) formal and informal groups in which people with similar gifts can relate, develop and learn to use their gifts; and (2) formal and informal groups in which participants have different interests, allowing them to use a variety of gifts to serve and encourage each other.

- *The church can provide spiritual instruction for families.* Churches can help families learn how to build relationships and have true Christian community in their homes. They can provide instruction to families regarding how they might express spiritual graces and gifts in their family life and in their neighborhood. Churches can distribute weekly Bible readings that encourage families to observe family worship time, which will draw the family closer to God and to each other. They can instruct families in wholesome, fun family activities that will help them build stronger relationships.

- *The church can provide ministry opportunities and social activities that bring together people of all ages.* We are told in the Bible that older believers should mentor younger ones. By providing regular opportunities for the body of Christ to gather as a family, we enable people in different age groups to form relationships. The result will be that younger people will gravitate toward older people for guidance in using their talents and spiritual gifts. Older people will see and encourage spiritual gifts in younger people. There will be opportunities for growth and service that may not exist in same-age groups. Opportunities for interaction among different generations might include multigenerational worship,[2] multigenerational social activities and mentoring programs.

- *Provide ministry opportunities outside the church. Churches can plan creative ministry and form ministry teams to serve in the local community, in other cities or in other countries.* Working together in a new location takes people out of their daily routines and habits and helps them build relationships and grow spiritually as they work together for God.

Whenever we work together for God in community, we will see the Holy Spirit move in our lives in wonderful ways. As we pray to the Holy Spirit for guidance, allow Him to move and follow His lead, we will feel our worth within the body of Christ, we will grow in our use of spiritual gifts, and we will express God's love in powerful ways in the world.

---

[2]An example of multigenerational worship is a local church's inclusion of various styles of music that appeal to people of different ages. In such worship, a church might include traditional hymns, contemporary songs and children's songs that all focus on the same worship theme. In addition to having the congregation sing the songs, the church might ask people of different ages to accompany or to help lead the singing. The church might also invite someone to tell the story behind a song from his or her generation. To ensure that the worship time speaks to and includes every age group, the church might set up a worship planning committee that includes individuals of various ages. Such multigenerational planning and participation helps persons of each generation learn to worship God through music; it helps these individuals learn to value people of all ages and to love each other; it encourages believers to develop appreciation for and learn from the experiences of Christians living at the time the songs were written; and it helps all worshipers present to feel validated and appreciated in the body of Christ.

The Challenge

May we always remember to ask the Holy Spirit to guide us to have the faith to follow His lead, to use our gifts with a heart of service, and to love and encourage each other.

SERVING GOD IN THE INSTITUTIONAL CHURCH

The Question

How can churches, church leaders and denominations remain focused on their primary spiritual calls and allow the Holy Spirit to perform His creative work among them—empowering them to share the good news, inspiring them in Charismatic worship and equipping them for prophetic ministry?

Background

As a movement, Pentecostalism has grown from a few tightly focused, small evangelistic organizations into a number of much larger, growing denominations. In the process, the Movement has entered the state where institutionalization has become evident.

Observations

At the stage in which institutionalization becomes apparent, a movement begins to focus on maintaining itself rather than continuing its original mission. Even though leadership may emphasize the earlier themes of the group, such as Spirit baptism and evangelism, the organization channels more and more energy into maintaining and managing its resources. Shifts in the group's emphases invariably occur as organization, indoctrination and administration take precedence over evangelizing, Charismatic expression and prophetic ministry.

As institutionalization becomes entrenched, the denominational leaders become more and more removed from the people in the local churches. Typically during this time, the leaders of a movement will seek to protect their own interests and positions. The spiritual health of the denomination becomes secondary to the personal interests of those with power. The leaders may begin to insulate themselves from the grassroots of the church by surrounding themselves with subordinates who are sympathetic to their interests. As the gap widens between the leaders and the people in the local churches, the laity become less involved and less concerned about the direction of the denomination. Eventually, the local churches also become more concerned with their own interests and less concerned with the denomination's mission. Thus, the end result is that the denomination begins to decline.

God's Word

"We will hold to the truth in love, becoming more and more in every way like Christ, who is the head of his body, the church. Under his direction, the whole body is fitted together perfectly. As each part does its own special work, it helps the other parts grow, so that the whole body is healthy and growing and full of love" (Ephesians 4:15, 16, *NLT*).

For Consideration

1. *Much of institutionalization develops as the denomination takes steps to ensure that the beliefs of the group are established and passed on to future generations.* Institutionalization is not all negative. Some of the changes are necessary to maintain large organizations or denominations. If the structures in place function properly, they clarify doctrine, guard against heretical teachings, and provide stability and lines of authority and accountability. Nevertheless, a movement begins to lose the dynamics that characterized it as a movement as institutionalization progresses.

2. *A key to balancing the institutionalizing effect that organizational regulations have on denominations are the local pastors and their churches.* In Pentecostal denominations in general, there are clear signs of advancing institutionalization. However, in a number

of North American Pentecostal denominations, the power base of local congregations and their pastors is becoming stronger. Many denominations openly recognize this as a reality. A number of denominational leaders have become aware of the lack of mutual communication between them and the local pastors, and they have begun to make efforts to correct this situation at regional and general meetings. These gatherings offer leaders excellent opportunities to cast a new vision for their respective areas of ministry by emphasizing themes and programs that move the hearts of the people and their pastors in the local churches. To ensure that the people have a voice in decision making, denominations are beginning to interview pastors and use surveys at the local church level. In order to add credibility to any new or renewed focus, churches and their denominations must evaluate their current programs and budgets to determine if these correspond to the areas that have been identified as being crucial to the life of the church.

3. *To ensure that Pentecostalism continues to flourish in North America, Pentecostal leaders and their people must face the challenge of discovering creative ways to revitalize and invigorate areas of ministry.* Denominations naturally have more shape and organization than do movements, but Pentecostal organizations have tried to maintain the dynamics of movements. Pentecostal denominations have made efforts to continue to allow for the creative move of the Holy Spirit. It cannot be denied that institutionalizing forces have had an effect on the older Pentecostal groups. Organization and centralized authority need to be balanced with the freedom to act and to take initiative within the understanding of God's will.

4. *Mature leaders are needed in order to have a good balance between the church's authority and the freedom that individuals and churches need in order to minister effectively.* The leaders of the first generation of Pentecostalism are gone, but a positive sign in the area of leadership in recent years has been the increasing influence of pastors of large congregations. Today, a number of these pastors serve in

positions of leadership at the denominational level and are filling a need for leaders who are closer to the front lines of ministry. As pastors, or having served recently as pastors, they are in touch with the work of local churches. They may be better equipped by the Holy Spirit to lead God's people and to counter the decrease of spiritual passion and fervency within the institutional walls of the church.

All communities, including communities of faith, must have structures. It is hard to see how the church could exist in this world without institutional forms. The church needs offices, leaders, polity and regulations. However, rigid institutional structures stifle spontaneity and the dynamics of faith. Like other institutions, the church has defects, but church structures are intended to enhance and protect the faith. In general, the institutional church successfully uplifts the faith more than it hinders and damages it. The institutional side of our faith serves to channel and stabilize our life in Jesus Christ.

As we serve God and others through our institutional organizations, we want to pray and submit to the Holy Spirit. We want to ask Him to empower and guide us individually and corporately, giving us wisdom and helping us to keep our focus on God's calls in our lives.

The Challenge

May we look unselfishly to the Holy Spirit for His guidance in personal, church and denominational expressions of our faith.

WORSHIPING GOD FROM OUR HEARTS

The Question

How can we allow the Holy Spirit to move among us so that we can worship God from our hearts?

Background

Throughout the Pentecostal and Charismatic Movements, participants' worship has been demonstrative and emotional in nature. As emotional worship, it often has included worship expressions such as raising one's hands in praise to God, shouting with joy, jubilant dancing, happy laughter, and tears of pain, sorrow or joy. It has sometimes included unusual reactions to the overwhelming presence and power of the Spirit, such as making jerking movements or falling into a trancelike state.

Many of these expressions of worship were more evident in early Pentecostalism. While some of these responses to the move of the Holy Spirit continue in newer Pentecostal denominations and Charismatic churches, others have become less common in the last two or three decades. In the United States, as the church has become more middle-class, people have tended to become more reserved in the emotional expression of their faith. People in the Pentecostal/Charismatic Movements often are now more similar to mainstream, secular American society, which generally does not encourage emotionalism and vulnerability in relationships with God or people.

The desire of early classical Pentecostals was to experience outpourings of the Spirit that would revitalize the church and change their communities. Their hopes were stirred during fervent worship services as the people sensed the presence of the Holy Spirit. As their worship became more intense, their commitment to change and willingness to work for it were reinforced and stimulated.

Many of the early Pentecostals were persecuted or ostracized in their communities. Worship gatherings became events where the members would be strengthened in their resolve to continue with the Movement. They often left a worship service emboldened to be more faithful to God and more committed to the mission of the church.

Observations

Crucial aspects of Pentecostal and Charismatic worship are fervency and freedom to praise God. An atmosphere of freedom creates boldness and excitement and provides healthy allowance for the whole person to get involved in worship. It serves as a powerful motivation for action, which is seen not only in worship but also in witnessing, missions, serving and giving.

Some Pentecostal churches have de-emphasized emotions because of the excesses that have occurred in worship and because of changes in our broader culture. Rather than eliminating outward emotional expression from worship, it would be good for Pentecostals and Charismatics to consider how they can invite the Spirit to move in worship gatherings and allow for a variety of expressions within a balanced and orderly environment.

God's Word

"Come, let us worship and bow down, let us kneel before the Lord our Maker" (Psalm 95:6).

"The twenty-four elders will fall down before Him who sits on the throne, and will worship Him who lives forever and ever, and will cast their crowns before the throne, saying, 'Worthy are You, our Lord and our God, to receive glory and honor and power; for You created all things, and because of Your will they existed, and were created'" (Revelation 4:10, 11).

Additional Scripture: Matthew 2:9-11

For Consideration

Here are some thoughts for consideration as we plan our worship and endeavor to allow the Spirit to move among us.

1. *When worshipers are allowed to express heartfelt desires in their worship of God, the Holy Spirit is allowed to move as He wills, and Pentecostal and Charismatic worship thrives.* When spontaneous praise is stifled, worship loses some of its dynamic. When believers come together and are encouraged to engage in expressive worship, the worship gathering becomes energized.

2. *Excessive emotional expressions can take away from Spirit-guided worship.* Leaders of worship gatherings should not allow

excesses or practices that create disorder; but when worshipers can freely express themselves within Scriptural guidelines, Pentecostal and Charismatic worship often creates a unique awareness of the presence of God.

3. *Wholehearted exuberant worship, often characterized by great joy and hope, attracts outsiders to the power of God.* During worship in Pentecostal and Charismatic churches, people may raise their hands, shout praises to God, dance in the Spirit, cry or laugh as they express themselves before the Lord. When such expressions are done in an orderly way and all people present are respected, those who are visiting often come to feel the power of God—a power that they want and need in their lives.

4. *God made us emotional people, and it is natural for us to express our emotions when we are worshiping God.* Since the Pentecostal and Charismatic Movements began, emotional expression has been an important aspect of their worship. It is not surprising, since all movements begin with strong emotions and a passion for change. Movements generally begin when people of similar interests and sentiments come together to effect change in society. These interests and sentiments are stimulated at group gatherings and rallies or meetings where emotional expression regarding issues is normal. The Pentecostal/Charismatic Movements are no different. These movements have consisted of groups of people who are impassioned about God's work in their lives through the Holy Spirit.

Some people may think that certain expressions of Pentecostal and Charismatic worship are emotional excess, especially since in the larger American society, outward emotions are generally discouraged. In the Christian church, some religious traditions view outward expression of emotions in public worship as being less respectful of God. As a result, people in American society often have few places to which they can go and honestly express their feelings. Many, however, still want a worship experience that allows them to express the way they feel and that creates an awareness of the presence of God.

5. *Pentecostal and Charismatic churches can offer a balanced worship style that facilitates encounters with the Holy Spirit and meaningful worship experiences.* By maintaining proper guidelines for Spirit-filled worship, Pentecostals can avoid both detrimental excesses and inflexible worship styles that stifle expressive worship. By striking a balance, a good worship environment can be created that invites worshipers to interact with the Holy Spirit on a deeper emotional level. This interaction can bring healing to wounded emotions and empowerment to believers. A church will thrive when the Holy Spirit heals worshipers and fills them with His power to serve and to live victoriously.

6. *Pentecostal and Charismatic worship can allow for a variety of expressions in worship.* There is no perfect formula or style for Spirit-led worship. Outward worship expressions vary according to peoples' personalities and backgrounds, the culture of the church, and how the Holy Spirit chooses to work in the lives of individuals and the church. The style of a person's worship does not indicate his or her spiritual condition. While some Pentecostal and Charismatic churches have a very relaxed, informal structure for worship, other churches have found ways to combine more formal, traditional liturgical worship and allow for the spontaneous move of the Holy Spirit. For Pentecostal and Charismatic churches, what is most important is not the specifics of our individual worship. What matters most is that we focus on God in our worship, allow the Holy Spirit to move, and honor and love all of those in the body of Christ, regardless of their particular style of worship.

As Spirit-led believers, we want to give our all through our worship of God in both private and public settings. We have a real opportunity through dynamic Spirit-led worship to express our love for God and to lead the way in serving our communities through the unique calls and gifts that God has given us.

The Challenge

May we always worship the Lord our God with our hearts, souls and minds, following the Holy Spirit's lead as we gather for worship and in every aspect of our lives.

ANTICIPATING THE RETURN OF CHRIST

The Question

Are we expectantly looking for Christ to return to earth?

Background

Pentecostals have traditionally seen themselves as living during the "last days." The last days is a time period initiated by the coming of the Spirit on the Day of Pentecost. It includes the time from the Day of Pentecost until the second coming of Christ.

After the Day of Pentecost, the centuries passed and many Christians became less inclined to actively pray for the Holy Spirit's power and to look for Jesus Christ's return during their lifetimes. At the dawn of the 20th century, a shift in spiritual thinking and experience took place when groups of Christians began to ask God for His blessing of spiritual empowerment—the Holy Spirit. This time period of spiritual renewal is often referred to as the beginning of a "latter rain"—an event predicted by the prophet in Joel 2:23. The occurrence of this new downpouring of the Holy Spirit confirmed for Pentecostals and Charismatics the belief that they were living in the last days, during the climax of history when Christ was going to return.

They began excitedly to tell people that the period of the "latter rain" had started. God was showering His spiritual power and gifts on them. As a result of their powerful encounters with the Holy Spirit, they experienced a profound spiritual intensity and felt assured that they were living in the last days and that the coming of Christ was going to happen very soon.

Observations

Regrettably, some Christians' enthusiasm and excitement about Christ's return have diminished. As people's economic status has risen and they have become increasingly more affluent and comfortable in their homes on earth, their lives are often driven by a desire to obtain wealth and prestige. Some Pentecostal and Charismatic pastors and members have been influenced by a "name-it-and-claim-it" type of religious thinking. This type of thinking promotes the assumption that if we want something and have faith for it, God will give it to us. Many mistakenly think that they are demonstrating great faith in God with their prayers for material wealth. This thinking, however, reflects a desire for the symbols of success, rather than a sacrificial love for God and others. As a result, recent years have seen many church-growth and "health-and-wealth" seminars have higher participation than prayer meetings, missionary meetings and mercy ministry work in the community.

The early message of Pentecostal Christians about the arrival of the last days and Jesus' soon return (maybe as soon as today) is often not a major theme in sermons and conversations today. The focus in more affluent nations is more on the here and now rather than on the second coming of the Lord. Fortunately, in many developing countries there still remains a future orientation among Christians. Those of us living more physically comfortable lives would benefit from some lessons our Christian families around the world could teach us. Their message still points ahead to a city whose builder and maker is God, where there will be no tears and death.

God's Word

"For the Lord Himself will descend from heaven with a shout, with the voice of the archangel and with the trumpet of God, and the dead in Christ will rise first. Then we who are alive and remain will be caught up together with them in the clouds to meet the Lord in the air, and so we shall always be with the Lord" (1 Thessalonians 4:16, 17).

Additional Scripture: Matthew 24:30, 31; 1 Corinthians 15:52

For Consideration

As we think about our lives on this earth, consider Biblical prophecy, and learn what it means to look for Christ's second coming, we might consider some of these factors.

1. *We want to embrace the reality of the second of coming of Jesus Christ and what it will mean to us and our world.* The Lord will return for His people. It will be a glorious event, for He will come with great power and glory (Matthew 24:30, 31), and all Christians will participate. His return will initiate the consummation of our salvation and we, along with all believers, will be united with the Lord forever.

No human knows when this event will occur. The exact time is God's business, not ours (Acts 1:6, 7). Our not knowing does not mean, however, that Christians should ignore the signs that point to the coming of Christ (Matthew 24). Our business is to be alert and watchful and to pursue a holy lifestyle. We need to be confident that Christ can return at any moment. Rather than trying to pinpoint the specific date, we need to use our time sharing the gospel with others and urging them to prepare for the coming of the Kingdom (Acts 1:8).

2. *We want to be excited about the future, realizing that our home on earth is only temporary and our home in heaven with God will be our permanent home.* Early Pentecostals saw themselves as a pilgrim people and believed that Jesus was coming "any day now." Today, if we are not careful, we may *not* see ourselves as pilgrims who are on a spiritual journey that leads to a wonderful home with God. If we immerse ourselves in material success, societal positions or even involvement in institutional church work, we can become isolated from the brokenness of our world. Such isolation can lead us to

become too comfortable and self-indulgent, looking to our present situation and to ourselves for complete fulfillment rather than looking to God. We may no longer fully appreciate how incredible our future home with God in heaven will be. We may forget that it is the only place of complete peace, health and happiness.

3. *While we look for Jesus Christ's return, we do not want to neglect the work He has given us on earth.* We do not want to think that since our permanent home is in heaven, we do not need to be concerned about matters on earth. God has given us much work to do while we are here. We are to spend our time learning about God, loving Him, showing His love to others and telling others about His plans for their lives. We are also to care for our families, for our neighbors in our communities and throughout the world, and for the earth, the home in which we all must live until Christ's return. We want to be expressions of God's love in the world, contributing to our world's being kinder and more God-focused. In doing so, we hope to leave our children an earthly home that is more whole and more at peace with God, should Christ's return be delayed. Through our relationships today and through our legacy, we want to be lights in a dark world, giving our human family a glimpse of the spiritual blessings that they will experience when Christ returns.

4. *While we live on earth, we want to place our hope in Jesus Christ.* We want to remember always that our hope is Jesus Christ, and our power comes from the Holy Spirit. We do not have to rely on our own intellects, efforts or wealth, but we can trust that God will always provide what we need in order to fulfill His purpose for our lives.

When focusing on Christ's soon coming, we are reminded of the hope that we have through His promised return. When Christ returns, we will have a new life. Every problem will be solved. Every pain and illness will be healed. There will be no more hunger and no more suffering. There will be no more death. Everything on earth will be healed and made new.

By studying and meditating on God's promises in His Word and by being diligent in serving Him during our lives on earth, we will be reminded daily of the hope that we have in Christ's expected return and in the promise of our future home in heaven. We can allow the Holy Spirit to encourage our hearts, giving us a firm conviction that Jesus is coming soon, that the great Day of Judgment is near, that the new Jerusalem will replace the earthly one, and that God's people will rule and reign with Jesus forever. We can confidently say, "Our Messiah, Jesus Christ, may return any day!"

The Challenge

May we place our hope in Christ and expectantly look for His return, as we follow the Spirit's lead, serving God and doing His work on earth.

CONCLUSION

Pentecostalism has a rich history. In its early years, the Movement had to overcome numerous difficulties. Sometimes its future was questionable in the eyes of many observers. Yet, those early Spirit-filled worshipers were convinced that God had His hand on them and that the Holy Spirit had given birth to their movement. Through persistent faith and the help of the Spirit, they overcame seemingly insurmountable difficulties and became a powerful force for God. Today, Pentecostalism reaches around the world.

Nevertheless, many new challenges confront the Pentecostal/Charismatic Movements in the 21st century. There are questions about the future of the Movement. Both external and internal forces must be addressed by the various Pentecostal and Charismatic groups and organizations as they attempt to fulfill their mission in the world.

In the past, Pentecostals had fewer monetary resources and met life's challenges through their dependence on the Holy Spirit. Today, many have more human and financial resources, and as a result, may need to relearn how to rely on the Holy Spirit for guidance and strength to do God's work in this multicultural, interconnected, complex world. Our future depends on our continued reliance on the Holy Spirit. Through the power of the Spirit, the Pentecostal and Charismatic Movements can face the challenges of the 21st century and remain vital forces for God.

CHAPTER 10—STUDY AND DISCUSSION

UNDERSTANDING AND COMMUNICATING THE TEACHINGS OF THE BIBLE

1. What is the purpose of the Bible?

2. How can we understand what the Bible is teaching us?

BEING AMBASSADORS FOR CHRIST IN TODAY'S WORLD

3. What are some specific ways in which your daily life can be a light for Christ?

4. What are some daily and weekly practices or routines that would help you remain true to your Christian beliefs and values?

RECEIVING THE SPIRIT'S EMPOWERMENT

5. How are Spirit baptism and speaking in other tongues relevant to each of our lives and the worship life of our churches?

6. How can churches today encourage people to seek the Spirit and be open to His empowerment through Spirit baptism?

EMBRACING THE MOVE OF THE SPIRIT IN OUR LIVES

7. In what ways do you most often experience the move of the Holy Spirit in your personal life? In the life of your church?

8. What are some areas of your personal life in which you would like to grow by inviting the Spirit to move and by following His lead?

9. What about areas of the life of your church?

SHARING THE SAVING LOVE OF CHRIST WITH OTHERS

10. What are some ways that you can share with others God's love and your own personal story of forgiveness and salvation?

ENCOURAGING THE USE OF SPIRITUAL GIFTS

11. What are some ways in which you can encourage your family and friends in their use of spiritual gifts?

12. What are some ways your church might encourage the development and use of spiritual gifts in its life and ministry?

SERVING GOD IN THE INSTITUTIONAL CHURCH

13. What ideas do you have for revitalizing the Christian church's work in the world today?

14. What ideas do you have regarding your local church's work in your community?

WORSHIPING GOD FROM OUR HEARTS

15. Describe worship you have experienced that has been very meaningful to you.

16. What are some ways that your church can encourage people to worship from their hearts?

ANTICIPATING THE RETURN OF CHRIST

17. What does it mean to your spiritual life to believe that Christ can return any day?

18. How does Christ's soon return affect the work we Christians do on earth?

Part Six

Personal Stories

We are telling you about what we ourselves have actually seen and heard, so that you may have fellowship with us. And our fellowship is with the Father and with his Son, Jesus Christ (1 John 1:3, *NLT*).

11

Personal Stories of Encounters With the Holy Spirit

P ersonal stories, or "testimonies," have been an important aspect of the Christian life since Jesus' time on earth. Since the death and resurrection of Christ, personal stories told by Christians have contributed greatly to our understanding and appreciation of God—the Father, Son and Holy Spirit. Through the sharing of their experiences, believers have helped illuminate, clarify and verify aspects of God's work in our lives and in the world.

In this chapter, several such testimonies are presented in order to demonstrate the wonderful stories that are such an integral part of the lives of those who have encountered the Holy Spirit. Through the telling and retelling of such stories, the faith is passed on to future generations. The testimonies in this chapter have been selected because they illustrate particular beliefs of Pentecostals and Charismatics, such as healing, speaking in tongues, leading of the Spirit, manifestations, and so forth.

Individuals who share their testimonies give us an intimate view of some of the most precious moments in their faith walk. In a sense, they are inviting the reader to join them in a walk on ground that is sacred to them. They are windows through which the Pentecostal/Charismatic faith can be seem more clearly.

Reading or hearing their stories can be compared to looking at stained glass windows from inside a building. In order to see the beauty through the windows and to see the light shining through the colored glass, one must be on the inside of the building. The personal stories shared here allow us an inside glimpse of the Spirit-led life. Thus, these testimonies may serve as colorful illustrations of the Spirit-filled experience and may contribute to the faith walk of individuals who desire a closer relationship with God. All personal stories have been obtained through interviews or through written statements unless otherwise footnoted. All names have been changed.

CONVERSION AND SPIRITUAL GRACES

When a person accepts Christ by faith and becomes a child of God, the act is so decisive that it can be described as *conversion.* This change is of such magnitude that it can be considered a "new birth." Becoming a Christian involves starting life all over again and going in a different direction.

[Conversion]
The Spirit leads Jack and Megan to Christ and their marriage is saved
—told by a pastor

Background

This personal story reveals the role of the Holy Spirit in drawing an unsaved couple to salvation and bringing healing into their marriage relationship. The minister who shares the story was the pastor of a Pentecostal church in the northwestern United States where the events took place.

The Story

Jack and Megan were on the verge of splitting up when they first came to the church where I was pastoring. Their marriage had deteriorated to the point that they both wanted a divorce. However, they had two wonderful, young boys. So both wanted to salvage their relationship if possible. Jack and Megan had tried different religious avenues for spiritual help and guidance, including various Protestant and Catholic churches, and even Mormonism. They had finally decided to give up. Then, Jack somehow heard about our church. After discussing it with Megan, they decided that they would visit the church. They were not sure why, but they felt this was their last opportunity to save their marriage.

Jack and Megan visited our church during a Sunday morning worship service. The service was typical for the church, with the Holy Spirit present as the congregation worshiped the Lord, but nothing unusual happened. I noticed this new couple visiting who did not actively participate in the worship. When I gave the altar call, this couple came forward. I went to them and asked their names. Then, after explaining the plan of salvation to them, I asked Jack and Megan if they wanted to accept Jesus Christ as their Savior. They said yes, and I led them in the sinner's prayer. After they had both accepted Jesus as their Savior, they shared that they needed the Lord to do a miracle in their marriage. Not knowing any details, I prayed for the Lord to work a miracle for them. Their countenances visibly changed as they expressed their newfound faith in the Lord. From that moment on, they became faithful in attendance. Eventually, they joined the church and became leaders in our congregation.

A few weeks later, Jack came to talk to me. He shared that when Megan and he came that first Sunday morning, they believed their marriage was over. However, they felt something drawing them to the church. The couple decided to try one more worship service, but agreed that if nothing changed for them that morning, they would separate and divorce.

Then, Jack shared that they now realized the Holy Spirit had drawn them to the church. That was why they felt as though they had to visit the church before they gave up on their marriage. The

Holy Spirit had drawn them to a Divine appointment that changed their lives forever. The last time I heard from them, Jack and Megan were still married and serving God together—over 10 years later. Praise the Lord!

[Conversion]

Kendall unknowingly points to the words that are his invitation to conversion
—told by Kendall, a retired minister

Background

Kendall, a retired minister, shared this testimony that demonstrates a dramatic and unusual work of the Holy Spirit in his conversion. When he was a young man in his 20s, he attended a revival service at the request of some friends. He had never been converted and had not been to a Pentecostal or Charismatic church before. He sat toward the back of the congregation.

The Story

When it was time for the minister to speak, Kendall was startled because the preacher left the front of the church and walked back to his pew. Though the two had never met, the minister, feeling led by the Holy Spirit, stood right in front of Kendall and handed his closed Bible to him. The preacher said, "I want you to pick the scripture that I will preach from tonight." Kendall just stared at the preacher in disbelief and took the Bible from him. He had never studied the Bible and had no idea what to do. Afraid to take his eyes off of the minister, he continued staring into the preacher's eyes as he held the Bible in both hands and let it fall open in his lap. Still gazing into the evangelist's eyes, Kendall took his right index finger and laid it on one of the pages of the Bible, oblivious to where he pointed.

The preacher and Kendall together looked down at the passage of Scripture he had selected. The minister took the Bible from him and returned to the pulpit. Then, he read the passage of Scripture to the rest of the congregation. It was the story of the Prodigal Son in Luke 15. As the evangelist preached on the Prodigal Son, Kendall was mesmerized by his words. He said, "That minister was preaching about me. I was the prodigal." When everyone was invited to pray at the altar, Kendall went forward, accepted Jesus as his Savior, and God called him into the ministry. He spent the rest of his life telling others that the heavenly Father was still calling prodigals like him to come home.

[Spiritual Obedience]

Kevin follows the Spirit's Guidance and is blessed
—told by Kevin, about his college days

Background

The Holy Spirit provides leadership and direction in our daily lives. Often we focus on the extraordinary works of the Spirit and overlook His interaction in the ordinary affairs of our life. This testimony demonstrates that obeying the Holy Spirit's leadership can result in unexpected blessings. A Pentecostal pastor shares this story that took place while he was attending college to prepare for the ministry.

The Story

During a break from college, I was attending a camp meeting service with some of the youth from my home church. We were planning to go out together for pizza after the service. I only had five one-dollar bills to last me all week. When it came time to give in the offering, I decided to give a dollar. That would barely leave me enough to eat out with the youth. When I reached in my wallet for the dollar, I felt the Holy Spirit impress me to give more. So, I reached for another dollar. As I reached for the second one, the Holy Spirit impressed me to give all I had. I gave the five dollars I had in the offering.

One of my friends saw me give all of my money in the offering. He knew I was short of cash, as college students often are. Without my knowing it, he turned to another of my friends and told him what I had given. He said, "God is going to bless him twofold." The other friend responded, "Twofold! God will bless him fourfold!"

After the service, we were enjoying the fellowship when the second friend came up to me and handed me $20. I asked, "What is this for?" Then, he related the conversation that my other friend and he had while discussing my giving. He told me, "When I said that God would bless you fourfold, I remembered that I owed you $20 from before you ever went to college. So here it is." Then I, too, remembered the long-forgotten debt. Later that night, I enjoyed a delicious dinner and rejoiced at the unusual way the Lord blessed me for following the Holy Spirit's leadership.

SPIRIT BAPTISM

Spirit baptism is experienced after conversion. Through this experience the Holy Spirit imparts power for witnessing and enables the believer to live a vibrant life of worship and service.

[Spirit Baptism]
Martha receives inner beauty
—told by Cathy, a pastor's wife

Background

During the early '70s, Bill and Cathy pastored a Pentecostal church in southern Georgia. Under their leadership, a revival broke out in the church that had a dynamic impact on the small town. People from the community were curious about reports of an unusual outpouring of the Holy Spirit, and folks who had never been to a Pentecostal church came to see what God was doing. In one month, over 92 new members joined the church. Many of these were new converts who came from non-Pentecostal backgrounds. Many of these new believers became hungry for the Holy Spirit, often filling the altars while praying to be baptized in the Holy Spirit. During the revival, many were filled with the Holy Spirit and spoke in other tongues as the Spirit moved upon them. Here are two testimonies shared by Bill and Cathy about "two wonderful women who were so hungry to receive and sought so sincerely to be filled with, the Spirit."

The Story

Martha was an intense seeker. She came to the altar at each opportunity, prayed at home and was so very hungry for God. Yet, she could not seem to break through hindrances and barriers and have a genuine encounter with the Holy Spirit.

One Sunday evening, there was a guest singing group at our church, and some followers of the group were in attendance. These followers were conservative in their religious practices, which was evident in their appearance. To Martha, a young, beautiful former Baptist girl, they really looked strange. She went to the altar again that night and prayed. As I prayed beside her, suddenly she stopped praying and whispered into my ear, "Sister Cathy, if I get the Holy Spirit, do I have to look like that?" I whispered back, "Not unless you want to!"

We resumed praying, and within minutes she was speaking in other tongues. The Comforter had come! Later, I asked her, "Martha, can you tell me what you were thinking?" She said, "I told the Lord, 'Lord, I don't want to look weird, but if that's what it takes for me to receive the baptism, I'm willing.' " She retained her attractiveness and now has an inward beauty to match her outward appearance.

[Spirit Baptism]

April expresses overwhelming joy when she encounters the Spirit
—told by Bill, a pastor

The Story

April was a very quiet-mannered young mother. She came from a Methodist background, and the emotional outbursts of some in the church were confusing her. She had many questions and fears. But she wanted the infilling of the Spirit. April would often say, "I could never respond to God that exuberantly." She sought intensely, but very quietly and reverently. We continually explained to her that God would work with her and bless her in a manner that agreed with her personality and temperament.

However, on the night she received Spirit baptism, we had to almost look twice to know if it was really April. This quiet and shy personality was suddenly highly demonstrative. It was as though she had been transformed into another person. The Holy Spirit did not come as a lamb, but more like a sweep of wind and fire. Her infilling was such an about-face experience that she and those of us around her would never forget it.[1]

SPEAKING IN OTHER TONGUES

Classical Pentecostals believe that speaking in an unknown tongue as the Holy Spirit gives the utterance is evidence of Spirit

---

[1]It is not uncommon for a person to manifest unusual behavior when experiencing the presence of the Holy Spirit. For more testimonies see Edith L. Blumhoffer, "Pentecost in My Soul": *Explorations in the Meaning of Pentecostal Experience in the Early Assemblies of God* (Springfield, MO: Gospel Publishing House, 1989). Especially see pp. 231-235.

baptism, and that unknown tongues can be a prayer language. They also believe that a Spirit-filled individual may speak on occasion through the inspiration of the Holy Spirit in a language that she or he has never studied or learned. This belief is based upon their understanding of the events in Acts 2.

[Gift of Tongues, Call to Conversion]

A Jewish man hears and understands a message in tongues

—told by Maria Woodworth-Etter, an evangelist

Background

Though it is a rare experience, testimonies do surface from time to time of individuals' speaking in earthly languages. Maria Woodworth-Etter recorded several such incidents in *A Diary of Signs and Wonders*. Though some people are skeptical of such reports, Woodworth-Etter received endorsements from such credible individuals as Stanley Smith and George B. Studd.[2]

The Story

During a meeting that Woodworth-Etter was conducting in Chicago, she described a message in tongues that was given during a service in which "hundreds of sinners were present." Among the unbelievers was a Jewish man who "sat with his head down as though he was stunned." He stood and stated that the message in tongues was for him, and that he understood it. When the invitation to pray was given, he came forward and prayed earnestly and repented of his sins. After praying, he testified that the person who spoke in tongues had spoken "pure Hebrew," telling him that he "must come down and acknowledge Jesus to be your Messiah." Woodworth-Etter stated that the man "through whom

---

[2]Maria Woodworth-Etter, *A Diary of Signs and Wonders* (Tulsa, OK: Harrison House, 1916) 7.

the Lord gave the message, testified that he had never studied languages, knew nothing about Hebrew and had never graduated from the grammar school."[3]

[Gifts of Tongues, Healing]

William's mother speaks Hebrew during surgery
—told by William Thomas, a denominational leader

Background

A story similar to the one related by Woodworth-Etter occurred almost 30 years ago in a small hospital in middle Georgia. William Thomas, a Pentecostal denominational leader, remembers the amazing events surrounding his mother's surgery. It happened when he was a child.

The Story

William's mother was scheduled for a surgery that was supposed to take only an hour and a half, but she developed some complications during the procedure. The surgery extended to five hours, and her condition grew worse. Late in the surgery her situation became more serious, and the doctors were having difficulty arousing her from the anesthesia. When she reached her lowest point and the physicians thought that they might lose her, an amazing event took place: she began to speak in tongues.

The anesthesiologist working on William's mother was a Jew who had studied in Israel. Her condition began improving, and she began waking up. When she was awake, the Jewish doctor asked her where she had studied Hebrew. She said that she had never studied Hebrew and that she only had a seventh-grade education. Startled by her reply, he said that at her lowest point during the surgery she had spoken in fluent Hebrew, calling on Jesus and asking Him for help. That was the point at which her condition improved.

---

[3]Woodworth-Etter 393.

[Gift of Tongues, Calls to Conversion, Gift of Prophecy]

Nurses from different countries hear their native languages
—told by Melissa about her uncle

Background

This testimony shared by Melissa is a powerful illustration of the witness of tongues to unbelievers. After suffering a heart attack, her uncle was dying in a hospital when these events happened. Here is her account of the story.

The Story

My uncle, who was 93 years old, suffered a serious heart attack, and they called the family in because he was expected to die at any moment. While they gathered at his bedside in the intensive care room, he began to speak in a most heavenly language! They were thankful for the Holy Spirit, who was comforting this precious saint of God as he faced death. One of the nurses came in and was shocked to hear my uncle speaking. She looked at the family and said, "I didn't realize that he spoke German." The family told her he did not. She responded that she was German, and he was telling her the plan of salvation in the most beautiful dialect of German that she had ever heard. The family began to praise the Lord that the Holy Spirit was speaking through my uncle in a language she could clearly understand.

His hospital in Florida had nurses in training from many countries. Several of the nurses came into the room to see what the excitement was about. Each nurse represented a different country and was surprised to hear a patient speaking in a language he had not studied. One of the nurses began to cry. She said that she was Vietnamese and that now he was telling her the plan of salvation in a language she could clearly understand. The Holy Spirit went on to tell of the love of God in the seven languages that were spoken by the nurses! It was like the Day of Pentecost!

Before dying, Melissa's uncle had a vision that demonstrated other works of the Holy Spirit, such as visions and prophecy. After speaking in tongues, her uncle opened his eyes and began to speak. Melissa testified that her uncle exhorted them "to keep their priorities straight," because the Lord was returning soon. Then he had a vision.

He looked up and asked the family if they could hear the heavenly music. He said that he wished they could see what he was seeing. There were saints from all ages praising the King of kings and the Lord of lords. They were saying, "Worthy is the Lamb! Holy! Holy! Holy!" Then he began to call names of people he could see with Jesus. Some of these had died while he was sick, and he did not realize they were in heaven. He then said something that meant the world to me! My father was in an accident when I was only six months old. He was paralyzed from the neck down for the remaining 24 years of his life. I never saw my Daddy walk, but my uncle did! He said, "Wouldn't you know it! Bee is the first one running to meet me!"

Her uncle then "closed his eyes and slipped into the very presence of Jesus."

[Spirit Baptism]
Teri receives an unexpected blessing while talking to God
—told by a minister, about his experiences in high school

Background

A Pentecostal minister had these experiences only a few months after his conversion and his receiving of Spirit baptism. Even though the events occurred almost 30 years ago, his telling of the story after all this time illustrates the limitless impact that encounters with the Holy Spirit can have on a person's life.

The Story

I was converted and later baptized in the Holy Spirit during my senior year in high school. Several of my friends also received the Holy Spirit about the same time. A young, devout Methodist girl, Teri, was often in the same classes with us. Before our conversions, we had thought she was very sweet, but overly religious. After our Spirit baptisms, our perspective changed. We began to admire her devotion, but still did not know her very well. During a class one day, we were discussing among ourselves the baptism in the Holy Spirit. Someone speculated that if Teri would receive the Spirit baptism, just imagine what a great Christian she could be.

We mustered our courage, and together we moved to where Teri was seated. She smiled at us, and we began to talk. We shared with her that we had become Christians, and she beamed as she related that she had already heard the good news. We told her that we also had been "baptized in the Holy Ghost" and spoke in tongues. Then we asked her if she would be interested in receiving the baptism of the Holy Spirit. We were shocked with her response. Her face seemed to glow as she said, "I already have received Him."

Teri then related her story to us. She attended a small Methodist church in our rural county. One Sunday afternoon, she went into the woods behind her house alone, to pray. After praying for some time, she suddenly felt a change happening in her prayers. She began speaking words that she did not understand and was somewhat perplexed by what was happening. Nevertheless, she continued to pray diligently for a while. When she finished, she anxiously hurried back to her house and went into her bedroom to search the Scriptures.

Teri had no idea what had happened and had never heard of such an occurrence at that time, but she believed the Bible would have an answer. As she studied the Book of Acts, she realized that her experience was similar to what the disciples experienced on the Day of Pentecost. That's when she realized that she had been baptized in the Holy Spirit and had spoken in tongues as the Spirit gave her an unexpected utterance. Then we knew the secret behind the glow on Teri's face.

SPIRITUAL GIFTS OF LEADERSHIP

Gifts of the Spirit are primarily intended for the benefit of the church as a whole, although they also benefit those who possess them and serve others with them. Believers who have leadership gifts should strive to use their gifts for the highest good of the church.

[Gifts of an Apostle, Service, Mercy]

God calls Carlos, a humble servant, to start a new church
—told by Graciela, a member of his church

Background

Carlos recently moved from Ecuador to a large metropolitan city in California. After completing his university studies, he began working in an inner-city ministry for young people. Here is Carlos' story, as told by a member of the church he pastors.

The Story

Brother Carlos was working in the youth recreation program, when some of the people in the neighborhood asked him if he would start a church. He immediately began having Spanish worship services in one of the English-speaking churches in the neighborhood. He was enthusiastic and dedicated in his work of building the church.

Brother Carlos lives in the neighborhood, and during the week he visits families. He is very kind, always checking to see if the church can do anything for us. If we cannot come to church because we are sick or have to work, Brother Carlos comes to our house to pray and to have church with us. If we do not have a car, he will drive us to the store or to the doctor. He loves the neighborhood children and always has time for them. Brother Carlos always reminds us how much God loves us. He is such a kind and humble man. My family is very blessed by his ministry. We give thanks to God for such a wonderful pastor.

[Gifts of Evangelism, Service, Encouragement (Exhortation)]
Brenda tells her neighbors about Christ
—told by Kathy, a friend of Brenda's

Background

Brenda, a single woman, lives in the Northeast and owns her own small business. She became a follower of Christ as an adult. As a result, she has a tremendous amount of gratefulness for the healing that God has brought about in her life. Everywhere she goes, she shares her excitement with people.

The Story

I met Brenda in a Bible study. Immediately, I knew that she was unique. She was very confident, yet extremely compassionate. Brenda was open about how God had helped her through some really difficult times. She attributed her current peace of mind to God's power in her life. I was amazed and inspired by her story.

Brenda is a conscientious person. She reads her Bible every day, poring over every word and getting excited by every truth she encounters. She does not miss an opportunity to tell people about Christ's love, whether it is a neighbor, a health care worker or someone she runs into at the grocery store. Brenda actively looks for opportunities to share the good news about Christ. When she goes on her daily walks, she prays for her neighbors. Brenda also invites friends to walk with her, takes baked goodies to the children in her neighborhood, invites friends to go to community activities with her, and leads a women's Bible study in her home.

I am amazed at how people are drawn to Brenda. They are really attentive to what she has to say. She is also very good at leading people to make a decision to follow Jesus Christ. I guess this is all part of her gift, her spiritual gift of evangelism. God sends the right people to Brenda, and she is open and honest and shares His love from her heart.

[Conversion/Spirit Baptism] ·
[Gifts of Evangelism, Teaching, Administrations, Service, Mercy, Encouragement (Exhortation)]

Raymond uses a variety of spiritual gifts in sharing God's "good news"
—told by his wife Elaine and by Kimberly, now an adult, one of the children whom he inspired

Background

Nearing the end of his combat duty during World War II, Raymond became a Christian. On the ship home, he met some Christian sailors who invited him to a Bible study. During the 19-day trip home, these dedicated young sailors explained the plan of salvation. Raymond understood it and accepted it for the first time. These young men also told him about the purpose of baptism in the Spirit.

The night he arrived in the States, Raymond received Spirit baptism in a worship service at a Pentecostal mission in California. The men who prayed for him to be filled with the Spirit guided him through God's Word and explained how that the Holy Spirit had come to live in him at conversion. They also explained that when he received Spirit baptism, he would then be empowered by the Holy Spirit to witness and preach for Christ. That day, Raymond came to understand that every believer was to carry out the primary mission of Christ—to share God's love and plan of salvation with others until everyone on earth had come to know Him. On that day Raymond's enthusiasm for evangelism was born.

The Story

God gave Raymond many spiritual gifts that he used as tools for evangelism. He worked hard to develop his spiritual gifts, studying to learn about a wide range of topics. He pursued higher education and was a professor of languages in a Christian college. There he inspired many faculty and students to share their faith with others. While on the faculty there, he served as an adviser for a dynamic ministry team that went out to share the plan of salvation with others. He trained students in soulwinning and helped them organize many ministries. These included jail ministries, house-to-house evangelism teams, street meetings, church rallies, child evangelism activities, and so forth.

Raymond became educated in cults and actively witnessed to their members, many of whom came to know Christ and went on to have dynamic ministries themselves. Because he wasn't a licensed cleric, his work inspired his denomination's laity to become actively involved in ministry in a wide variety of ways. He set up denominational programs for training people how to share their faith, and he traveled around the world, lecturing on evangelism, lay apologetics and cult evangelism.

Raymond also actively participated in service and mercy ministries, such as visiting the sick and the discouraged in hospitals and nursing homes. He always had time to spend with children and young people, always ready with a smile and a pocket full of candy to show them that he cared. He considered all of this work to be part of the divine call to be God's witness "to the ends of the earth" (Acts 1:8, *NIV*).

As Raymond served others by listening, providing encouragement and praying with them, he always kept his primary purpose in mind. In everything he did, Raymond told people about Jesus' love for them and encouraged them to give their lives to Christ so that they could have eternal life and experience the joy he had. He shared with them these scriptures that tell of God's forgiveness and salvation: Luke 18:10-14; 19:7-10; 23:39-43; John 8:3-11. When people gave their hearts and lives to Christ, he urged them to seek the empowerment of the Holy Spirit in their lives so that they too could be powerful witnesses for Jesus Christ in our world. Raymond continued until the end of his life on earth to endeavor to be God's witness. He continued to go "into all the world and preach the gospel to every creature" (Mark 16:15, *NKJV*).

[Gift of Administrations, Meditating in the Spirit]
The Holy Spirit guides Anna in the quiet of the morning
—told by Anna, an artist and homemaker

Background

Anna is a 46-year-old woman with the gift of administrations, which she uses in many creative ways. People often describe Anna as a visionary or an organizer. Anna has a God-given ability to see the large picture, break it down into smaller components, and then make a plan. Her Christian service often involves making plans for, and assisting with, solving problems, meeting an individual's need, starting a Christian ministry, beginning a community initiative or managing her family's household.

For Anna to be most effective in using her gift, she needs to work with and have the support of others with complementary gifts— such as, apostles, pastors and persons with gifts of service. Anna's husband, Kyle, has the gifts of encouragement and service, which work well with hers in Christian ministry. Here is what Anna has to say about her gift:

The Story

I enjoy the work that God sends my way. A lot of people who have the spiritual gift of administrations seem to use their gift as part of their duties for a particular position. Since I am a home-maker, the work that I do is often more project-based. I find it exciting to look at a particular situation or set of problems and to imagine all the possibilities, whether it's envisioning and planning a ministry in the church, designing curriculum, planning a family activity, or working on a piece of art. Just imagining all that God is going to do is so thrilling!

I have learned that one of the most essential components of serving God is to stop and listen to Him. I must allow the Holy Spirit to speak to me and lead me, or I will get off track with my own dreams, agendas or even fears. In order to hear the Holy Spirit's voice, I must create space in my daily routine for listening to God. I have learned that if I am quiet in the evening before going to bed, and quiet in the morning when I get up, I am able to hear the Spirit's voice of guidance more clearly. I believe that during the night as I sleep, the Holy Spirit gives me creative ideas, reveals truths to me and makes me aware of God's desires for my life. The next morning when I wake up, if I am very still, new ideas and solutions come to me. I start out my day with peace and confidence, knowing that God is leading me. All I need to do is listen and follow His lead.

Sometimes, this means stopping, praying and waiting for Him to move. If I do not wait on Him, I may move too fast and create a lot of trouble for myself. When I do not allow God to reach out to me in the quiet, I often feel stressed and overwhelmed by the wide variety of roles that I play. Because I have not allowed God to encourage me, I tend to get easily discouraged when others do not notice or appreciate the less visible, supportive work that I do. But if I listen closely to God, I am able to know and feel that God sees and cares. I have the assurance that He will supply all I need—all of the wisdom, knowledge, ability, resources and people that are needed for a particular task.

I have also learned that after I have gone out in the world and completed a creative project, I must return to that very quiet place once again. It's time to allow the Holy Spirit to heal my tired body and mind, to renew my spirit and to begin preparing me for my next exciting work.

SPIRITUAL GIFTS FOR PRACTICAL SERVICE

The Holy Spirit equips God's children with gifts of service so that they can do a variety of helpful deeds and can minister to the needs of the poor, the needy and the sick. They are to exercise their gifts in a spirit of simplicity, sincerity and generosity.

[Gift of Encouragement (Exhortation)]

Amanda shares her joy and love with the church
—told by Jennifer, a youth leader

Background

Amanda is a 12-year-old girl whom God uses through her gift of encouragement. According to Jennifer, a youth leader in Amanda's church, Amanda uses her spiritual gift wherever she goes. Even though she struggles with Down's syndrome, Amanda actively shares her loves with those around her. Her friendliness continually reminds her church family of just how much God cares for everyone, and that each one of us has so much to celebrate. Here is Jennifer's story:

The Story

I want to thank God for Amanda's ministry in my life. Every Sunday she arrives at church early with her mother, who teaches Sunday school. When I arrive, Amanda is standing in the entry, waiting to say hello and give me a big hug. I really love Amanda; she is such an inspiration to me. No matter how difficult a week I may have, with struggles in the workplace or challenges with my health, Amanda always reminds me that I am loved. What a gift she is to our church family!

[Gift of Helps]

Ellen serves the Body of Christ through her faithful service
—told by Laticia

Background

Laticia tells of listening to a sermon about honorable service to God and being faithful in this service.

The Story

I was sitting, sort of half-listening to a sermon, when the minister began to talk about a conversation he had with another pastor, and I perked up. The two clergymen were discussing people in churches who faithfully use their spiritual gifts in service to the body of Christ. In the discussion, the other pastor indicated that if there were any person in her local church she would like to honor, it would be Ellen. She said that every Wednesday night for years, Ellen had come to church early and laid out the dishes, flatware and cups for the weekly fellowship dinner. Each week, Ellen did what God called her to do, and she did it faithfully. This pastor believed that Ellen's spiritual gift was a real blessing to the church and that she deserved great honor.

Since I have heard this story, whenever I start to think that my tasks of service are unimportant or are keeping me from "real" ministry, I remember Ellen. I am inspired to go out of my way to thank the "Ellens" in my life as I come into contact with them.

[Gifts of Giving and Service]

Alex provides financial and practical assistance to Geoffrey

—told by Maria, Alex's wife

Background

Alex, a young man just out of college, worked for a bank in Colorado when he met his friend, Geoffrey, at church. Alex's wife, Maria, tells the story.

The Story

My husband, Alex, is a caring person. He's always helping out someone in need; he must have the spiritual gifts of giving and serving. A particular story of his helping Geoffrey comes to mind. Alex met Geoffrey one Sunday when he visited our church. Alex saw that Geoffrey was a kind, simple man who did not have a lot of money, and that a lot of people took advantage of him because of his mental disability. So he started taking Geoffrey to lunch each week and took him shopping for toiletries every two weeks. The two developed a good friendship that both enjoyed. Alex and Geoffrey continued their weekly lunches until Geoffrey moved to another city to live near family.

SPIRITUAL GIFTS OF POWER

Testimonies of healing are commonplace in Pentecostal and Charismatic churches. Most Pentecostals and Charismatics have heard someone describe a miraculous healing, a manifestation or some other work of the Holy Spirit. Here are some dramatic testimonies that demonstrate various works of the Holy Spirit, such as healing, words of wisdom and knowledge, spiritual leadings, prophecy, discernment, and other Spirit manifestations. Many more testimonies could be related, but the intent here is to provide a few illustrative testimonies of the ongoing, supernatural works of the Holy Spirit.

[Gift of Healings]

Parents pray for God to heal their baby
—told by the parents of Joshua

Background

Many times healing takes place outside of a worship service. In this case, a minister tells how the intercessory prayers of many people contributed to the healing of his son.

The Story

Our first son, Josh, was about six months old when his mother and I noticed that he was not responding to sound. He had a history of ear infections, so we assumed he had developed another ear infection that was temporarily blocking his hearing. So we made an appointment with his doctor, thinking that we would get an antibiotic and everything would be fine.

After the doctor examined Josh, he informed us that our son was not suffering from an ear infection, but that his hearing impairment was more serious than that. The doctor suggested we have a brain stem test done to determine the extent of Josh's hearing disorder. An appointment was made with the ear specialist on the following Monday.

Of course, my wife and I were terribly concerned. Josh was a beautiful child with bright blue eyes and curly blonde hair. The thought of having a deaf child was overwhelming. When we returned home from the doctor's office, I began to call friends and family to ask them to pray for a healing miracle. The weekend was very long, and the anxiety was building.

On Monday afternoon, we made the trip to see the specialist. We arrived at his office, and he began to prepare Josh for the test immediately. The nurse took Josh into the examination room, and my wife and I were left alone in the waiting area. After about 45 minutes, the specialist came into the waiting area with the news. His exact words: "I don't know what has happened since Friday, but today there is nothing at all wrong with his hearing. Josh is fine!"

Today, Josh is a wonderful 17-year-old young man who is gifted musically. He has always been a blessing from the Lord, and we are indeed grateful that God touched our son.

[Gift of Healings]

God spares Melissa's life and repairs her shattered leg
—told by Melissa, a teacher

Background

When Melissa was a young teacher and a minister's wife, she was in a tragic accident that almost took her life. She relates the story of her dynamic recovery as a result of the faithful praying of people who rallied around her family.

The Story

"Great Is Thy Faithfulness" has always been one of my favorite songs. The faithfulness of God was proven to me in 1976 when I was in a car accident and was not expected to live. A driver who went into a diabetic coma while driving crashed into my car. Rescue workers had to extract me from the car and take me to a local hospital. The medical team said that my injuries were so severe I would be sent to a larger hospital in Chattanooga, Tennessee. They told my husband, Ryan, that they did not expect me to live. The doctor said that, at best, he would give me a 50 percent chance to survive. He told Ryan that if I did live, I would be paralyzed on the left side of my body and would have serious eye damage. My femur (thigh bone) was shattered into over a hundred pieces. The doctor said it would take two to five years to repair it; and if I ever walked again, there would be a noticeable limp. He told Ryan that his main concern was that I lived!

My family and many members of our church gathered in the Intensive Care waiting room. They joined hands and began to pray, for they believed that "by His stripes we are healed" (Isaiah 53:5). While they were praying, the doctor came in and asked to talk to my husband. He explained that while they were doing an extensive test, the left side of my body began to move! Ryan was told that I was coming out of the coma and that I would live! God had answered their prayers! When I was too weak to pray for myself, someone was praying for me!

The doctor told Ryan that my leg would require surgery. He explained that he would need to place a rod in the area where the bone had been shattered. Ryan told him to do whatever he needed to do and that he knew God would complete the healing. We were expecting the surgery on the next day, but the doctor said that he was going to wait a day. He continued to postpone the surgery for a week. Finally, Ryan asked him why the delay. The doctor showed my husband the Xrays of the femur on the day of the wreck, and the Xrays of the bone a week later. God was bringing every piece of the bone back together! Ryan began to praise the Lord! Then the doctor said that he did not believe that God had done it. Ryan asked him who he thought had done it. The doctor explained that at times the body decides to re-create itself. Ryan told him that the great Creator was taking care of me, and that if He chose to re-create, He could! The doctor did not know how to reply.

God continued healing me, and four months after the accident, I walked into the doctor's office! I was not supposed to be able to walk for two to five years. God had brought every piece of the shattered femur back together without surgery, and the doctor said that it was stronger than before the wreck! He looked at Ryan and said, "Your God has done the work, but you will have to pay me for it."

Ryan responded, "You will get the pay, but God will get the glory!"

It has been 25 years since the accident, and I have never had any problems with it. There is no limp or pain! To God be all the glory for His faithfulness!

[Gifts of Faith, Speaking in Tongues, Healings]
The Spirit gives Amy faith to trust God for healing
—told by a pastor

Background

Pentecostals and Charismatics often emphasize the need to be sensitive to the leading of the Holy Spirit. This emphasis is related to their belief that the Holy Spirit is active in the affairs of Spirit-filled people and that the Spirit desires to perform signs and wonders through them. This poignant story from a pastor illustrates Spirit-led ministry that results in dynamic manifestations of healing. It demonstrates the overpowering presence of the Spirit that often accompanies a healing experience.

The Story

From 1985 to 1987, I pastored a church in the South. Sister Amy, 81, was an elderly member who had trusted the Lord for her physical healing for 60 years. When she was sick, Amy trusted God until she was healed. One day she told me her story.

When Amy was 21, she was dying with hardening of the liver. The doctors were limited in what they could do at that time, and they gave her up to die. While she was lying in her bed one day, the Lord visited her and said, "Amy, you have trusted Me with your soul. If you trust Me with both your soul and your body, I will heal you!" Weeping, she made a promise to the Lord that she would trust Him with both soul and body. She was completely restored to full health, and began her faith walk in divine healing.

While serving as her pastor, I was called to her house one day to pray for her. A large, painful knot had formed on her side. For several days we prayed, but the knot continued to grow. A woman in our church who worked for a gynecologist took a urine sample to their lab. The doctor said that she was full of infection and would die within a few days if the condition was not treated. She became so weak she was completely bedridden. Her daughters and the ladies from the church put adult diapers on her and added "draw sheets" under her to move her in bed.

On a Wednesday evening, I received a call that Amy was about to leave this world. I had a fever of 103 degrees, and usually I would not make a visit while being so sick; but I felt an urgency to pray with Sister Amy. I rushed to her house and went to her room. Hearing that I was running a fever, she told me I should not have gotten out of the house. I told her that I wanted to come, and let her know what a joy it had been to be her pastor.

I prayed a prayer of comfort for Amy and went to sit in the living room. A little later, she called me and asked me to pray for her, so I prayed another pastoral prayer of comfort. This happened two more times. The last time was different. As I stepped to the door, the presence of the Holy Spirit manifested Himself over me, and I doubled over. When I straightened up, I was shaking under the power of God and praying in the Spirit. Standing by Amy's bed, I waved my hands over her. I never touched her, but the Spirit did! She began to shake and pray in the Spirit. She raised her hands and began to wave them before the Lord. Suddenly Amy sat up in bed, laid hands on my forehead and cursed the fever I had. That night the Lord healed both of us, and Amy was in church the next service!

[Gift of Faith]

Co-eds pray to find a lost contact lens

—told by Laura, a student studying in Europe

Background

Laura was traveling and studying in Spain with a group of college students from Oklahoma. After a month of speaking in churches and seeing the sites in Spain, they decided to take a train back to the city of Madrid to meet up with some of the church members that they had met during their stay. They planned to spend a few weeks with these church friends until it was time for them to fly back to the United States or to move on to the next destination in Europe. Laura was just beginning her trip; in a few weeks she was scheduled to begin her studies in Spanish in another city. This is her story.

The Story

My friends and I arrived in Madrid, got off the train and unloaded our luggage. We were unable to get in touch with our friends from church, so we called another pastor in the city. His wife answered the phone and invited us to stay in their apartment until everyone at the other church returned from a funeral. We hailed a small taxi, loaded our stuff in the trunk and on top of the cab, then squeezed in. After we had unloaded the luggage at the pastor's home, and had carried most of it to the upstairs apartment, I noticed that I was not able to see very well. I thought, *Oh, no, my contact lens is off-center*. Then I realized that my contact was not even in my eye! I began to cry—I was tired, I was in a country where I barely spoke the language, and this was just the beginning of the trip. What was I to do?

The pastor's wife, Señora Rivera, who spoke English, told me not to worry. She reminded me that God cares about everything, even small things, like contact lenses. She said that we would pray . . . that when two or three are gathered in His name, God is with them. We stopped, joined hands and prayed for a few seconds, then we went down to retrieve the rest of the luggage. As we were paying the cab driver, one of my girlfriends happened to look at the ground and see my contact lens wedged under the edge of the wheel of the taxi, where it must have rolled. The small lens was the same color as the pavement, and the lens was unharmed! It was a miracle!

I have never forgotten that day. When I have doubts about the power of prayer or about God caring for the small things in my life, I remember that day. I recall the words of Señora Rivera, her amazing faith and my contact lens miracle!

SPIRITUAL GIFTS OF REVELATION

Many of God's children face problems, challenges and crises. The Lord may give insight or knowledge to meet the need at hand. Such insight is not due to human knowledge or insight, but is a revelation given by the Holy Spirit.

[Gifts of Prophecy (a Vision), Healings]

Ted sees a prophetic vision about his father's healing
—told by Ted's brother Charles

Background

This amazing account has encouraged numerous people in the Louisville, Kentucky, area, where Charles is a well-respected, retired high school teacher. He was deeply impacted by the powerful manifestation of the work of the Spirit through the healing of his father. A remarkable aspect of Charles' story is his brother Ted's vision that preceded the miracle.

At age 42, Charles' father, Thomas, received the shocking news that he had tuberculosis. Specialists confirmed the doctor's diagnosis that Thomas had only about six months to live. When Thomas was only 9, his father had died of the same disease. The doctor's prognosis devastated Thomas. For the first time ever, Charles saw his dad cry, overwhelmed with the thought of leaving his young family without a husband or father. Thomas, however, "sought out a second opinion by petitioning heaven's door."

Remembering the Biblical account of the healing of the king in Isaiah 38, the devastated father asked God to "grant him 20 more years" to raise his family of three boys and two girls. God graciously heard his prayer, healed Thomas and gave him strength. His request was honored, and he enjoyed his family for 23 more years. Then Thomas once again faced another battle for his life. Charles' own words provide a poignant picture of the amazing events that transpired through the Holy Spirit's intervention. Here Charles takes up the story.

The Story

Twenty-three years later, my dad was gravely ill again. After a period of hospitalization, he was sent home to die. Except for my youngest brother, Ted, all of my family was at home seated around my dad's bed. We knew that Daddy would not make it through the night. He was curled up in bed in a fetal position, breathing laboriously, unable to speak and semiconscious.

Ted was in Virginia, where he pastored a small church. The phone rang, and Ted began the conversation by saying he had been fasting and praying for Dad. He told me of an incident that left me staggering in unbelief; but there was no unbelief on his end of the line. Ted boldly proclaimed that God had given him a vision. He said he was wide-awake, and he saw what resembled a color television screen. He continued: "I saw Dad lying in the bed in a fetal state. After a while, Daddy straightened out on the bed. In a few minutes, Daddy sat up on the edge of the bed and asked Mother to bring him his clothes. He dressed, went down to the family room and sat in his easy chair."

Then my brother gave the clincher line to this astounding account: "The Lord is going to give Daddy another 10 years." Well, this was almost more than an unbelieving heart could endure; but not to be unkind, I told Ted I would relay the message to the family.

In my unbelief, I hesitated to add to the grief and sorrow already engulfing the room by sharing Ted's vision. But in the face of my silence, I saw Dad stretch out in the bed. In a matter of minutes, I saw him sit up on the side of the bed and ask Mother to get his clothes. He said he was going to the family room. Needless to say, my heart was in my throat as everything took place just as my brother had prophesied.

Seven years later, on January 7, 1985, my dad passed away. After the funeral, Mother quietly remarked to me, "You know, Charles, Ted said Thomas would have 10 years, and it's been only seven." Instantly, the answer came to me.

"Mama," I replied, "Remember when Daddy asked God for 20 more years? Twenty-three years later, the hospital sent him home to die. Add the three extra years of Dad's 20-year request to the seven, and you have 10 more years." A faint but satisfied smile etched my mother's sad face.

[Gifts of a "Word of Knowledge," Healings]

Richard receives a message from God about Sue's cancer
—told by Richard, an evangelist

Background

Sometimes a word of knowledge, or a message of knowledge, may precede an act of healing. During the late '70s, Richard, an evangelist, was conducting a revival in a Pentecostal church in Georgia.

The Story

One night during the revival, a woman named Sue came through the prayer line, asking God for healing. According to the evangelist's testimony, she "had cancer that had caused her to waste away," even though she had received all the medical treatments that were available at the time. Sue taught an adult Sunday school class and was esteemed as "an anointed woman of God" who had "great faith."

The evangelist said that when Sue came forward for prayer, "the Lord told me to tell her that her sickness was not unto death." He was extremely reluctant to tell her this, because he thought that if she died, he would be classified as a "false prophet" and lose his credibility as a minister. He said, "The Lord told me again to give her the message. Finally, I obeyed the Lord." After praying for Sue, he did not hear the outcome of the matter for some time.

Several years later while attending a regional camp meeting, a healthy, vivacious woman walked up to greet him. He rejoiced to see Sue for the first time since she came through the prayer line. He said, "The Lord had restored her health, and she was walking in the divine healing power of God. She is still alive to this day. Praise the Lord!"

[Gifts of a "Word of Knowledge," Healings]
James is skeptical about a man's healing
—told by James

Background

This testimony also demonstrates the gift of a word (or message) of knowledge that accompanied a work of healing. In this story, the miracle became a faith-building experience for the young man who shared these events.

The Story

The guest speaker for the revival was a well-known evangelist who conducted tent meetings and healing services throughout the Deep South. During the altar service, the evangelist stated that someone in the service had a problem with his or her hearing, and that the person should come forward to receive healing. A middle-aged man stepped forward and stated that he was deaf in one ear. The evangelist prayed for him to be healed. After the prayer, the evangelist whispered softly toward the damaged ear to see if the man had been healed. The man replied that he could now hear; he had been healed. The congregation began celebrating his healing.

James, a new believer, was skeptical of the healing. He was new to the Pentecostal faith and had never seen anyone healed like that. He thought that the man might have felt pressured to say he was healed, or would have been embarrassed to say that he was not healed. When the revival was over, he returned to work the next week. One of his coworkers attended the same church and had been at the revival services. As they discussed the services, James asked his friend what he had thought of the revival. He was surprised when his coworker told him, "My uncle from another town came to one of the services. He had been deaf in one ear for as long as I have known him, and God healed him that night when the evangelist prayed for him. Now he can hear out of that ear." This testimony deeply impacted James and helped him to become established in his newfound faith in Christ.

[Gift of a "Word of Knowledge," Conversion, Spirit Baptism]

The Holy Spirit exposes sin
—told by a military chaplain

Background

A minister who was serving as a chaplain to the military in Europe shared this testimony.

The Story

An executive of a civilian support agency to the military brought a male employee of the company to a worship service at the center where I was pastoring. The employee had been talking about suicide, and his friend thought that we could help him. I was not informed of the nature of the problem. When the altar service began, the man came forward, and I went to him and started to pray.

The Lord revealed to me specifics about the addictive sins that he was involved in. As I shared these things, his spirit broke and he began to repent. He was saved that night. As he continued to pray and weep for an extended time, I prayed for him to receive the Holy Spirit, and he was baptized in the Holy Spirit. Later, he shared how shocked he was that God had revealed his problems to me, and he became a faithful believer.

[Gift of Discernings of Spirits]

Frank receives a message of discernment
—told by Frank, a pastor in the Midwest

Background

This testimony illustrates the gift of discernment of spirits at work in the spiritual deliverance of an individual. At the church Frank pastored in the Midwest, a woman new to the church came forward during the altar service. Standing in the altar area, she appeared to be praying in tongues. Pastor Frank felt the Holy Spirit prompting him that the woman was actually chanting to the devil. He asked the musicians to stop playing. Then he told the congregation that the woman was demon-possessed and that the Lord was going to deliver her. He said that if anyone was uncomfortable with the situation, they could leave the service. Pastor Frank relates the events.

The Story

As I looked at her, she glared at me defiantly as though there was an evil spirit all over her. Then, I jumped across the altar and landed in front of her. I began to rebuke the evil spirit and cast out the evil presence. She screamed and fell to the floor, weeping. After some time of being broken before God, she arose. Then she testified that she had been possessed with a demonic presence that had tormented her for two years. After her deliverance, she was in total soundness of mind, and she expressed appreciation to God for deliverance. She became a faithful believer after that time.

SPIRITUAL GIFTS FOR WORSHIP

Many spiritual gifts are manifested in Spirit-inspired worship. Their purpose is to strengthen the congregation, both spiritually and numerically. As a result, they glorify Jesus Christ and prepare us for His return.

[Sign of the Spirit's Presence]

A visual manifestation of the Holy Spirit
—told by a Lee College alumnus

Background

The Holy Spirit sometimes manifests Himself in unusual ways. See how the Spirit's manifestation strengthens faith in God.

The Story

At Lee College in the mid-70s, two other guys and I met in a dormitory room one evening to pray. After we had prayed in the Spirit for a while, we all three stood up. For a few moments, we stared around the room in silence, and then looked at each other. One of my friends began rubbing his eyes, saying, "Guys, I think something is wrong with my eyes!" I was relieved to hear his words, because I thought that I was seeing things. I said, "Do you see a haze?" He said, "Yes. Do you see it too?" I replied, "Yes." The third fellow who was silent during all of this said, "I see it too."

What we were seeing amazed us. The entire room was filled

from top to bottom with a fog-like haze. I had thought my eyes were playing tricks on me, or that my vision had become distorted. We slowly became aware that we were experiencing something super-natural. I said, "I've never seen anything like this before." The previously silent friend said, "I've seen it before, at my home church." I asked, "What is it?" He replied, "It is a manifestation of the glory of God." We just stood there in the haze, praising God and enjoying His presence, until the haze slowly disappeared from the room. This event impacted my life dramatically and became a cornerstone experience in my faith walk with the Lord. During times when I struggled with doubt, I would reflect on this experience and remind myself of how great God is.

[Conversion / Spirit Baptism]
[Spiritual Graces/Spiritual Empowerment and Guidance/Christian Community (Gifts of Leadership, Practical Service, Power, Revelation, Worship)]

Amazing encounters with the Spirit

Background

Several years ago, a large Christian fellowship in the eastern United States experienced a powerful, dynamic move of the Holy Spirit. During a weeklong, concentrated time of prayer and worship, individuals received spiritual revitalization. Amazing things began to happen. The Holy Spirit inspired major changes in individuals' lives. He empowered this fellowship and other churches to do things they had never dreamed possible.

The original membership of this fellowship consisted of a wide variety of people. It included individuals from Pentecostal/ Charismatic backgrounds, as well as those from other Christian backgrounds. It included older and younger people from different cultural, educational and socioeconomic backgrounds. It was a diverse group of individuals with unique abilities and gifts. During this special time of worship, God blessed them, inspiring and giving them the abilities to bring about powerful positive changes in the world.

Here is the story of how some people, just like you and me, paused from the busyness of their daily lives in order to worship God, and how God then changed their lives forever.

The Story

It was spring, and the Easter season was approaching. It was one of our fellowship's regular evening worship times. We were all praying. The astonishing events began when someone spoke a message in tongues. Someone else gave an interpretation of the message. I do not remember exactly what the message was, but I do remember that it had a profound emotional and spiritual effect on those of us present. From that moment on, so much began to change for us. This first move of the Holy Spirit began a weeklong journey of spiritual experiences that would alter and set the course for the rest of our lives.

That week people just wanted to pray and be present with God. After our first encounter with the Holy Spirit that night, many people decided to stay late and pray. Many prayed far into the night; some stayed all night. Their dedication to prayer, meditation and praise continued all week. Many people took a vacation from their jobs and their university studies. Often individuals forgot to eat meals; they just wanted to worship God and listen to the Holy Spirit. Others would go home, sleep a few hours, then return early the next day to be with God. When people came, they often sat for hours in complete silence. They just sat and enjoyed the presence of God.

During the worship gatherings, the Holy Spirit moved in a powerful way. Words cannot describe the excitement we felt, nor the tremendous transformations that took place that week. As we sat in our seats and prayed, we could feel waves of spiritual power come over us. The pastor was sensitive to the move of the Holy Spirit, and at appropriate times, he would give us words of encouragement inspired by the Spirit. He never planned the services, but just allowed the Holy Spirit to lead. There were no two services the same, with the Holy Spirit leading in each one.

At other times, individuals present would speak Spirit-inspired messages in languages unknown to them. International university students who were present excitedly reported that they heard their own languages being spoken. Some individuals in the worship gatherings received interpretations from the Holy Spirit and shared them with us. Prophecies were also given. Some people told about visions they saw. Some shared testimonies of God's work in their lives. Other individuals repented, gave confessions and repaired fractured relationships with others.

When we arrived at the place of worship, we would hear the Holy Spirit give so many messages of encouragement, see so many people praying, hear such amazing testimonies and feel God's amazing power! As soon as we entered the room, we could immediately feel the presence and power of the Holy Spirit. A young woman said that at times it felt like she was dreaming, because she had never seen such a "miraculous outpouring of the Holy Spirit." Another woman who did not have a Pentecostal background said, "I know this is from God. No person could work up this revival!"

During the week, God changed hearts and lives and called many people to their life work. Many were healed of illnesses and disabilities. For some, healing occurred after they returned to their homes to rest. Relationships were also healed. Conflicts were resolved, and individuals and families began to work together in harmony to do God's work. People were inspired to generosity, giving freely to God's work. This enabled the fellowship to later expand its ministry in the world.

Many people said that God had caused them to change directions and move toward a particular type of ministry and service. Among those who received their special calls that week were two women who were called to be missionaries and educators in Asian countries.

One was a Spanish teacher, who earlier had felt that God had called her to be a missionary, but she did not know where she should go. During this week of meditation and renewal, God gave her guidance through a message delivered by the Holy Spirit. He told her that she was to go to Asia to work with the poor. She immediately began making plans to go and ended up serving as a missionary for years—sharing the good news of Christ's love, helping the poor and establishing a Christian girls' school. God sent the other young woman called to full-time mission work to another Asian country, where she also established a school, teaching children about God's love for them.

An example of God's move that week was a young man whose ministry call was confirmed by the Holy Spirit. He became a pastor, established a Christian counseling center and became a great leader in his denomination. Over the years, his ministry and service to others have touched thousands of lives. Still another person present in the meetings was inspired to pursue her life's work by teaching children with disabilities. Her love and compassion for others have inspired hundreds of children and their families. Many other individuals present during the revival were called, and went on to do what some would consider to be ordinary work in society, but they did it as they were empowered by the Holy Spirit. In secular jobs and in their family lives, they have touched and ministered to countless people, impacting the world around them in positive ways.

One of the most significant things that occurred that week was that so many people said their thinking had changed, they wanted a closer relationship with God, and they were committed to following His leading in their lives. As a result of the week's events, many people began to reevaluate priorities and to change directions in their lives. I, too, was inspired by the Holy Spirit to seek a closer relationship with God. God revealed to me that He would direct my life step-by-step, if I would put my trust in Him and obey Him. After sitting that week in the presence of God for hours, I have never doubted that God is real and that His Holy Spirit directs His people when they are sensitive to Him. As a result, I have always had a sense of peace and assurance that God is with me. I believe that my experiences with the Spirit that week have impacted every aspect of my entire life—my relationship with God, my work and my family life.

In the worship gatherings, people came to Christ, and the good news began to spread. During this week of life-changing empowerment, many people were drawn to worship. One person described the power of the Holy Spirit to be like a magnet "pulling the people in." Many came out of curiosity, were drawn to a relationship with Christ and began to desire the Spirit's empowerment. By the end of the week, almost everyone who had attended the spontaneous worship/prayer time had committed their lives to Jesus Christ. Many were filled with the Spirit and were empowered for the service to which He was calling them. People reported that God had revitalized their love and passion for Christian service.

The spiritual power received during this time began to spread quickly. Individuals in the community heard of the move of God and came to see and experience it. They returned to their churches and shared the exciting news. As international students went to their home countries and new missionaries went out, reports of God's work began to be sent back from around the world. They told that when their families and churches heard about their encounters with the Holy Spirit, they also began to pray for such moves of the Spirit in their lives and communities.

One student from Latin America reported that God was moving so powerfully that amazing miracles were occurring in her community. Hundreds had been converted. People who could not see, those who could not walk, and those who could not hear had been healed. Among those touched were hundreds of people in a nearby quarantined site, who were healed of Hansen's disease. A missionary in Europe reported a spiritual revival there. People were coming to

Christ in unprecedented numbers. God's healing power was spreading around the world!

SOME CONCLUDING THOUGHTS

As I think back on this time of spiritual blessings and what has happened since, I am keenly aware of the fact that God has grown the seeds He planted in our lives and in our Christian community that week. My life has been affected, along with people in my church and community, and people around the world. It is almost unbelievable how God has taken something that seemed so small—our taking time to pray and listen to the Holy Spirit—and has turned it into something so enormous! As one of my friends said, this time in our lives will always be one of our "most precious memories." I think that we will see and feel the effects of this week's spiritual blessings and awakenings for generations—in fact, for eternity.

These personal stories so graciously shared by many people remind us of how the Holy Spirit still works in our lives and in the world today. He gives us assurance that a full and complete life, promised by Christ and experienced by the early Christians, is still available for God's people today. As the various testimonies indicate, the Holy Spirit has a special role in our entire Christian experience. He opens our eyes so that we can understand and receive Jesus as our Savior.

To most people in the first century, Jesus was either a false prophet or a revolutionary rabbi; but to His disciples, Jesus was the Son of God, the Savior of the world. They did not come to this conviction by merely listening to what He said or observing what He did. As Paul says, God reveals truth about Himself through the Spirit (1 Corinthians 2:9-12). When Peter confessed Jesus to be the Son of God, Jesus said to him, "Flesh and blood did not reveal this to you" (Matthew 16:17). Through the Holy Spirit, God makes

Jesus Christ known and convinces people of the truth of the gospel. Faith energized by the Spirit enables us to receive salvation.

It is, therefore, by the Spirit that we enter the Christian life. Yet the work of the Spirit is broader than what He does in conversion. Life in the Spirit encompasses a total lifestyle, including Spirit baptism and fruit and gifts of the Spirit. A Spirit-led and empowered life becomes a reality as we serve God in the community of faith and in the world. There is no other way for the Spirit-filled Christian. The Cross is central to our salvation and to our living holy, Christlike lives. The fruit of the Spirit is the essence of our Christian walk. Being directed by the Spirit makes us open to the profound experience of baptism in the Spirit and to the flourishing of charismatic power and spiritual gifts through us.

Truly the nurture and empowerment of the Holy Spirit gives us deep roots in Christ and enables us to walk the path of spiritual growth and service. In short, encounters with the Holy Spirit are miracles of God's grace that transform our lives profoundly, empowering us to be conformed more and more to the person and ministry of Jesus Christ.

CHAPTER 11—STUDY AND DISCUSSION

PERSONAL STORIES

1. Is there a particular personal story in this chapter that you enjoyed reading? How has it impacted you?

2. What is your story? How has the Holy Spirit moved in your life?

3. What are some special ways the Holy Spirit has moved in the life of your church?

REFLECTION

4. What are some things that you have learned in this *Encountering the Holy Spirit* study?

5. What impact has this study had on you?

Our Prayer

Spirit of Truth,

*As you guide us and walk with us
on our paths of spiritual growth and service,*

*Move in the depths of our hearts and give us
a love for God's Word,
a compassion for the lost,
a zeal for holiness,
a dedication to a life of prayer, and
a yearning for the appearing again of Jesus Christ.*

*May we always praise You and enjoy
a life with You forever .*

*In the name of the
Father, Son and Holy Spirit we pray.
Amen.*

May "the grace of the Lord Jesus Christ, and the love of God,
and the fellowship of the Holy Spirit, be with you all."
2 Corinthians 13:14

Part Seven

Appendix

Glossary

Apostle—Literally, one sent forth as a messenger, but the word *apostle* in the New Testament is used in a broad and restricted sense. The broad usage refers to an agent or messenger (2 Corinthians 8:23; Philippians 2:25), but in its restricted sense it applies primarily to the Twelve and to Paul, who after the resurrection of Christ assumed the leadership of the church.

Apostolic age, Age of the apostles—The time from Pentecost (about 30 A.D.) to the death of the apostle John (about 100 A.D.), during which period the apostles had great influence on the Christian churches.

Age of the Spirit, Age of fulfillment, Messianic age, Last days, Charismatic age—Terms to describe the period of time initiated by the first coming of Christ and the outpouring of the Holy Spirit on the Day of Pentecost. The period from Pentecost to the second coming of Christ can be described by any of the terms listed above.

Altar service—In many churches, a part of the larger worship service. Frequently, at the conclusion of the sermon, the pastor invites the congregation to come to the altar area for repentance, rededication and prayer.

Anointing of the Holy Spirit, Spirit anointing—Terms widely used by Pentecostals and Charismatics to speak about the Spirit's endowment of believers with Pentecostal power for witnessing and evangelizing. Jesus said, "The Spirit of the Lord . . . anointed Me" (Luke 4:18). Peter told about the anointing of Jesus by the Holy Spirit (Acts 10:38).

Anointing with oil—A symbol of anointing with the Holy

Spirit, especially associated with the outpouring of the Spirit (see 1 Samuel 10:1-9; 16:13; Isaiah 61:1). Oil may be used in praying for the recovery of the sick (Mark 6:13; James 5:14).

Apologetic value—Something that has value for explaining and giving clear reasons for a belief or a doctrinal position.

Baptism *by* the Holy Spirit, Conversion baptism—Terms that refer to conversion as being a distinct experience from baptism in the Spirit. A person is baptized by the Spirit into the body of Christ, or experiences conversion baptism, at the moment of salvation. *See also* **Conversion**.

Baptism *in* the Holy Spirit, Spirit baptism, Gift of the Spirit, Blessing of empowerment—A variety of terms that refer to the powerful, Pentecostal anointing by the Spirit that one may experience subsequent to, or after conversion.

Baptism in water, Baptism with water, Water baptism—Terms that signify the believer's identification with the death, burial and resurrection of Christ. Water baptism shows by an external and visible means what happens to a person spiritually in conversion.

Baptism *of* the Holy Spirit—An ambiguous phrase that fails to indicate whether the Holy Spirit is the agent or the element of Spirit baptism. "Baptism *in* the Spirit" expresses more accurately the idea of immersion in the Spirit.

Baptism *with* the Holy Spirit—A possible translation of the Greek phrase "*baptisma en tō hagiō pneumati*," but "baptism *in* the Spirit" seems to express better the meaning of the Greek.

Believer (New Testament and modern times) —*See* **Christian**.

Believer (Old Testament)—An individual in the Old

Testament who was saved by faith in the promised Christ.

Bestow—To convey as a gift.

Body of Christ, The Church—The people of God.

Canon of the New Testament—A sacred collection of 27 books that belong to our New Testament.

Cessationism—The view that teaches that spiritual gifts—especially the more extraordinary ones such as tongues, prophecies and miracles—ceased at the end of the apostolic age. *See also* **Continuationism**.

cf.—Compare.

Charisma—*noun, singular (plural—charismata).* A term used almost exclusively by Paul in the New Testament; it is a term that can be translated "grace-gift" since it is closely connected to divine grace (*charis*). In its broad meaning the term refers to God's blessings such as salvation, deliverance from mortal danger, or divine favor. When used with a restricted meaning, however, it refers to spiritual gifts bestowed upon believers for Christian service.

Charismatic—*noun.* A person who identifies with the Pentecostal/Charismatic Movements that began in the 1960s within the mainline and historic Protestant and Catholic churches. Some Charismatics began to disassociate themselves from their Pentecostal roots and now have their own distinct theologies, cultures and styles of worship.

Charismatic—*adjective.* A term that describes those who emphasize empowerment by the Holy Spirit and spiritual gifts for ministry, as do both Pentecostals and Charismatics. Personal encounters with the Holy Spirit form the basis of their faith and theology. Their experiences include such spiritual manifestations as prophecies, *glossolalia*, miraculous signs and healings.

Charismatic dimensions of the Holy Spirit's work— Dynamic, life-changing encounters with God, many of which involve Spirit baptism and the gifts of the Spirit. This distinct emphasis shows that the Spirit and His works are an experienced reality that have a crucial role in the life and ministry of God's people.

Charismatic leaders—*See* **Gifts of leadership.**

Charismatic Movement—A movement that began in the '60s in the mainline Protestant denominations and has been called "the new Pentecost" (Neo-Pentecostalism). It was a major influence in the spread of the Pentecostal experience in the mainline denominations. Many of the early leaders were virtually Pentecostal in doctrine, but now the Charismatic Movement has some different theological beliefs and ethos than classical Pentecostalism. *See also* **Pentecostal churches, Pentecostalism.**

Charismatic power—Divinely given power to witness, evangelize, and to exercise gifts of the Spirit, especially those outlined in 1 Corinthians 12.

Christian, Believer, Saint—One who trusts in Jesus Christ as personal Savior (Acts 16:31) and is devoted to Him.

The Church, Christian community—The Greek word *ekklēsia,* translated "church," which refers to the assembly of God's people. In the majority of the cases *ekklēsia* refers to a local congregation of believers, but in a few places it has in view the universal church to which all believers belong. *See also* **Body of Christ.**

Clothed in the Spirit—A phrase that stresses the divine side of Spirit baptism. The believer does not put on the Spirit, but the Spirit clothes the person with His power and presence.

Continuationism—The view that all of the gifts of the Spirit, including the so-called extraordinary gifts or sign gifts, have a legitimate and vital place in the life and ministry of the church today. None of the spiritual gifts were withdrawn at the end of the apostolic age. *See also* **Cessationism**.

Conversion, Salvation, Being saved, New birth—Closely related terms that indicate one has become a follower of Christ. Literally conversion means "to turn." In the positive sense it means to turn from the undesirable to the desirable. When used of unbelievers, they turn from sin through faith and repentance that enable them to receive the saving grace of God (Acts 3:19). Thus they repudiate sin and accept Christ as Lord by the help of the Holy Spirit and are saved from the guilt of sin and eternal death. *See also* **Regeneration**.

Conviction—The necessary condition to repentance and conversion. The Holy Spirit brings unbelievers to the realization of their guilt and to the conviction that without Christ they are lost.

Day of Pentecost—*See* **Pentecost**.

Devotions, Prayer, Meditation, Contemplative time, Bible study—Devotions, private or public, that involve worship and may include such spiritual practices as prayer, meditation, contemplation and Bible study.

Diakonia—*See* **Gifts of the Spirit**.

Discernings of spirits—*See* **Gift of discernings of spirits**.

Disciple—A term used for all of Christ's followers, but in its restricted usage the term applied to the Twelve who were called out of the greater company of disciples to hear Jesus expound the mysteries of God's kingdom.

Doctrine, Teachings—The central themes of Scripture, including the instruction given by Jesus and the apostles. The early disciples in Jerusalem devoted themselves to the teaching of the apostles (Acts 2:42; cf. 2 Timothy 3:16).

Doctrine of Subsequence, Postconversion encounters with the Spirit—Terms that describe a distinct and separate work of the Spirit from His work in conversion. After the salvation experience, a believer may be baptized in the Spirit.

Domata—*See* **Gifts of the Spirit**.

Dove—A symbol of the Holy Spirit. The coming down of the Spirit like a dove affirmed by a visual sign the beginning of Jesus' Spirit-filled ministry (Luke 3:22).

Edification, Spiritual enlightenment, Building up, Encouragement—Terms that indicate that believers are spiritually strengthened. The ascended Christ gave gifts of leadership to some believers for the purpose of their equipping the saints for this work of "building up" the body of Christ (Ephesians 4:11, 12).

Empowerment—Spirit-given ability to bear witness to Jesus Christ and His saving work, to withstand the power of Satan, and to do signs and wonders.

Encounter with the Spirit—An experience effected by the Holy Spirit. A vital encounter occurs at Christian conversion and subsequent encounters through Spirit baptism and the use of spiritual gifts.

Endowments of the Spirit, Spiritual endowments—*See* **Gifts of the Spirit**.

Energēmata—*See* **Gifts of the Spirit**.

Evangelical—One who holds to the basic teaching of Scripture such as the Trinity, deity of Christ, salvation by faith, personal conversion, authority of the Bible and the importance of preaching.

Evangelism—The bringing of good news, especially the announcement of the essentials for Christian salvation provided by God through His Son, Jesus Christ. *See also* **Witness**.

Evangelist—One who has the gift of evangelism. *See also* **Evangelism**, **Gift of evangelism.**

Evil spirit, **Demon**—A messenger or agent of Satan. The disciples of Jesus were empowered by the Holy Spirit to cast out evil spirits (Matthew 10:8; Luke 9:1; 10:17-20), and Paul urges Christians to withstand the evil forces of darkness (Ephesians 6:12).

Exhortation, **Encouragement**—One of the gifts of the Spirit (Romans 12:8) but also an aspect of prophesying (1 Corinthians 14:3). The operation of this gift offers consolation, comfort and encouragement. *See also* **Gift of exhortation**, **Gift of teaching**, **Gift of prophecy**.

Faith—A noun that corresponds to the verb *believe* and is regularly used for the relationship into which the gospel calls people—that of trust in Christ for salvation. "The faith" may refer to the body of truths believed (Galatians 1:23; 1 Timothy 4:1, 6; Jude 3). *See also* **Gift of faith**.

ff.—Following.

Filled with the Spirit, **Full of the Spirit**, **Fullness of the Spirit**, **Spirit-Filled Life**— Terms that describe the Charismatic or dynamic activity of the Holy Spirit, referring specifically to prophetic inspiration and empowerment for serving and worshiping the Lord.

Fruit of the Spirit, **Spiritual fruit**, **Spiritual graces**— Behavioral qualities and attitudes produced by the Holy

Spirit in Christians, particularly seen in the treatment of others (Galatians 5:22, 23; Ephesians 5:9).

Fulfillment—The realization of God's promises. For example, Joel 2:28-32 had predicted the outpouring of the Holy Spirit. The experience of the disciples on the Day of Pentecost was the initial fulfillment of that prophecy.

Fullness of time—A specific time or date in history that has arrived according to God's plan (Galatians 4:4).

Gift of administrations—A spiritual gift that is similar to the gift of leadership, enabling a person to preside over affairs of the congregation or provide leadership in other ministries.

Gift of apostle—*See* **Apostle**.

Gift of discernings of spirits, Gift of discernment—An intense illumination by the Holy Spirit that enables a believer to know whether a manifestation is of the Holy Spirit or not and, furthermore, the ability to know what is in the human heart.

Gift of evangelism—A spiritual gift that particularly equips a believer for bringing the gospel to the unsaved and winning converts to the Christian faith. *See also* **Evangelism, Evangelist**.

Gift of exhortation—The gift of being able to give wise counsel and speaking words of comfort and encouragement. *See also* **Exhortation**.

Gift of faith—An endowment by the Holy Spirit that enables a believer to trust God for extraordinary manifestations of His power.

Gift of giving—A gift of the Spirit that enables a believer to share his or her resources for the benefit of others, whether food, clothing, money or possessions.

Gift of healing—*See* **Gifts of healings**.

Gift of helps—*See* **Gift of service**.

Gift of interpretation, Gift of interpretation of tongues—The companion gift of speaking in tongues. When this gift is exercised, the significance of what is said in tongues is given in the language of those who are present.

Gift of knowledge, Word of knowledge, Words of knowledge, Message of knowledge—A Spirit-given capacity to express knowledge obtained only by revelation.

Gift of mercy—See **Gift of showing mercy**.

Gift of "One who leads"—*See* **One who leads**.

Gift of pastor—*See* **Pastor**.

Gift of prophecy, Prophetic charisma—Through inspired speaking, a Spirit-given capacity to offer edification, exhortation, and consolation to God's people (1 Corinthians 14:3). *See also* **Prophecy, Prophesy**.

Gift of service, Gift of helps—Two gifts of the Spirit that overlap in their function and are the Spirit's endowments of individuals with great capacity as servants and helpers of those in need (Romans 12:7). They involve the loving care and treatment of others.

Gift of showing mercy, Gift of mercy—A Spirit-given capacity to express empathy to the needy in concrete ways, such as caring for the sick, providing for the poor, and tending to the aged and the handicapped.

Gift of teaching—The Spirit-given ability to instruct others in the Christian faith.

Gift of the Spirit—An expression used for Spirit baptism. As salvation is a gift of God, so is "baptism" or "immersion" in the Spirit (Acts 2:38; 10:45).

Gift of tongues, Gift of speaking in tongues—A Spirit-given capacity to speak in different kinds of languages, either human or angelic; but since they are unknown by the speaker, tongues in a worship gathering require interpretation so that the congregation may be edified. *See also* **Speaking in other tongues**.

Gift of wisdom, Word of wisdom, Words of wisdom, Message of wisdom—A Spirit-given ability to speak a word or message full of wisdom, often taking the form of silencing opponents or offering special guidance in trying circumstances.

Gift of workings of miracles—A spiritual endowment to do miraculous works to glorify God and minister to human needs. Jesus worked miracles because He was moved by compassion (Matthew 15:32; Mark 8:2).

Gifts of healings—Spirit-given power that enables a person to bring about extraordinary healings of all kinds of ailments, whether physical or mental.

Gifts of leadership—Spiritual gifts that enable believers to serve as spiritual leaders for the edification of the body of Christ. Among them are those who are identified as apostles, prophets, teachers, pastors and evangelists.

Gifts of power—Demonstrations of the immediate presence of God through divine breakthroughs of miraculous power. Such demonstrations occur in the gifts of faith, healings and miracles.

Gifts of practical service, Gifts for practical service—Spiritual gifts that equip believers to perform deeds of service to members of their community of faith and others who need assistance, encouragement and understanding.

Gifts of revelation—Spiritual gifts that involve knowledge or wisdom that is given by the Holy Spirit. Two such gifts are a word of knowledge and a word of wisdom.

Gifts of the Spirit, Spiritual gifts, Gifts of grace, *Charismata, Diakonia, Domata, Energēmata, Phanerōsis tou Pneumatos, Pneumatika*—A variety of terms that refer to spiritual or Charismatic gifts bestowed upon Christians by the Holy Spirit to enable them to fulfill their function as a member of Christ's body.

Gifts of worship, Gifts for worship—Spiritual gifts that are regularly manifested in congregational worship, such as gifts of prophecy, discernings of spirits, tongues and interpretation.

Glorification—The consummation of the salvation of believers resulting in the transformation of their bodies, and each believer will be conformed to the glorified Savior (Romans 8:29,30; 1 Peter 5:4).

Glorify—A term that expresses honor and praise, especially to God.

Glory—A term that refers to the revelation or manifestation of the person and nature of God. The glory of God was revealed in the events surrounding the birth of Christ (Luke 2:9, 14, 32). During much of Christ's earthly ministry the divine glory was veiled, except for a glimpse at the Transfiguration (9:28ff.).

Glossolalia—*See* **Speaking in other tongues**.

God the Father, The Father, The Creator—Terms for the first person of the Trinity.

God the Son, Jesus Christ, Savior, Messiah—Titles for the second person of the Trinity, who is equal with the Father and the Holy Spirit in power and glory and through whom was accomplished God's saving and redeeming purpose.

Gospel, the—A word in the New Testament for the message of Christ. It means "good news" and consists of teachings about His life and its significance for the salvation of humankind.

Great Commission—A command of Jesus to every Christian to become a witness to the gospel until He returns (Matthew 28:19, 20; Mark 16:15-18; Luke 24:46-49; John 20:21-23; Acts 1:4, 5, 8).

Half-believers—A description by some Biblical scholars of the disciples of Acts 19:1-7. But obviously those disciples were full-fledged Christians who had not yet received Spirit baptism.

Healing—*See* **Gifts of healings**.

Holy living, Holiness, Godly living, Christlike living, Righteous living, Righteousness, Sanctified living— Terms that underscore the importance of our being like Jesus in thought, word and deed in both our private and public life. Such a lifestyle has a dynamic, ongoing dimension in which the Holy Spirit transforms our lives and provides strength to live a holy life (Galatians 5:16, 22, 23; 2 Corinthians 12:18).

Holy Spirit, Holy Ghost, Spirit of God, The Spirit, One Spirit—The third person of the Trinity. The Holy Spirit is equal with the Father and the Son. He is God, and knows all things, is all-powerful and is everywhere. He is a personal being. He anointed Jesus for His ministry, dwells in each Christian, and bestows spiritual gifts upon them. As the disciples at Pentecost, believers may be filled and empowered by the Holy Spirit to serve and worship God. *See also* **Personal being**.

Holy vessels—Objects like the Tabernacle and its contents that were classed as holy, or sacred, because they were used entirely in the service of God.

Imposition of hands—*See* **Laying on of hands**.

Indwelling of the Holy Spirit—The presence of the Holy Spirit in the life of believers from the moment of conversion. His presence in their lives is the stamp of divine ownership on believers (Ephesians 1:13).

Initial physical sign, **Initial physical evidence**—*Glossolalia*, a form of inspired speech that because of its demonstrative character serves as the first audible, visible sign of the reception of baptism in the Spirit.

Intercede—A word that means "to appeal" or "to petition," with an emphasis on drawing near to God in prayer on behalf of others (Romans 8:26, 34; 1 Timothy 2:1-4).

Last days—*See* **Age of the Spirit**.

Laying on of hands, **Imposition of hands**—A religious act that signifies the imparting of a special blessing. In Antioch, Paul and Barnabas were consecrated by the laying on of hands for the preaching of the gospel in the Gentile world (Acts 13:3).

Leader—*See* **One who leads**, **Gifts of leadership**.

Lord's Supper—One of the ordinances of the church, which was introduced by Christ. The bread and the cup in the Supper signify His sacrificial death, and the eating and drinking anticipate the final messianic meal when the divine work of salvation will be consummated. Christians often refer to the observance of the Lord's Supper as "Communion," "Holy Communion," or "Holy Eucharist."

Manifestation—A term used by Paul to speak of the gifts of the Spirit, which are all actions of the Spirit and demonstrate His presence. Some gifts are more dramatic than others (1 Corinthians 12:7-11).

Ministry—A broad term used in the New Testament that indicates that each believer is to function as a servant of Christ (Romans 12:6-8; 1 Corinthians 12:28; Ephesians 4:11). *See also the various gifts of the Spirit listed in this glossary.*

Miracles—*See* **Gift of workings of miracles**.

Mission in the world—The church's responsibility to preach the gospel and "make disciples" of all nations. *See also* **Great Commission**.

Narrative theology—The understanding that the Biblical narratives are not merely accounts of historical events, but that they also teach Christian doctrine (1 Corinthians 10:11). For example, the narrative accounts in the Book of Acts about the outpouring of the Spirit serve to instruct the church as to what is normative Christian experience.

One accord—A striking way of expressing unity, suggesting one mind and purpose (Acts 1:14; 2:1).

One who leads—A gift that stands in the list in Romans 12:6-8 and one who has been equipped by the Spirit for leadership in the church.

Paganism—Beliefs and practices that are identified with idolatry and sensual pleasures.

Paradigm, Paradigmatic—A model, pattern or example. A Biblical passage may serve as a model, such as the account of Jesus' empowerment with the Spirit at the Jordan River. That event demonstrated what the disciples would later receive on the Day of Pentecost (Luke 3:21, 22; Acts 2:1-4).

Pastor—One who exercises among believers the gift of pastor (Ephesians 4:11) and functions as a shepherd, guarding the truth, leading his people in worship, and ministering to their needs.

Pentecost, Day of Pentecost—One of three major feasts in early Israel. It was also known as the Feast of Harvest, Weeks, and Pentecost. This feast was celebrated in early summer, 50 days or seven weeks after the first day of unleavened bread. On the first Pentecost after the resurrection of Jesus, the Holy Spirit was poured out on the church. This event was the beginning of the fulfillment of Joel's prophecy (Joel 2:28, 29).

Pentecost Sunday, Feast of Pentecost—A day that celebrates the coming of the Holy Spirit on the Day of Pentecost. This Christian celebration or "feast" takes place 50 days after Easter. It originally coincided with the Jewish Feast of Weeks, or *Shavuot* (Exodus 34:22; Deuteronomy 16:10; 1 Corinthians 16:8), and has been celebrated since at least the third century A.D. Some Christian churches refer to this day as "Whitsunday."

Pentecostal—*noun.* A person who has received the Holy Spirit according to the pattern in Acts 2, 10 and 19.

Pentecostal—*adjective.* A term that describes those believers who emphasize baptism in the Spirit after conversion, spiritual gifts (such as *glossolalia*, prophecy, faith and healing), expressive worship, and dynamic evangelism.

Pentecostal churches (classical)—Churches that had their origin in the U.S. at the beginning of the 20th century and which emphasize a postconversion experience known as "baptism in the Holy Spirit" and spiritual gifts continuing to be manifested in the life of the believer. *See also* **Pentecostalism, Charismatic Movement**.

Pentecostal experience—An experience that encompasses baptism in the Spirit, manifestations of spiritual gifts,

Charismatic expressions in worship, and fervent evangelism.

Pentecostal lifestyle—A Christian lifestyle that includes submission to the Spirit, expression of spiritual graces, and service to others through the use of spiritual gifts (Acts 2:42-47).

Pentecostalism, Pentecostal Movement—The largest group of Protestant Christians in the world. The Pentecostal Movement is international in scope and includes many denominations, parachurch groups and independent congregations. This movement has a distinctive understanding of the Holy Spirit's work in the life of the individual Christian and in the life of the church, and a ministerial concern for fulfilling the Great Commission (Matthew 28:19, 20). *See also* **Pentecostal churches, Charismatic Movement**.

Personal being—A being such as the Holy Spirit, who performs the actions of a person: teaches (John 14:26), testifies (John 15:26), directs (Acts 8:29), and warns (1 Timothy 4:1). He has the characteristics of personality: intellect (Romans 8:27), emotions (Ephesians 4:30) and will (1 Corinthians 12:11).

Phanerōsis—*See* **Gifts of the Spirit, Manifestation**.

Pneuma—*See* **Wind**.

Pneumatika—*See* **Gifts of the Spirit**.

Possession of the Spirit—*See* **Filled with the Spirit**.

Prayer language—*See* **Speaking in other tongues**.

Prophecy—*noun*. A spiritual gift that enables a believer to speak words inspired by the Holy Spirit. A prophetic message may be predictive, referring to future events, or it may speak to a need or situation in the church at the time.

Prophesy—*verb*. A term for speaking spontaneous, inspired words, a revelation given by the Holy Spirit.

Prophet—One who has the gift of prophecy. *See also* **Gift of prophecy.**

Prophetic charisma—*See* **Gift of prophecy.**

Refilled with the Spirit—An experience that may occur over and over again so that the Christian is empowered to meet new challenges and situations. *See also* **Filled with the Spirit.**

Regeneration, Spiritual transformation, Renewal of hearts—A profound spiritual change that is likened to and called a "new birth." This change affects the moral and spiritual nature of the believer and is so radical that it can be said that he or she is a "new creation" (2 Corinthians 5:17, *NKJV*). *See also* **Conversion.**

Renewal of hearts—*See* **Conversion, Regeneration.**

Repentance—A doctrine clearly set forth in the New Testament. It is a change of mind and convictions rooted in the fear of God and sorrow for offenses against Him, which when accompanied by faith in Christ results in turning from sin to God.

Resurrection—An event that is at the heart of the Christian faith and message, the miracle of Christ's resurrection. When Christ returns, believers will receive a new resurrection body "like His body of glory" (see Philippians 3:21); but when a person accepts Christ as Savior, he experiences the renewing grace of the Holy Spirit, which may be described as "spiritual resurrection" or life from the dead (see Romans 6:13).

Revelation—*See* **Gifts of revelation.**

Righteous living—*See* **Holy living.**

Ruach—*See* **Wind**.

Saint—In the New Testament, it's the same as *Christian*. All Christians are identified as saints because they are in Jesus Christ. *See also* **Christian**.

Salvation—*See* **Conversion, Regeneration**.

Sanctification—A term meaning the breaking of the power of sin so that we may be holy and pure as God's children in the world. To put it another way, it is being set free from the dominion of sin by the Holy Spirit so that we may live in obedience to Christ in contrast to our former sin-dominated lives. *See also* **Holy living**.

Saved—*See* **Conversion, Regeneration**.

Service, Ministry—*See* **Ministry**, **Gift of Service**, **Gifts of Practical Service**.

Sin, Wrongdoings, Mistakes, Imperfection—Anything we may do or any attitude we may have that displeases God. In short, sin is anything contrary to the character of God. *See also* **Unbeliever**.

Soothsayers, Fortune-tellers—Terms for people who use demonic occult powers. Individuals have sought out such people to obtain knowledge about the future and for help in the affairs of life, either for their own benefit or for the harm of others.

Soteriological aspects of the Spirit—The involvement of the Holy in the believer's experience of salvation.

Speaking in other tongues, Speaking in tongues, Speaking with tongues, Speaking in unknown languages, *Glossolalia*, Prayer language, Praying in the Spirit, Praying in tongues—Terms that refer to speaking under the inspiration of the Spirit in a language, either human or angelic, but the language is unknown by the speaker. This manifestation serves various purposes: a sign of Spirit baptism, a sign to unbelievers, a spiritual gift accompanied by interpretation for the edification of the congregation, and a means of prayer and private devotion.

Spirit baptism—*See* **Baptism in the Holy Spirit**.

Spirit-filled life—*See* **Filled with the Spirit**.

Spirit of witness—The Holy Spirit, who bears witness to Christ (John 15:26) and takes the things of Christ and makes them known to us (16:13-15). He also bears witness with our spirit that we are children of God (Romans 8:15, 16). Furthermore, He enables believers to bear witness to the good news of Christ (Acts 1:8).

Spiritual fruit—*See* **Fruit of the Spirit**.

Spiritual gifts—*See* **Gifts of the Spirit**.

Spiritual graces—*See* **Fruit of the Spirit**.

Spiritual transformation—*See* **Conversion, Regeneration**.

Submission to one another—A term expressing the showing of mutual respect for one another, that is, submitting to other believers out of reverence for Christ (Ephesians 5:21). It is unbecoming for believers to seek to manipulate others or to insist on getting their way.

Subsequent to, Postconversion—*See* **Doctrine of Subsequence**.

Teacher—One who has the gift of teaching. *See also* **Gift of teaching**.

Testify—*See* **Witness**.

Testimony, Personal story—An individual's sharing or telling of his or her spiritual life experiences and how God has blessed them. An individual's testimony, or story, may include gratitude and appreciation for blessings such as salvation, sanctification, Spirit baptism, healings, spiritual guidance and the hope of heaven.

Those who lead—*See* **One who leads**.

Tongues—*See* **Speaking in other tongues**.

Tongues of fire, Flames of fire—A supernatural manifestation on the Day of Pentecost. The tongues that appeared to be like fire and rested on each of the disciples, demonstrating God's presence and glory.

Trinity, Triune God, Godhead—*See* **God the Father, God the Son, Holy Spirit**.

Unbeliever, Unsaved, Non-Christian, Sinner—Words to describe those who have not accepted Jesus Christ as their Savior from the bondage of sin and death. When non-Christians are referred to as "sinners," it should not be taken that Christians cannot sin. If they do sin, they fail to please God. However, God is always willing to forgive sin, but a Christian should not assume that sin is a light matter.

Ungodliness—The opposite of godliness, showing no reverence for sacred things and without any respect for God. An ungodly person does contrary to God's demands. *See also* **Sin, Unbeliever, Holy living**.

Utterance—The act of expressing oneself in words. *For a definition of Spirit-inspired utterance, see* **Speaking in other tongues, Prophecy**.

Vision—A means by which God reveals His word or will to His people. At times a vision took the form of a dream, such as Jacob's dream of the angels ascending and descending on the heavenly ladder (Genesis 28:12).

Water Baptism—*See* **Baptism in Water**.

Wind, *Ruach*, *Pneuma*—The Hebrew *ruach* and the Greek *pneuma*, two words meaning either "spirit" or "wind" (breath). The coming of the Holy Spirit on the Day of Pentecost is described as a noise "like a violent, rushing wind" (Acts 2:2).

Witness, Testify—To attest to or to tell about something that one knows and can confirm with a degree of authority. In the New Testament apostles were witnesses (Acts 1:21, 22), and all believers were to be God's witnesses (Acts 1:8; 13:31; Matthew 28:19, 20). *See also* **Testimony**.

Word of knowledge—*See* **Gift of knowledge**.

Word of wisdom—*See* **Gift of wisdom**.

Resources

GENERAL TOPICS
General Theology of the Holy Spirit

Arrington, French L. *Christian Doctrine: A Pentecostal Perspective.* 3 Vols. Cleveland, TN: Pathway, 1992-1994.

Berkhof, Hendrikus. *The Doctrine of the Holy Spirit.* Atlanta: John Knox, 1976, 1964.

Bruner, Frederick Dale. *A Theology of the Holy Spirit: The Pentecostal Experience and the New Testament Witness.* Grand Rapids: Eerdmans, 1970.

Carr, Wesley. "Towards a Contemporary Theology of the Holy Spirit." *Scottish Journal of Theology* 28, No. 6 (1975): 501-516.

Harper, George W. "Renewal and Causality: Some Thoughts on a Conceptual Framework for a Charismatic Theology." *Journal of Ecumenical Studies* 24, No. 1 (1987): 93-103.

Jensen, Robert W. "You Wonder Where the Spirit Went?" *Pro Ecclesia* 2 (1993): 296-304.

Kraft, Charles H. *Christianity With Power: Your World View and Your Experience of the Supernatural.* Ann Arbor, MI: Vine Books, 1989.

Land, Steven J. *Pentecostal Spirituality: A Passion for the Kingdom.* Sheffield, U.K.: Sheffield Academic Press, 1993.

Meynell, Hugo. "Two Directions for Pneumatology." *Religious Studies Bulletin* 2, No. 3 (1982): 101-116.

Moltmann, Jürgen. *The Church in the Power of the Spirit: A Contribution to Messianic Ecclesiology.* Trans. Margaret Kohl. New York: Harper & Row, 1977.

_____. *The Spirit of Life: A Universal Affirmation.* Trans. Margaret Kohl. Minneapolis: Fortress, 1992.

Placher, William C. *Narratives of a Vulnerable God: Christ, Theology and Scripture.* Louisville, KY: Westminster/John Knox, 1994.

Reynolds, Blair. *Toward a Process Pneumatology.* Selinsgrove, PA: Susquehanna UP, 1990.

Sirks, George J. "The Cinderella of Theology: The Doctrine of the Holy Spirit." *Harvard Theological Review* 50 (1957): 77-90.

Sontag, Frederick. "Should Theology Today Be Charismatic?" *Journal of the Evangelical Theological Society* 30 (1987): 199-203.

Thielicke, Helmut. *A Theology of the Spirit.* Vol. 3 of *The Evangelical Faith.* Ed. and trans. Geoffrey W. Bromiley. Grand Rapids: Eerdmans, 1982.

The Person of the Holy Spirit and the Trinity

Carter, Charles W. *The Person and Ministry of the Holy Spirit: A Wesleyan Perspective.* Grand Rapids: Baker, 1974.

Coffey, David. "Holy Spirit as the Mutual Love of the Father and the Son." *Theological Studies* 51 (1990): 193-229.

Congar, Yves M.J. *I Believe in the Holy Spirit.* 3 vols. New York: Seabury, 1983.

_____. *The Word and the Spirit*. Trans. David Smith. San Francisco: Harper & Row, 1986.

Del Colle, Ralph. *Christ and the Spirit: Spirit-Christology in Trinitarian Perspective*. New York: Oxford UP, 1994.

Gelpi, Donald L. *The Divine Mother: A Trinitarian Theology of the Holy Spirit*. Lanham, MD: UP of America, 1984.

Green, Michael. *I Believe in the Holy Spirit*. Grand Rapids: Eerdmans, 1975.

Gresham, John L. "The Social Model of the Trinity and Its Critics." *Scottish Journal of Theology* 46, No. 3 (1993): 325-343.

Hanson, R.P.C. "The Divinity of the Holy Spirit." *Church Quarterly* 1 (1969): 298-306.

Johnson, Elizabeth A. *She Who Is: The Mystery of God in Feminist Theological Discourse*. New York: Crossroad, 1992.

LaCugna, Catherine Mowry. *God for Us: The Trinity and Christian Life*. San Francisco: HarperCollins, 1993.

Moltmann, Jürgen. *The Trinity and the Kingdom*. San Francisco: Harper & Row, 1981.

Palma, Anthony D. *The Holy Spirit: A Pentecostal Perspective*. Springfield, MO: Legion, 2001.

Peters, Ted. *God as Trinity: Relationality and Temporality in Divine Life*. Louisville, KY: Westminster/John Knox, 1993.

Plantinga, Cornelius. *The Hodgson-Welch Debate and the Social Analogy of the Trinity*. Ph.D. dissertation, Princeton Theological Seminary, 1982.

Reich, K. Helmut. "The Doctrine of the Trinity as a Model for Structuring the Relations Between Science and Theology." *Zygon* 30 (1995): 383-405.

Rosato, Philip J. *The Spirit as Lord: The Pneumatology of Karl Barth*. Edinburgh: T&T Clark, 1981.

Schweizer, Eduard. *The Holy Spirit*. Philadelphia: Fortress, 1980.

Welker, Michael. *God the Spirit*. Trans. John F. Hoffmeyer. Minneapolis: Fortress, 1994.

Studies on Books of the Bible

Entire Bible

Black, Matthew, and H.H. Rowley, eds. *Peake's Commentary on the Bible*. New York: T. Nelson, 1962.

Full Life Study Bible (King James Version). Grand Rapids: Zondervan, 1992. (2003: Published under title: *Life in the Spirit Study Bible*)

Full Life Study Bible (New International Version). Grand Rapids: Zondervan, 1992. (2003: Published under title: *Life in the Spirit Study Bible*)

Stronstad, Roger. *Spirit, Scripture and Theology*. Baguio City, Philippines: Asia Pacific Theological Seminary Press, 1995.

Old Testament

See the category, "The Holy Spirit and The Old Testament."

New Testament

This section includes general resources on the New Testament, as well as resources specifically covering the Gospels of Matthew, Mark and John. For resources on the Gospel of Luke, see the category "Luke and Acts."

Arrington, French L. *New Testament Exegesis: Examples*. Washington, DC: UP of America, 1977.

_____ and Roger Stronstad, eds. *Full Life Bible Commentary to the New Testament: An International Commentary for Spirit-Filled Christians*. Grand Rapids: Zondervan, 1999. (2003: Published under title: Life in the Spirit New Testament Commentary)

Burge, Gary M. *The Anointed Community: The Holy Spirit in the Johannine Tradition*. Grand Rapids: Eerdmans, 1987.

Ewert, David. *The Holy Spirit in the New Testament*. Scottdale, PA: Herald, 1983.

Friedrich, Gerhard, ed. *Theological Dictionary of the New Testament*. Vol. 6. Grand Rapids: Eerdmans, 1968.

Han, Yung Chul, ed. *Transforming Power: Dimensions of the Gospel*. Cleveland, TN: Pathway, 2001.

Käsemann, Ernst. *New Testament Questions of Today*. Philadelphia: Fortress, 1969.

Suurmond, Jean-Jacques. *Word and Spirit at Play: Towards a Charismatic Theology*. Grand Rapids: Eerdmans, 1995.

Swete, Henry Barclay. *The Holy Spirit in the New Testament*. Grand Rapids: Baker, 1976.

Luke and Acts

Arrington, French L. *The Acts of the Apostles: An Introduction and Commentary*. Peabody, MA: Hendrickson, 1988.

Grizzle, Trevor. *Church Aflame: An Exposition of Acts 1-12*. Cleveland, TN: Pathway, 2000.

Haenchen, Ernst. *The Acts of the Apostles*. Philadelphia: Westminster, 1971.

Marshall, I. Howard. *The Acts of the Apostles: An Introduction and Commentary*. Grand Rapids: Eerdmans, 1980.

Menzies, Robert P. *The Development of Early Christian Pneumatology: With Special Reference to Luke-Acts.* (JSNT Supplement Series, vol. 54) Sheffield: JSOT Press, 1991.

Russell, Walt. "The Anointing With the Holy Spirit in Luke-Acts." *Trinity Journal* ns 7, No. 1 (1986): 47-63.

Shepherd, William H., Jr. *The Narrative Function of the Holy Spirit as a Character in Luke- Acts.* Atlanta: Scholars, 1994.

Stronstad, Roger. "The Holy Spirit in Luke-Acts, Part I." *Paraclete* 23, No.1 (1989): 8-13; and "The Holy Spirit in Luke-Acts: A Synthesis of Luke's Pneumatology, Part II." *Paraclete* 23, No. 2 (1989): 18-26.

_____. *The Charismatic Theology of St. Luke.* Peabody, MA: Hendrickson, 1984.

Turner, Max B. "Spirit Endowment in Luke-Acts: Some Linguistic Considerations." *Biblical and Historical Essays From London Bible College.* Ed. Harold H. Rowdon. London: London Bible College, 1981: 45-63.

Epistles

Arrington, French L. *Divine Order in the Church: A Study of 1 Corinthians.* Cleveland, TN: Pathway, 1978.

_____. *The Ministry of Reconciliation: A Study of 2 Corinthians.* Grand Rapids: Baker, 1980; Cleveland, TN: Pathway, 1998.

Barrett, Charles K. *A Commentary on the First Epistle to the Corinthians.* New York: Harper & Row, 1968.

Fee, Gordon D. *God's Empowering Presence: The Holy Spirit in the Letters of Paul.* Peabody, MA: Hendrickson, 1994.

Kroeger, Richard, and Catherine Clark Kroeger. "An Inquiry Into Evidence of Maenadism in the Corinthian Congregation."

Society of Biblical Literature Seminar Papers, No. 14. Missoula, MT: Scholars, 1978: 331-338.

Pearson, Birger A. *The Pneumatikos-Psychikos Terminology in 1 Corinthians: A Study in the Theology of the Corinthian Opponents of Paul and Its Relation to Gnosticism. Society of Biblical Literature Seminar Papers,* No. 12. Missoula, MT: Scholars, 1973.

Schmithals, Walter. *Gnosticism in Corinth: An Investigation of the Letters to the Corinthians.* Trans. John E. Steely. Nashville, TN: Abingdon, 1971.

Scroggs, Robin. "Paul and the Eschatological Woman." *Journal of the American Academy of Religion* 40 (1972): 283-303.

Church History and the Pentecostal/Charismatic Movements

Collections and Internet Links

Hal Bernard Dixon Jr. Pentecostal Research Center. Lee University, 260 11th St., N.E., Cleveland, TN 37311. (*http://faculty.leeu.edu/~drc/*). 260 11th Stree, N.E., Cleveland, TN 37311, (423) 614-8676. email: *dixon_research@leeuniversity.edu*

Note: The Hal Bernard Dixon Jr. Pentecostal Research Center contains materials concerning the Pentecostal, Charismatic and Holiness Movements, as well as the archives of the Church of God (Cleveland, Tennessee). The Research Center collects, organizes and preserves materials that show the origin, history, development and theology of the Church of God, other Pentecostal denominations and Charismatic ministries.

Denominations and Fellowships Links

Pentecostal/Charismatic Churches of North America,

(*http://www.pccna.org*). Provides links to member organizations and other related sites.

Pneuma Foundation (*http://www.pneumafoundation.com/links_fellows.shtml*). Provides links to several Pentecostal/Charismatic denominations and fellowships.

Print Resources

Archer, Kenneth J. "Pentecostal Hermeneutics: Retrospect and Prospect." *Journal of Pentecostal Theology* 8 (1996): 63-81.

Bartleman, Frank. *How Pentecost Came to Los Angeles*, 1925. Reprinted in *Witness to Pentecost: The Life of Frank Bartleman*. New York: Garland Publishing, 1985. Also reprinted and edited by various publishers under the following titles: *What Really Happened at Azusa Street?* 1962; *Another Wave Rolls In!* 1962, 1970, 1971, 1980; *Another Wave of Revival*, 1982; *Azusa Street*, 1980, 2000.

Burgess, Stanley M., Gary B. McGee, and Patrick H. Alexander, eds. *Dictionary of Pentecostal and Charismatic Movements*. Grand Rapids: Zondervan, 1988.

_____. *The Holy Spirit: Eastern Christian Traditions*. Peabody, MA: Hendrickson, 1989.

_____ and Eduard M. Van Der Maas, eds. *The New International Dictionary of Pentecostal and Charismatic Movements*. Grand Rapids: Zondervan, 2002.

Campbell, Theodore C. "The Doctrine of the Holy Spirit in the Theology of Athanasius." *Scottish Journal of Theology* 27 (1974): 408-440.

Campenhausen, Hans von. *Ecclesiastical Authority and Spiritual Power in the Church of the First Three Centuries*. Trans. J.A. Baker. Stanford, CA: Stanford UP, 1969.

Conn, Charles W. *Like a Mighty Army: A History of the Church of*

God, Definitive Edition, 1886-1995. Cleveland, TN: Pathway, 1996.

Culpepper, Robert H. *Evaluating the Charismatic Movement.* Valley Forge, PA: Judson, 1977.

Dayton, Donald W. "The Evolution of Pentecostalism." *Covenant Quarterly* (1974): 28-40.

De Soyres, John. *Montanism and the Primitive Church: A Study in the Ecclesiastical History of the Second Century.* Lexington, KY: American Theological Library Association, 1965.

Eaves, Lindon, and Lora Gross. "Exploring the Concept of Spirit as a Model for the God-World Relationship in the Age of Genetics." *Zygon* 27 (1992): 261-285.

Forbes, Christopher. "Early Christian Inspired Speech and Hellenistic Popular Religion." *Novum Testamentum* 28, No. 3 (1986): 257-270.

Garrett, Clarke. *Spirit Possession and Popular Religion From the Camisards to the Shakers.* Baltimore: Johns Hopkins UP, 1987.

Gelpi, Donald L. *Pentecostalism: A Theological Viewpoint.* New York: Paulist, 1971.

Knox, Ronald Arbuthnott. *Enthusiasm: A Chapter in the History of Religion.* New York: Oxford UP, 1950.

MacArthur, John F., Jr. *The Charismatics: A Doctrinal Perspective.* Grand Rapids: Zondervan, 1978.

Nichol, John T. *Pentecostalism: A Descriptive History of the Origin, Growth and Message of a Twentieth Century Religious Movement.* New York: Harper & Row, 1966.

O'Conner, Edward D. *The Pentecostal Movement in the Catholic Church.* Notre Dame, IN: Ave Maria, 1971.

_____, ed. *Perspectives on Charismatic Renewal.* South

Bend, IN: U of Notre Dame P, 1975.

Robeck, Cecil Melvin, Jr. "Montanism: A Problematic Spirit Movement." *Paraclete* 15, No. 3 (1981): 24-29.

Schnackenberg, Rudolf. *The Church in the New Testament.* New York: Seabury, 1966.

Snyder, H.A. "The Church as Holy and Charismatic." *Wesleyan Theological Journal* 15 (1980): 7-32.

Spittler, Russell P., ed. *Perspectives on the New Pentecostalism.* Grand Rapids: Baker, 1976.

Stam, John E. "Charismatic Theology in the Apostolic Tradition of Hippolytus." *Current Issues in Biblical and Patristic Interpretation.* Ed. G.F. Hawthorne. Grand Rapids: Eerdmans, 1975: 267-276.

Stephanou, Eusebius A. "The Charismata in the Early Church Fathers." *Greek Orthodox Theological Review* 21 (1976): 125-146.

Strachan, Gordon. *The Pentecostal Theology of Edward Irving.* Peabody, MA: Hendrickson, 1988.

Swete, Henry B. *The Holy Spirit in the Ancient Church: A Study of Christian Teaching in the Age of the Fathers.* Grand Rapids: Baker, 1966.

Synan, Vinson, ed. *Aspects of Pentecostal-Charismatic Origins.* Plainfield, NJ: Logos International, 1975.

_____. *The Holiness-Pentecostal Tradition: Charismatic Movements in the 20th Century*, 2d ed. Grand Rapids: Eerdmans, 1997.

Trevett, Christine. "Prophecy and Anti-Episcopal Activity: A Third Error Combated by Ignatius?" *Journal of Ecclesiastical History* 34 (1983): 1-18.

Wagner, C. Peter. *Look Out! The Pentecostals Are Coming.* Altamonte Springs, FL, Strang Communications, 1986.

Waldvogel, Edith L. *The "Overcoming Life": A Study of the Reformed Evangelical Origins of Pentecostalism.* Thesis, Harvard University. Cambridge, MA: Waldvogel, 1977.

Watkins-Jones, H. *The Holy Spirit From Arminius to Wesley.* London: Epworth, 1929.

_____. *The Holy Spirit in the Medieval Church.* London: Epworth, 1922.

Williams, J. Rodman. *The Era of the Spirit.* Plainfield, NJ: Logos International, 1971.

_____. *The Pentecostal Reality.* Plainfield, NJ: Logos International, 1972.

_____. *Renewal Theology.* 3 vols. Grand Rapids: Zondervan.

Vol. 1: *God, the World and Redemption*, 1988.

Vol. 2: *Salvation, the Holy Spirit, and Christian Living*, 1990.

Vol. 3: *The Church, the Kingdom, and Last Things*, 1992.

THE HOLY SPIRIT AND THE OLD TESTAMENT

Brunner, Emil. *The Christian Doctrine of Creation and Redemption.* Vol. 2 of *Dogmatics.* Trans. Olive Wyon. Philadelphia: Westminster, 1952.

Maloney, George A. *The Spirit Broods Over the World.* New York: Alba House, 1993.

McQueen, Larry R. *Joel and the Spirit: The Cry of a Prophetic Hermeneutic.* Sheffield, England: Sheffield Academic Press, 1995.

Moltmann, Jürgen. *God in Creation: A New Theology of Creation and the Spirit of God.* San Francisco: Harper & Row, 1985.

CONVERSION AND SPIRITUAL FRUIT

Conversion

Del Colle, Ralph. "Spirit-Christology: Dogmatic Foundations for Pentecostal-Charismatic Spirituality." *Journal of Pentecostal Theology* No. 3 (1993): 91-112.

Dunn, James D.G. *Jesus and the Spirit: A Study of the Religious and Charismatic Experience of Jesus and the First Christians as Reflected in the New Testament.* Philadelphia: Westminster, 1975; Grand Rapids: Eerdmans, 1997.

Gause, R. Hollis. *Living in the Spirit: The Way of Salvation.* Cleveland, TN: Pathway, 1980.

Gillespie, V. Bailey. *The Dynamics of Religious Conversion: Identity and Transformation.* Birmingham, AL: Religious Education, 1991.

Haight, Roger. "The Case for Spirit Christology." *Theological Studies* 53 (1992): 257-287.

Smith, Gordon T. *Beginning Well: Christian Conversion & Authentic Transformation.* Downers Grove, IL: InterVarsity, 2001.

Spiritual Fruit and Christian Living

Foster, Richard J. *Celebration of Discipline: The Path to Spiritual Growth.* San Francisco: Harper & Row, 1988, 1978.

_____. *Freedom of Simplicity.* New York: Harper & Row, 1981.

_____. *Prayer: Finding the Heart's True Home.* San Francisco: HarperSanFrancisco, 1992.

Kenneson, Philip D. *Life on the Vine: Cultivating the Fruit of the Christian Community.* Downers Grove, IL: InterVarsity, 1999.

Newman, Paul W. *A Spirit Christology: Recovering the Biblical Paradigm of Christian Faith.* Lanham, MD: UP of America, 1987.

Ogilvie, Lloyd John. *The Magnificent Vision: Seeing Yourself Through the Eyes of Christ.* Ann Arbor, MI: Servant Publications, 1991.

Zoschak, Greg. *Fruit of the Spirit.* Tulsa, OK: Harrison House, 1987.

SPIRIT BAPTISM
General

Basham, Don. *A Handbook on Holy Spirit Baptism: 37 Questions and Answers on the Baptism in the Holy Spirit and Speaking in Tongues.* Monroeville, PA: Whitaker, 1969.

Bennett, Dennis J. *Nine O'Clock in the Morning.* Plainfield, NJ: Logos International, 1970.

Blumhofer, Edith L., compiler. *"Pentecost in My Soul": Explorations in the Meaning of Pentecostal Experience in the Assemblies of God.* Springfield, MO: Gospel Publishing House, 1989.

Cross, Terry L., and Emerson B. Powery, eds. *The Spirit and the Mind: Essays in Informed Pentecostalism.* Lanham, MD: UP of America, 2000.

Dunn, James D.G. "Baptism in the Spirit: A Response to Pentecostal Scholarship on Luke-Acts." *Journal of Pentecostal*

Theology No. 3 (1993): 3-27.

_____. *Baptism in the Holy Spirit: A Re-Examination of the New Testament Teaching on the Gift of the Spirit in Relation to Pentecostalism Today*. Naperville, IL: Allenson, 1970.

Lederle, Henry I. *Treasures Old and New: Interpretations of "Spirit Baptism" in the Charismatic Renewal Movement*. Peabody, MA: Hendrickson, 1988.

McDonnell, Kilian, and George T. Montague. *Christian Initiation and Baptism in the Holy Spirit: Evidence From the First Eight Centuries*. Collegeville, MN: Liturgical, 1990.

Muhlen, Heribert. *A Charismatic Theology: Initiation in the Spirit*. New York: Paulist, 1978.

Palma, Anthony D. *Baptism in the Holy Spirit*. Springfield, MO: Gospel Publishing House, 1999.

Stott, John R.W. *The Baptism and Fullness of the Holy Spirit Today*. London: InterVarsity, 1975.

Williams, J. Rodman. *The Gift of the Holy Spirit Today*. Plainfield, NJ: Logos International, 1980.

Speaking in Other Tongues

Barnett, Donald L., and J.P. McGregor. *Speaking in Other Tongues: A Scholarly Defense*. Seattle, WA: Community Chapel Publications, 1986.

Christenson, Larry. *Speaking in Tongues and Its Significance for the Church*. Minneapolis: Bethany Fellowship, 1968.

_____. *Speaking in Tongues: A Gift for the Body of Christ*. Minneapolis: Bethany House, 1968, 1987.

Christie-Murray, David. *Voices From the Gods: Speaking With*

Tongues. London: Routledge & Kegan Paul, 1978.

Coulson, Jesse E., and Ray W. Johnson. "Glossolalia and Internal-External Locus of Control." *Journal of Psychology and Theology* 5 (1977): 312-317.

Cullen, Peter J. "Euphoria, Praise and Thanksgiving: Rejoicing in the Spirit in Luke-Acts." *Journal of Pentecostal Theology* 6 (1995): 13-24.

Cutten, George B. *Speaking With Tongues, Historically and Psychologically Considered*. New Haven, CT: Yale UP, 1927.

Dunn, James D.G. "Spirit-Baptism and Pentecostalism." *Scottish Journal of Theology* 23 (1970): 397-407.

Ervin, Howard M. *"These Are Not Drunken As Ye Suppose" (Acts 2:15)*. Plainfield, NJ: Logos International, 1968.

Esler, Philip F. "Glossolalia and the Admission of Gentiles Into the Early Christian Community." *Biblical Theology Bulletin* 22 (1992): 136-142. Also in *The First Christians in Their Social Worlds: Social Scientific Approaches to New Testament Interpretation*. New York: Routledge, 1994.

Goodman, Felicitas D. *Speaking in Tongues: A Cross-Cultural Study of Glossolalia*. Chicago: U of Chicago P, 1972.

Green, William M. "Glossolalia in the Second Century." *Restoration Quarterly* 16, No. 3/4 (1973): 231-239.

Johanson, Bruce C. "Tongues, a Sign for Unbelievers: A Structural and Exegetical Study of 1 Corinthians 14:20-25." *New Testament Studies* 25 (1979): 180-203.

Kelsey, Morton T. *Tongue Speaking: An Experiment in Spiritual Experience*. Garden City, NY: Doubleday, 1964.

Kildahl, John P. *The Psychology of Speaking in Tongues*. New York: Harper & Row, 1972.

Macchia, Frank D. "The Question of Tongues as Initial Evidence: A Review of Initial Evidence." Ed. Gary B. McGee. *Journal of Pentecostal Theology* 2 (1993): 117-127.

MacDonald, William G. *Glossolalia in the New Testament.* Springfield, MO: Gospel Publishing House, 1964.

Malony, H. Newton, and A. Adams Lovekin. *Glossolalia: Behavioral Science Perspectives on Speaking in Tongues.* New York: Oxford UP, 1985.

Martin, Dale B. "Tongues of Angels and Other Status Indicators." *Journal of the American Academy of Religion* 59 (1991): 547-589.

McGee, Gary B., ed. *Initial Evidence: Historical and Biblical Perspectives on the Pentecostal Doctrine of Spirit Baptism.* Peabody, MA: Hendrickson, 1991.

Menzies, Robert P. "Coming to Terms With an Evangelical Heritage."

"Part 1: Pentecostals and the Issue of Subsequence." *Paraclete* 28 (1994): 18-28.

"Part 2: Pentecostals and Evidential Tongues." *Paraclete* 29 (1994): 1-10.

Mills, Watson E., ed. *Speaking in Tongues: A Guide to Research in Glossolalia.* Grand Rapids: Eerdmans, 1986.

Poythress, Vern S. "The Nature of Corinthian Glossolalia: Possible Options." *Westminster Theological Journal* 40 (1977): 130-135.

Richardson, William E. "Liturgical Order and Glossolalia in 1 Corinthians 14:26c-33a." *New Testament Studies* 32, No. 1 (1986): 144-153.

Rogers, Cleon L., Jr. "The Gift of Tongues in the Post-Apostolic Church (A.D. 100-400)." *Bibliotheca Sacra* 122 (1965): 134-143.

Samarin, William J. *Tongues of Men and Angels: The Religious Language of Pentecostalism*. New York: Macmillan, 1972.

Sherrill, John L. *They Speak With Other Tongues*. New York: McGraw Hill, 1964.

Stagg, Frank E., E. Glenn Hinson, and Wayne Edward Oates. *Glossolalia: Tongue Speaking in Biblical, Historical and Psychological Perspective*. New York: Abingdon, 1967.

Swindoll, Charles R. *Tongues: An Answer to Charismatic Confusion*. Anaheim, CA: Insight for Living, 1998.

Thomas, Robert L. "Tongues . . . Will Cease: [1 Corinthians 13.]" *Journal of the Evangelical Theological Society* 17 (1974): 81-89.

Tugwell, Simon. "The Gift of Tongues in the New Testament." *Expository Times* 84 (1973): 137-140.

Wedderburn, A.J.M. "Romans 8:26—Towards a Theology of Glossolalia." *Scottish Journal of Theology* 28, No. 4 (1975): 369-377.

White, R. Fowler. "Richard Gaffin and Wayne Grudem on 1 Corinthians 13:10: A Comparison of Cessationist and Noncessationist Argumentation [Duration of Prophecy Gift]." *Journal of the Evangelical Theological Society* 35 (1992), 173-181.

Wiebe, Phillip H. "The Pentecostal Initial Evidence Doctrine." *Journal of the Evangelical Theological Society* 27 (1984): 465-472.

_____. *Tongues of the Spirit: A Study of Pentecostal Glossolalia and Related Phenomena*. Cardiff: U of Wales P, 1981.

SPIRITUAL GIFTS

General

Bittlinger, Arnold. *Gifts and Graces: A Commentary on 1 Corinthians 12—14*. Trans. from German by Herbert Klassen and supervised by Michael Harper. Grand Rapids: Eerdmans, 1967.

_____. *Gifts and Ministries*. Grand Rapids: Eerdmans, 1973.

Elbert, Paul. "Calvin and the Spiritual Gifts." *Journal of the Evangelical Theological Society* 22 (1979): 235-256. Also in *Essays on Apostolic Themes*. Peabody, MA: Hendrickson, 1985: 115-143.

_____. "The Perfect Tense in Matthew 16:19 and Three Charismata." *Journal of the Evangelical Theological Society* 17 (1974): 149-155.

Floris, Andrew T. "Chrysostom and the Charismata." *Paraclete* 5, No. 1 (1971), 17-22.

Fowler, Stuart. "The Continuance of the Charismata." *Evangelical Quarterly* 45 (1973): 172-183.

Franklin, L. David. *Spiritual Gifts in Tertullian*. Ph.D. dissertation, St. Louis University, 1989.

Fung, Ronald Y.K. "Charismatic versus Organized Ministry: An Examination of an Alleged Antithesis." *Evangelical Quarterly* 52 (1980): 195-214.

_____. "Function or Office: A Survey of the New Testament Evidence." *Evangelical Review of Theology* 8, No. 1 (1984): 16-39.

_____. "Ministry, Community and Spiritual Gifts: [In Pauline Theology]." *Evangelical Quarterly* 56 (1984): 3-20.

Graves, Robert W. "Tongues Shall Cease: A Critical Study of the Supposed Cessation of the Charismata." *Paraclete* 17, No. 4 (Fall 1983): 20-28.

Koenig, John. *Charismata: God's Gifts for God's People.* Philadelphia: Westminster, 1978.

Kydd, Ronald. "Novatian's De Triniate, 29: Evidence of the Charismatic?" *Scottish Journal of Theology* 30, No. 4 (1977): 313-318.

_____. "Origen and the Gifts of the Spirit." *Eglise et Theologie* 13 (Jan. 1982): 111- 116.

_____. *Charismatic Gifts in the Early Church: An Exploration Into the Gifts During the First Three Centuries of the Early Church.* Peabody, MA: Hendrickson, 1984.

Lombard, H.A. "Charisma and Church Office." *Neotestamentica* 10, No. 1 (1976): 31-52. Also in *Ministry in the Pauline Letters.* Pretoria: New Testament Society of South Africa, 1976: 31-52.

Robinson, Donald W.B. "Charismata versus Pneumatika: Paul's Method of Discussion." *Reformed Theological Review* 31 (1972): 49-55.

Ruthven, Jon Mark. "The Cessation of the Charismata."

Part 1: "A Survey of a Prevailing Viewpoint." *Paraclete* 3, No. 2 (Spring 1969): 23-30.

Part 2: "An Evaluation of Some Popular Presuppositions." *Paraclete* 3, No. 3 (Summer 1969): 21-27.

Part 3: "A Biblical Defense for Continuation of the Charismata." *Paraclete* 3, No. 4 (Fall 1969): 20-28.

_____. *On the Cessation of Charismata: The Protestant Polemic on Postbiblical Miracles.* Sheffield, UK: Sheffield Academic Press, 1993.

Schatzmann, Siegfried. *A Pauline Theology of Charismata.* Peabody, MA: Hendrickson, 1987.

Thomas, R.B. *You Are Gifted.* Cleveland, TN: Pathway, 1985.

Thomas, Robert L. *Understanding Spiritual Gifts: A Verse-by-Verse Study of First Corinthians 12—14.* Grand Rapids: Kregel, 1999.

Gifts of Leadership

Apostles, Prophets, Teachers, Pastors, Evangelists, Those Who Lead, Administrations and Help. See also other related categories, such as "Gifts for Practical Service," "Gifts of Revelation" and "Gifts for Worship."

General

Furnish, Victor Paul. "Prophets, Apostles and Preachers: A Study of the Biblical Concept of Preaching." *Interpretation* 17 (1963): 48-60.

Trigg, Joseph W. "The Charismatic Intellectual: Origen's Understanding of Religious Leadership." *Church History* 50 (1981): 5-19.

Apostles

Agnew, Francis H. "The Origin of the NT Apostle-Concept: A Review of Research." *Journal of Biblical Literature* 105, No. 1 (1986): 75-96.

Brown, Schuyler. "Apostleship in the New Testament as an Historical and Theological Problem." *New Testament Studies* 30 (1984): 474-480.

Schmithals, W. *The Office of Apostle in the Early Church.* Trans. J.E. Steely. Nashville, TN: Abingdon, 1971.

Schnackenberg, Rudolf. "Apostles Before and During Paul's

Time." *Apostolic History and the Gospel: Biblical and Historical Essays Presented to F.F. Bruce on His 60th Birthday.* Ed. W. Ward Gasque and Ralph P. Martin. Grand Rapids: Eerdmans, 1970.

Young, J.E. "That Some Should Be Apostles." *Evangelical Quarterly* 48 (1976): 96-104.

Prophets

See the categories "Gifts of Revelation" and "Gifts for Worship."

Teachers / Preachers / Evangelists

Lawless, Elaine J. *Handmaidens of the Lord: Pentecostal Women Preachers and Traditional Religion.* Philadelphia: U of Pennsylvania P, 1988.

Mittelberg, Mark. *Building a Contagious Church: Revolutionizing the Way We View and Do Evangelism.* Grand Rapids: Zondervan, 2000.

Plake, David. *The Ministry of Teaching: [A Practical Guide for Developing Your Gift of Teaching].* Springfield, MO: Gospel Publishing House, 1982.

Scott, Robert B.Y. "Is Preaching Prophecy?" *Canadian Journal of Theology* 1 (1955): 11- 18.

Zuck, Roy B. *Spirit-Filled Teaching: The Power of The Holy Spirit in Your Ministry.* Ed. Charles R. Swindoll. Dallas: Word, 1998.

Pastors

Carter, Kenneth H. *The Gifted Pastor: Finding and Using Your Spiritual Gifts.* Nashville, TN: Abingdon, 2001.

Fisher, David H. *21st Century Pastor: A Vision Based on the Ministry of Paul.* Grand Rapids: Zondervan, 1996.

Administrations / Helps

Campbell, Thomas C. *The Gift of Administration: Theological Bases for Ministry*. Philadelphia: Westminster, 1981.

Engstrom, Theodore Wilhelm. *Your Gift of Administration: How to Discover and Use It*. New York: T. Nelson, 1983; London: MARC, 1985.

Gifts for Practical Service

Service, Exhortation, Giving, Showing Mercy

Service

Funk, Virgil C., ed. *Pastoral Musician*. (Pastoral Music in Practice, 5). Washington, DC: Pastoral, 1990.

Getz, Gene A. *Serving One Another*. Wheaton, IL: Victor, 1984.

Shelly, Judith Allen. *Spiritual Care: A Guide for Caregivers*. Downers Grove, IL: InterVarsity, 2000.

Underwood, B.E. *The Gifts of the Spirit: Supernatural Equipment for Christian Service*. Franklin Springs, GA: Advocate, 1967.

Veith, Gene Edward. *The Gift of Art: The Place of the Arts in Scripture*. Downers Grove, IL: InterVarsity, 1983.

Whaley, Vernon M. *Understanding Music & Worship in the Local Church*. Wheaton, IL: Evangelical Training Association, 1995.

Exhortation (Encouragement)

Crabb, Lawrence J. *Encouragement: The Key to Caring*. Grand Rapids: Zondervan, 1984.

Doering, Jeanne. *Your Power of Encouragement*. Chicago: Moody, 1985.

Getz, Gene A. *Encouraging One Another*. Wheaton, IL: Victor, 1981.

Huggett, Joyce. *Listening to Others: How One Woman Discovered a Healing Art*. Downers Grove, IL: InterVarsity, 1989.

Littauer, Florence. *Silver Boxes: The Gift of Encouragement*. Dallas: Word, 1989.

Giving

Fisher, Wallace E. *All the Good Gifts: On Doing Biblical Stewardship*. Minneapolis: Augsburg, 1979.

Showing Mercy

Grantham, Rudolph E. *Lay Shepherding: A Guide for Visiting the Sick, the Aged, the Troubled and the Bereaved*. Valley Forge, PA: Judson, 1980.

Keller, Timothy J. *Ministries of Mercy: The Call of the Jericho Road*. Grand Rapids: Ministry Resources Library/Zondervan, 1989.

Klinken, Jaap van. *Diakonia: Mutual Helping With Justice and Compassion*. Grand Rapids: Eerdmans, 1990.

Maxwell, Katie. *Bedside Manners: A Practical Guide to Visiting the Ill*. Grand Rapids: Baker, 1990.

Gifts of Power

Faith, Healings, Workings of Miracles

Faith / Healings

Hayford, Jack W., with Nathaniel Cleave. *God's Way to Wholeness: Divine Healing by the Power of the Holy Spirit*. Nashville, TN: T. Nelson, 1993.

Kelsey, Morton T. *Healing and Christianity in Ancient Thought and Modern Times*. New York: Harper & Row, 1973.

Maust, John. "Charismatic Leaders Seeking Faith for Their Own Healing." *Christianity Today* 24 (April 4, 1980): 44-46.

Thomas, Gary. "Doctors Who Pray: How the Medical Community Is Discovering the Healing Power of Prayer." *Christianity Today* 41 (Jan. 6, 1997): 20-24, 26-28, 30.

Thomas, Leo, and Jan Alkire. *Healing Ministry: A Practical Guide.* Kansas City, MO: Sheed & Ward, 1994.

Workings of Miracles

Grudem, Wayne A., ed. *Are Miraculous Gifts for Today? Four Views.* Grand Rapids: Zondervan, 1996.

Jensen, Peter F. "Calvin, Charismatics and Miracles." *Evangelical Quarterly* 51 (1979): 131- 144.

Warfield, Benjamin Breckinridge. *Counterfeit Miracles.* New York: C. Scribner's, 1918; London: Banner of Truth Trust, 1972.

Woodworth-Etter, Maria. *A Diary of Signs and Wonders.* Tulsa, OK: Harrison House, 1980, c. 1916.

Gifts of Revelation

Wisdom, Knowledge, Discernment, Prophecy

See also the related categories: "Gifts of Leadership" and "Gifts for Worship."

General

Burns, J. Lanier. "A Reemphasis on the Purpose of Sign Gifts." *Bibliotheca Sacra* 132 (1975): 242-249.

Grudem, Wayne A. "Does God Still Give Revelation Today?" *Charisma and Christian Life* 18, No. 2 (1992): 38-44.

Wisdom / Knowledge / Discernment

DeGrandis, Robert, with Mrs. Jessie Borrello. *Word of Knowledge: A Charismatic Gift.* Hauppauge, NY: Living Flame, 1989.

Johnson, J. Foy. "The Word of Knowledge: [1 Corinthians 12:4-11]." *Conference on the Holy Spirit Digest*, Vol. 1. Springfield, MO: Gospel Publishing House, 1983: 221-224.

Parker, Stephen E. *Led by the Spirit: Toward a Practical Theology of Pentecostal Discernment and Decision Making. (Journal of Pentecostal Theology.* Supplement series, vol. 2). Sheffield, England: Sheffield Academic Press, 1996.

Prophecy

Beker, Johan Christiaan. *Prophecy and the Spirit in the Apostolic Fathers*. Ph.D. dissertation, University of Chicago, 1955.

Crone, Theodore M. *Early Christian Prophecy: A Study of Its Origin and Function.* Baltimore: St. Mary's UP, 1973.

Gillespie, Thomas W. *The First Theologians: A Study in Early Christian Prophecy.* Grand Rapids: Eerdmans, 1994.

Grudem, Wayne A. "Why Christians Can Still Prophesy." *Christianity Today* 32 (Sept. 16, 1988): 29-31.

_____. *The Gift of Prophecy in the New Testament and Today.* Eugene, OR: Wipf and Stock, 1999; Eastbourne, England: Kingsway, 1988.

Klawiter, Frederick Charles. *The New Prophecy in Early Christianity: The Origin, Nature and Development of Montanism, A.D. 165-220.* Ph.D. dissertation, University of Chicago, 1975.

Osiek, Carolyn. "Christian Prophecy: Once Upon a Time?" *Currents in Theology and Mission* 17 (1990): 291-297.

Robeck, Cecil Melvin, Jr. "The Gift of Prophecy in Acts and Paul." *Studies in Biblical Theology* 4 (1974): 15-35; 5 (1975): 37-54.

_____. *The Role and Function of Prophetic Gifts for the Church at Carthage, A.D. 202-258.* Ph.D. dissertation, Fuller Theological Seminary, 1985.

Thomas, Robert L. "Prophecy Rediscovered? A Review of the Gift of Prophecy in the New Testament and Today [by W.A. Grudem, 1988]." *Bibliotheca Sacra* 149 (1992): 83-96.

_____. "The Spiritual Gift of Prophecy in Revelations 22:18." *Journal of the Evangelical Theological Society* 32, No. 2 (1989): 201-216.

Wire, Antoinette Clark. *The Corinthian Women Prophets: A Reconstruction Through Paul's Rhetoric.* Minneapolis: Fortress, 1990.

Gifts for Worship

Prophecy, Discernings of Spirits, Speaking in Tongues, Interpretation of Tongues

This category includes gifts commonly used in demonstrative ways in public worship. For other spiritual gifts used in worship, please see other spiritual gift categories.

General

Arrington, French L. *Divine Order in the Church [A Study of 1 Corinthians].* Cleveland, TN: Pathway, 1978.

Ramm, Bernard L. *The Witness of the Spirit: An Essay on the Contemporary Relevance of the Internal Witness of the Holy Spirit.* Grand Rapids: Eerdmans, 1960.

Schweizer, Eduard. "The Service of Worship: An Exposition of 1 Corinthians 14." *Interpretation* 13 (1959): 400-408.

_____. *Church Order in the New Testament.* London: SCM Press, 1961; Naperville, IL: Alec R. Allenson, 1961.

Prophecy in Worship

See also the related category: "Gifts of Revelation."

Ash, James L., Jr. "The Decline of Ecstatic Prophecy in the Early Church." *Theological Studies* 37 (1976): 227-252.

Callan, Terrance. "Prophecy and Ecstasy in Greco-Roman Religion and in 1 Corinthians." *Novum Testamentum* 27 (1985): 125-140.

Grudem, Wayne A. *The Gift of Prophecy in 1 Corinthians*. Lanham, MD: UP of America, 1982.

Discernings of Spirits in Worship

Gee, Donald. *Is It God? Tests for Evaluating the Supernatural*. Springfield, MO: Gospel Publishing House, 1972.

Morse, Christopher. *Not Every Spirit: A Dogmatics of Christian Disbelief*. Valley Forge, PA: Trinity Press International, 1994.

Speaking in Tongues / Interpretation of Tongues in Worship

See also the related category: "Spirit Baptism."

Grudem, Wayne A. "1 Corinthians 14:20-25: Prophecy and Tongues as Signs of God's Attitude." *Westminster Theological Journal* 41 (1979): 381-396.

Harpur, Thomas William. "The Gift of Tongues and Interpretation." *Canadian Journal of Theology* 12 (1966): 164-171.

Thiselton, Anthony C. "The 'Interpretation' of Tongues: A New Suggestion in the Light of Greek Usage in Philo and Josephus." *Journal of Theological Studies* ns 30 (1979): 15-36.

Scripture Index

Acts

Acts

1 COR

Subject Index

Disabilities and limitations, 155-157, 210-211, 343-344, 442

Discernings of spirits. *See* Gifts of the Spirit – Specific gifts – Gifts for worship

Disciples, 88-91, 124-127, 136-143, 156-162, 473
in Ephesus, 168-170

Doctrine, 19-20, 28, 40-41, 63-66, 83, 85-86, 106, 116-117, 139-140, 171-178, 295-297, 378-382, 386-387, 406, 474

Doctrine of subsequence, 83, 87, 89, 92, 254-255, 474

Domata, 239, 264, 279

Edification, 61, 87, 159, 171, 174, 180, 248-250, 266, 291, 331, 335, 341, 347, 474

Empowerment, 96, 101, 118, 137-138, 140, 174, 183, 197, 204-207, 218-220, 222-224, 384-387, 391, 394-396, 440-441, 458-463, 474. *See also* Baptism in the Holy Spirit

Encounters with the Spirit, 29-30, 35, 40-43, 55-57, 92-96, 118-122, 125-145, 147-148, 156-170, 183-184, 197-200, 216-217, 237-238, 286-301, 323-346, 396, 423-463, 474

Encouragement. *See* Edification; Exhortation

Energēmata, 239-240, 264, 330, 479

Enlightenment, spiritual. *See* Edification

Evangelical, 87-88, 386, 474

Evangelism, 206-207, 213-215, 218-220, 343, 394-396, 437-440, 476. *See also* Gifts of the Spirit – Specific gifts – Gifts of leadership; Witness

Evangelist(s). *See* Evangelism; Gifts of the Spirit – Specific gifts – Gifts of leadership

Evil spirit, 339-340, 366, 456, 475

Exhortation, 338, 347-348. *See also* Gifts of the Spirit – Specific gifts – Gifts for practical service

Faith, 55-58, 71-72, 101, 128-132, 190-193, 295-297, 327, 475. *See also* Gifts of the Spirit – Specific gifts – Gifts of power

Faith – Resources, 513-514

Father, The. *See* God the Father

Filled with the Spirit, 33, 83, 89, 91, 95-97, 99, 101, 110, 115, 127, 142-144, 153, 157-158, 182, 190-202, 197-202, 215-217, 222-225, 475. *See also* Refilled with the Spirit

Flames of fire. *See* Tongues of fire

Fortune tellers. *See* Soothsayers

Fruit of the Spirit, 211-212, 224, 475

Fulfillment, 39-44, 93-94, 123-126, 159, 206-207, 476

Full of the Spirit. *See* Filled with the Spirit

Fullness of the Spirit. *See* Filled with the Spirit

Fruit of the Spirit, 69-73, 76, 250, 252-254, 269